Franccois Frédeeric Roget

An Introduction to old French

I0084614

Franccois Frédeeric Roget

An Introduction to old French

ISBN/EAN: 9783741103797

Manufactured in Europe, USA, Canada, Australia, Japa

Cover: Foto ©Thomas Meinert / pixelio.de

Manufactured and distributed by brebook publishing software
(www.brebook.com)

Franccois Frédeeric Roget

An Introduction to old French

AN INTRODUCTION TO OLD FRENCH

BY THE SAME AUTHOR

Third Edition.

First Steps in French History, Literature, and Philology.

'Hommes de Lettres' Series of French Classics.

Vol. I. : Voltaire's Short Prose Tales.

In Preparation.

Old French Commentary and Phonetics.

The History and Literature of the Anglo-Norman Dialect.

Handbook of Romance Philology.

AN INTRODUCTION TO

OLD FRENCH

BY

F. F. ROGET

GRADUATE OF GENEVA UNIVERSITY, LECTURER ON THE FRENCH
LANGUAGE AND LITERATURE, AND ON ROMANCE PHILOLOGY
IN THE UNIVERSITY OF ST. ANDREWS

THIRD EDITION

WILLIAMS AND NORGATE

14, HENRIETTA STREET, COVENT GARDEN, LONDON
20, SOUTH FREDERICK STREET, EDINBURGH
AND 7, BROAD STREET, OXFORD

1896

PREFACE TO FIRST EDITION

THIS book contains no independent research and little scientific method. Suggested by some acquaintance with the difficulties of students who begin to read Old French, it has been written for the convenience of candidates for the L.L.A. title of St. Andrews University, and perchance may be found useful by students working under the Cambridge University scheme for a tripos in Mediæval and Modern Languages.

Professor Crombie, of St. Andrews, for his kind encouragement, and Mr. G. Saintsbury, for a timely hint regarding the scope of this work, have my thanks.

The excellent works of Bartsch (*Chrestomathie de l'ancien français*) and of Clédat (*Grammaire élémentaire de la vieille langue française*) have, more directly than any other sources, afforded me guidance and help. Those books should be resorted to by students who may have a taste for more scholarship than can be offered in this Introduction to a phase of language, in which the philologist and the literary critic will find well-nigh inexhaustible material.

But for fear of being found inaccurate by the learned, and yet abstruse by the learners, I should trust altogether to the excellence of the subject for a recommendation to the critics, whose judgment a book on Old French studies cannot escape.

In the selection of fragments of Old French texts, and in the construction of the Glossary, I have attempted to provide those studying French literature in the works of G. Saintsbury, Staaff, and Vinet, with the means of understanding the Old French extracts found in those Manuals.

F. F. R.

EDINBURGH, *24th November* 1886.

PREFACE TO SECOND EDITION

SOME time ago, at our publisher's, Paterfamilias stepped in. He wanted a book on Old French for his daughter. This volume was handed to him, as the only one extant in English. He looked at the Preface, and read : *This book contains no independent research and little scientific method.* He shook his head, and laid down the book. Such a humble beginning would not do for his daughter.

Yet the sale of the first edition—not a small one— was rapid, considering to what a limited circle it could appeal. This second edition is as humble as the first.

It is not a treatise on phonetics; it is not an Old French grammar properly so called; it is not a corpus of properly edited texts, nor is it a learned etymological dictionary. It is just an introduction to Old French. The works of Clédat and of Bartsch were the acknowledged basis of the first issue. I have now collated my writing with such authorities as Schwan, Suchier, and Darmesteter, of more recent date. This work is no longer the only one of its kind in English. There appeared, in 1892, *Specimens of Old French*, by Paget Toynbee, Clarendon Press, 750 pages. This is a very good piece of work.

I particularly wish to acknowledge a flattering *critique* with which, in a special periodical, the late H. Koerting, Professor of Romance Philology in the University of Leipzig, honoured the first edition.

Since writing, the Universities of St. Andrews, Aberdeen, and Edinburgh have made provision for the teaching of French, its literature, and its philology as a part of the curriculum for Graduation in Arts.

F. F. R.

St. Andrews, *February* 1894.

TABLE OF CONTENTS

FIRST BOOK

THE LANGUAGE AND ITS EARLIEST MONUMENTS

CHAPTER I

CHAPTER II

SECOND BOOK

GRAMMAR

First Part—Flexions

CHAPTER I

Contents

Second Part—Syntax

CHAPTER I

CHAPTER II

CHAPTER III

Contents

CHAPTER IV

CHAPTER V

THIRD BOOK

PREMIÈRE PARTIE—PROSE

Deuxième Partie—Poésie

TROISIÈME PARTIE

FIRST BOOK

THE LANGUAGE AND ITS EARLIEST MONUMENTS

FIRST BOOK

THE LANGUAGE AND ITS EARLIEST MONUMENTS[1]

CHAPTER I

ORIGIN, DIALECTS

OLD French may be divided into three successive Periods, the Period of Formation, the Flourishing Period, and the Period of Decay.

The First extends over the first thousand years of the Christian Era. It is contemporaneous with the earliest Middle Ages, and its origin can be traced back to the conquest of Gaul by Rome. When the Roman Republic was still in existence the *Lingua Romana* of its soldiers, merchants, and colonists came into contact with the Celtic dialects of Gaul. The campaigns of Julius Cæsar (57-51 B.C.) may be considered as the first link in the chain of historical events which were to bring about the formation of a French language. The *Lingua Romana* became the prevalent speech of the language-making masses of Gaul, Celtiberia, and Italy (to say nothing of its lesser homes by right of conquest), though the invasion of the Barbarians

[1] It would be idle to read even this elementary work on Old French without previous acquaintance with the historical aspect of the Modern language. Eugène's *The Student's Comparative French Grammar*, and Roget's *First Steps in French History, Literature, and Philology*, both published by Messrs. Williams & Norgate, are recommended as books in which the treatment of Modern French is such as to lead quite smoothly to a subsequent study of Old French.

brought into play a new linguistic factor. By the fourth
century A.D., Celtic had been overpowered by its invader
and driven to out-of-the-way districts ; Latin, the literary
dialect of Cicero, was written, but little spoken out of the
governing and educated caste ; it was a class-language.
The *Lingua Romana* altered much in the different areas of
the vast territories it had spread over. It was assuming
local peculiarities which prepared for its splitting into different dialects, when the Teutonic element burst upon the
scenes, and acted as an ultimate dissolvent. (486 A.D.)

From that day the processes of decay, which till then
might be considered as modifications within the *Lingua
Romana,* assumed a regenerative character, and became the
starting-point of a new language (Romance, Gallo-Roman).

A Germanic tribe, the leading military and political
agent in the plains of Northern Gaul, that of the Franks,
has had the honour of seeing its name affixed to the
language. This Germanic title has little affected the
language itself. Teutonic influences can be traced in
goodly number in the vocabulary, in the phonetics, and in
the etymology of Old French ; Latin words have been pre-
sented with meanings after the analogy of Teutonic corresponding terms. But the grammatical framework of the
language, and its syntax, which developed only in the later
stage of Old French, are wholly and absolutely Latin in
origin and Latin in character.

It seems reasonable to believe that at no time, not even before 842, the date of the first Old French document known
to history, the destructive process obtained the upper hand
over the constructive one. It is evident, from the way in
which it spread over so many peoples and lands so distant,
that the *Lingua Romana Rustica* contained a principle of
remarkable vitality. It was sufficiently strong to maintain
its supremacy in spite of the heavy odds arrayed against
it in consequence of the breakdown of the Empire. It
regulated its own decay, it absorbed what it could not
reject, it upheld the high standard of linguistic efficiency
which distinguishes the Indo-European races. It is also
clear from the character of the first literary documents of

Old French and from the wealth and spontaneousness of its literature, that a fair amount of popular culture was extant among the masses of society in which language has its centre and whence it borrows its leverage. There was, in the fresh and vivid imagination of the people, an abundant supply of language-producing power. Unfettered by the weight of a set language with stereotyped forms and with a literature, this power preserved its elasticity, had free play, and bore fruits. Those fruits, in Gaul like elsewhere, ran into types; dialects, whose primary causes are obscure, were formed. In the valleys of the Rhône and of the Garonne, in the whole country, very nearly the half of Modern France, verging towards the Mediterranean and the Bay of Biscay, from the mountains of Auvergne southwards, early French was not French: it inclined towards the Italian and the Spanish modifications of Romance on which it bordered. These Southern Dialects, known under the collective name of *Langue d'Oc*, fell out of the race for existence when a centre of political and military power showed itself to be placed in the Frankish portion of France, near enough for the absorption of the Mediterranean border into the circle over which it radiated. What in the *Langue d'Oc* had affinities with the *Langue d'Oïl* strengthened the Northern invader by as much against its Southern neighbour. Political troubles and military invasion debarred the Southern speech of its national significance, it lost its literary standing, and died out as a body of language (thirteenth century). Nowadays *Provençal* is on the one hand a *patois*, on the other a study for literary antiquarians and philologists.

Its adversary, the *Langue d'Oïl*, has had a triumphant career. It has become one of the very foremost culture-languages of Europe. Geographically, to it belonged the valleys of the Saône (looking westwards from the bed of the river), the Loire, the Seine, the Upper Scheldt, and the Upper Meuse. Scholars recognise four Dialects in it. These divisions are well marked in the central Middle Ages. In the earlier and in the latter, from confusion in one case, from obliteration in the other, they are less dis-

tinguishable.   They are more convenient in a classification
than exhaustive from a philological point of view.   For
all round the area strictly belonging to these dialects,
North of them in Belgium, and East towards Alsace and
Switzerland, also within their respective provinces, there
exist not only local forms, but whole dialects that are distinguishable from any of the four leading ones.

In the eleventh, twelfth, and thirteenth centuries, a
process of natural selection took place among the dialects
of the *Langue d'Oïl.* The one at the centre of political
power came out victorious. It is likely that, linguistically,
it was the worthiest of a supremacy which was really
obtained by agencies of the political order. The other
dialects were by degrees incorporated, for all the Northern
dialects have much in common. Their extinction was an
absorption rather than a destruction. As for local literature, it died a natural death when talent ceased to use
local dialects as a channel for literary expression. By the
time the conquering dialect had laid down Old French
characteristics, the centralisation of literature in its hand
was completely effected. Arrested in their upward development, the defeated dialects sank to the rank of *patois*
(sixteenth century).

The most western of the four was that of Normandy (we
should say that of Neustria, for the name of Norman is a
misnomer as applied to a Gallo-Roman dialect). Submitted
to direct Scandinavian influence by the invasion of the
Norsemen, it stoutly resisted foreign contamination : so
stoutly, that when the Normans invaded England they
imported the language of France instead of their own, long
since forgotten. That they were in reality only a numeric-
ally weak Teutonic colony in a mass of Gallic people is
shown by the slight mark they have put on their adoptive
speech. When the Norman dialect crossed the Channel
with William the Conqueror's standards (1066 A.D.), it fell
under Anglo-Saxon influence. It developed then into what
has been called 'Anglo-Norman,' while Norman proper
lost its identity into that of French.

Norman literature was great, and of a strikingly epic

character. It was cultivated both in its Continental home and at the Court of the Kings of England. Norman French differs from its fellow-dialects in some peculiarities which do not affect the material of speech, but only its shape. The area occupied by this dialect and its sub-dialects is far more extended than its name implies. From La Rochelle on the ocean, right across the Loire and the Seine, to the English Channel and Picardy, with the exception of Celtic Brittany, proofs have been found of the undisputed supremacy of Norman French.

Its Northern neighbour is the dialect of Picardy. In what is now Belgium, it bordered on Walloon (a fellow-dialect), Flemish, and Dutch. Its main dialectical features are a preference for hard consonantal sounds and the persistence in pronunciation of the diphthong *oi*. It uses hard *c* and *k* rather than soft *c* or *ch*, a guttural *g* and *ch* instead of the sibilant *s*. A Neo-Latin ending -*iemes* in the First Person Plural of the Imperfect was superseded by the generic Old French contraction -*ions* or -*iuns* (Norman).

The Burgundian dialect is the main dialect in the *Langue d'Oil*; it is so closely bound up with the fourth dialect, the one spoken in Paris and the country round it, that some scholars have merged them into one. It touches on the East the Germanic districts of the Vosges, enters into contact in the South with the *Langue d'Oc*, and is separated from Norman French in the West by the dialect of *Isle-de-France*. Out of France proper, under the name of *Franco-Provençal*, it occupies, jointly with *Langue d'Oc*, Romance Switzerland and Savoy.

Though French Switzerland and Savoy are geographically distinct from Burgundy proper, and have escaped on the whole French political influence and interference, they were, in their best mediæval days, either well in the scope of Burgundian literary and social life, or (this is the case of Savoy) without a real local literature.

Burgundian uses *ch* in words where Picard has hard *c* or *k*. It has a Past Definite of First Conjugation in : -*ai*, -*ais*, -*ait*, the diphthong *oi* in the Imperfect (-*oie*, -*oies*, -*oit*) succeeding an early Neo-Latin form in -*eve*, -*eves*, -*evet* (Latin

-abam, -abas, -abat). A Third Person Plural of Past Definite in *-arent,* Neo-Latin also, gave way to the later form *-erent.*

The fourth and last dialect among the leading sub-divisions of the *Langue d'Oïl* is the dialect of *Isle-de-France*—that is, of Paris and the province of which Paris was the capital. It may be called Francic, by a convenient misappropriation of terms, justified by the accepted, though equally faulty, expression—Norman French. This dialect is open to the accusation of being a conception of Old French students rather than a tangible reality. *Isle-de-France* is the meeting-place of the three dialects above mentioned, rather than the cradle of an aggressive and sharply defined speech. It was a centre of assimilation and compromise, having in common with all dialects of the *Langue d'Oïl* the same substratum, and making its own the borrowings it gathered from West, North, and East. It was, so to say, neutral, and attained to excellence by the subservience of all. It can hardly be said that, either in literature or in phonology and morphology, it has a single feature that it does not hold in common with one or another of its neighbours. The instrument of its might did not reside in its literature, or in its linguistic aptness. As said before, the reasons of its gradual spread over France are of the political order. These began to take effect in 987, when Hugh Capet, Count of *Isle-de-France,* became King of France. The gradual formation, even before the year 1200, of the University of Paris gave the colouring of legitimacy to the claim of Parisian to being paramount in letters. The work of unification was complete at the close of the Middle Ages, when Old French turned into Modern French. So rapid was the gravitation setting in literature towards Paris under the Capetian Kings that the expression Old French on the whole applies to the speech of *Isle-de-France.*

On looking back upon the dialects thus rapidly reviewed, one is struck by the comparative insignificance of their differences. This reveals the powerful Romance unity underlying them. It points also to the difficulties still affecting Old French studies. It is by no means easy to establish distinctions between the dialects, owing to dearth of early documents, owing to utter confusion in the alphabetical notation of sounds in manuscripts, and owing to the action and reaction, exchanges and combinations from dialect to dialect and from century to century. Dialects and local literature are still an open question; where the firm foothold of science begins is in the study of the oral forms deposited in the mediæval national literature of France.

The outburst of literary production coincides with what is, philologically speaking, the 'Flourishing Period of Old French' (twelfth and thirteenth centuries).

Old French is before all things a spoken language. It has the features of a language that is more spoken than written. It was formed in a happy unconsciousness of grammar, in a fortunate ignorance of the fact that each Latin form, which gave birth to a corresponding Old French form, was once part of a systematic whole, of a linguistic scheme reducible to Declension, Conjugation, and Syntax. That is why, from a philological standpoint, it can be called a pure speech, a natural product of the phonetic influences at work in the areas where it arose— influences which have been generalised into rules and codified by philologists.

No uniform orthographical system was devised in the Middle Ages. Now that Old French studies have so much gained in popularity and trustworthiness, it will be the task of scholars to agree on a consistent orthography, if it can be done without unduly assimilating to one type the diversities in pronunciation at different times and in different places. There could be no absolute standard of right and wrong in the graphic notation of a language still engaged in the process of generalising its phonetic laws. Pronunciation varied remarkably between the ninth and sixteenth centuries.

Another stumbling-block is looseness in the construction of the Old French sentence. Like Homer, it has what we should call superfluous particles, and on the other side it leaves relations often unexpressed. While we express every

shade of syntax in the structure of our clauses, Old French
left much to the voice, to the tone, and to gesture; less so,
however, in its later periods than in its earlier ones. Further-
more, the wealth of words in Old French is perplexing;
they are much more numerous than one could expect, and
their meanings are somewhat uncertain—not only subject to
alterations in the course of time, but to local applications
of a confusing character, to say nothing of the idiosyncrasies
of the individual writer. Such a plentiful word-supply has
hitherto made it impossible to publish a final dictionary of
Old French; even against many of the words actually collected notes of interrogation must be allowed to stand.

The culminating point of Old French was reached when
it had evolved its ' half-synthetic system' in the twelfth
century. For an account of the growth of this system,
works bearing on the history of the French language must
be consulted, also for the stupendous mass of literature the
language thus shaped brought forth. A brief exposition of
the half-synthetic system will be found in the grammatical
part of this book. Suffice it to say at present that work-
able Noun Declensions with two cases, a complete Conjugation, and a correct Syntax gave a linguistic organisation
expansive and elastic enough to meet all the wants of the
age. But not only was intelligible speaking made easy:
artistic composition was also provided for. For two centuries Mediæval French was the polite language of Europe,
more so than Modern French is; for the Old language had
no rivalry to fear from its still shapeless fellow-languages
of the Roman stock. *Provençal* alone, earlier mature than
French, entered the lists against it for a while.

But the half-synthetic system had no finality in itself. It
stood, so to say, on the furthest outside edge of the synthetic
system of language; insufficient allowance was made in it
for wear and tear in the forms of a language early burdened
with an enormous literature, and unfixed by the steadying
influence of antique and wide-spread culture. The elements
of analysis it contained took the upper hand; the synthetic
machinery lost the subtle flexional distinctions on which it
rested.

In the fourteenth and fifteenth centuries the day of Modern French began to dawn. A period of linguistic decay set in; literature, purely spontaneous and national, shared the fate of the language. Italian and Spanish, reaching philological finality, burst forth in the literary sky of Europe; French, for a while, was outshone. It lost its cases, it thinned down its vowel-system, it sifted its vocabulary, it defined more closely the significancy of its words, it absorbed a great many terms directly from classical Latin; to its stores of words expressing feeling and action it added those expressive of reflection and thought; it lost or divorced in meaning its double forms derived from some Latin words of the Third Declension. But in two points it remained synthetic : it preserved the system of verbal inflections of Old French, and its inflected Personal Pronouns, with a few phonetic alterations. This transformation dates from the fourteenth century. It was complete in the sixteenth. Then French took a new departure, and entered upon its Modern course.[1]

There is in the Old language a main distinction to be made between the early dialects and the later literary speech. In the former, the distinction between *Langue d'Oïl* and *Langue d'Oc* is only faintly drawn. Latin is, then, a nearer analogy than Modern French; and the literary monuments, invaluable as links in the breach, are insignificant in respect of their contents. Yet, from the linguist's point of view, they are of much account. Their grammar is not too transitory, too uncertain, to be of value. They must not be overlooked; men of learning view them with respect, and even the amateur philologist could ill afford to brush aside such an instructive page of the history of language.

[1] On Old French literature read *La Littérature française au Moyen Age*, by Gaston Paris. Second edition, 1890, 300 pages. There is a good and handy *Glossaire de la Langue d'Oïl*, by Dr. A. Bos, 1891, 466 pages. The standard dictionary of Old French, *Dictionnaire de l'ancienne Langue française et de tous ses Dialectes du IXme au XVme siècle*, by Frederic Godefroy, has now for several years been in course of publication, and approaches completion.

CHAPTER II

The Earliest Monuments

THE very earliest written monuments are the *Cassel Glossary* and the *Glossary of Reichenau*.[1] They both belong to the eighth century. The first is a collection of words in Romance, with their translation into High German, and arranged into chapters according to their meaning. The first chapter deals with the names of the human body and its parts, the second with domestic animals, the third with housekeeping, the fourth with clothing, the fifth with household articles, the sixth with miscellaneous words, the seventh with connected expressions. Its authorship is unknown, and the mode of its composition is disputed.

As for the *Glossary of Reichenau*, it consists of two parts. In the first we have glosses interpreting in Romance portions of the Latin text of the Vulgate. In the second we find, in alphabetical order, words taken from all departments of thought, without reference to any particular text. The author's aim was obviously to facilitate the reading of the Bible to priests who were bad scholars. But instead of giving in the Gallo-Roman of the day the equivalent of the classical Latin words he wished to explain, he added classical suffixes to the Romance stems. We pick here and there glosses in which the Romance is at once distinguishable in its pseudo-Latin garb :—

Latin.	*Romance.*	*Modern French.*
femur.	coxa.	cuisse.
(in) cartallo.	(in) panario.	(dans le) panier.
sarcina.	bisatia.	besace.
onerati.	carcati.	chargés.
rerum.	causarum.	(des) choses.
pallium.	drappum.	drap.

[1] See the complete text of these in *Altfranzösisches Uebungsbuch*, by W. Foerster and E. Koschwitz, *erster Theil: die ältesten Sprach-denkmäler*. Heilbronn. 167 pages.

Latin.	*Romance.*	*Modern French.*
arundine.	ros.	roseau.
gratia.	merces.	merci.
mutuare.	impruntare.	emprunter.
pruina.	gelata.	gelée.
caseum.	formaticum.	fromage.
galea.	helmus.	heaume.
novacula.	rasorium.	rasoir.
oves.	berbices.	brebis.
rostrum.	beccus.	bec.
sortileus.	sorcerus.	sorcier.
tugurium.	cavana.	cabane.
vespertiliones.	calves sorices.	chauves-souris.
viscera.	intralia.	entrailles.
semel.	una vice.	une fois.
segetes.	messes.	moisson.
reus.	culpabilis.	coupable.
litus.	ripa.	rive.
pueros.	infantes.	enfants.
in foro.	in mercato.	(au) marché.
regit.	gubernat.	(il) gouverne.

SERMENTS DE STRASBOURG

Next to the *Cassel Glossary* and to that of Reichenau in chronological order, but far above them in order of importance, stand the *Strasburg Oaths* of 842.[1]

The chronicler says that on the 16th day before the Calends of March, Ludwig the German and Charles the Bald met in the town of Strasburg and swore the following Oath, Lewis in the Romance, Charles in the German language.

[1] See, for the text, Foerster and Koschwitz, as already quoted. For an unpretending, but handy, commentary, see *Les Serments de Strasbourg*, by Armand Gasté. Paris, 1888, 38 pages. For a thorough-going inquiry into the questions of phonetics and grammar, see *Commentar zu den ältesten französischen Sprachdenkmälern*, by Dr. E. Koschwitz. Heilbronn. Gaston Paris has hitherto published only an *Introduction à un commentaire grammatical*, which is not printed separately.

'Pro deo amur et pro christian poblo et nostro commun salvament, d'ist di in avant, in quant deus savir et podir me dunat, si salvarai eo cist meon fradre Karlo et in aiudha et in cadhuna cosa, si cum om per dreit son fradra salvar dift, in o quid il mi altresi fazet, et ab Ludher nul plaid nunqua prindrai, qui meon vol cist meon fradre Karle in damno sit.'

When the kings had thus pledged their faith to each other, the followers of each bound themselves to enforce the oath as follows :

'Si Lodhuvigs sagrament, que son fradre Karlo jurat, conservat, et Karlus meos sendra de sue part lo suon fraint, si io returnar non l'int pois, ne io ne nëuls, cui eo returnar int pois, in nulla aiudha contra Lodhuwig nun li iv er.'

We shall now imitate the cleric of the *Glossary of Reichenau*, and affix to the Romance stems the Latin flexions.

Lingua Romana :—1. ' Pro Dei amore et pro christiani popli et nostro communi salvamento, de isto die in abante, in quanto Deus sapere et potere mí donat, sic salvare habeo (salvabo) ego ecce istum meum fratrem Karlum, et in adjutu et in catuna causa, sic quomodo homo per drictum suum fratrem salvare debet, in hoc quid ille mihi alteris sic faciat, et apud Lotharium nullum placitum numquam prehenhere habeo quod, mea voluntate, ecce isti meo fratri Karlo in damno sit.'

2. ' Si Ludovicus sacramentum quod suo fratri Karlo juravit, conservat, et Karlus, meus senior, de sua parte illud suum frangit, si ego retornare non illum inde possum, nec ego nec nullus quem ego retornare (avertere) inde possum, in nullo adjutu contra Ludovicum non illi ibi ero.'

By comparing the Romance text with our pseudo-Latin setting of the Oaths, we may lay bare the processes of Romance word-formation and grammar, which in due course resulted in Old French. The process took place in the sounds, not in the signs. Hence we may first ask ourselves whether in the paleograph of the Oaths we have an exact graphic representation of the phonetic state of the language in the ninth century. The answer must be in the negative. A phonetic script would show that *christian* stands for *chrestien*, *in* for *en*, *cist* for *cest*, *prindrai* for *prendrai*, *savir* for *saver*, *podir* for *poder*. In the endings, too, the different vowel-signs *a*, *o*, *u*, *e* of Latin, all stand for the same sound, Old French *e*.

It follows that old documents, like these Oaths, are a perpetual study with phoneticians and paleographists, and through the labour thus spent have been wrought out the corner-stones of Romance philology—the art of properly interpreting the symbols of sound, and that of properly editing the ancient texts.

We now give a version of the Oaths, in which we have endeavoured to visibly restore the pronunciation of the period. Vowels thus marked : *ēu̯, āi̯,* etc., form diphthongs (two vowel sounds of unequal stress, uttered so as to form one syllable) ; *ōu̯* stands for Modern *ou*, a monophthong ; *u* for Modern *u*, a simple vowel ; *ue*, *ui*, *ia* are not diphthongs. We shall use our phonetic version as a reference in our brief grammatical commentary.

Phonetic Version :—1. ' Por dēu̯ amōu̯r e por crestïian poble e nostre commun salvement, d est di en avant, en quant Dēus saver e poder me dōu̯net, si salverāi̯ ēo cest mēon fredre Karle e en aïude e en cadune cose, si com om per drēit son fredre salver deft, en o que il me altresi fazet, e ab Ludher nul plāi̯d nonque prendrāi̯, qui, mēon vol, cest mēon fredre Karle en damne sēit.'

2. ' Se Lodhuvigs sagrement, que son fredre Karle jurat, conservet, e Karles mēes sendre de sūe part le sūon frāi̯nt, se eo retōu̯rner non l ent pōis, ne ēo, ne nēuls cui ēo retourner ent pōis, en nulle aïude contre Lodhuvig non li iv er.'

In reading this version aloud, all consonants should be sounded : *i* before *a* should have the consonantal sound of y in English ' yard ' ; *u* before *e* and *i* should have the consonantal sound of *u* in English ' to conquer ' (to conqver).

GRAMMATICAL COMMENTARY

Deu stands to the next word *amour* in the relation of a genitive : Latin *dei*, French *de dieu*.

Crestiian poble stands in the same relation to *salvement*: Latin *christiani populi*, French *du peuple chrétien.*

Saver e poder are best taken as infinitives used substantively.

Me should be read as a dative to *dounet* : Latin *mihi.*

Si, a frequent expletive in Old French : Latin *sic.*

Salverai, an example of the new Romance future, which replaced the future of classical Latin.

Cadune, a combination of Greek κατὰ (cata) and Latin *unus.* Greek κατὰ subsists to the present day in *Provençal* and *Franco-provençal.* Old French *chaiins.*

Deft, for Latin *debet* (phonetic *devd* or *deft*).

Me, accusative case, governed by *fazet*, for *salvet.*

Fazet, present subjunctive, Latin *faciat* (phonetic *fakjat*). This verb stands here instead of *salvet.* As it stands for *salvet*, so as to avoid repetition, it governs the same case as that verb would, the Accusative.

Ab, from Latin *apud*, Old French *ot*, in the sense of *avec.*

Cest meon fredre stands to *seit* in the relation of a dative. Latin *isti meo fratri*, French *à mon frère-ci.*

Seit, subjunctive present.

Jurat, preterite, Latin *juravit*, French *jura.* *Son fredre* is in dative.

Conservet, present indicative : Latin *conservat*, French *conserve.*

Notice throughout that (1) the Masculine Nominative Singular ends in *s*, whenever the Latin ended in *s* (*deüs*, from *deus* ; *Lodhuvigs*, from *Ludovicus* ; *karles*, from *carolus* ; *mēes*, from *meus* ; *neüls*, from *nullus*) ; (2) the Masculine Nominative Singular has no final *s* when the Latin did not end in *s* (*eo*, from *ego* ; *om*, from *homo* ; *il*, from *ille* ; *qui*, from *qui* ; *sendre*, from *senior*) ; (3) there are no Nominatives Plural in the Oaths (either masculine or feminine) ; (4) the nouns before which modern *de* is understood (Latin genitive), those before which modern *à* is understood (Latin Dative), and those which are direct objects to verbs (Latin Accusative) or governed by prepositions (Latin Accusative, Dative, Ablative) all end in *e*, or on the stem consonant, except a few monosyllables (*poble, nostre, fredre*, *karle, aïude, cose, altre, damne,* to which may be added the feminine forms *cadune, sue, nulle,* the adverbial forms *ne, nonque,* the pronominal *le, que, me,* the prepositional *contre,* the conjunctional *se; amour,* from *amor-e, crestiian,* from *christian-o; commun,* from *commun-i, salvement,* from *salvament-o, est,* from *isto, quant,* from *quant-o, cest,* from *eccist-um, dreit,* from *direct-um, Ludher,* from *Ludher-o, plaid,* from *placitum, nul,* from *null-um, vol,* from *vell-e, cest,* from *eccist-i, sagrement,* from *sacrament-um, part,* from *part-e, Lodhuvig,* from *Lodhuvig-um;* the exceptions are *deũ,* from *dei, di,* from *die,* on the one hand, and *mẽon,* from *meum, son,* from *suum, sũon,* from *suum* in tonic position, on the other hand).

Without further entering upon the discussion of the forms in these fundamental documents, we now affix their equivalents in Old French of the later centuries, in which the bulk of Old French literature is written.

1. 'Por deu amor et por christïen peuple et nostre commun sauvement, de cest jorn en avant, en cant dex saveir et pooir me doin, si salverai jo cest mon freire Karle et en aïe et en chascune cose, si com on par droit son freire salver deit, en ceu ke il me autresi faice, et ot Luther nul plaid onque prendrai, qui mon voil cestui mon freire en dan seit.'

2. 'Si Ludovics *le* sairement que *a* son freire Karle jurat, conservet, et Karles mes sire de seie part le suen fraint, se jo retorner ne l'ent pois, ne jo ne nuls ki jo retorner ent pois, en nulle aïe cuntre Ludovic li i serai.'

In the second fragment we have introduced the Definite Article and the Preposition *a.* The appearance of this Old French *pastiche* could be varied almost *ad infinitum* by adopting some other of the numerous forms of the words composing it. As it stands, it can no doubt be understood at a glance.

It is interesting to roughly divide the words of the Oaths into three classes.

We have a few words (*est, cadun, o, ab*) which have not even become accepted Old French words of the literary period. They are the dying gasp of latinity.

Then there are a few other words (*di, altresi, nonque, vol, er*) which have not passed from Old French into Modern French.

Few words are of quite unclassical origin, being altogether from the *Lingua Romana* or from Low-Latin. The larger number are of unimpeachable latinity in their stems.

In the same way we may like to see in what proportion syntheticism stands to analysis in the Oaths. The former is quite paramount. 'Case' makes itself felt in every line, Suffixes are shorn off, but Prepositions in their stead are wholly unrepresented, the Article is not forthcoming, the Subj. Personal Pronoun alone is freely used for emphasis.

In Modern French the Oaths read as follows :—

1. 'Pour l'amour de Dieu et pour le salut du peuple chrétien, et notre commun salut, de ce jour en avant, autant que Dieu me donne savoir et pouvoir, je sauverai mon frère Charles et en aide et en chaque chose (ainsi qu'on doit, selon la justice, sauver son frère) à condition qu'il en fasse autant pour moi, et je ne ferai avec Lothaire aucun accord qui, par ma volonté, porte préjudice à mon frère Charles ici présent.'

2. 'Si Louis garde le serment qu'il a juré à son frère Charles, et que Charles mon maître de son côté viole le sien, si je ne l'en puis détourner, ni moi ni personne que j'en puis détourner, ne lui serons en aide contre Louis.'

It is not our intention to study any more closely than the Oaths the documents we still have to review in the class which philologists call, for convenience' sake, the Pre-Old French, Neo-Latin, or Romance class.

The next two fragments belong to the tenth century ; we have nothing so ancient in the *Langue d'Oil*, whose characteristics are plainly visible in them, whilst the language of the Oaths occupies an undefined position antecedent to both *Langue D'Oc* and *Langue D'Oil*. We may therefore say that the fragments now under consideration are written in an archaic dialect of Old French. Latin analogy in them has not yet fully given way to that recasting of it which we must call French analogy, and it is from the combination of the two that the fragments derive their interest.

The one of the fragments, known as the *Chant d'Eulalie,*
or as the *Cantilène de Ste Eulalie,* is written in verse. It
is very short, consisting of no more than twenty-nine lines.
The other is less important: it is a pulpit paraphrase about
the prophet Jonah. It is called the *Fragment de Valen-
ciennes,* and presents a text broken at almost regular
intervals by whole sentences in Latin.

Both monuments are of decidedly Northern penman-
ship—

Chant d'Eulalie.

1 'Buona pulcella fut Eulalia,
  bel auret corps, bellezour anima.

3 Voldrent la veintre li do inimi,
  voldrent la faire dïaule servir.

5 Elle non eskoltet les mals conselliers,
  qu'elle do raneiet, chi maent sus en ciel,

7 Ne por or ned argent ne paramenz.
  por manatce regiel ne preiement,

9 Ni ule cose non la pouret omque pleier,
  la polle sempre non amast lo do menestier.

11 E por o fut presentede Maximiien,
  chi rex eret a cels dis soure pagiens.

13 Il li enortet, dont lei nonque chielt,
  qued elle fuiet lo nom chrestiien.

15 Ell' ent adunet lo suon element.
  melz sostendreiet les empedementz,

17 Qu'elle perdesse sa virginitet:
  poros furet morte a grand honestet.

19 Enz enl fou la getterent, çom arde tost.
  elle colpes non auret, poro nos coist.

21 A czo nos voldret concreidre li rex pagiens,
  ad une spede li roveret tolir lo chief.

23 La domnizelle celle kose non contredist,
  volt lo seule lazsier, si ruovet Krist.

25 In figure de colomb volat a ciel.
  tuit oram, que por nos degnet preier,

27 Qued auuisset de nos Christus mercit
  post la mort et a lui nos laist venir

29 Par souue clementia.'

The Modern French translation runs as follows :—

'Eulalie fut bonne pucelle : elle avait beau corps, âme plus belle. Les ennemis de Dieu voulurent la vaincre, voulurent la faire servir le diable. Elle n'écoute les mauvais conseillers, qu'elle renie Dieu qui demeure sus au ciel, ni pour or, ni pour argent, ni parure. Par menace de roi, ni prière, ni aucune chose, on ne put jamais plier la jeune fille qu'elle n'aimât pas le service de Dieu. Et pour cela elle fut présentée à Maximien, qui était en ces jours roi sur les païens. Il l'exhorte, ce dont ne chaut à elle, qu'elle fuie le nom chrétien. Elle en fortifia la sienne volonté. Plutôt elle supporterait les fers que de perdre sa virginité. Pour cela elle mourut en grande honnêteté. Ils la jetèrent dans le feu, de façon qu'elle brûle tôt. Elle n'avait aucune coulpe, aussi ne brûla-t-elle pas. A cela le roi païen ne voulut se fier : il ordonna de lui ôter la tête avec l'épée. La demoiselle n'y contredit ; elle veut laisser le siècle, si Christ l'ordonne ; en figure de colombe elle vola au ciel. Prions tous qu'elle daigne pour nous prier que Christ ait merci de nous après la mort, et nous laisse venir à lui par sa clémence.'

PHILOLOGICAL EXPLANATIONS

Verse 1. *Buona*, from Latin *bona*, is an instance of dialectic intensification of radical vowels. The correct form is *bon*, and *buon, buen, boen, boin* should be rejected.

2. *Auret* is in form a Pluperfect, from Latin *habuerat* (*hábverat*), in sense an Imperfect. Other like forms in our text are : *pouret*, from *potuerat* (*pótverat*) ; *furet*, from *fúerat* ; *voldret*, from *voluerat* (*vólverat*) ; *roveret*, from *ropáverat*. This synthetic Pluperfect after Latin analogy is Neo-Latin only, not Old French proper. Like the Modern Verb-forms in -*ent*, its -*et* would not be accented, and sometimes would be altogether mute.

Bellezour is from a Low-Latin *bellatiorem*. A Neo-Latin Comparative ; it is not an isolated formation, but one of a whole series dealt with elsewhere.

Anima has two syllables : Old French will say and write : *anma, aneme, ame*.

3. *Voldrent* is Past Definite from Latin *voluerunt* with consonnified *u* (*vólverunt*), which throws the accent back upon the first syllable. Modern French, by saying *voulurent* (accent on penultimate) has, unwittingly, restored the classical Latin analogy. The *d* is an auxiliary consonant. Such appear quite regularly in a whole class of French so-called Irregular Verbs, between *l* and *r*, and between *n* and *r* (Old French, *toldre*; Modern French, *craindre*).

Veintre, for an older *veinctre*, from Latin *vincere*, shows the auxiliary consonant *t*.

Li inimi, Nom. Plur., has no *s* in agreement with 'rule of *s*.'

4. *Diaule*, for *diable*, is parallel to *peule*, for *peuple*.

5. *Non*, for the sake of the metre, is by some considered to be an etymological spelling at variance with the atonic pronunciation in force : pronounce *n'*.

Eskoltet, for *auscultat*; the last syllable is mute.

Mals, for Latin Accusative, Plural *malos*, keeps the rule of *s*.

6. *Raneiet*, a Present of Subjunct. for Latin *reneget*. Old French : *renoier, reneier, regnier, raneier*, 'to disown.' The simple Verb is *nier, noier, neier, neger*, the last being the most ancient Infinitive. This Verb, like many others, has both a strong radical vowel and a weak radical vowel.

Maent has one syllable, and is written later *maint*, from Latin *manet*, with a strong Infinitive, *maindre*, and a weak one, *manoir*. It has only one representative in the Modern language, *manant*.

Sus, not from Latin *sub*, 'under,' a Preposition, but from *susum*, 'above,' an Adverb. Old French often spells them identically.

8. *Regiel*, from *regale*, has not yet lost its medial consonant, nor bound together its vowels with the semi-vocal *y* heard in Old French *roial* (pr.: *roiyal*, and *redgel*).

Priement, a Noun, from Verb *prier* (*preier, proier*), which has also the Nouns *priere* (*preiere, proiere*) and *pri*, all with the same sense of 'prayer.' This Verb is another instance of weak and strong radical vowel.

9. *Ule* is more correct after a negation than the *nul* and *nculs* of the Oaths. It was short-lived. *Aucun* takes its place in the Modern language. Another reading is: *niule* in one word, equal to *neule*.

Pouret, from *pótrerat*, has accent on the stem. It has the temporal force of an Imperfect or Past Definite. A similar transfer of force has made of the Subjunctive Pluperfect in Latin an Imperfect in French, Old and Modern.

Between the ninth and tenth line a Conjunction, *que*, called for by Modern usage, has to be understood, as often happens in Old French.

10. *Polle*, Latin *puella*, or *pucllula*, 'a young girl.'

Sempre, from Latin *semper*, means 'always,' 'still,' 'at once.'

Amast has a weak radical vowel, as it is not accented. This was according to rule. Vowel-intensification should be accompanied and caused by accentuation. But the rule became unsettled. *Amast* is from *amásset*.

Lo do menestier, synthetic for *lo menestier de deu*. See above, *li do inimi*, in text.

11. *Presentede*, fem. of Past Part. *presentet*, Latin *presentatu* (*s*).

Maximiien, synthetic for: *a Maximiien*.

12. *Eret*, Imperfect of *estre*, with unaccented termination, directly formed from Latin *erat*, and of Neo-Latin coinage, an alternative to *estoit*, of purely Old French analogy. Forms: *iert, ere*.

Soure, from *super*, has numerous forms, formed with *u, o*, and *e*.

Pagiens. The *i*, as in *regiel*, may be purely orthographic, and not phonetic. This noun has *s* according to rule, and comes from *paganos*.

13. *Enortet*, for a barbarous *inortat*, equivalent to classical *exhortatur*.

Lei, like *li* in same line, is an Objective case, *lei* being distinctly Feminine. They are both in the Dative.

Nonque, from *nunquam*.

Chielt, from Latin *calet*, Old French *chalt, chaut, çaut*, *chault*, a favourite impersonal expression, meaning : ' I do not care.' The Modern French equivalent here is : *dont elle n'a cure.*

14. *Fuiet*, a present of the Subjunctive, from Latin *fugiat*. This is another example to add to those we have already had of the modification of the termination -*at* to -*et*.

15. *Ent* is the *int* of the Oaths.

Adunct, Old French *aüner*, means ' to collect,' ' to brace up,' from Low-Latin *adunare*, ' to make one.'

16. *Melz* from *melius*. Modern : *mieux*.

Sostendreiet, the first appearance of the Conditional Mood, non-existent in Latin, and formed by French on the lines of its own analogy, by the suffixing of a temporal ending (the Imperfect of *avoir*) to the Infinitive, with ensuing acquirement of modal force. Modern French is *soutiendrait.*

17. *Perdesse*, Modern *perdisse*, classical Latin *perdidisset*, Low-Latin *perdisset*, a Pluperfect in Latin, an Imperfect in French, Subjunctive Mood in both languages.

18. *Poros*, the *o* in *os* is *o* seen above, meaning ' this.' The *s* is an enclitic form of *se*, the Verb being used reflexively. Read in three words : *por o s.*

Furet, from *fuerat*, literally ' she had been,' practically ' she was.' We have a compound tense here, while Modern French would say *mourut*, in Past Definite.

A, a Preposition used for *avec*, from Latin *apud.*

19. *Enz* is an Adverb, and means ' inside, well in.' It strengthens the following Preposition *en.*

Enl is for *en le.*

Com must be read as meaning *pour que.*

Arde, a Present Subjunctive of a Verb *ardoir*, lost to Modern French, save in *ardent.*

20. *Colpes*, from Latin *culpas*, Old French *coupe*, ' sin.'

Auret, or *avret*, from *hábverat*, see above, line 2.

No stands for *non, n'.*

S, for the Reflective Pronoun *se.*

Coist, from Infinitive *coire* or *cuire*, ' to cook,' transitive and intransitive. *Se coire* means ' to feel pain.' *Coist* is a Past Definite for Latin *coxit*.

21. *Czo* is the same in meaning as *o*. It is the Latin *ecce hoc*.

Voldret, from Latin *volucrat* changed to *vólverat*, Pluperfect with a Past Definite's meaning.

Concreidre, Latin *concredere*. Modern French has lost this compound, which is here reflective, *nos* being for *non se*.

Pagiens, from Latin Nominative *paganus*, has the *s* required by rule of Old French declension.

22. *Spede*, for *esped*, Latin *spatha*.

Roveret, from *ropáverat*, with the force of a Past Definite, a verb of Germanic origin.

Tolir, a weak Infinitive from the Low-Latin *tollēre*, with accent on the penult. The classical Infin. *tollĕre* has produced the strong Infinitive *toldre*. Both are lost to Modern French.

Chief, or *chef*, from Latin *caput*, 'the head,' forthcoming in Modern French.

23. *Contredist*, Latin *contradixit*, a Past Definite.

24. *Volt*, for Latin *volŭit*, is also a Past Definite.

Seule, from Latin *saec(u)lum*; compare *peule* and *d'iaule*.

Lazsier, from Latin *laxare*, with a new meaning. Forms : *laissier*, *laisser*, *laxier*, *lacier*, *leissier*, *lessier*, *lesser*. The Modern compound *délaisser* translates the simple Verb in our text.

Ruovet, with Infinitive *rover*, from Teutonic *ropan*.

25. *Volat*, Past Definite; Latin *volavit*.

26. *Tuit*, from Latin *toti*, has, in consequence, no final *s*.

Orám, from Latin *orémus*, is a Neo-Latin reproduction of First Person Plural Subjunctive Present. The simple *orer* is not forthcoming in the Modern language.

Degnet is a Present Subjunctive. The Infinitive is *deignier*, with many variations; Latin : *dignari*.

27. *Auuisset* reproduces Latin Pluperfect *habuisset*, and is, in our text, an Imperfect of Subjunctive. Another form is *ouist*, more contracted. They are both Neo-Latin only. Old French says *eüst* or *euïst*.

Mercit, from *mercedem*.

28. *Post* is Latin *post*. Old French : *pues, puez, puis, puys, pois, pos, poyst*.

Laist, from Latin *laxet,* Present of the Subjunctive.

29. *Souue,* a form of the Possessive Adjective in the Feminine.

The use everywhere of diphthong *ci* for *oi* shows this hymn to have been written in the Western dominions of the Langue d'Oïl. It affords scope for studies of verse and of metre, as well as of comparative grammar. There is a little more 'analysis' than in the Oaths: the Indefinite Article appears once, the Definite is frequent, the Prepositions *de* and *a* are used, and Subjective Personal Pronouns are freely placed before Verbs. In tenses and moods Latin etymology still reigns supreme. There is yet no independent body of French analogy.

Our next extract is in no respect more typically French than Eulalia's canticle. If anything, it is the reverse, for the Romance text is not continuous. The monkish writer breaks away into more familiar Latin at every moment, and, what is worse, gaps in the sense are not rare. As the Latin context is absolutely necessary to make sense of the Romance fragments, we shall give it in Modern French and in square brackets. This will make it intelligible to students who do not read Latin, and keep it distinct from the Romance we wish to examine. *Il,* in the formula *il dit, dit-il,* stands for *le livre*: the Bible.

FRAGMENT DE VALENCIENNES

[Il eut miséricorde] si cum il [toujours] solt haveir de [le pécheur] e [ainsi il libéra] (les Ninivites) de cel peril quet il [avait décrété] que [sur] els metreiet. [Et Jonas fut affligé d'une grande affliction, et il s'irrita: et il pria Dieu, et il dit: la mort pour moi est meilleure que la vie]. Dunc, ço [il dit], si fut [le prophète Jonas] mult correcious e mult ireist [parce que Dieu eut pitié des Ninivites] e lor [péché] lor [remit]: saveiet [que cette pénitence] astreiet [la destruction des Juifs] e ne doceiet [ceux-ci. Aussi il déplorait] lor salut, cum il [faisait la perdition des Juifs], ne si cum [nous lisons] e le [Evangile] que [notre Maître pleura sur Jérusalem . . . Et Jonas sortit de la ville et

s'assit pour voir ce qui arriverait à la cité]. Dunc, ço
[dit-il, quand Jonas le prophète] cel [peuple eut] pretiet e
convers . . . si escit foers de la [cité] et si sist [vers
l'orient de la cité] e si avardevet [si Dieu détruirait la
ville, ou miséricordieux] astreiet u ne fereiet. [Et le
Seigneur fit monter un lierre au dessus de la tête de Jonas,
pour lui donner de l'ombre ; . . . le prophète Jonas avait]
mult laboret et mult penet a cel [peuple], ço [il dit] ; e
[il faisait] grant iholt, et eret mult las : [aussi le Seigneur
éleva] un edre sore sen cheue quet umbre li fesist e
repauser si podist. [Et Jonas se réjouit du lierre], mult
[il se réjouit], ço [il dit], por que deus cel edre li donat a
sun soueir et a sun repausement. [Et le Seigneur commanda à un ver qui frappa le lierre et le déssécha ; et Dieu
fit souffler un vent chaud sur la tête de Jonas, et il dit : il
vaut mieux que je meure]. Dunc, ço [il dit], si [ordonne]
deus ad un verme que percussist cel edre sost que cil [était
assis] ; e cum cilg eedre fu seche, si vint grancesmes iholt
[sur la tête de Jonas, et il dit : j'aime mieux mourir que
vivre. Et le Seigneur dit à Jonas : T'affliges-tu à bon
droit de ce lierre, et il répondit : Je m'en afflige à bon
droit. Maintenant par] cel edre dunt cil tel [ombre eut],
si [vous devez entendre les Juifs] chi [restent desséchés et
arides, parce qu'ils renient le Fils de Dieu], por quet il en
cele duretie et en cele encredulitet permessïent, si cum
dist e le [Evangile selon Matthieu] de avant dist ; e por
els es doliants, car ço [les prophètes voyaient par l'esprit],
que, [quand les peuples viendraient à la foi], si astreient li
[Juifs] perdut, si cum il ore sunt. [Et le Seigneur dit :
Tu t'affliges de ce lierre, et je n'épargnerais pas la cité de
Ninive où il y a tant d'hommes qui ne peuvent distinguer
leur main droite de leur gauche]? Dunc si [Dieu dit au
prophète Jonas : tu douls mult (de cel edre) . . . e io ne
dolreie de [tant de milliers d'hommes] si perdut erent?
. . . [De plus] en ceste [chose] ore [vous pouvez voir
combien la miséricorde et la pitié de Dieu sont grandes] :
cil [voulait] delir [les hommes] de cele [cité] et tote la
[cité il voulait] comburir [et anéantir. Mais comme] per
cele [menace expiation] fisïent, si achederent [leur pardon

et la rémission de leurs péchés. Le Dieu tout-puissant qui est miséricordieux et clément], cum ço [il vit] quet il se erent convers [de leur mauvaise voie], et sis penteiet de cel mel que fait [ils avaient, leur pardonna et ils furent ainsi libres] de cel peril quet il [avait décrété] que [sur] els mettreiet. [Vous pouvez] ore [voir] et entelgir [de quelle utilité est le repentir à ceux] chi sil feent cum faire lo deent, e cum cil lo fisïent dunt ore aveist odit. E poro si vos avient de pécher, faciest cest [pénitence] quet oi comenciest; ne aiet nïuls male [volonté contre] sem peer; . . . aiest cherté [entre vous, parce que la charité couvre une multitude de péchés]; seietst unanimes [dans le service de Dieu], et en tot [vous serez récompensés; faites vost almosnes, ne si cum faire [vous devez]; cert, ço [vous savez que vous pouvez] acheder ço que li preirets; preiest li que de cest [péril il nous délivre] chi [de si grands maux avons faits, et qu'il nous garantisse des païens] e de mals [chrétiens. Demandez] li que cest [fruit], que mostret nos [il a], quel nos [conserve et qu'à maturité] conduire lo posciomes, e cels [aumônes] ent [puissions faire telles] que [nous] lui ent [puissions plaire. Demandez] li que [il nous accorde la rémission de tous nos péchés, et nous fasse parvenir aux joies éternelles . . .

Students who have consulted in the Bible the short book of the prophet Jonah, and compared it with this homily, will easily understand the course followed by the unknown ecclesiastic whose notes are of such value to modern philology. He quotes a biblical passage, then he explains it in the French vernacular of his day.

GRAMMATICAL COMMENTARY

Solt, from Latin *soluit, solvit,* is a word whose loss the Modern language should regret. It is equivalent to : *avoir coutume.* Infinitive is : *soloir, souloir, suloir.*

Haveir stands for *avoir.*

Els is for Modern *eux,* and it is the Objective case of

Masculine Plural. The vocalisation of *l* has at no time taken place in the Feminine.

Metreiet is a Conditional formed like *sostendreiet*, already mentioned. *Astreiet*, from *estre*, and *fereiet*, both lower down in our text, are formed in the same way. In texts of later date the same person appears without *e*, and ends in *-eit* or in *-oit*, according to the dialect in question. Students recognise without difficulty the Verb *mettre*, to put, with a sense still close to that of Latin *mittere*, to send.

Dunc appears as : *donc, doncq, dont, don, dom, denques, dumques*, etc. From Latin *de unquam*.

Co is the Neuter Demonstrative Pronoun from Latin *ecce hoc*. *Czo*, seen in Eulalia's canticle, and the forms *iceo, cco, iço, iceu, icé, iché*, have the same meaning and origin.

Mult, from Latin *multum*, 'much,' is still used instead of *beaucoup* and *très* in some archaic phrases.

Correcious is the modern *courroucé*.

Ireist, Modern *irrité*, and connected with Old French Past Participle *iré, irié*, Infinitive *irer*, is the Latin *iratus*.

Lor appears here twice in the same clause, first as an Adjective of possession, then as a Personal Pronoun in Dative Plural. The proper value of the Latin *illorum* is much generalised in the French Personal Pronoun, while the Possessive, which is in other respects logically conceived, adds after a while in the Plural a non-etymological *s*.

Saveiet and *doceiet* are Imperfects, in which we detect the same suffix as in the Conditional Present. This is quite regular, since the Conditional is, in formation and often in use, the Imperfect of the Future. The *e* preceding the *t* is an intercalary letter peculiar to this text. *Saveiet* is Modern *savait*.

Doceiet, from Latin *docebat*, Infinitive *docēre*, to teach, has no heir in Modern French. It was a short-lived Neo-Latin formation.

Astreiet is one of the three alternative forms for the Future of *estre*, with the Conditional suffix instead of the pure Future suffix. The only one that has survived is derived from a Low-Latin Infinitive, *essère*, being in Old

French *seroie*, Modern *serais*, with spurious *s*. *Astreiet*, or *estreiet* (*esteroit*), is from the Old French Infinitive *estre*. As for the Future, *ere, ers, ert, crmes, ertes, erent*, from Latin *ero, eris, erit, erimus, eritis, erunt*, the most etymological of the three, it has not produced any Conditional, and some of its persons are not to be found in paleographic monuments.

Ne si appears twice in this text as a composite co-ordinative Conjunction. *Ne si cum* must be read as equivalent to *aussi comme, aussi* referring to the antecedent, and *comme* introducing a fresh statement. This gives to *ne* an affirmative value, instead of the negative one it should hold on the strength of its etymology.

E stands for *en*, Preposition meaning 'in.'

Pretiet has led to several conjectures; it is better to connect it with Latin *praedicatus*, Modern *prêché*, than with anything else.

Convers, Modern *converti*, is from Latin *conversus*. These Participles *pretiet* and *convers* connected with an Auxiliary, in Latin in the text (*eut* in our Modern French translation), form a compound tense that corresponds to the Past Anterior, thus breaking away distinctly from Latin syntheticism.

Escit, is a Past Definite for Latin *exiit, exīt*, or *exīvit*. Old French has the Verb *issir, isir, iscir, yssir, eissir, escir, exir*. Modern French has kept only the Past Participle *issu*, and the Noun *issue*, its Feminine. *Issant* is a term of heraldry. The Latin Present *exĭt*, with accent on first syllable, produced *ist* regularly.

Foers, from Latin *foris*. Old French *fors, for, fores*, means with ensuing *de*, 'out of.' A locative Adverb in Latin, it is used in Modern French to mean: 'except,' 'save'; but it is archaic even then. *Si*, from Latin *sic*, occurs here three times: and so he went out, and so he sat, and so he waited (an epic or familiar use of the expletive *si*).

Sist, Third Person of Past Definite, and the Plural, *sisdrent*, point to a Perfect: *sistit, sistĕrunt*, from Infinitive *sistere*. The same stem appears in Past Participle *sis*.

Avardevet contains a root which the *Lingua Romana* may have had, but which it did not get from Latin. French *garder* is from Germanic *warten*, and, as in other words of the same origin, there is a swaying in the beginning between *w* and *gu*. The simple Verb, *garder*, has also in Old French the form *warder*; English has both, to ward, and to guard. For 'to look,' Old French has the compound *esgarder*, and *aeswarder*; our *avardevet* is akin to it, and from an Infinitive *avardar*, 'to watch,' 'to wait.' The suffix is the Latin ending -*ābat* in a Neo-Latin shape; for the suffix -*ēbat* we have in this fragment -*eiet*.

U is for *ou*, Latin *aut*, meaning 'or,' here 'and.'

Fereiet, one of the Conditionals mentioned above : Verb *faire*.

Laboret, Latin *laboratu* (*s*), is used here in the sense of Modern *travaillé*, wider than that of Modern *labourer*. In connection with preceding *habebat* (*il avait* in our intercalated Modern French translation) it forms a Pluperfect which is analytical after French analogy instead of being synthetical, as the Latin equivalent *laboraverat* would be. We have, therefore, in the text, so far as form goes, examples of French and of Latin Pluperfect.

Penet, Low-Latin *poenātu* (*s*), with a meaning still associated with that of the Latin deponent : *punior* or *poenior*; Modern : *peiné*.

Cholt, written *iholt* in the text, is from Latin *calidus*, Modern *chaud*, Old French forms being : *caut*, *cholt*, *chault*, *chaut*.

Eret, Latin *erat*. One reason for the arising of the Modern French form of Imperfect, *était*, is the similitude of Latin Imperfect and Latin Future : no distinction could be made in Old French between them : hence the substitution of *était* for the one, and of *sera* for the other.

Sore, Modern *sur*, Latin *super*, has been seen in Eulalia's canticle.

Edre, from Latin *hedera*, 'ivy.' The article has been agglutinated to the word in later times : *lierre*, instead of *l'ierre*, hence Modern *le lierre*.

Cheue, or *Cheve*, Latin *caput*, 'head.'

Fesist, from *fecisset,* a Pluperfect in Latin, is in our text an Imperfect of Subjunctive.

Podist, from a barbarous *podisset.* Same tense and mood as preceding word. Modern verb *pouvoir.*

A in the sense of Modern *pour.*

Soueir has afforded scope for much discussion among philologists. First connected with Latin *sudarium* or *siparium,* it is now set down to be an Infinite used substantively, and connected either with Latin *sedere,* 'to sit,' or with *sopire,* 'to sleep.'

Repausement, Low-Latin *repausamentum,* meaning *repos,* is lost to Modern French.

Percussist, with Infinitive *percutre,* is from Latin Pluperfect *percussisset,* Infinitive *percutere,* 'to strike.' Modern French has lost *percutre,* but it has -*percuter* in composition, with an analogical Imperfect Subjunctive -*percutât.*

Cilg for *cil.* Notice how consistently *cil* stands for Subjective case, and *cel* for Objective case.

Vint, from Latin *venit,* is what it was to remain.

Grancesmes, from Latin *grandissimus,* is a Neo-Latin Superlative of the Latin synthetic type; a later form is *grandisme.* Several of these were at a time scattered up and down the language.

Dunt is the *dont* of the Canticle. It comes from *de unde,* and, etymologically, would be spelt *d'ont.*

Permessïent is open to controversy. The sense demands a Third Person Plural of the Imperfect of the Indicative. The Latin Verb is *permanere,* 'to remain.'

Dist, forthcoming twice in this sentence, is, in the first case, for Latin *dixit,* that is a Past Definite. In the second case it corresponds to a Latin Past Participle *dicĭtum* or *dixtum,* which is not classical; *dict* or *dit,* from *dictum,* is the normal Past Participle.

Es stands for *est.*

Doliants comes from a corrupt form of Latin *dolens,* the Present Participle of *doleo,* 'I suffer.' The Old French Infinitive is *doloir* or *douloir.* Modern French has lost this excellent word. Other forms of Present Participle are *dolent, dolant.*

Perdut, Nominative Plural, from Low-Latin *perdúti* : the rule of *s* is carefully observed. *Perduts* would represent Latin *perdutos*.

Ore, also written *or*, *ores*, is an Adverb, derived from the Noun *hore* (*ore*, *heure*, *eure*, *hure*, *ure*), which is the Latin *hora*, 'an hour.' It enters as component into many Adverbs of time, and means 'now,' 'at present.'

Douls, Second Person of Present Tense of *douloir*, seen above.

Dolreie, Conditional of same Verb.

Erent. *-ent* is atonic, as in its Modern equivalent *étaient*.

Ceste, Modern *cette*, from *ecce ista* (*m*) like *cele*, Modern *celle*, from *ecce illa* (*m*). They are Adjective-Pronouns, that is, they fill at will either capacity, and are well exemplified in this sentence and the next, in which they stand in contrast to each other; the first expresses the nearer, and the second the remoter, Object.

Delir, with an Infinitive in *-ir*, from Latin *delēre*, has been replaced in Modern French by *détruire*, its synonym, in Old French, *destruire*.

Comburir is an irregularly-formed Infinitive. French Infinitives in *-er*, *-ir*, *-oir*, should come only from Latin Infinitives accented on the penultima. Those accented on the antepenultima should end on the atonic ending *-re* in French. *Comburir*, from Latin *combúrĕre*, breaks the law, while *delir*, from *delēre*, obeys it. *Comburere* should give : *combourre*, as *currere* gave *courre*.

Fisient is the Third Person Plural of the Imperfect of the Indicative of *faire*. The Latin *faciebant* corresponds to it.

Achederent, Plural Past Definite of *acheder*, *acheter*, 'to purchase.'

Convers, Latin *conversos*, whence it is a direct formation ; while Modern French says *convertis*, from its own Infinitive *convertir*. The interest of the word arises from its construction with *se*, the Reflective Pronoun, *estre* (*être*) being used as Auxiliary, just as reflective verbs are conjugated in the Modern language.

Sis is a contraction of *les*, Personal Pronoun, with *si*, the expletive from *sic*.

Penteiet, which would generally be *penteit* or *pentoit,* is another instance of the *e* intercalated in the Imperfects of the text. From Latin *poenitebat,* it is used impersonally according to Latin grammar, being here in the singular.

Mel for *mal,* Latin *malum* ; other forms : *mau, miel.*

Entelgir, from Latin *intelligere,* which became *intelgire* by accent displacement, metathesis of *g* and loss of penultimate *e.*

Sil, a contraction of Expletive *si* with the Objective Personal Pronoun *le.*

Feent has the accent on the first syllable; it is the Third Person Plural Present Indicative of *faire,* the Low-Latin equivalent being *facunt.* Other more usual forms are the monosyllabic *funt* and *font.* *Facunt* is for classical *faciunt.*

Deent, analogical to *feent,* is from Latin *debent.*

Aveist, from Latin *habetis,* with the accent on the second syllable, like its Modern descendant *avez.* The word is dissyllabic, *st* being for *z* and *ei* diphthongal for modern *e.*

Odit is Latin *auditum.* It is Neo-Latin for Old French *oï,* Infin. at first *odir,* then *oyir, oÿr, oïr.* *Aveist odit* is an example of French analysis in contrast with the synthetic *audivistis* of classical Latin, which means the same thing.

Avient, from Old French Infinitive *avenir* ; the *d* of the Modern *advenir* was introduced at the Revival of Letters. The Pronoun is omitted. *Avient = il advient.*

Faciest is, in the Second Person Plural, the same tense as the *fazet* of the Oaths. It has the accent on the second syllable, unlike *fazet,* owing to the Latin law of accent.

Oi, from Latin *hodie,* meaning ' to-day' (itself a compound for *hoc die*), has the forms *ui, hoi, hui.*

Comenciest, with an Infinitive *comencier* or *comencer* (forms: *comensier, commenchier, cumancer, cummancer, commencier, commenchier, commencer*) from the Latin Preposition *cum* in composition with *initiare,* is the Second Person Plural of the Present Subjunctive.

Aiet, from Latin *habeat,* is the Third Person Singular Present Subjunctive for Modern French *ait.*

Aiest, a little lower down, is the Second Person Plural of same Tense and Mood, from *habeatis.* It has the accent

C

on the last syllable, while *aiet* has it on the first, as evident in form *ait*. Other forms are: *aiets, aies, aieiz, aiez.*

Sem is for *son*, Possessive Pronoun.

Peer, from Latin *parem*, has the forms : *per, peir, picr, par*. It is the Modern *pair* and the English ' peer.' It has a restricted use in Modern French, and a very wide one in Old French, in the sense of *compagnon*.

Cherté, from Latin *caritatem*, with by-form *chierté*, has partly lost its place in Modern French to *charité*.

Seietst, an isolated form for Old French *soies, soieiz, soiez*, Present Subjunctive Second Person Plural, used imperatively.

Unanimes is a learned word, which the writer of our text may have coined himself from Latin *unanimus*. It is an unwrought word, it is thrust into the text in a crude condition, such as it was in Latin, and it has never undergone recoinage at the hands of the people.

Faites, from *facitis*, is identical with the *faites* of the Modern language.

Vost stands for Modern *vos*, with forms, *vos, voz*.

Almosnes, from *eleemosunas*, a Greek word naturalised in Rome and less corrupted in French than in the English ' alms.' Modern French *aumône*.

Ne si is here affirmative, and was discussed before.

Cert, from Latin *certis*, with form *chert*, lives on in Modern *certes* as an Adverb, and as an Adjective has been ousted by *certain*.

Preirets is the Second Person Plural Future of the Old French *preier*, or *proier*, or *prier*, mentioned before. *Preiest* that follows is the same person of the Present Subjunctive used imperatively.

Mostret is the Past Participle of an Infinitive with many forms: *monstrer, moustrer, mustrer, monstreir*. It comes from Latin *monstrare*, to show, Modern *montrer*.

Qel is a contraction of the Conjunction *que* with the Objective Personal Pronoun *le*.

Posciomes, the First Person Plural Present Subjunctive of *pooir* or *podir* already seen more than once; it comes from a barbarous Latin form: *possiomus*.

Ent, already several times seen, must be translated here, first by *en*, and further on by *par elles*.

Of the early documents of the pre-literary period three can be neglected here: the one is known under the name of *Sponsus*, the other is the *Epître de St. Etienne*, and the third is the *Paraphrase du Cantique de Salomon*.

Of greater importance are the *Passion du Christ* and the *Vie de St. Léger*.

The *Passion du Christ*, the first in date of the numerous Old French amplifications of this subject, is a poem containing 516 octosyllabic lines. It is remarkable for a dash of *Langue d'Oc* or *Provençal* in its language, and therefore cannot be offered as a pure sample of the *Langue d'Oïl* in the tenth century.

The form derived from the Latin Pluperfect occurs several times:—

vidra is from	*viderat.*
veggra	,,	*venerat.*
fura, fure	,,	*fuerat.*
voldrat	,,	*voluerat.*
fedre	,,	*fecerat.*
agre	,,	*habuerat.*

These are not the only 'Latinisms.' Such occur repeatedly in the flexions and in the interior phonetics of words. As for the metre in which this fragment of a sacred epic is written, it is the eight-syllabled line. As the poem was meant to be sung, the requirements of music helped to insure the regularity of the metre. Within each stanza the full compass of the melody was developed, and the repetition of it in every set of four lines gave to the poem the monotony appertaining to Church lyrics.

The *Vie de St. Léger*, with the mention of which we close our study of the monuments of the pre-literary period, consists of some 240 lines in the same eight-syllabled metre, divided into stanzas of six lines each. It gives an account of the life, merits, and death of St. Leodegar, whose martyrdom appealed to the devotional feeling of ecclesiastic poets. But it does not appear that he was a privileged object of their respect; for, says the unknown romancer, 'as we have to praise the Lord God and to do honour to his saints, we sing of the saints who for his sake underwent heavy trials, and the time has come for us to sing of St. Leodegar.'

The fragment that has reached us is therefore a single portrait from an otherwise lost gallery. It stands chronologically near the 'Passion of Christ.'[1]

[1] For all the ancient documents treated of or mentioned in this chapter, and a few more, see, for the texts, *Altfranzösisches Uebungsbuch, erster Theil, Die ältesten Sprachdenkmäler*, by Foerster and Koschwitz. For the *Apparatus Criticus* see *Commentar zu den ältesten französischen Sprachdenkmälern*, by Dr. E. Koschwitz. The phonetics of Old French should be studied in *Grammatik des Altfranzösischen*, §§ 1-333, by Dr. Eduard Schwan, second edition. An excellent exposition of the general phonetics of French, including Old French, will be found in *Cours de Grammaire Historique de la Langue française, première partie, phonétique*, by Arsène Darmesteter. The history of French pronunciation from the sixteenth century will be found in *De la Prononciation française depuis le commencement du XVI. siècle*, by Ch. Thurot. The phonetic development in the *Langue d'Oc* appears jointly with that of *Langue d'Oïl* in Suchier's *Die französische und provenzalische Sprache* (Gröber's *Grundriss der Romanischen Philologie*). There is a very good and compact phonetical treatise at the beginning of *La Langue et la Littérature française depuis le IXème siècle jusqu'au XIVème siècle, Textes et Glossaire*, par Karl Bartsch, *précédés d'une Grammaire de l'ancien français*, par Adolf Horning. Paris, 1887.

SECOND BOOK

GRAMMAR

FIRST PART—FLEXIONS

SECOND PART—SYNTAX

SECOND BOOK

GRAMMAR

FIRST PART—FLEXIONS

No acquaintance with the Old French flexional system can be thorough that is not based upon a serious previous study of the phonetics controlling the passage of words from Latin to Romance, and from Romance to Old French. In consequence, the best Old French Grammars append to grammar properly so-called a treatise on the alterations undergone in the mouth of the speaker, both by the stems and the flexions making up the material of the ancient French speech.

We have already indicated the most easily accessible works on French phonetics.

For a study of grammatical flexions upon a plan more extensive and deeper laid than ours, one should turn to Hermann Suchier's *Die französische und provenzalische Sprache und ihre Mundarten* in Gröber's *Grundriss der Romanischen Philologie*. In Schwan's *Grammatik des Altfranzösischen*, the §§ 334 to 535, or *Formenlehre*, deal with the Old French flexions, and the second volume, which appeared this year [1894], of A. Darmesteter's *Cours de Grammaire Historique* treats of the same subject under the title *Morphologie*. These are the latest works; they are compact, trustworthy, written by masters in the science, and each in about 200 pages exhausts, from an expositor's point of view, what lies within this province of Romance philology. The history of Old French flexions extends from the eleventh century to the fifteenth. It is not in the nature of language that it should, during a period of some five centuries, make no change in its grammar. Generally speaking, we shall find in Early Old French etymological flexions, in Middle Old French regular flexions, and in Late Old French decaying or confused flexions, which may be grouped under the common name analogical flexions.

CHAPTER I

THE DEFINITE ARTICLE

THE Latin forms lying at the foundation of this Article are the case-forms of the Demonstrative Pronoun and Adjective *ille*. The same forms lie at the foundation of the Pronoun of the third person and of the corresponding Possessive Adjective of plurality. The Latin *ille* had, in latter days of classical Latin, and in the *Lingua Romana*, seen its use much increased, and its substantial value diminished. As an Adjective and Article its accent was merged into that of the following word; as a Pronoun it preserved better its tonic independence. It does not appear that any rules of Latin accent were violated : their gradual transformation accounts for the loss of the accentual stress in *ille*, for its displacement in some forms of Old and Modern French, and for its preservation in other forms.

The Article and Personal Pronouns must have a marked tendency to become enclitic or proclitic. They are liable to contraction with preceding or following words. Contraction of the Article with the vowel of the following word is called elision in the Modern language. In the Old, when it took place, the apostrophe being practically non-existent, the amalgamation was fully carried out in writing, as in speech. Contraction with the preceding word is a more thorough process, the two words becoming incorporated into one with ensuing phonetic change. These contractions are far more common in Old French than in Modern French, and point to an early and thorough corruption of the Latin *ille*, when it was pressed into service to show Gender analytically for inflections lost in Nouns.

Articles were, to a great extent, dispensed with in the earliest stage of French. *Ille* went through the mass of its phonetic changes as Personal Pronoun and as Demonstrative Adjective rather than as Article. Its inflected syllable alone appears in the Article. In spite of the many functions thrown upon the French offsprings of the Latin *ille*, they have fallen away less from the Latin paradigm of case-inflections than the Nouns. They have still in their vowels traces of 'case,' visible as a rule only in the consonantal terminations of French. *Le, la, li, les, lui, leur*, etc. are proofs of this, though some vowel changes visible in Old French are purely local.

Principal forms of Old French Definite Article.

Simple Nominative forms.

	Masc.	*Fem.*
Sing.	li, le, lo.	la, li, le.
Plur.	li, les, le.	les, li.

Simple Accusative forms.

Sing.	le, lo, lou.	la, le, lai.
Plur.	les, los.	les.

Contracted Genitive forms.

Sing.	del, dou, du, do.	de la, de le, de lai.
Plur.	dels, des.	dels, des.

Contracted Dat. forms.

Sing.	al, au.	a la, a le, ai lai.
Plur.	als, as, aus, aux.	als, as, aus.

Contracted Locative forms.

enl, el, equivalent to *en le, en la.*
ou, u, o, same origin.
enls, els, es, ens, equivalent to *en les.*

It is a question whether there has been a Neuter form of the Article. If so, it is *le*, and being identical with the Masculine can hardly be distinguished from it. Evidence on this point is mostly drawn from the absence of *s* at the end of some Nouns, Neuter in Latin, and preceded by *le* in

French. The absence of *s* in the Nominative Singular and Accusative Plural would show that these Nouns have not been assimilated to the Masculine Nouns 'of the same declension, and that therefore *le* is Neuter. But this is very uncertain.

CHAPTER II

INDEFINITE ARTICLE

THIS is from the Latin *unus*, a declinable Numeral, used indeterminately.

Nominative forms.

	Masc.	Fem.
Sing.	uns, un, ung.	une.
Plur.	un.	unes.

Objective (Accusative) forms.

Sing.	un, ung, unt, u.	une.
Plur.	uns.	unes.

There are no contracted Gen. and Dat. forms, as in the Definite Article. The Plural of the Indef. Art. was at length partly replaced by the Partitive Article of Modern Grammar, identical in form and origin with the Genitive case of the Definite Article, and not separable from it in Old French. All Articles are subject to the principles of declension explained in the next chapter.

CHAPTER III

THE NOUN

THE declension of the Old French Noun is a relic of the Latin system of Noun declension. For practical purposes, the Latin system may be considered as reduced to three declensions instead of five, to two genders instead of three (Neuter being lost), and to two case-inflections instead of four or five distinct ones. Of those Latin cases, one remained distinct, the Nominative; the others were merged into one, called the Objective case or the Oblique case, and more directly derived from the Latin Accusative than from any other oblique case.

Accordingly, Nouns must be divided into two Genders, three Declensions, and two Cases.

I. FEMININE NOUNS

Declension derived from the First Latin Declension, and partly from the Third

This declension is the most rudimentary in Old French, because it is the frailest in Latin. *Rosa, rosae, rosâ*, have nothing substantial enough in their endings to convey distinct case-relations when phonetically impoverished, *rosam* lost its *m* in Latin even; *rosis, rosas* have a poor protection against decay in their *s*. The result is that all inflectional vowels in that declension became *e* in Old French; *m* was altogether lost, *s* subsisted with difficulty and precariously in the Objective case of the Plural. The declension is then, etymologically—

	Sing.	*Plur.*
Subj.	rose (for *rosa*).	rose (for *rosae*).
Obj.	rose (for *rosam*).	roses (for *rosas*).

The poverty of this type will strike every one. The final *e* fast becoming mute, the final *s* gradually ceasing to be heard, the accent resting always on the same syllable, everything made for uniformity. This declension was the first to reduce itself to the Modern French uninflectedness. For a while it formed its plural like feminine nouns of the third declension, and then confusion ensued.

We find in very Old French purely Roman forms like *corona* (for *coronam*) in the Objective case; we find forms after the analogy of the second declension, like *terres* (from a fictitious *terrus*) in the Subject case of the Singular.

Taking irregularities into account, and using one word only as paradigm, a historical table of endings would be shown thus:—

	Sing.	*Plur.*
Subj.	rose (rosa, roses).	(rose) roses.
Obj.	rose (rosa).	roses.

A peculiar feature of this declension is an Accusative in
-*ain*. Its origin is doubtful. Some philologists attribute
it to Teutonic influences, others see in it a reproduction
of the Latin Accus. in -*am*. Others seek its explanation
in a Low-Latin form in -*ánem*, replacing the regular flexion
in -*am*, become meaningless by phonetic decay. By this
last hypothesis, a feature of Old French declension, resting
on the place of Latin accent in oblique cases, is very
plausibly introduced into this class of words. This type
runs thus :—

	Sing.	*Plur.*
Subj.	ante.	antains.
Obj.	antain.	antains.

A Low-Latin declension, reconstituted from these Old
French forms, would be ;—

ánta.	*antánes.*
antánem.	*antánes.*

Examples are the old French forms :—

Subj.	pute.	Berte.	Eve.	pinte.	none.
Obj.	putain.	Bertain.	Evain.	pintain.	nonain.

Such forms are rare, and lost ground gradually.

The noun *suer* may be placed here on account of similarity
in declension with *ante, antain*.

Latin.

	Sing.	*Plur.*
Nom.	*sóror.*	*soróres.*
Acc.	*sorórem.*	*soróres.*

Old French.

Subj.	suer.	serors.
Obj.	seror.	serors.

The above applies to Nouns, Feminine in Latin as well
as in French, belonging almost all to the first Latin declension. Two classes yet remain to be considered : Nouns
primitively Neuter in Latin and made Feminine by a false
analogy ; Nouns Feminine in Latin, but belonging to the
third declension. The former category, by a series of

barbarisms, was assimilated to Feminine Nouns in *a* and and received the Objective flexion in *s* on a scheme as follows :—

Low-Latin pattern.

Sing.	*Plur.*
animalia.	*animalia.*
animaliam.	*animalias.*

Old French equivalent.

Subj.	almaille.	almailles.
Obj.	almaille.	almailles.

The latter category had in Latin a Nominative Singular ending in *s*. It lost that *s* in Old French, by assimilation to feminine nouns ending in *a*, while forcing upon these the *s* of its Nominative Plural.

Latin.

	Sing.	*Plur.*
Nom.	*finis.*	*fines.*
Acc.	*finem.*	*fines.*

Old French.

Nom.	fin.	fins.
Acc.	fin.	fins.

II. MASCULINE NOUNS

Declension derived from the Second Latin Declension

This declension is the triumph of the rule of *s*, resting on the fact that a very large number of Latin Nouns in all five declensions, except Sing. of first, ends in *s* in the Nominative Singular, and, in the principal oblique case of the Plural, the Accusative. This prominent feature, recurring in so many words of so many declensions, is the foundation on which the bulk of the Old French declension is built; the element, common to all, which made possible the merging of the five Latin declensions into what is practically one French declension, with a few collateral formations dependent on accent.

Subject to what we know of the extreme caducity of the Latin final *m* and final *s*, the Latin second declension, as restored by Old French, would be :—

	Sing.	Plur.
Nom.	*amicus.*	*amici.*
Accus.	*amicum.*	*amicos.*

The corresponding Old French formation is :—

	Sing.	Plur.
Subj.	amis.	ami.
Obj.	ami.	amis.

The principle is absolute and sweeping. Applicable at first, strictly speaking, only to the Latin Nouns of second declension ending in *s* in Nom. Sing., and in Accusative and Dative Plural, it has come to embrace Latin Nouns which do not displace the accent in the oblique cases of 2nd, 3rd, 4th, and 5th Latin declensions, ending in -*er*, -*us*, -*um*, -*u*, -*es*, -*is*, etc. In the long run, even Nouns displacing the accent in oblique cases came under the *s* rule, with more or less regularity. It ended by holding sway over the whole field of French ' case,' till it became the sign of the Plural in the Modern tongue.

Examples :—

Latin.

	Sing.	Plur.
Nom.	*murus.*	*muri.*
Accus.	*murum.*	*muros.*

Old French.

	Sing.	Plur.
Subj.	murs.	mur.
Obj.	mur.	murs.

Low-Latin.

	Sing.	Plur.
Nom.	*soliculus.*	*soliculi.*
Accus.	*soliculum.*	*soliculos.*

Old French.

Subj.	solaus.	solel.
Obj.	solel.	solaus.

(The change of *l* to *u* before *s* is normal.)

Whatever orthographical or phonetic changes the bulk of the word may undergo, whatever parasitic letters it may adopt, the principle holds good in the flexion. Its irresistible influence is seen in the following examples, taken from words which, in Latin, do not belong to the 2nd declension :—

Latin (*Singular only*).

Nom.	*panis.*	*fructus.*	*dies.*
Accus.	*panem.*	*fructum.*	*diem.*

Old French (*Singular only*).

Subj.	pains.	fruits (fruiz).	dis.
Obj.	pain.	fruit.	di.

In the Plural, when the Latin ends in *s* in *both* Cases, the assimilation to the flexion of Nouns in *-us* is still more evident :—

Latin (*Plural only*).

Nom.	*panes.*	*fructus.*	*dies.*
Accus.	*panes.*	*fructus.*	*dies.*

Old French (*Plural only*).

Subj.	pain.	fruit.	di.
Obj.	pains.	fruits (fruiz).	dis.

It would be rash, however, to say that assimilation was not preceded by a more etymological scheme. In the case of Latin Nouns ending in *-er*, like *magister*, we have evidence of a correct paradigm, as follows :—

Latin.

	Sing.	*Plur.*
Nom.	*liber.*	*libri.*
Accus.	*librum.*	*libros.*

Old French.

	Sing.	*Plur.*
Subj.	livre.	livre.
Obj.	livre.	livres.

But this was soon swept away by the levelling rule of *s*. This rule is carefully observed in critical editions of old Texts, and, as it is well-nigh universal, students will very rarely be at a loss to know whether they have an Object or a Subject to deal with. On doubtful cases light is thrown by the termination of the Verb, or by the flexion of the accompanying Adjective or Article.

In the first French declension, we had Latin Neuter Nouns by assimilation only; here, in the second, we have them as Nouns of the Latin second declension. Their Latin cases were :—

Latin.

	Sing.	*Plur.*
Nom.	*vinum.*	*vina.*
Accus.	*vinum.*	*vina.*

Phonetically, this would give in

Old French.

	Sing.	*Plur.*
Subj.	vin.	vine.
Obj.	vin.	vine.

But this type has very doubtful credentials. An analogy either with Masc. Nouns in -*us* or Fem. Nouns in *a* was established very early, and entailed the application of the rule of *s*. The type has, however, survived in :—

Latin.

	Sing.	*Plur.*
Nom.	*cornu.*	*cornua.*
Accus.	*cornu.*	*cornua.*

French.

	Sing.	
Subj.	cor.	corne.
Obj.	cor.	corne.

In Modern French those two forms are no longer equivalent in meaning, a separate sense having been allotted to each.

The first and second Latin declensions shifted in one case only the accent towards the flexion; that was in the Genitive Plur.: *rosárum, dominórum.* By the laws of phonetic change, these flexions were liable to confusion with the similar endings : *-órum, -órem, -óris,* etc. They have produced forms in Old French, but very few, and of a temporary character. Preserved in Modern French in a few cases like *chandeleur* (*candelarum*), *leur* (*illorum*), and in some geographical names they have, in other cases, not outlived the Neo-Latin period of Old French. Instances are : *la geste francor* (*gesta francorum*), *la gent paienor* (*gens paganorum*), *le tens ancianor* (*tempus antianorum*), *Sarrasinor, diablor, Macedonor, crestianor, vavassor, al tens Pascor.*

In the *s* declension the Vocative has sometimes *s,* but generally has not. It was not clear whether that case was of the nature of the Subject or of that of the Object.

In this declension the intrusion of the double consonants *z* and *x* calls for our attention. *Z* and *x* were either substituted for the normal *s* arbitrarily, and are equivalent to it, or else they were used with a purpose. In words ending with a dental, *z* is in its place, provided the dental is not written ; so is *x* when a preceding *l* has been vocalised. In that case *x* stands for *-ux,* as *chevex,* for *cheveux,* once *chevux,* earlier yet *cheveus,* and *chevels* at the very beginning. A very late spelling, *cheveulx,* is a useless complication.

S falls before *ts* (*z*) as in *oz,* for *osts, Criz* and *Cris* for *Crists.*

Before *s, m* becomes *n,* as in *nons* for *noms.* Mute consonants are dropped before *s,* ex. : *sans* for *sancs ; sers* for *serfs ; cols* for *colps.*

Latin words, whose sibilant in the inflection is tacked immediately on to the stem, like *voc-s,* forming *vox* in Latin, *vois, voiz* in Old French, do not show visible traces of the *s* declension. The same in general applies to Latin words with a sibilant at the end of their stem, like *sens-us ; vic-es* (sibilant *c,* French *fois*). If the sibilant is not preserved

D

in the Latin oblique cases, the general rules resume sway, for instance: *rois, roi*; *roi, rois.* Nouns from Latin Neuters in *-us* became early undeclinable: ex.: *cors, corps* from *corpus*; *tens, temps* from *tempus.*

The *s* is omitted arbitrarily in several texts, even in old ones, in the Subject Singular. By degrees it disappears from the Singular altogether. As a set-off it appears in both cases of the Plural (end of fourteenth century).

We have collected here the leading facts about the rule of *s.* It applies to Pronouns with limitations, to Numerals, to Adjectives, and also to Nouns of the next declension.

III. MASCULINE NOUNS

Nouns are in Latin parisyllabic or imparisyllabic. With reference to our subject, a parisyllabic noun is one in which the Accusative form has the same number of syllables as the Nominative: the accent being on the same syllable in both cases. An imparisyllabic noun is one in which the Accusative form is by one, or by more than one syllable, longer in the Accusative than in the Nominative.

DECLENSION DERIVED FROM THE THIRD LATIN DECLENSION

A large number of Nouns derived from Latin prototypes of the 3rd declension were assimilated in Old French to Nouns derived from the 2nd Latin declension, and have been dealt with. These, as a rule, are parisyllabic Nouns, which accounts for the assimilation. We have nothing to do with them here. The remaining ones can, in Latin, be divided into two classes. I. Those that form their Accusative case by adding a syllable to the Nominative Stem but without displacing the accent; II. Those which add one or several syllables and do displace the accent towards the inflection. Both classes are imparisyllabic, but the mobility of the tonic accent divides them sharply enough into two groups. Example: *árbor*, gen. *árbŏris*, gives in French: '*árbre*'; but *lábor*, gen. *labóris* gives in French '*labeúr.*'

Now the centre of gravity of an original French word is always situated in the syllable which, in Latin, had the tonic accent. Hence, when the accent is movable, there appear two centres of phonetic growth in the same word, but in different cases, and these variations become means of case-distinction in Old French. This case-distinction cannot be called flexional, because the new token of case is not a separable suffix: it is part and substance of the Latin stem. It does not admit of a generalisation in its process of formation, because it is controlled in each instance by the phonetic affinities of each word liable to it. A Latin root with two differently accented stems produces two Old French forms, each with its function, on purely organic principles. This declension is the triumph of the tonic accent, as the former is the triumph of the rule of s.

On a smaller scale were the phonetic changes in imparisyllabic Latin Nouns which did not displace the accent. Yet this too sufficed to bring about case-distinction. But it was not a barrier powerful enough against the inroad of analogy. These nouns succumbed first. Their Subjectives were lost one by one, and the remaining Objectives submitted to the inevitable rule of s. As for the stronger class, the language rejected one of their accentually differentiated forms, or, losing ultimately the consciousness of case, it saved occasionally both forms by giving them different meanings.

The s declension may be called the Weak Old French declension, and the 'accentual' declension may be called the Strong declension.

It is not possible, from the nature of its principle, to give a generalised paradigm applicable to the words of this declension.

I. *Imparisyllabic Nouns without Accent Variation.*

(*a*) Example of Noun *imparisyllabic* in Latin, with *immovable* accent, and Nominative ending in *s* in the Singular.

Latin.

	Sing.	Plur.
Nom.	cómes.	cómite(s).
Accus.	cómite(m).	cómites.

Old French.

	Sing.	*Plur.*
Subj.	cuens.	comte.
Obj.	comte.	comtes.

(*b*) Example of same, with Nominative free from final *s*.

Latin.

Nom.	*hómo.*	*hómine(s).*
Accus.	*hómine(m).*	*hómines.*

Old French.

Subj.	hom.	homme.
Obj.	homme.	hommes.

This group of *Masculine* Nouns does not keep the Latin *s* in the Nominative Plural, because *all* masculine nouns follow the second declension in the Subjective Plural.

It would be a mistake to think that all Latin words of this group transmitted to Old French have produced forms originally differently sounded. A large number of Latin Nominatives were simply destroyed and laid aside, the Neo-Latin form for the oblique cases alone surviving.

Some forms of the *s* declension are liable to be mistaken for forms of this group, for instance, when *l* is vocalised before an inflectional or stem *s*. The following paradigm belongs to the *s* declension :—

Latin (*Singular only*).

Nom.	*natális.*	*Accus.*	*natálem.*

French (*Singular only*).

Subj.	noeus.	*Obj.*	noel.

The same occurs in *travaux* for *travals*, *faus* for *fals*, *chevax* for *chevals*, etc.

Forms like :—

Subj.	bous,	cos,
Obj.	bouc,	cok,

introduced by analogy in words of Germanic and Celtic origin, are of doubtful classification.

As for Latin Datives and Ablatives in *-ibus*, like *hominibus*, *pectóribus*, causing a secondary accent to obliterate the primary one, they became corrupt before French was in existence.

II. *Imparisyllabic Nouns with Accent Variation.*

This group alone can be properly called the 'accentual' declension.

There is the radically accented form and the inflectionally accented form, as follows :—

Latin.

	Sing.	*Plur.*
Nom.	*venátor.*	*venatóre(s).*
Accus.	*venatóre(m).*	*venatóres.*

Old French.

Subj.	venere.	veneor.
Obj.	veneor.	veneors.

Latin.

Nom.	*látro.*	*latróne(s).*
Accus.	*latróne(m).*	*latrónes.*

Old French.

Subj.	lerre.	larron.
Obj.	larron.	larrons.

The stem and flexion accents are foremost in the Singular. The complete absence of the stem accent in the Plural is the weak point of this declension. Hence an analogy with the second declension established itself in the Subjective plural, and extinguished the Latin *s*. The nouns following this 'accentual' declension are all masculine names of persons, some of them designating classes of human beings, and others being proper names of individuals.

1. From Latin in *-átor*, Acc. *-atórem*, or from presumed Low-Latin words in *-átor* ; also Old French words inflected by analogy on that pattern :—

Subject.	Object.
pechere.	pecheor.
salvere.	salveor.
emperere.	empereor.
criere.	creator.
jugiere.	jugeor.
juglere.	jugleor.
donere.	doneor.
poignere.	poigneor.
vengiere.	vengeor.
chantere.	chanteor.
salvere.	salveor.
trovere.	troveor.
trompere.	trompeor.
baillere.	bailleor.
amere.	ameor.
parlere.	parleor.
enginiere.	engineor.

2. From Low-Latin in *-ítor*, Accus. *-itórem* :—

traïtre.	traïtor.

3. From Latin in *-or*, Accus. *-órem* :—

ancestre.	ancessor.
pastre.	pastor.
sire.	seignor.

4. From Latin or Low-Latin in *-o*, Accus. *-ónem* :—

gar.	garson.
ber.	baron.
compain.	compaignon.
fel.	felon.
gloz.	gloton.
lerre.	larron.
drac.	dragon.
bris.	bricon.
mes.	maison.
faux.	faucon.
brac.	bracon.

5. From various Latin endings :—

Subject.	Object.
enfes.	enfant.
abes.	abbé.
niès.	neveu.
poverte.	poverté.
poeste.	poesté.

A Noun belonging properly to another class has an Objective on this pattern. It is *prestre* (Latin *présbyter*), Objective *preveire, provoire* (from *presbýterum*). Parallel instances can be found.

Examples of proper names with imparisyllabic Objective are :—*Guene*, Object. *Ganelon* ; *Pierre, Pierron* ; *Estevenc, Estevenon* ; *Charle, Charlon*. This supposes a Low-Latin Subject. *Cárolus*, Object. *Carolónem*, as barbarous as the first declension forms in -*ain*.

The rule of *s* in time broke the regularity of the accentual declension by intruding itself upon the Subject Sing. as if it ended in Latin in -*us* or -*is* or some such Nom. suffix. This compels us to give another set of paradigms and of endings in which the spurious *s* and some orthographic by-forms appear :—

I. Latin -*tor*, Accus. -*tórem.*

	Sing.	*Plur.*
Subj.	-iere, -eres, -ere (rr)	-ëor, -ëour, -ëur.
Obj.	-ëor, -ëour, -ëur.	-ëors, -ëours, -ëurs.

II. Latin in -*o*, -*ónem.*

	Sing.	*Plur.*
Subj.	lerres, lerre.	larron.
Obj.	larron, ladron, ladrun.	larrons.

An example of the extensive alterations undergone by words of this type appears in the following :—

	Sing.	*Plur.*
Subj.	{ sendra, sinre. *usually* : sire, sires, sieur. *later* : seigneur.	seignor, etc.
Obj.	{ seignor, seignour. seigneur, senior. sennior, seinor.	seignors, etc.

This is an Adjective in the comparative degree in Latin, but a Noun in Old French.

To sum up, this declension, resting upon Latin or Low-Latin words alternately accented, embraces only a small portion of the Old French Nouns; many a Latin word of this class can show in Old French only the one or the other of the two forms; the rule of *s* engrafted itself upon this class by degrees, and finally effaced the memory of tonic differentiation as a case characteristic. Then a unification took place in each word by the expulsion of the one or the other of the different forms. In *peintre, chantre, sire, maire, traître, ancêtre, moindre, pire, prêtre, on,* all in use at this day, the Nominative forms have become the Modern Nouns.

When the Old French Subject has survived till the Fourteenth Century, it forms a Plural by adding *s*. When the Object has survived it adds *s* in the same way. When both have survived in distinct meanings they both take *s*. In that way the rule of *s* emerges as the cardinal fact of Old French declension, and the one it has most clearly bequeathed to the Modern tongue.

CHAPTER IV

THE ADJECTIVE

THE declension of the Adjective is a chapter in the declension of the Noun. The lines laid down for the one are a frame-work in which must be considered as set all we have to add about the other. As Latin reproduced in its

Adjective-declension the features of its Substantive-declension, so Old French carries out in the former the principles underlying the latter. The difference is this: we divided Nouns into three declensions, and each Noun was allotted to one of the three, while Adjectives belong to the first declension by their feminine, when they have a distinct flexion for it; to the second by their masculine, when it ended in -*us* in Latin; or to the third when their Latin forms were either parisyllabic or imparisyllabic, without flexions whereby to distinguish Masculine and Feminine. Neuter is almost entirely out of count throughout the three declensions. So we have two adjective declensions: the first showing gender by flexion and corresponding to the first and second declensions of Nouns; the second corresponding to the third declension of Nouns and subdivided into two groups, the parisyllabic group and the accent-displacing group, both without inflections for gender.

I. FIRST DECLENSION OF ADJECTIVES

The Latin Prototype is as follows :—

Singular.

	Masc.	*Fem.*
Nom.	bonus.	bona.
Accus.	bonum.	bonam.

Plural.

	Masc.	*Fem.*
Nom.	boni.	bonae.
Accus.	bonos.	bonas.

The Old French etymological type is :—

Singular.

	Masc.	**Fem.**
Subj.	bons.	bone.
Obj.	bon.	bone.

Plural.

	Masc.	**Fem.**
Subj.	bon.	bone.
Obj.	bons.	bones.

The Masculine remained as it is here. The Feminine Plural soon lost its regular nominative, and, as in fem. Substantives, substituted for it the form *bones*, under the same influence (the plural *s* of the Latin third declension in the Nom.).

Here is the same paradigm, but applied to a class of Adjectives in which the working of phonetic laws has obliterated the distinct gender-flexion of the femin. by compelling the masc. to end in *e* (*voyelle d'appui*).

Singular.

	Masc.	*Fem.*
Subj.	tiedes (*tépidus*).	(*tépida*) tiede.
Obj.	tiede (*tépidum*).	(*tépidam*) tiede.

Plural.

Subj.	tiede (*tépidi*).	(*tépidae*) tiedes.
Obj.	tiedes (*tépidos*).	(*tépidas*) tiedes.

If the isolated forms that can be interpreted as neuters warrant the setting up of a separate scheme for that gender, the Neuter would run thus :—

	Singular.	*Plural.*
Subj.	bon (*bonum*).	(*bona*) bone.
Obj.	bon (*bonum*).	(*bona*) bone.

This is tantamount to the absence of all flexion.

Latin Adjectives with Nom. Sing. in -*er*, -*a*, -*um*, were gradually assimilated to those with Nom. in -*us* which follow the paradigm *tiede*.

II. SECOND DECLENSION OF ADJECTIVES

First Group—Parisyllabic

To the first group belong a large class of Latin Adjectives with case-inflections identical with those of the third declension of Latin Nouns, but with no distinct flexion for the Femin., though they have one for the Neuter form.

These Latin Adjectives do not add a syllable in the

Accusative, nor do they displace the accent. If they were Nouns, they would belong in Old French, by an easy assimilation, to the second declension of Nouns. The absence of a distinct Femin. having allowed more prominence to the Latin Neuter, we shall admit it in our first etymological paradigm :—

Latin.

Singular.

	Masc.—Fem.	*Neuter.*
Nom.	*grandis.*	*grande.*
Accus.	*grandem.*	*grande.*

Plural.

	Masc.—Fem.	*Neuter.*
Nom.	*grandes.*	*grandia.*
Accus.	*grandes.*	*grandia*

Old French.

Singular

Subj.	granz.	grant.
Obj.	grant.	grant.

Plural.

	Masc.—Fem.	*Neuter.*
Subj.	granz.	grande.
Obj.	granz.	grande.

This scheme, however, is more ideal than real. The rule of *s* made itself felt in the case-endings, assimilating them to those of the second Noun-declension, obliterating the Neuter and distinguishing the Feminine. The declension became :—

Singular.

	Masc.	*Fem.*
Subj.	granz.	grant.
Obj.	grant.	grant.

Plural.

Subj.	grant.	granz.
Obj.	granz	granz.

At last an 'analogical' *e* became the sign of the Fem.; and the *s* was common to both genders in the Plural.

Here is a paradigm with phonetic modifications :—

	Singular. Masc.—Fem.	*Plural.* Masc.—Fem.
Subj.	loiaus.	loiaus.
Obj.	loial.	loiaus.

To this first group were assimilated Adjectives like *aigre*, from Latin *acer, acris, acre*, and those which do not distinctly fall under the next class.

Second Group—Imparisyllabic.

To the second group belong Adjectives which throw forward the accent in the oblique cases. These, too, have in Latin no inflection for the Feminine. Their difference from the first group was little more than nominal, because the process known as 'stem unification' soon extinguished the Nominative stem, bearing the stem accent, and replaced it by the stem of the Accusative form, bearing the flexion accent. With them we decidedly overstep the line that separates Adjectives proper from Present Participles, and from Comparatives. The Present Participle was declined in Latin : so it was declined in Old French, but barbarously. By stem unification a first paradigm like this arose :—

Low-Latin.

	Singular.	*Plural.*
Nom.	amáns.	amántes.
Accus.	amántem.	amántes.

Old French.

Subj.	amans, z.	amanz.
Obj.	amant.	amanz.

Thus, the important distinction that would have arisen from the preservation of the classical Latin Nom. accented on the first syllable is lost. Once the stem of the Latin Nom. was got rid of, this group of Adjectives was declined

like *granz*, to which we refer the reader for application of
the rule of *s*, and for the distinct Feminine. A large
number of Latin Present Participles, which have become
Adjectives in Old French, fill this group.

The declension of the Present Participle in Old French
brought about in the modern language the class of words
called Verbal Adjectives, whilst the declension was discon-
tinued for the Present Participle proper, but Old French is
not responsible for the introduction of an inflected femin.
in Verbal Adjectives.

Remarks on Past Participles, etc.

Past Participles, whose last letter in the Masculine is a
sounded vowel, follow the first declension of Adjectives.
Some of these preserved originally the Latin *t*, and dropped
it gradually. For instance: *cantatus* gave *chantet*, Fem.
chantede; then *chanté*, Fem. *chantée*. Here is a full paradigm:—

Early Old French.

Singular.

	Masc.	*Fem.*
Subj.	portets (portez).	portede.
Obj.	portet.	portede.

Plural.

Subj.	portet.	portedes.
Obj.	portez.	portedes.

As for Past Participles ending with a consonant—that
is, with a *t* or an *s* having organic life in it, they did not
lose it, and conform to the paradigm *bon, bone*.

Example: *uvert*, Fem. *uverte*; *mis*, Fem. *mise*.

Comparatives of the synthetic type derived from Latin
have, properly, no special feminine flexion, as the Latin
did not hand down any, but those which survived long
enough received the analogical *e* imposed by degrees
on all Adjectives. Superlatives of the same kind
ended organically in *e*, and therefore do not show a
flexional *e*.

A complete treatment of the declension of Adjectives would require a study of changes taking place before the flexional *e* in the letters terminating the stem. For instance, the change of *t* to *d* in Past Participles, of *c* to *ch* in some Adjectives, calls for the student's attention. But we must refer him to the works on the History of the Language for this matter. We have in view a practical, rather than a theoretical, survey of Old French.

Some Adjectives are indeclinable for the same reasons as Substantives, and they are subject to the same orthographic peculiarities. *Fals,* for instance, Modern *faux,* was always *fals* in masculine, being from the Latin *fals-us,* but in the feminine it was regularly declined.

As for orthography, the principal peculiarity is, that the consonant preceding the flexional *s* was dropped, and *ts, z, x, s* were confused, though, strictly speaking, they are not interchangeable. *Frans* stood for *Francs, loiax* for *loiaus, portets* for *portez,* etc.

It must be borne in mind that in the end *the rule of e* for Adjectives became as sweeping as *the rule of s* for Nouns, and that the latter also took as thorough a hold on Adjectives as it had taken on Substantives.

The *analogical s* and the *analogical e,* at first etymological only, now almost purely mechanical, by their assimilative force, so completely drove out of the field all other declensional agencies, that they are, in the Modern Language, the only survival of a flexional system for Substantive and Adjective Nouns.

CHAPTER V

DEGREES OF COMPARISON

THESE call for attention in one respect only. We have mentioned before that some Old French Comparatives and Superlatives are formed directly from the Latin by corruption, while the mass of them follow a new analogy, unprecedented in Latin, which can be called the periphrastic or analytic comparison. The former have a suffix of comparison, the latter have none.

COMPARATIVES

The Latin flexions were *-ior* for masc. and fem., *-ius* for the neuter.

The first gave rise to declinable Adjectives, the second to indeclinable Neuters and Adverbs.

Here is the type, both in Latin and Old French:—

Latin.
Singular.

	Masc.—Fem.	Neuter.
Nom.	grándior.	grándius.
Accus.	grandiórem.	grándius.

Plural.

	Masc.—Fem.	Neuter.
Nom.	grandióre(s).	grandióra.
Accus.	grandióres.	grandióra.

Old French.
Singular.

Subj.	graindre.	grainz.
Obj.	graignor.	grainz.

Plural.

Subj.	graignor.	—
Obj.	graignors.	—

Here is a list of such Comparatives:—

Positive.	Comparative.	Comparative.
	Subjective case.	
	Masc.—Fem.	Neuter.
bons.	mildre.	mielz.
	mieldre.	mieus.
	mieudre.	mix.
	miaure.	
Latin. bónus.	mélior.	mélius.

	Positive.	Comparative.	Comparative.
		Objective case.	
		Masc.—Fem.	*Neuter.*
	bon.	meillor.	—
		meilleur.	—
		millor.	—
Latin.	*bónum.*	*meliórem.*	*mélius.*
		Subjective case.	
	mals.	pire.	piz.
Latin.	*málus.*	*péjor.*	*péjus.*
		Objective case.	
	mal.	pëor.	piz.
Latin.	*málum.*	*pejórem.*	*péjus.*
		Subjective case.	
	(petit) parvs.	mendre.	meins.
Latin.	*párvus.*	*mínor.*	*mínus.*
		Objective case.	
	parv.	menor.	moins.
Latin.	*párvum.*	*minórem.*	*mínus.*
		Subjective case.	
	magnes.	maire.	—
Latin.	*mágnus.*	*május.*	*május.*
		Objective case.	
	magne.	mäor.	—
Latin.	*mágnum.*	*majórem.*	*május.*

The above are all subject to dialectic and orthographic peculiarities. This is the case in almost all words quoted in this work, but for the sake of brevity and precision we must neglect such particulars.

In the following words the principle of an inflectional comparison is markedly, but less systematically, carried out.

bel.	Comparative	belleisor.
fort.	„	forçor.
gent.	„	genzor
halt.	„	halçor.
plus.	„	plusor.
sire.	„	seignor.
joindre.	„	joignor.

These Comparatives fall under the third declension of Nouns, in the group that throws forward the accent to distinguish the subjective from the objective case, but with stem unification.

SUPERLATIVES

The Latin flexion was: *-issĭmus, a, um.* The short *i* fell, leaving *-ismus*, which is represented in the following Superlatives :—

pesmes	from	pessimus.
grandismes	,,	grandissimus.
grantesmes	,,	,,
seintismes	,,	sanctissimus.
altismes	,,	altissimus, etc.

These follow the first declension of Adjectives.

CHAPTER VI

NUMERALS

NUMERALS which in the Modern language have a feminine flexion or a plural flexion were declinable in Old French.

CARDINAL NUMERALS

The first three of these, declinable in Latin, passed into Old French without losing that feature.

Un follows the first declension of Adjectives. The paradigm has been given under the heading : Indefinite Article. It has a plural, chiefly as Indefinite Pronoun.

Dui, Modern *deux*, was declined after a Low-Latin pattern somewhat divergent from the classical one.

Low-Latin.

	Masc.	*Fem.*
Nom.	dui.	duas.
Acc.	duos.	duas.

Old French.

Subj.	dui.	{ dos.
Obj.	dos, deus.	{ deus, deues.

E

The feminine was not long preserved distinct from the masculine.

Trei, Modern *trois*, belongs to the first declension of Adjectives, like *dui*.

Old French.

	Masc.	*Fem.*
Subj.	trei, troi.	{ treis, trois.
Obj.	treis, trois, trais.	{ troie.

The other Cardinals, up to one hundred, are undeclinable; here is a list of them :—

quatre, chatre, quaor.   trente deus.
cinc, chunc, cienq.   trente treis.
sis, seis.   quarante, charante.
sept, set, seat.   cinquante, chiunkante.
uit, oit, vit, ut.   soissante, sissante.
nuef, nef, nof, nos.   setante, septante.
dis, dez, deis.   oitante, octante.
onze, ouse.   nonante, nunante.
deuze, doce, dusce.   cent, cens, chens.
treize, trese, troize.   cent e vint.
quatorze, kators.   dui cent, deus cens.
quinze, chinze, quince.   troi cent, trois cenz.
seize, seze, sese.   cinc cent, cinc cenz.
dis et set, deiz et seit.   wit cenz e seisante e sis (866).
dis e uit, dis et huis.   mil, mile, mille, milie.
dis e nof, dis e nuef.   mil e wit cenz.
vint, nins (plural).   trois mile.
vint e un.   mil milie (1,000,000).
vint e dels, etc.   dis fies cent mile.
trente, treante.   mil foiz mile mile (1,000,000,000).
trente e un.

Quatre and *cinq* are found with an *s*, which is not etymological, and may be declensional.

The Celtic method of counting by twenties is prevalent alongside the usual one of counting by tens. Hence: *quatre vint, quatre vint e cinq, cinq vint, dix vint, six vinz.* The *s* is arbitrarily resorted to or omitted. The rule of Modern

French on this Numeral is unknown to the Old language. Old French is more systematic in the addition of *s* to *cent*; it appears as a rule in the plural objective case. This Numeral was fully declined in Latin, while the above-mentioned one was not declined at all.

Mil is derived from Latin *mille*, and is a singular; *mile* is from *milia*, and is a neuter plural. Old French has no larger unit than *mil*.

A declinable Numeral from Latin *ambo* must be treated separately; it means 'both.'

Am is the subject case in masculine.

Ambes is the object case in both genders.

This form gave way to a combination of *ambe* with *dui*, *andui*.

Andui (anduit, andoi, andau) are subject masc.

Andos, andeus are subject fem.

Andos (andeus, andus, andels) are object masc. or fem.

A less contracted form is:—

ambedui, subject.

ambedous, object.

ORDINAL NUMERALS

These are declinable throughout, and belong to the first class of Adjectives.

Masc.	*Fem.*
prins.	prime.
primiers.	primiere.
primerains.	primeraine.
seconz.	seconde.
tierz.	tierse (tierc, tert).
troisiemes.	troisieme (tierceinne).
quarz.	quarte (carz, quairt, quatrime)
quinz.	quinte.
cinquimes, cinquimes.	
sistes.	siste (sist).
simes, sesimes, sisiemes.	
sedmes.	seme (seme).
septimes.	

Masc.	Fem.
{ uidmes. { oitimes.	oidme (oime, uitme).
{ nuemes. { nofimes.	neume (noeme, nofme).
{ dismes. { disimes, dissiemes.	disme (dime).
onzimes.	onzime (unzime).
dozismes.	dozisme (dudzime).
trezimes.	trezime.
quatorzismes.	quatorzime.
quintismes.	quinsime.
sesimes.	sesime (sezme).
diziseptimes (disietime).	
dise-uitme.	
diz et nuevisme (disenofme).	
vintisme (vintiesme).	
vint unime (vyntysme premer).	
vinti-deusime.	
vingt et troisieme.	
vint et quart.	
vinte cinkisme.	
vinte sisme.	
trentisme.	
quarantisme.	
cinquantisme.	
centisme.	

The Ordinals show some arbitrariness in the carrying out of the declension principle, and their derivation from Latin is not always in keeping with the best phonetic traditions; this proves that they were sparely handled by the people. The Modern flexion in *-ieme* is an often forthcoming alternative to its earlier shape *-isme*; and the suffix *-ain*, preserved in words like *douzaine*, *vingtaine*, is an Ordinal flexion often substituted for that in *-isme*. *Unieme* and *deuxieme* are of purely French coinage, while *uidme* and *nuelme* are from Low-Latin forms (*octimus* and *novimus*), whose classical equivalents have produced the Nouns *uitieve* and *noive*. From eleven upwards the suffix is added to the Cardinal Numeral.

FRACTIONAL NUMERALS

Mi, feminine *mie*, or *mei*, feminine *meie*, from Latin *mediu* (m) is an Adjective and means 'mid'; instance: al mie nuit = at midnight.

Demi, Latin *dimidiu* (m), half, is unhampered in Old French by the Modern rule on its agreement.

For $\frac{1}{3}$, li tiers, la tierce part, are used.

   „ $\frac{1}{4}$, li quart, li quartier.

   „ $\frac{1}{5}$, li quint.

   „ $\frac{1}{6}$, la siste part.

   „ $\frac{1}{7}$, la setme partie.

   „ $\frac{1}{8}$, l'uintains.

   „ $\frac{1}{10}$, li disme.

   „ $\frac{1}{16}$, la sezme partie.

   „ $\frac{1}{100}$, li centisme, which appears in the Modern language to express the hundredth part of a franc.

MULTIPLICATIVE NUMERALS

These are (Objective forms only):
   simple.
   doble, double, duble, doule.
   treble, trible, tresble.
   quadruple, etc.

The suffix *-ple, -ble* is the Latin *-plex*, acc. *-plicem*. All Multiplicatives are of learned formation.

DISTRIBUTIVE NUMERALS

The following are derived from Latin:

sengle, sangle, seingle.	Latin	singuli.
bin (authority doubtful).	„	bini.
terne, tarne, trine.	„	terni.
querne, quarne.	„	quaterni.
quinne.	„	quini.
' sinne.	„	seni.

COLLECTIVE NUMERALS

These are Substantives. *Cent* and *milier* often stand together, ex.: Païen l'assallent a milier et a cent. Collectives in *-aine* like *quartaine, tierccinne, quarenteine*, etc., are very numerous, and have most of them been handed down to the Modern language.

CHAPTER VII

THE PRONOUN

IN any spoken sentence, the words used as Articles, as Pronouns, or Adjective Pronouns, and as Auxiliaries, stand in tonic position or in atonic position (accented or unaccented). They possess, therefore, as spoken words, two sets of forms—those belonging to their tonic use, and those belonging to their atonic use. As written words, however, they need not show distinctly the two forms, because phonetic difference may lack graphic signs revealing it to the eye. Aphæresis is frequent in atonic position.

FIRST SECTION—PERSONAL PRONOUNS

Of these, the Pronouns for the first and for the second person can be treated together, along with the Reflective of the third, for they alone are exclusively used as Personal Pronouns.

A further division is necessary. The Pronouns for the first and second person, and the Reflective Pronoun, hold in common a characteristic belonging to both numbers alike, but which has a graphic notation in the Singular only. This characteristic, fully developed in Modern French, where it has brought about the distinction of Pronouns as *Disjunctive* or *Conjunctive*, has its origin in the distinction of Pronouns in Latin as *accented* or *atonic*. The atonic Latin forms are the parents of the Conjunctive forms of modern grammarians, and the accented Latin forms have given birth to the modern Disjunctive Pronouns. The former are synthetically inflected, the latter show analytically (by Prepositions) the relation they bear to the other terms of their clause.

PRONOUNS OF THE FIRST TWO PERSONS IN THE SINGULAR

The Latin prototypes are thus:

	First Person.	*Second Person.*	*Reflect. Pron.*
Nom.	*ego.*	*tu.*	—
Accus.	*me.*	*te.*	*se.*
Dat.	*mi* (*mihi*).	*ti* (*tibi*).	*si* (*sibi*).

Modern French has made of these the *atonic* forms :

Subj.	je.	tu.	—
Dir. Obj.	me.	te.	se.
Ind. Obj.	me.	te.	se.

These forms are atonic ; in other words, in a sentence they appear closely bound up with the Verb and sacrifice their accent to that close alliance. But Personal Pronouns are often called upon to stand by themselves, to follow Prepositions, which are themselves atonic, or to assert personality by emphasis. In popular Latin, the forms *mē, tē, sē*, accented, were used in those capacities. Now, *me, te, se*, accented, will give in French *moi, toi, soi*. Hence we have :

Accented Pronouns—Latin prototype :

mê.   tê.   sê.

Modern French in all cases.

moi.   toi.   soi.

Now let us confine ourselves to Old French. We find, at the earliest period, that the atonic forms, standing in close connection with a verb, do not pronounce their vowel, whether they precede or follow the verb form, and no accented word may stand between them and the verb to which they syntactically belong. By exception, however, the Subject forms *je, tu,* like *il, elle,* pl. *il, elles,* could stand as accented forms in isolation from their verb.

From the twelfth century we find the accented pronouns and atonic pronouns fully developed.

Accented Pronouns.

		I.	II.	III.
Sing.	*Subj.*	eo.	tu.	—
	Obj.	mei.	tei.	sei.
		moi.	toi.	soi.

Atonic Pronouns.

		I.	II.	III.
Sing.	*Subj.*	jo, je.	tu.	—
	Obj.	me.	te.	se.

Such is, free from all disturbing influences, and in its simplest expression, the mode of formation of these Personal Pronouns. Now we give them again with dialectic forms and irregularities.

First Person Singular.

Subject.	*Object.*
eo, eu, io, jeo.	me ; mi.
jieo, jo, ju.	m ; moi.
jou, je, ge, gie.	mei.

Second Person Singular.

tu.	te, t ; ti, toi, tei, tai.

The Subject forms *je, tu* may stand in tonic position, and need not then yield their place to *moi, toi,* as the Modern language requires.

REFLECTIVE PRONOUN IN BOTH NUMBERS

Singular Object.	*Plural Object.*
se ; si, soi, sei.	se ; si, soi, sei.

PRONOUNS OF THE PLURAL FOR FIRST AND SECOND PERSONS

The confusion that overtook the Latin flexions of these has obliterated all case-endings in Old French. The distinction between accented and atonic forms exists, but has no graphic presentment, and all forms are practically reduced to one in each Pronoun.

First Person Plural.

<table>
<tr><td>*Subject.*</td><td>*Object.*</td></tr>
<tr><td>no, nos, nous, nus.</td><td>nos, nous, nus.</td></tr>
</table>

Second Person Plural.

vo, vos, vous, vus.   vos, vous, vus.

PRONOUN OF THIRD PERSON, SINGULAR AND PLURAL.

This Pronoun is derived from a Latin Demonstrative, which has produced in French: (1) a Personal Pronoun; (2) an Article; (3) a Demonstrative Adjective-Pronoun; (4) a Possessive Adjective (*il*; *le*; *cil*; *leur*).

It resembles the preceding Pronouns in so far as it is either *atonic* or *accented* like them. It differs from them in so far as it shows gender.

The variations in the accentuation of the Latin Pronoun are open to controversy. Yet three facts remain positive: (1) in tonic position it was accented on the first syllable, except in the genitive case; (2) it was accented on the inflection by transference of accent from the stem, when the stem was lost in popular Latin; (3) it was not accented at all in atonic position.

Hence three sets of forms in Old French.

First Set (Accented).

Latin Prototype.

	Masc.	*Fem.*	*Neuter.*
Nom. Sing.	*ílle.*	*illa.*	*íllu(d).*
Nom. Plur.	*illi.*	*illae.*	*illa.*
Accus. Sing.	*íllu(m).*	*illa(m).*	*íllu(d).*
Accus. Plur.	*íllos.*	*illas.*	*illa.*

Old French.

	Masc.	*Fem.*	*Neuter.*
Subj. Sing.	**il.**	ele.	[el].
Subj. Plur.	**il.**	eles.	—
Dir. Obj. Sing.	[el].	[ele].	[el].
Dir. Obj. Plur.	els, eus.	eles.	—

The forms in square brackets were of an evanescent character.

The next set differs from this one by the place of the accent.

Second Set (Semi-tonic).
Latin Prototype.

	Masc.	Fem.	Neuter.
Dat. Sing.	illú (illúi, illúic).	illú (illéi).	illú (illúi).
Gen. Plur.	illórum.	illárum.	illórum.

Old French.

Ind. Obj. Sing.	lui.	lei.	—
Ind. Obj. Plur.	lor.	lor.	

Third Set (Atonic).
Latin Prototype.

	Masc.	Fem.	Neuter.
Accus. Sing.	illum.	illam.	illud.
Accus. Plur.	illos.	illas.	illa.

Old French.

Dir. Obj. Sing.	lo, le.	la.	lo.
Dir. Obj. Plur.	les.	les.	—

In the following table, the pure etymological forms above singled out are put beside their numerous Old French kindred. Neuter forms are omitted.

Singular.

	Masc.	Fem.
Subj.	il; el; ill, illi.	ele, elle, ela, el.
Obj.	lui; loi, li, lu, lli, l.	lei, lu.
	lo, lou, le.	la, le, le.

Plural.

Subj.	il; ils; ilz; els, eus, eulx.	eles, elles, els, el.
Obj.	els, elz, elx, eus, als, aus.	eles, elles, elz.
	ax, eaus, euls, eux.	les.
	les, los, ls.	
Ind. Obj.	lor, lour, lur, leur.	

CONTRACTED PRONOUNS

This process, already studied in the Definite Article, is still more extensively practised in the Personal Pronoun.

The Modern language has not sanctioned the contraction of Personal Pronouns :—

del, deu, du	stands for Modern		de le.
jel	„	„	je le.
nel, nu, no	„	„	ne le.
sim	„	„	si me.
nem, nen	„	„	ne me.
jes, jos	„	„	je les.
jot	„	„	je te.
mes	„	„	me les.
tes	„	„	te les.
ses	„	„	se les.
nes	„	„	ne les.
quis	„	„	qui les.
sis, ses	„	„	si les.
nes, nos	„	„	ne se.
quis	„	„	qui se.
sis	„	„	si se.
tum	„	„	tu me.
tus	„	„	tu les.
kil	„	„	qu'il.
quel	„	„	que le.
eissis	„	„	ainsi les.
nol	„	„	ne lui, ne le.
quou	„	„	qui le.
sil	„	„	si le.
çol	„	„	ce le.
kit, quit	„	„	qui te.
etc	„	„	etc.

SECOND SECTION—POSSESSIVE PRONOUN AND POSSESSIVE ADJECTIVE

It is not convenient to separate these in a grammar of Old French, as they were not etymologically distinct in the language. So we speak of the Old French *Adjective-Pronoun.*

It has two sets of forms, phonetically distinct. The one is original, the legitimate corruption of a Latin prototype.

The other, though derived from the same source, is a Gallo-Roman aftergrowth and reserved in the Modern language for the Pronoun proper. There is thus a splitting into two, or a divarication of the Latin Possessive. This branching of a Latin word into two French ones, not an unusual phenomenon, took place here in the objective case.

ADJECTIVE-PRONOUNS OF FIRST, SECOND, AND THIRD PERSONS OF THE SINGULAR NUMBER

These have not an identical root-vowel in Latin, but stem unification gradually took place, along with flexion unification in the cases. *Tuus* and *suus* were assimilated to *meus*, and a monosyllabic word was easily obtained by the slurring of the vowels, and by the additional influence of the sounds *mj*, *sv*, and *tv*, represented by *me-*, *su-*, and *tu-*. The customary intensification of free accented vowels into a diphthong accounts sufficiently, taken in connection with the above, for the Old French forms. The persistence of the essentially corruptible final *m* occurs in other monosyllables.

Latin Prototype.
Singular.

	Masc.	Fem.	Neuter.
Nom.	meus.	mea.	meum.
Accus.	meum.	meam.	meum.

Plural.

Nom.	mei.	meae.	mea.
Accus.	meos.	meas.	mea.

First set of forms—early, atonic:

Masculine Singular.

	First Person.	Second Person.	Third Person.
Subj.	mes.	tes.	ses.
	mis.	tis.	sis.
	meos.	—	sos, suos.
Obj.	mon.	ton.	son.
	mun.	tun.	sun.
	men.	ten.	sen, sem.
	meon	tom, to.	som, so.

Feminine Singular.

	First Person.	Second Person.	Third Person.
Subj.	ma, me.	ta, te.	sa, se.
Obj.	(Same forms as Subject.)		

Masculine Plural.

	First Person.	Second Person.	Third Person.
Subj.	mi.	tui, ti.	sui, si.
Obj.	mes, mis.	tes, tis.	ses, sis.

Feminine Plural.

	First Person.	Second Person.	Third Person.
Subj.	mes, mis.	tes, tis.	ses, sis.
Obj.	(Same forms as Subject.)		

The process that has replaced all subjective forms in Modern French by the objective ones made itself felt in later Middle Ages.

Elision of final *a* in feminine was the rule: *t'ame* or *tame* standing for *ton âme*; *m'amie* for *mon amie*; *symage* or *s'ymage* for *son image*, etc.

Second set of forms—later, accented :

This set is remarkable for the suffix *-en*, which forms a new stem with the root of each Pronoun, and is duly declined by *s* and *e*.

This set is more specially pronominal, and has in the feminine a complicated diphthong written *-oie* and *-eie*, and pronounced most likely with a semi-vowel like this: *oye, eye.*

Masculine Singular.

	First Person.	Second Person.	Third Person.
Subj.	miens.	tuens.	suens.
	mens, men.	tiens.	siens.
Obj.	mien.	tuen, tien.	suen, sien.

Feminine Singular.

	First Person.	Second Person.	Third Person.
Subj.	moie.	toie, toe.	soie, soe.
	meie.	teie, tene.	seie, sieue.
Obj.	(Same forms.)		

Masculine Plural.

	First Person.	Second Person.	Third Person.
Subj.	mien.	tuen.	suen.
Obj.	miens.	tuens.	suens.

Feminine Plural.

	First Person.	Second Person.	Third Person.
Subj.	meies.	teies.	seies.
Obj.	(Same forms.)		

ADJECTIVE-PRONOUNS OF FIRST AND SECOND PERSONS OF THE PLURAL NUMBER

These, like the preceding ones, have branched off in Old French into two sets of forms, phonetically distinct, but with a common origin and functionally confused.

Latin prototype.

Singular.

	Masc.	Fem.	Neuter.
Nom.	noster.	nostra.	nostrum.
Accus.	nostrum.	nostra.	nostrum.

Plural.

Nom.	nostri.	nostrae.	nostra.
Accus.	nostros.	nostras.	nostra.

The Latin *vester* had a Low-Latin form *voster*.

Of the two sets of forms, the first, strictly derived from the Latin, has come to be used pronominally only in Modern French, the second, an abbreviation aiming at speed of utterance, is now the Plural of the Adjective.

First set of forms—atonic or accented, early :

Masculine Singular.

	First Person.	Second Person.
Subj.	nostre.	vostre.
Obj.	nostre.	vostre.

(Same form for Feminine Singular.)

Masculine Plural.

Subj.	nostre.	vostre.
Obj.	nostres.	vostres.

Feminine Plural.

Subj. } *Obj.* }	nostres.	vostres.

Second set of forms—atonic only, later:

Masculine Singular.

Subj.	noz.	voz (*z* for *sts*).
Obj.	no.	vo.

(Same forms for Feminine Singular.)

Masculine Plural.

Subj.	no.	vo.
Obj.	nos.	vos.

(Same forms for Feminine Plural.)

The type of declension in both sets is that of the first declension of Adjectives without gender-flexion, and without assimilation in Nom. Sing. to Latin Nouns in *-us*.

ADJECTIVE-PRONOUN OF THIRD PERSON PLURAL

The Latin genitive plural *illorum* has given birth to this Pronoun. With the primitive sense and function of 'of them,' it passed to that of 'their,' and was declined as a Possessive Adjective in its own right from the end of the thirteenth century only. Hence:—

Singular and Plural.

Subj.
Obj. } lor, lour, lur, leur.

Later Plural.

Subj.
Obj. } lors, lours, lurs, leurs.   No feminine flexion.

THIRD SECTION—THE DEMONSTRATIVE ADJECTIVE-PRONOUNS

Old French has two of these, formed on similar lines from two Latin prototypes, one of which expresses the nearer, and the other the further, object of thought.

ADJECTIVE-PRONOUN OF NEARER OBJECT

This is the Modern Adjective: *ce, cet, cette, ces.* Latin had an Adjective-Pronoun: *iste*, which is strengthened by prefixing to it *ecce*, a demonstrative particle, also placed before the Adjective-Pronouns *is* and *ille*. In the *Lingua Romana*, the connection of the particle with the Pronoun became universal, and thus the foundation was laid for embodying the particle inseparably in the Old French Pronoun.

Ecciste was declined thus:—

Singular.

	Masc.	Fem.	Neuter.
Nom.	ecc*í*ste.	ecc*í*sta.	ecc*í*stud.
Accus.	ecc*í*stum.	ecc*í*stam.	ecc*í*stud.
Dat. (Romance)	eccist*ú*i.	eccist*é*i.	eccist*ú*i.

Plural.

	Masc.	Fem.	Neuter.
Nom.	ecc*í*sti.	ecc*í*stae.	ecc*í*sta.
Accus.	ecc*í*stos.	ecc*í*stas.	ecc*í*sta.
Dat.	ecc*í*stis.	ecc*í*stis.	ecc*í*stis.

Neuter and Dative Plural came to nothing.

Old French, early forms—tonic, now extinct:

Singular.

	Masc.	Fem.
Subj.	icist.	iceste.
Obj.	{[icest.] / icestui.	iceste. / [icestei.]

Plural.

	Masc.	Fem.
Subj.	icist.	icestes.
Obj.	icez.	icestes.

Old French, later forms—atonic, now extant in *ce*, etc.:

Singular.

Subj.	cist, cis.	ceste, cette.
Obj.	cest, cet, ce.	ceste, cette.
	cestui, cesti.	cestei, cesti.

Plural.

Subj.	cist.	cestes, cez, ces.
Obj.	cez, ces.	cestes, cez, ces.

C becomes dialectically *ch* throughout the declension:— *chist*, *chest*, *chestui*, etc. *Cettui*, found sporadically in the language since the Revival of Letters is then an archaïsm.

ADJECTIVE-PRONOUN OF FURTHER OBJECT

This came from a Latin paradigm, obtainable by substituting *ille* for *iste* in the above.

Old French, early forms—tonic, now extinct:

Singular.

	Masc.	*Fem.*
Subj.	iciL	icele.
Obj.	{ [icel.] { icelui.	icele. [icelei.]

Plural.

Subj.	icil.	iceles.
Obj.	icels, iceus.	iceles.

Old French, later forms—atonic, now partly extant:

Singular.

	Masc.	*Fem.*
Subj.	cil, chil, chel.	cele, celle, cella.
forms with *s*—	cis, chis, cilz, ceus.	cilla, ciel, chele.
	cieux, chius.	—
	chieus, chiex.	—
Obj.	cel, ciel.	same as Subject.

Plural.

	— *Masc.*	*Fem.*
Subj.	cil, chil, cilz.	celes, celles, cheles.
Obj.	cels, celz, chels.	celes, celles, cheles.
	cheux, çax, ceus.	

The form *icelui* developed into an independent Pronoun, preserved in Modern French, with a plural borrowed from the above :—

Singular.

	Masc.	*Fem.*
Subj. and Obj.	celui, chelui, celluy.	celei, celi, cheli.

Plural.

Subj. and Obj.	ceos, ceus, ceuz. ceaus, chiaus, ceaz.	celx, ceulx, çaus. celles.

F

THE DEMONSTRATIVE PRONOUN OF THE NEUTER

A third Latin Demonstrative—*hic*, with *hoc* in the neuter—has produced, when connected with *ecce*, an Old French Neuter, *iceo, iço, iceu, icé, iché,* or, with aphæresis of the *i* : *ceo, ço, çou, chou, ceu, ce, che.* In the Modern language it is much in use.

The Latin *hoc* without *ecce* appears here and there in the earliest period as : *o, hoc, huec, aec,* and, in composition, with prepositions, in : *avuec, poruec, senuec.* In the later period, it appears as particle of affirmation in *o je, o tu, o il, o nos*; ultimately *o il* alone survived in this use; hence *langue d'oïl* and Modern *oui.*

FOURTH SECTION—THE RELATIVE PRONOUN

I. The Latin *qui*, with complete declension of case and flexion of gender in its own tongue, is reduced in Old French to three distinct forms, and has dropped all movable suffixes of case, number, and gender. Yet these three leading forms admit of the following classification :—

Subj. Sing. and Plur. qui, ki, chi.   *Subj. Sing. Neut.* que, quei, quoi.

Dir. Obj.   que, ke, qued.

Ind. Obj.   cui, coi, quoi   (from Latin *cui*, originally a Dative case or Indirect Object only).

A feminine *que*, from Latin *quae*, is found in the earliest period. Later the form for the Indirect Object stands often for the Direct Object.

II. The relative *liquels*, feminine *laquel, la quele,* of French coinage, offers no difficulty.

III. *Dont, dunt,* is noticed elsewhere as an Adverb.

FIFTH SECTION—THE INTERROGATIVE PRONOUN

This Pronoun is practically identical with the Relative in origin and forms.

Qui, ki, chi alone is used interrogatively in the Subjective case, and *quoi, koi, quei* appears as Interrogative in the Neuter beside *que.* The Neuter *quoi* is related to *que,* like *me* to *moi, te* to *toi, se* to *soi,* and originated with the Romance form *qued,* in tonic position, standing for classical *quid.*

The interrogatives *quels,* feminine *quele,* from Latin *qualis,* and *li quel,* are regular in their declension. (Second declension of adjectives, parisyllabic group.)

SIXTH SECTION—THE INDEFINITE ADJECTIVE-PRONOUNS

These follow the declension of the Noun or Adjective to which they naturally belong. Two are interesting by their double Objective forms on the pattern of *cestui, celui, lui,* and *cui.* They are :—

Old French.		*Low-Latin.*	
altre	altre. altrui.	alter	*alterum.* *alterui.*
nuls	nul. nului.	*nullus*	*nullum.* *nullui.*

So *li chevals altrui* meant 'the other's horse.' Now, *autrui* is a Pronoun in its own right.

Here is a list of Indefinite Pronouns peculiar to Old French :—

Old French.	*Low-Latin.*	*English.*
al, el.	*alu (aliud).*	else.
alquant alkant } plural. auquant	*aliquanti.*	some.
molt, molz (plural).	*multi.*	many.
nëisuns, nesuns.	*nec ipse unus.*	none.
cadhun.	*catunu(m).*	each.
altel, autel, otel. itel, aital.	*aliud talem* *aeque talem* }	such, like.
eps, es, eis, *fem.* epsa, essa. }	*ipse.*	self.

Old French.	Low-Latin.	English.
nïent, neant, noiant, nent, }	*nec entem.*	{ something. anything. nothing.
quant, *fem.* quante.	*quantum.*	all that, what.
trestots.	*trans-totus.*	all, every.
nului.	*nullui.*	none.
alques.	*aliquod(s).*	a little.

The following ones appear in the Old language in a form that is now changed :—

Old French.	*Modern.*
alcuns, alquns (alqu'un), etc.	aucun.
chasque, chesque, etc.	chaque.
chascuns, chaucuns (chasqu'un).	chacun.
meint, maint.	maint.
mesme, mëisme, medisme.	même.
hom, om, on, etc. (nomin. only).	on.
riens, ren.	rien, chose.
tels, tex.	tel.
toz, *plur.* tuit, toit.	tout.
un, ung, unt, hun.	un.

Several of the above are real Nouns, some are used as Adverbs, and others, according to the Syntax used, are either negative or affirmative in meaning.

CHAPTER VIII

THE UNDECLINABLE PARTS OF SPEECH

FIRST SECTION—ADVERBS

THESE are remarkable in many instances for the addition of an Old French *s*, which, when it is not excused by some foregoing corruption of the classical Adverb in Latin, must be traced back to the adverbial Accusatives of Romance, or laid down to the appearance in the early period of a generally-accepted ' adverbial *s.*'

Onques from *unquam*, and *ores* from *adhoram*, are examples in point.

As for Adverbs in -*ment*, this ending, before being a suffix, was a regular Noun. The Adjectives it followed, and affected adverbially, agreed with it as they would with any other *feminine* Substantive, and when the connection grew to actual amalgamation, phonetic laws obtained sway over it. Examples :—

bon	produced	bone-ment (bonement).
privé	,,	priveement.
cointe	,,	cointement.
beau	,,	belement.
delivre	,,	delivrement.
diligent	,,	diligentment (diligenment).
loyal	,,	loyalment (loyaument).
grand	,,	grandment (granment).
gent	,,	gentement.
briés	,,	briément.

In Nouns like *tremblement, traveillement, penement,* of which the Old language has a great number, -*ment* is, of course, a Noun-suffix, and the preceding *e,* if not always etymological, is phonetically a binding-vowel distinct from the *e* of the feminine Adjective amalgamated with -*ment,* Latin *mente.* This remark is intended as a hint to beginners not to be led away by appearances or superficial analogies—a valuable caution when reading Old French, because the Modern language often suggests false points of comparison with the Old.

In the following list we give principally Adverbs of time, manner, and place. A large number are convertible into Prepositions without further alteration, and into Conjunctions by the addition of *que.*

I. Adverbs extinct or obsolete nowadays are :—

Old French.	*Modern.*	*English.*
a bandon.	à volonté.	at will.
abans.	auparavant.	before, formerly
ades.	aussitôt.	at once, directly.
adun.	ensemble.	together.
ainc, ainques.	jamais.	ever.
ainçois, enceiz.	avant, plutôt.	before, rather.
ains, einz.	avant, mais.	before.
alsi, alsiment.	aussi, également.	also.
amont.	en haut.	upwards.
antan.	l'an passé.	last year.
anuit.	cette nuit.	that night, to-night.
apermenmes.	sur le champ.	at once.
as, es, *etc.*	voici.	here is, here are.
atant.	alors.	then, now.
au main, main.	le matin.	in the morning.
auques, alques.	un peu.	a little, somewhat.
autresi, altresi.	de même.	similarly, alike.
aval.	en bas.	downwards.
çaiens, ceans.	ici dedans.	inside, herein.
desanz.	auparavant.	before.
detrés.	derrière.	behind, backward.
dont.	d'où.	hence.
durement.	beaucoup.	much, heavily.
endementres, endementiers.	pendant ce temps.	meanwhile.
eneslepas.	sur le champ.	immediately.
enqui, encui.	ici, là.	here, there.
ensement.	de même.	alike.
ensorquetot.	surtout.	above all.
ensus.	en haut.	above.
entresait.	entièrement, aussitôt.	quite, at once.
enviz.	malgré soi.	under compulsion.
enz.	dedans.	inside.
erranment.	sur le champ.	immediately.
es, ez.	voici, voilà.	here is, there is.
este-vus.	voici.	here is.
faitement.	ainsi.	thus so.

Old French.	Modern.	English.
finablement.	enfin.	lastly, at last.
gens, gienz.	rien.	nothing.
hui, hoi.	aujourd'hui.	to-day.
idonc, adonc.	alors.	then.
iki, iqui, enqui.	là, ici.	there.
iloec, illueques.	là.	there.
ja, jai.	déjà, jadis.	already, formerly.
jus, jos.	en bas.	down.
laienz, leans.	là-dedans.	inside, therein.
lassus.	là-haut.	thereon.
longues.	longtemps.	long.
luec, lués, loés.	aussitôt.	immediately.
mar.	par malheur.	by misfortune.
meshui.	désormais.	henceforth.
mont.	beaucoup, très.	much, many.
mult, moult.	très, beaucoup.	very.
nai.	non.	nay.
neïs.	même, pas même.	even
nenil.	non.	no.
oan, ouan.	cette année.	this year.
oidi.	aujourd'hui.	to-day.
onques, oncque.	jamais.	ever.
orains.	tout à l'heure.	a while ago.
ore, or, ores.	maintenant.	now.
petit.	peu.	a little.
petitet, petitelet.	très-peu.	a very little.
pieça.	il y a longtemps.	long ago.
primes.	premièrement.	firstly.
puer.	en dehors, en vain.	outside, in vain.
pro, prou.	assez, beaucoup.	enough, much.
qui, ki.	là.	there.
rechief, de rechief.	de nouveau.	anew.
redre.	en arrière.	backward.
res à res.	tout près.	close.
sainglement.	séparément.	singly.
sempre.	toujours, aussitôt.	always, at once.
sevels, sevals.	au moins.	at least.
tantost.	aussitôt.	directly.

Old French.	Modern.	English.
tostens.	toujours.	always.
totevoies.	de toute manière.	by all means.
toudis.	toujours.	every day.
veals, viaus.	au moins.	at least.
voirs, voirement.	vraiment.	really, truly.

II. Adverbs common to Old and Modern French are :—

Old French.	Modern French.
acertes.	certes, sérieusement.
aillors.	ailleurs.
assés, aisses, sez.	assez, beaucoup.
ausi, assi.	aussi.
autrefoïz.	quelquefois.
autretant.	autant.
ben, beyn.	bien.
ça, sai.	ici.
cert, certe.	certainement.
ci, chi.	ici.
coment, comant.	comment.
demesmes.	de même.
desi.	d'ici.
desja.	déjà.
desoremés.	désormais.
doresanavant.	dorénavant.
encor, ancor.	encore.
ensamble, ensems.	ensemble, avec.
entraviers.	en travers.
entretant.	pendant ce temps.
envers.	à l'envers, à la renverse.
especial, par especial.	spécialement.
forment, fortment.	beaucoup.
gaires, guerres.	guère, beaucoup.
icy, ichi.	ici.
jameis.	jamais.
lai.	là.
lau *contract. for* la u.	là où.

Old French.	*Modern French.*
lor, lors.	alors.
meins, mains.	moins.
meintenant.	tout de suite.
mi, mei, permi.	au milieu.
ne, ned.	ne (negat. particle).
nun, nom.	non.
oïl, oï.	oui.
ou, o, ou.	où.
plus, plux.	plus.
po, pou.	peu.
quant, cant.	combien, quand.
sovent.	souvent.
tant, tan, itant.	tant, tellement.
tart.	tard.
tost.	tôt, vite.
tousjours.	toujours.
vechi.	voici.
vela.	voilà.
vez.	voici, voilà.
volentiers.	volontiers.

The above lists are purely formal in their arrangement, and by no means established on an etymological basis. Adverbs, and for the matter of that, Prepositions and Conjunctions, Indefinite Pronouns, and Interjections, draw upon the other Parts of Speech and upon one another for their formation.

The suffix *-ment* is sometimes spelt: *mant, mand, manz*, etc.

The Pronominal Adverbs are *en, y,* and *dont.*

En is from *inde*; it has the forms *en, an, ent, ant, int, em.*

Y is from *ibi*; it has the forms, *i, iv, hi.*

Contractions with *en* are: *sin* for *si en, quin* for *qui en, nen* for *ne en.*

A contraction with *y* is: *noi* for *no i, ne* . . . *y.*

Dont from *de unde* has: *dont, dunt, dons, dom, dunc.*

The three appear as Indirect Objects in the Personal and Relative Pronouns, defective in consequence of the phonetic impoverishment of later Latinity.

ADVERBS OF NEGATION

Non, nen, no, ne, from Latin *non,* is found in early documents. The formations *ne . . . pas, ne . . . point, ne . . . mie, ne . . . goutte, ne . . . grain,* etc., emphatic at first, then purely negational, supersede altogether the simple negation.

Ne, reduced to a mere negative or dubitative particle, appears in atonic position in many syntactical combinations.

Nient or *noient* is equivalent in meaning to *rien, nullement,* when it is used adverbially.

SECOND SECTION—PREPOSITIONS

I. Prepositions lost to the Modern language :—

Old French.	*Modern French.*
ab, a, from Lat. *b.*	avec.
ains, anz.	avant.
aprof.	auprès de, après.
atot.	avec.
avers.	à côté de.
deci en, deci a.	jusqu'à.
dedesoz.	sous.
defors.	dehors de.
dejoste, dejuste.	à côté de.
delez, dalés.	à côté de.
desor.	sur, dessus.
empor, en pur.	pour, à cause de.
emprés.	auprès de, après.
endroit, endreit.	quant à, vers.
en mi.	au milieu de.
estre.	outre.
fors.	dehors, excepté.
joste, juste.	près de.
lon, lunc.	près de.
o, ob, od, ot (Lat. *apud*).	avec.
otot.	avec.
pués, puys.	après, depuis.
sus, suz.	sur.
tres.	depuis.

II. Prepositions possessed in common by the Old and the Modern language :—

Old French.	*Modern French.*
a (Latin *ad*).	à, avec, par, sur.
apriés.	après.
avan.	avant, devant.
avoec.	avec.
chiez.	chez.
cuntre.	contre, vers.
davant.	devant, avant.
de coste, encoste.	à côté de.
dedenz.	au dedans de, dans.
dedesus.	au dessus de.
dedevant.	au devant de.
dens.	dans.
derrier.	derrière.
des (Latin *de ipso*).	dès, depuis.
desoz.	au dessous de, sous.
desus.	au dessus de, sur.
devers.	vers.
en, ant, int, ens, en.	en, dans.
encontre.	contre, vers.
entor.	autour de.
entre, antre.	entre, parmi.
environ, anviron.	autour de.
maugré.	malgré.
oultre, ultre.	au delà de, outre.
par, per.	par, à travers.
por.	pour.
prez, priés.	près de.
selonc.	selon, le long de.
sens, sainz.	sans, excepté.
sor, sour.	sur, plus que.
soz, souz.	sous.
viers.	envers, contre.

THIRD SECTION—CONJUNCTIONS

Old French.	*Modern French.*
a ce que.	afin que.
adonc.	alors.
affin que.	afin que.
assavoir.	c'est à dire.
au plus tost que.	aussitôt que.
car, quer.	car, donc.
com, come.	comme, que.
delors que.	depuis que.
demantres que.	pendant que.
dent, den.	puis, ensuite.
desi que.	jusqu'à ce que.
devant que.	avant que.
donc, donques.	donc, alors.
dusques, jusque.	jusqu'à ce que.
ensi que.	tandis que, pour que.
entresi que.	jusqu'à ce que.
entresque.	tandis que.
essi . . . que.	de sorte que.
et, e.	et.
fors que.	excepté que.
in quant.	autant que.
ja si . . . ne.	quelque . . . que.
ja soit ce que.	quoique.
meis, mais, mes.	mais, plus.
mais que.	pourvu que,
ne.	et, ni.
ne . . . ne	ni . . . ni.
neporquant.	pourtant.
ne poruec.	néanmoins.
ne . . . si . . . que.	ne . . . pas tant . . . que.
ou, o, ou.	ou.
ou que.	quelque part que.
parke.	pour que.
parke . . . ne.	à moins que . . . ne.
por ce que.	parce que.
porro que.	parce que.

Old French.	Modern French.
puesque.	parce que, depuis que.
puissedi que.	puisque.
quandius.	autant que.
quanque, quant que.	tout ce que, autant que.
quant.	quand, lorsque.
quant que.	tant que.
que, ke, quet.	que, car.
que que.	pendant que.
que . . . que.	tantôt . . . tantôt.
quoi que.	quoique, pendant que.
se . . . non.	sauf.
si, se.	ainsi, si, comme.
si come.	comme, que.
si ne.	sans.
si que.	comme.
si, se, set.	si (English ' if ').
tant cum.	tant que.
tantost que.	aussitôt que.
tôt maintenant que.	aussitôt que.
touteffois.	en tous cas, toutefois.
tresque, tros que.	jusqu'à ce que.
usque.	jusqu'à ce que.

FOURTH SECTION—INTERJECTIONS

Old French.	Modern French.
a.	ah, ha.
ahi, aï, ai.	hélas.
aia.	eh bien.
aimmi.	malheur à moi.
allas, halas, alais.	hélas.
aoi.	—
avoi.	—
dea.	vrai, bien, diable.
diva.	va dire, dis donc.
e.	—
enne.	
es, ais.	voilà.

Old French.	Modern French.
fi.	fi
ha.	—
hahay, hai, hai.	—
haro, haré, hari.	haro
hau.	—
hei.	hé.
hola.	holla.
o.	oh, o.
ohi.	hélas.
os.	—
va.	eh bien, hé.

A few of these are Interjections only in name.

Allas, for instance, contains the Adjective *las*, and is found in the Feminine when put in the mouth of a woman, as in *lasse medre!* (poor mother!). *Diva* contains parts of the Verbs *aller* and *dire*. Exclamations like *caitif mei, las mei*, are elliptical (poor me!).

CHAPTER IX

THE VERB

WE can give only a short sketch of the Verb-forms and of the peculiarities of conjugation in Old French. The subject is a vast one, forms are too numerous to be compressed into an elementary work like this, and their classification is not yet uniform.

The Auxiliaries, the four conjugations of so-called Regular Verbs, the so-called Irregular conjugations with some consideration of 'analogy,' of 'strengthening' and 'weakening,' of the growth of Verbs in their 'organic' types, regardless of dialectic, orthographic, and inorganic side-forms, this is a sufficient budget for a practical grammar of Old French. Let it be remembered that the study of etymology and phonetics is not our aim.

FIRST SECTION—THE AUXILIARIES

These present, at the outset of our chapter on Verbs, the partly synthetic, partly analytic conjugation which is characteristic of the Old French language, and of the Modern language.

The forms of *aveir* and of *estre*, early evolved, and most frequently used either in tonic or in atonic position, became what we may call centres of analogy. In any language the most frequently used word-forms may become such centres, and assimilate other forms to themselves. Assimilation by analogical force may occur in two ways. The stem of less frequently used words may by phonetic attraction be assimilated to a powerful type: there arises then a centre of stem analogy. The flexions of more unusual application may yield to a similar action put forth by well-established flexions: there arises then a centre of flexion analogy. *Les, mes, tes, ses*; *sont, font, vont, ont*; *mettait, était*; *disait, lisait* are groups in which this principle has been at work.

VERB ESTRE.

This is derived partly from the corresponding forms of classical Latin, partly from Low-Latin formations, partly from a root foreign to the Latin verb.

The Imperfect of the Indicative has two parallel sets of forms.

The Future has three sets of forms, and the Conditional Present has two.

There are instances of a Pluperfect of synthetic make on the Latin Pattern.

We print the Latin with phonetic alterations.

Estre.   Latin : *essere* for *esse.*

Indicative.

	Main-form.	By-forms.	Phonetic Latin.
Present.	sui.		som, sui.
	es.	iés.	es.
	est.	es.	est.
	somes, sons.	sommes, esmes, ermes.	somus.
	estes.	iestes.	estis.
	sont.	sunt, son.	sont.

	Main-form.	By-forms.	Phonetic Latin.
Imperfect I.	ere.	iere, eret.	éra.
	eres.	ieres.	éras.
	eret.	ere, iere, ert, iert.	érat.
	erions.	—	erómus.
	eriez.	—	erétis.
	erent.	ierent.	érant.
Imperfect II.	estoie.	esteie.	estába, estéa.
	estoies.	esteies.	estábas, estéas.
	estoit.	esteit.	estábat, estéat.
	estiens.	estions, estion.	estiámus.
	estiez.	estieiz, esties.	estiátis.
	estoient.	—	estéant.
Past Definite.	fui.	fu, fuis, fuz.	fui.
	fus.	fuz.	fosti.
	fut.	fu, fud, fo.	foit.
	fumes.	—	fóimus.
	fustes.	—	fóstis.
	furent.	fuirent.	fórunt.
Future I.	serai.	—	esserábjo.
	seras.	—	etc.
	serat.	sera, serad, serrat.	
	serons.	serrums.	
	serez.	sereiz, serés, seroiz, serrez.	
	seront.	serunt.	
Future II.	er.	ier, ierc.	ero.
	ieres.	iers.	eris.
	er.	ert, iert.	erit.
	ermes.	—	érimus.
	(ertes).	—	(éritis).
	ierent.	—	erunt.
Future III.	estrai.	—	esterábjo.
	estras.	—	etc.
	estrat.	—	
	estrons.	—	
	estrez	—	
	estront.	—	

Conditional.

Main-form.	By-forms.	Phonetic Latin.
Present I.		
seroie.	sereie.	esserabéa.
seroies.	sereies.	etc.
seroit.	sereiet.	
seriens.	serions	
seriez.	serieiz, seriés.	
seroient.	—	
Present II.		
estroie.	—	esterabéa.
estroies.	—	etc.
esteroit.	astreit.	
—	—	
—	—	
—	astreient.	

Subjunctive.

	By-forms.	Phonetic Latin.
Present.		
soie.	seie.	sea.
soies.	seies.	seas.
soit.	seiet, sit, sia, sie.	seat.
soiens.	soions.	seámus.
soiez.	soieiz, soiés, seietst.	seátis.
soient.	—	seant.
Imperfect.		
fusse.	fuisse.	fosse.
fusses.	fuisses.	fosses.
fust.	fuisset, fus.	fosset.
fussiens.	fussions, fuissons.	fossiómus.
fussiez.	fussieiz, fussiés	fossiétis.
fussent.	—	fossent.

Imperative.

sois.	—	sea.
soiens.	soions.	seámus.
soiez.	soieiz, soiés.	seátis.

Gerund and Present Participle.

estant.	—	estánte. estándo.

Past Participle.

Main-form.	By-forms.	Phonetic Latin.
estet.	esteit, esté.	estátu.

Infinitive.

	Main-form.	By-forms.	Phonetic Latin.
I.	estre.	—	éssere.
II.	ester.	—	estáre.

Compound tenses are omitted, their components being given above and elsewhere.

When there are two or several sets of forms for one tense, those closest to Latin are the most corruptible and belong to the earlier phases of the literature.

The Latin Pluperfect appears in the Third Person only: it is *furet, fure* or *fura,* from *fuerat,* with the tense value of the Modern Preterite.

VERB AVOIR. PHONETIC LATIN : ABERE.

Indicative.

	Main-form.	By-forms.	Phonetic Latin.
Present.	ai.	ay, ey, hay, ays.	ábjo.
	as.	—	ábes.
	at, o.	ad, a, ait, adz, ha.	ábet.
	avons.	avuns, avon, avum, avomes, avommes, avem.	abómus.
	avez.	aveiz, avés.	abétis.
	ont.	unt, ant, an.	ábunt.
Imperfect.	avoie.	aveie.	abéa.
	avoies.	aveies.	abéas.
	avoit.	aveit, aveid.	abéat.
	aviens.	avions, avion.	abeámus.
	aviez.	avieiz, aviés.	abeátis.
	avoient.	aveient.	abéant.

Indicative.

Main-form.	By-forms.	Phonetic Latin.

Past Definite.

Main-form.	By-forms.	Phonetic Latin.
oi.	eu.	ábui.
eüs.	oüs.	abuíst.
ot.	{ out, aut, oth, og, ab, eust. }	ábuit,
eümes.	oümes.	abvúmus.
eüstes.	oüstes.	abvústis.
orent.	{ ourent, augrent, urent, eurent. }	ábverunt.

Future.

averai.	{ avrai, aurai, arai, avrais, arais. }	aberábjo.
averas.	avras, auras, aras.	etc.
averat.	averad, avera, averait.	
averons.	avruns, avrum.	
averez.	avroiz, arés.	
averont.	—	

Conditional.

Present.

averoie.	avreie.	aberabéa.
averoies.	avreies.	etc.
averoit.	avreit.	
averiens.	avrions.	
averiez.	avrieiz, avriés.	
averoieut.	—	

Subjunctive.

Present.

aie.	—	ábja.
aies.	—	ábjas.
ait.	aiet.	ábjat.
aiens.	aions, aion.	abjámus.
aiez.	aieiz, aiés, aiest.	abjátis.
aient.	—	ábjant.

Imperfect.

eüsse.	oüsse, euise.	abuísse.
eüsses.	oüsses.	abuísses.
eüst.	euïst, auuisset, ouist.	abuísset.
eüssiens.	eüssions.	abuissiómus.
eüssiez.	eüssieiz, eüssiés.	abuissiétis
eüssent.	euïssent.	abuíssent.

Imperative.

Main-form.	By-forms.	Latin.
aic.	—	ábjas.
aiens.	aions.	abjámus.
aiez.	aieiz, aiés.	abjátis.

Gerund and Present Participle

I. aiant.	—	abiánte.
II. avant.	—	{ abénte. abéndo.

Past Participle.

eüt.	eü, oüt, oï.	abútu.

The Latin Pluperfect produced a Neo-Latin tense found in the third person only : *auret, auuret, agre* (Latin *habuerat*).

SECOND SECTION—THE SO-CALLED FOUR REGULAR
CONJUGATIONS

Philologists reduce the ordinary four Latin conjugations to two. A similar upsetting of the teaching of Modern grammarians must be resorted to in the handling of the Old French Verbs. The superficial line between Regular and Irregular Verbs must be done away with, and two main principles must be recognised as shaping the whole process of conjugation. These are (1) that, etymological forms being given as a starting point, analogical forms may supersede these ; (2) that accent variation prevails in the old language, as a means of conjugation, to an extent unknown in the modern. We have already become familiar with accent variation in the declension of substantives. It is accompanied by vowel intensification and vowel attenuation when the position and nature of the vowels concerned admit of this.

We place analogy first because it is this process which

led to the Modern conjugation, and established its stems and flexions. Some types, when once clearly evolved, put forth an assimilative power that shaped uniformly, and generalised into classes, feebler types which otherwise would have remained individual and irreducible to a common standard. This tendency that makes for unity, hardly discernible in the Neo-Latin French Verb, becomes more and more sweeping with the progress of time, till its pace was slackened by what must be called, in comparison with the earlier state of affairs, the 'fixation' of the French language by literature and culture. The assimilation of less frequent phonetic formations to the preferred ones of the same order obscured etymologies. Now it has altogether thrown into the background and shrouded the working of the second principle of Old French conjugation.

We place accent variation second because its part was a decreasing one as time wore on. Verb forms are indeed still either parisyllabic or imparisyllabic, and their accent is still movable; but, along with uniformity in flexion, stem unification, as in Nouns, has taken place, expelling, as a rule, the one or the other of the two accent stems, so as to destroy the accent conjugation which corresponded to the accent declension. In *savoir*, for instance, the two stems *sav-* and *sai(v-)* still exist, but in almost all Verbs, as in *aimer*, where the stem *aim-* has everywhere superseded *am-*, there is only one stem throughout the conjugation.

Going back to Latin, as for Noun forms, we therefore distinguish parisyllabic Verb forms, in which the accent falls on the same syllable as in the verb stem, and imparisyllabic forms, in which it falls on one of the terminational syllables. If the vowel of the verb stem undergoes in Old French intensification, we agree to call *strong* the forms in which this occurs. If, on the contrary, by the moving of the accent on to the termination the root vowel is set free from intensification, we agree to call such forms *weak* forms, or attenuated forms.

The Latin terminations which are accented and have produced Old French accented flexions are, *-ávi* [*évi*],

-édi, -ívi (endings of perfect); *-ándo, -ántem* (Gerund and Present Participle); *-átum, -ítum, -útum* (Past Participle); *-ámus, -átis* (First and Second Persons Plur. Pres. Indicative); *-ábam*, etc. (Imperfect Indic.); *-ássem*, etc. (Pluperfect Subj.); *-ísco*, etc. (Inchoative termination); the Romance Future and Conditional endings, and the Infinitive endings *-áre, -ére, -íre.*

The other Latin terminations contained in Old French do not bear any accent; they therefore admit of strong Verb forms.

Latin verbs have not all in the Perfect the accented terminations *-ávi, -édi, -ívi,* quoted above. Some have the non-accented terminations *-si, -i, -ui.* The latter are often designated as *primary* verbs, and the former as *secondary.*

Properly speaking, all Old French verbs consist of both weak and strong forms, but in some the root vowel is not visibly and outwardly affected by the accent. We shall call these *terminational* verbs, and the others *accentual* verbs.

For instance, *chanter* is a terminational Verb compared with *boivre* (unaccented weak *a* throughout stem of first, against accented strong *oi* in some forms of second); the Imperfect of *tenir* is a weak tense compared with its Past Definite, and, in the Present, *nous tenons* is a weak person compared with *il tient.*

THE TERMINATIONAL CONJUGATION

The test for finding what verbs belong to this conjugation is not the ending of the Infinitive, for the endings, *-er, -ir,* and *-re,* are all represented in this conjugation. But a rough and ready criterion is afforded in the Imperfect Indicative compared with the Present. If after the apocope of the suffix *-oie* in the former we obtain a stem which is identical, in the First Person Singular, with that of the latter, the verb in question is terminational. Thus, *je chantoie* holding *chant-* in common with *je chant,* the verb is terminational, but *amoie* being *aim* in the Present, this verb is accentual.

The terminational conjugation is throughout purely terminational: it never visibly strengthens the root vowel, 1 owever much the accent may rest upon it.

First Terminational Type containing Verbs with -er in the Infinitive.

Secondary Verb chanter. Latin: cantáre.

Indicative.

	Main-form.	By-forms.	Phonetic Latin.
Present.	chant.	—	cánto.
	chantes.	—	cántas.
	chantet.	chante, -ed, -at, -a.	cántat.
	chantons.	-ums, -om, -um, -am.	cantómus.
	chantez.	chanteiz, chantés.	cantátis.
	chantent.	chanten.	cántant.
Imperfect.	chantoie.	chanteie, etc.	cantábam, cantéa.
	chantoies.	chantoes, chantoues.	cantábas, cantéas.
	chantoit.	{ chantot, chantout, chantevet. }	cantábat, cantéat.
	chantiens.	chantions.	canteámus.
	chantiez.	chantiez, chantiés.	canteátis.
	chantoient.	chantovent, chantaient.	cantábant, cantéant.
Past Definite.	chantai.	chantais.	cantái.
	chantas.	chantes.	cantásti.
	chantat.	chantad, -a. -et, ed.	cantávit.
	chantames.	chantasmes.	cantávimus.
	chantastes.	chantaistes.	cantástis.
	chanterent.	chantarent.	cantárunt.
Future.	chanterai.	chantarai.	cantar ábjo.
	chanteras.	—	etc.
	chanterat.	{ chanterad, chantera, chanterait. }	
	chanterons.	chanterom.	
	chanterez.	{ chantereiz, chanterés, chanteroiz. }	
	chanteront.	chanterunt.	

Conditional.

	Main-form.	By-forms.	Phonetic Latin.
Present.	chanteroie.	chantereie.	cantar abéa.
	chanteroies.	chantereies.	etc.
	chanteroit.	chantereiet.	
	chanteriens.	chanterions.	
	chanteriez.	chanterieiz, chanteriés.	
	chanteroient.	—	

Subjunctive.

Present.	chant.	chante.	cánte.
	chanz.	chantes.	cántes.
	chantet.	chante.	cántet.
	chantiens.	chantions.	cantiómus.
	chantiez.	chantieiz, chantiés.	cantiétis.
	chantent.	—	cántent.
Imperfect.	chantasse.	chantaisse, chantaixe.	cantássem.
	chantasses.	chantaisses.	cantásses.
	chantast.	chantas, chantat.	cantásset.
	chantassiens.	chantassions.	cantassiómus.
	chantassiez.	chantassieiz, chantassiés.	cantassiétis.
	chantassent.	—	cantássent.

Imperative.

chante.	chant.	cánta.
chantons.	—	cantómus.
chantez.	chanteiz, chantés.	cantátis.

Infinitive.

chanter.	chanteir, chantar.	cantáre.

Gerund and Present Participle.

chantant.	chantan.	cantánte, cantándo.

Past Participle.

chantet.	chanté, -eit, -ei, -ed, -etz, -at, -ad.	cantátus, -u.
fem. chantede	chantee, chanteie, chantete.	—

Observations.—I. This Conjugation has a synthetic Pluperfect from Latin, occurring occasionally in documents; instances are: *roveret* from *ropaverat* and *laisera* from *laxaverat.*

Fully reconstituted, that Pluperfect might run thus:—

rovére.	rovérons.
rovéres.	rovérez.
rovéret.	rovérent.

The temporal idea of that evanescent form was not distinct from that of the Past Definite.

II. Besides the Imperfect given above, which is the normal formation (subject to the equivalence : $ai=ei=oi$). we have other sets of Imperfect forms from the Latin flexion *-abam.* Compared with our paradigm they are early or local. They are:—

(1) In the South-East of France—

chantéve.	chantiens.
chantéves.	chantiez.
chantévet.	chantévent.

(2) In the North-West—

chantoe.	chantions.
chantoes.	chantiez.
chantout.	chantoent.

III. The epithesis of an *e* mute in the First Person Singular of Present Indicative is general from the fifteenth century only. That of an *s* is not unknown, but it is quite irregular. *E* is often dropped in the Third Person, and *t* still more so. The apocope of *e* is the rule in the First Person of Present Subjunctive, while the *t* of the Third Person is not corruptible. The flexion may phonetically affect the last consonant of the stem. The flexion is altogether dropped in the Third Person Singular of the Present Subjunctive, when the root ends on a dental. Ex.: *gart, chant.*

IV. There is an Infinitive form in *-ier* in many Verbs. Its *i* appears in the Indicative and in the Imperative, and frequently in the Past Participle. **Ex.**: *culchiez, chacierent, traitié, corocier*.

V. Contracted Futures are frequent by suppression of atonic *e* in the Infinitive. *Dorrai* stands for *donnĕr-ai, demourra* for *demourera*. In *dorrai* there is assimilation of *n* to following *r*. Sometimes *r* is transposed; *mousterrai* stands for *moustrerai*.

VI. Imperfects of the Subjunctive with endings *-issiens, -isois, -isiez, -issiés*, etc., instead of the regular *-assiens, -asois, -asiez, assiés*, are formed by analogy with the next conjugation, or are corruptions from an original *-ess-*, from Latin *-ass-*. **Ex.**: *passisoiz* for *passasois* (passassiez).

Second Terminational Type containing Verbs with -re in the Infinitive.

Secondary Verb vendre.   Latin : véndere.

Indicative.

	Main-form.	By-forms.	Phonetic Latin.
Present	vend.	– –	véndo.
	venz.	vens.	véndis.
	vend.	vendet.	véndit.
	vendons.	vendon, vendum, vendem.	vendómus.
	vendez.	vendeiz, vendés.	vendétis.
	vendent.	—	véndunt.
Imperfect	vendoie.	vendeie, vendoys.	vendéa.
	vendoies.	vendeies.	vendéas.
	vendoit.	vendeiet, vendeit, vendïet.	vendéat.
	vendiens.	vendion(s), vendium.	vendeámus.
	vendiez.	vendieiz, vendiés.	vendeátis.
	vendoient.	—	vendéant.
Past Definite	vendi.	—	vendéi.
	vendis.	vendies.	vendésti.
	vendit.	vendi, vended, vendet, vendiet.	vendéit.
	vendimes.	—	vendeímus.
	vendistes.	—	vendeístis.
	vendirent.	vendierent.	vendérunt.

Indicative.

Main-form.	By-forms.	Phonetic Latin.

Future.

vendrai.	venderai, venderais.	vendre ábjo.
vendras.	venderas.	etc.
vendrat.	vendra, vendrait.	
vendrons.	vendron, vendrum.	
vendrez.	{ vendreiz, vendrés, vendroiz.	
vendront.	vendrunt.	

Conditional.

Present.

vendroie.	vendreie, -eroie, -ereie.	vendre abéa.
vendroies.	vendreies.	etc.
vendroit.	vendreiet.	
vendriens.	vendrions, vendrium.	
vendriez.	vendrieiz, vendriés.	
vendroient.	—	

Subjunctive.

Present.

vende.	—	vénda.
vendes.	—	véndas.
vendet.	vende.	véndat.
vendiens.	vendions, vendium.	vendiómus.
vendiez.	vendieiz, vendiés.	vendiétis.
vendent.	—	véndant.

Imperfect.

vendisse.	—	vendísse.
vendisses.	—	vendísses.
vendist.	vendiest.	vendísset.
vendissiens.	vendissions, vendissium.	vendissémus.
vendissiez.	vendissieiz, vendissiés.	vendissétis.
vendissent.	—	vendíssent.

Imperative.

vend.	—	vénde.
vendons.	—	vendómus.
vendez.	vendeis, vendés,	vendétis.

Infinitive.

| vendre. | — | véndere. |

Gerund and Present Participle.

Main-form.	By-forms.	Phonetic Latin.
vendant.	—	vendándo.
		vendánte.

Past Participle.

vendut.	vendu, vendud, venduit.	vendutus, -u.
fem. vendue.	—	—

Third Terminational Type containing Verbs with -ir in the Infinitive.

This Conjugation must be subdivided into two classes, of which the first, the Pure class, or the Non-Inchoative class, fastens the flexion immediately on to the stem of the Verb, while the second, the Inchoative class, inserts the element -ss- of Latin origin between stem and flexion, wherever the nature of the tense admits of the idea expressed by that element. This second class is also called the 'Mixed Class,' as it follows the first class for all tenses which reject the inchoative -ss-, from Latin sc, Greek σκ, of unknown origin.

First Class: Pure Class.

Secondary Verb partir.   Latin : partíre.

Indicative.

Main-form.	By-forms.	Phonetic Latin.
part.	—	párto.
parz.	pars.	pártis.
part.	—	pártit.
partons.	parton, partum.	partómus.
partez.	parteiz, partés.	partétis.
partent.	partunt.	pártunt.

(Present.)

Indicative.

Main-form.	By-forms.	Phonetic Latin.
Imperfect.		
partoie.	parteie, partoys.	partéa.
partoies.	parteies.	partéas.
partoit.	partiet.	partéat.
partiens.	partions, partion, partium.	parteámus.
partiez.	partieiz, partiés.	parteátis.
partoient.	—	partéant.
Past Definite.		
parti.	partit.	partíi
partis.	—	partiísti.
partit.	parti, partid.	partívit.
partimes.	—	partímmus.
partistes.	—	partístis.
partirent.	—	partírunt.
Future.		
partirai.	—	partir ábjo.
partiras.	—	etc.
partirat.	partira, partirad, partirait.	
partirons.	partiron, partirum.	
partirez.	partireiz, partirés, partiroiz.	
partiront.	partirunt.	

Conditional.

Present.		
partiroie.	partireie.	partir abéa.
partiroies.	partireies.	etc.
partiroit.	—	
partiriens.	partirion(s), partirium.	
partiriez.	partirieiz, partiriés.	
partiroient.	—	

Subjunctive.

Present.		
parte.	—	pártja.
partes.	partas.	pártjas.
partet.	parte.	pártjat.
partiens.	partions, partium.	partjámus.
partiez.	partieiz, partiés.	partjátis.
partent.	—	pártjant.

Subjunctive.

Main-form.	By-forms.	Phonetic Latin.
partisse.	—	partísse.
partisses.	—	partísses.
partist.	—	partísset.
partissiens.	partissions, partissium.	partissémus.
partissiez.	partissieiz, partissiés.	partissétis.
partissent.	partisent.	partíssent.

(marked Imperfect, bracketed)

Imperative.

part.	—	parti.
partons.	—	partómus.
partez.	parteiz, partés.	partétis.

Infinitive.

partir.	—	partíre.

Gerund and Present Participle.

partant.	—	{ partando.
		{ partante.

Past Participle.

partit.	parti, partid.	partítus, -u
fem. partie.	partide, partidet.	

Second Class : Inchoative Class.

The Inchoative Tenses are the following :—

Verb florir.   Latin : florére.

Indicative.

Main-form.	By-forms.	Phonetic Latin.
floris.	flori.	florísco.
floris.	—	floríscis.
florist.	florissed.	floríscit.
florissons.	—	floriscómus.
florissez.	—	floriscétis.
florissent.	florissen.	floríscunt.

(marked Present, bracketed)

Indicative.

Main-form.	By-forms.	Phonetic Latin.
Imperfect. florissoie.	florisscie.	floriscéa.
florissoies.	etc.	etc.
florissoit.		
florissiens.		
florissiez.		
florissoient.		

Subjunctive.

Present.		
florisse.	—	florísca.
florisses.	—	etc.
florist.	florisse.	
florissiens.	—	
florissiez.	—	
florissent.	—	

Gerund and Present Participle.

florissant.	—	floriscándo. floriscánte.

The remaining tenses are identical in form with those of the Pure class.

Observations.—I. Some Eastern dialects had an uncontracted Imperfect that was not accepted in the literary dialect. It runs thus, on the lines of the Latin flexion -*ibam* :—

partive.	partiens.
partives.	partiez.
partivet.	partivent.

II. Some Verbs float somewhat arbitrarily between the Pure forms and the Inchoative forms. For instance : *guaresist* and *attendrisist* are Inchoative Imperfects of the Subjunctive, without etymological authority, this, like the Past Definite, being a Non-Inchoative tense.

III. The *i* of the Infinitive becomes atonic in the Future, and disappears often altogether after an *r*; *guarra* is for *guarira*. Metathesis of *r* occurs in *sofrir* and elsewhere: *soferrai* stands for *sofrirai* (*sofrerai*).

IV. Some Past Participles end in -*cit*, -*ert* or -*u*. Exam.: *ofert, sofert, coilleit, benëeit* (*ei* = *oi*), *feru, sentu, vestu*.

EXAMPLES OF VERBS IN TERMINATIONAL CONJUGATION

I.	II.	III.
colchier	fendre.	sortir.
changier.	pendre.	atenebrir.
garder.	rendre, etc.	garir.
marchier.	entendre.	perir.
regreter.	repondre.	seisir.
sejorner.	battre.	escharnir.
regarder, etc.	rompre.	plevir.

THE ACCENTUAL CONJUGATION

The Accentual Conjugation contains Verbs whose Infinitive ends in -*oir*, and also Verbs ending in -*er*, -*re*, -*ir*, like the Verbs of the Terminational Conjugation. No Verbs are strong in the whole of their conjugation, because in no Verb does the accent remain throughout on the same syllable. So Verbs belonging to this conjugation are verbs whose root-vowel is strong when it is accented and weak when the accent is withdrawn. The strengthening of the root-vowel may affect the inflection. An acquaintance with the modes of strengthening will afford a less mechanical means of distinguishing the accentual conjugation than the test indicated in our first remarks on Terminational Verbs.

FIRST ACCENTUAL TYPE

This differs from the corresponding Terminational type in the following tenses only :—

Secondary Verb amer.

Present Indicative.	Present Subjunctive.	Imperative.
je aim.	j'aim.	—
tu aimes	aimes.	aime.
il aime.	aim.	aim.
nos amons.	amiens.	amons.
vos amez.	amiez.	amez.
il aiment.	aiment.	aiment.

In those three tenses the stem-accented forms have *ai-*, the others *a-*.

The process of vowel-strengthening is worked out as follows :—

a	becomes	*ai, e*,	ex. : *amer, j'aim*; *laver, lef*.
e	„	*ai, oi, ei*,	ex. : *mener, je meine*.
e	„	*ie*,	ex. : *lever, je lieve*.
o	„	*uo, cu, ue, oe*,	ex. : *demorer, je demeure*.
o	„	*oi*,	ex. : *doner, je doin*.
ei	„	*i*,	ex. : *preier, je prie*.
oi	„	*ui*,	ex. : *apoier, j'apuie*.

The substitution of *u* for *l* in forms like *baut* for *balt* (from *ballier*), *esmervaut* for *esmervalt* (from *esmerveller*), *soue* from *soldre* (*sourre*), is not a strengthening.

The same remark holds good with respect to numerous Verbs which have by-forms of a dialectic character in which their root-vowel is made into a diphthong : thus *vuidier* and *voider* for *vider*.

There is often only vowel-change or orthographic uncertainty, like *trichier* and *trecher*, *tenser* and *tanser*.

Under the working of stem analogy some accentual Verbs in -*er* became double-stemmed Verbs in the Infinitive with a double conjugation throughout; ex. : *preuver* and *prouver*, *demourer* and *demeurer*, *plourer* and *pleurer*, *trouver* and *treuver* (confused diphthongs).

But originally and properly speaking, for the diphthong

H

ou of these Verbs stood a primitive weak *o*; *eu* was strong, and they were conjugated thus :—

> *Demourer, demourant, nos demourons*, etc., **but** *ie demeur, tu demeures, il demeure.*
> *Plourer*, **but** *il ploure*, etc.
> *Prouver*, **but** *il preuve*, etc.
> *Trouver*, **but** *il treuve*, etc.

Ou is always a monophthong in Modern French.

In the same way *lever* gave *il lieve* (*lief*), *mener* gave *il meine* (*moine*), *peser* gave *il peise* (*poise*).

Hence in Modern Grammars the badly explained, or unexplained alternances : mener, *je mène*, peser, *je pèse*, lever, *je lève*, appear in logical sequence with Old French, and are philologically justified.

In some accentual Verbs the stem has two syllables. In their strong forms the accent falls on the second syllable and preserves it. In their weak forms the accent is on the termination. There is then nothing to preserve the second syllable of the stem : so its vowel, now atonic, drops out. Ex. :

Strong Forms.	Weak Forms.
je manjue.	*mangier* (no *u*).
je parole.	*parler* (no *o*).
il raisonne.	*nous raisnons* (no *o*).
tu desjunes.	*vous disnez* (no *u*).
Imperat. *aiue.*	*aidons* (no *u*).

The second syllable of the stem is seen to disappear in the weak forms.

SECOND ACCENTUAL TYPE

The infinitive ends in -*ir*. The root-vowel is affected in the same tenses as in the First Accentual Type, and in the same way :—

> *e* becomes *ie*, ex. : *ferir, je fier.*
> *o* „ *ue*, ex. : *soffrir, je sueffre.*
> *o* „ *oe*, ex. : *ovrir, j'oevre.*

Verbs in *-ir* with the Pres. Indic. Sing. in *-e*, and Past Part. in *-ert* (Latin *-ertum*), are best classified under this head :—

Secondary Verb soffrir.

Pres. Indic.	*Infinitive.*
je sueffre.	soffrir.
tu sueffres.	*Pres. Part.*
il sueffre.	soffrant.
nos soffrons.	*Past Part.*
vos soffrez.	soffert, etc.
il sueffrent.	

REMARKABLE VERBS OF THE TERMINATIONAL CONJUGATION, AND OF THE FIRST AND SECOND ACCENTUAL TYPES

VERB ALER.

Indicative Present.
S. 1. vai, voi, vois, vais.
2. vas.
3. vait, vet, va, vat.

P. 3. vont, vunt.

Future.
S. 1. irai, irrai.

Subjunctive Present.
S. 1. aille, voise.
3. voist, alge, auge, alget, alt, aut.
P. 3. algent.

Imperative.
S. 2. va, vai.

Past Participle.
alet, alé.

VERB DONER.

Indicative Present.
S. 1. doing, duins.

Subjunctive Present.
S. 1. doingne.

2. doinses.
3. dunget, dunge, dont, donst, doint, doinst.

P. 3. doiguent.

VERB ESTER.

Indicative Present.
S. 1. estois.

Imperfect.
S. 3. stout.

Past Definite.
S. 3. estut, istud.
P. 3. esturent, esterent.

Subjunctive Imperfect.
S. 3. estëust.

VERBS LAISSIER AND LAIER.

Indicative Present.
S. 3. lait, laist.

Future.
S. 1. lairai, lerrai, lerai.

VERB TROVER.

Indicative Present.
S. 1. truis, treuve.

Subjunctive Present.
S. 1. truisse.
3. truist, truisse.

VERB SIVRE.

Indicative Present.
S. 1. siu.
3. sieut, suit.

Imperative.
S. 2. suis.

Present Participle.
sivant.

Past Definite.
S. 1. sewi, siuvi, sivi.
P. 3. sivirent.

Past Participle.
soüt, sëu, siwi.

VERB ROMPRE.

Past Participle.

Anal. form : rompu.

Ety. form : rot, rut.

VERB FAILLIR OR FALIR.

Indicative Present.
S. 2. fals, faus.
3. falt, fat, faut, fault.

Future.
S. 1. faurai, faurrai,
faudrai, fauldrai.

VERB HAIR.

Indicative Present.
S. 1. he, has, hais.
3. het.
P. 3. heent.

Future.
S. 1. harrai.
Subjunctive Present.
S. 3. hace.

VERB ISSIR OR ISTRE.

Indicative Present.
S. 3. ist, eist.
P. 3. issent, iscent.

Subjunctive Present.
S. 1. isse.

Imperative.
S. 2. is.

Future.
S. 1. istrai, isterai, eistrai.

Past Participle.
issu, eissuz.

VERB OÏR OR ODÏR.

Indicative Present.
S. 1. oi, oz.
2. os, oz, oys.
3. ot, oit.
P. 1. oons.
2. oēz, oës.
3. oënt.

Imperfect.
S. 1. ooie, oioye.

Future.
S. 1. orrai, orai.

Subjunctive Present.
S. 1. oie.

Imperative.
S. 2. oz.

VERB CHAOIR.

Indicative Present.
S. 3. chiet, kiet, ciet, quiet.
P. 3. chedent, chieent.

Imperfect.
S. 1. chaoie, chaeie.

Past Definite.
S. 3. chaï.
P. 3. cheïrent, chaürent.

Future.
S. 1. charrai.

Subjunctive Present.
S. 1. chiee.

Imperfect.
S. 1. caïsse.

Past Participle.
chëut, chëu, këu,
chaït, chaeit,
chaet.

THIRD ACCENTUAL TYPE.

The Infinitive ends in *-re*, *-oir*, or *-ir*. Its root-vowel is affected in the following manner :

The process of the First and Second Accentual Types

which strengthens the root-vowel into a diphthong, is accompanied in this type by other characteristics.

Confused diphthongs made their appearance with some regularity, and a feature, the adjunction of corroborative consonants to the stem, is prominent. Also, and this is the most distinctive feature of all, the Preterite (Primary Latin Perfect in *-si, -i, -ui*), is almost always strong.

Practically this Type is better viewed as a Defective Etymological Conjugation. It consists mostly of Verbs which have etymological forms that cannot be reduced to one common standard.

Regarding vowel-strengthening :

a	becomes	*ai,*	ex. : *manoir, maint.*
e	„	*ie, i,*	ex. : *tenir, tiènt, tint.*
e	„	*oi,*	ex. : *devoir, doit.*
o	„	*eu,*	ex. : *corre, queurt.*
o	„	*ue,*	ex. : *morir, muert.*

The confusion in diphthongs is thus :

$$o\begin{cases} ou & \text{becomes } eu, & \text{ex. : } mouvoir, meut. \\ ou & „ \quad oe, ue, & \text{ex. : } pouoir, poet, puet. \\ ou & „ \quad ui, & \text{ex. : } pouoir, puist. \end{cases}$$

au for *al*, *ou* for *ol*, are not accentual workings.

Regarding corroborative consonants :

creindre,	from Low-Latin *cremere,*	has a *d.*	
fraindre	„	*frangere,* has a *d.*	
joindre	„	*jungere*	„ *d.*
roembre	„	*redimere*	„ *b.*
semondre	„	*submovere*	„ *d.*
boivre	„	*bibere*	„ *v.*
conoistre	„	*cognoscere*	„ *t.*
croistre	„	*crescere*	„ *t.*
beneistre	„	Low-Latin *benediscere,* has a *t.*	
		Etc. etc.	

The additional consonants, considered in their mechanical

function, are helps to pronunciation. The *v* of *boivre* is etymological.

TYPES OF TENSES AFFECTED

Present Indicative of creindre and savoir.

je criem.	je sai.
tu criens.	tu sais.
il crient.	il sait.
nos cremons.	nos savons.
vos cremez.	vos savez.
il criement.	il saivent.

Past Definite of devoir, voir, and ardre.

je dui.	vi.	ars.
tu deüs.	veïs.	arsis.
il deüt.	vit.	arst.
nos deümes.	veïmes.	arsimes.
vos deüstes.	veïstes.	arsistes.
il deürent.	virent.	arstrent.

Present Subjunctive of devoir and venir.

je deive.	je veigne.
tu deives.	tu veignes.
il deive.	il veigne.
nos deviens.	nos veniens.
vos deviez.	vos veniez.
il deivent.	il veignent.

Imperfect Subjunctive of voir, dire, and devoir.

je vëisse.	desisse.	dëusse.
tu vëisses.	desisses.	dëusses.
il vëist.	desist.	dëust.
nos vëissiens.	desissiens.	dëussiens.
vos vëissiez.	desissiez.	dëussiez.
il vëissent.	desissent.	dëussent.

Imperative of tenir, savoir, and voir.

tien.	saiche.	voi.
tenons.	sachions.	veons.
tenez.	sachiez.	veez.

Past Participle of ardre, ceindre, and manoir.

ars.	ceint.	mes.

Infinitives.

toldre.	maindre.	boivre.

We have said that verbs of this conjugation could not be reduced to a common standard. A study of each form would lead us into philological disquisitions out of place in this work, and which, after all, though accounting for the diversity of formation, could not reduce it to uniformity. So we must draw up a list of *Simple* Verbs and of a few *Compound* ones of the Third Accentual Type, and be satisfied with the general principles we have laid down. Yet the first person of the Past Definite of these Verbs can be used to divide them into three leading classes.

The *First Class* form in Latin (or corrupt Latin) their first person of the Perfect in -*i*, and have an *i* in Old French at the end of their Past Definite stem. *Vi*, of *voir*, typifies them (Latin *vidi*).

The *Second Class* form in Latin (or corrupt Latin) their first person of the Perfect in -*si*, in Old French *s*. *Ars*, of *ardre*, represents them (Latin *arsi*).

The *Third Class* form in Latin (or corrupt Latin) their first person of the Perfect in -*ui*, in Old French *ui*. *Dui*, of *devoir*, exemplifies them (Latin *debui*).

In the following tables it will be found that the verb forms were etymological to begin with, that is, shaped in their growth by their Latin or Low-Latin original; then, the laws of phonetics acted upon them; and, lastly, analogy within the reconstituted language further broke down individual distinctions. The forms here given are those that are actually forthcoming in the Old French language, and are the product of etymology, phonetics, and analogy working together.

PRIMARY VERBS AND PRIMARY FORMS OF SOME SECONDARY VERBS

First Class.

VERB TENIR.

Indicative Present.

S. 1. teing, tieng, tieing, tien, teins.
  2. tiens.
  3. tient, tent.
P. 1. tenons.
  2. tenez.
  3. tienent, tiennent.

Past Definite.

S. 1. tinc, ting, tins.
  2. tenis.
  3. tint.
P. 3. tindrent.

Future.

S. 1. tendrai, tenrai, tanrai.

Conditional.

S. 1. tendroie, tendreie.

Subjunctive Present.

S. 1. tienge, tiegne, teigne, teyne.

Imperfect.

S. 1. tenisse.

Imperative.

S. 1. tien.

Past Participle.

tenut, tenu.

VERB VENIR.

Indicative Present.

S. 1. vieng, vienc.
  2. viens, vienz.
  3. vient, vieu.
P. 1. venons.
  2. venez.
  3. vienent, viennent.

Imperfect.

S. 1. venoie.

Past Definite.

S. 1. vinc, ving, vins.
  2. venis.
  3. vint.
P. 1. venimes, venismes.
  2. venistes.
  3. vindrent.

Pluperfect (Neo-Latin).

S. 3. veggra.

Future.

S. 1. vendrai, venrai, vanrai, viendray, verrai.

Conditional.

S. 1. vendroie, vendreie.

Subjunctive Present.

S. 1. vienge, viegne, veigne, vigne, vienne.

Imperfect.

S. 1. venisse.

Imperative.

S. 2. vien, ven.

Past Participle.

venut, venu.

VERB VËOIR.

Indicative Present.
S. 1. voi, vei, vai, voys.
2. vois.
3. voit, veit, vait.
P. 1. vëons.
2. veez.
3. voient.

Imperfect.
S. 1. vëoie.

Past Definite.
S. 1. vi, veiz.
2. veïs, veïz.
3. vit, vid, veit, vey.
P. 1. vëimes, vëismes.
2. vëistes.
3. virent, veirent.

Pluperfect (Neo-Latin).
S. 3. vidra.

Future.
S. 1. verrai, verai, vairai.

Conditional.
S. 1. verroie, verreie.

Subjunctive Present.
S. 1. voie, veie.
3. veied.

Imperfect.
S. 1. vëisse.
3. vidist, vist, vedest.

Imperative.
S. 2. voi.
P. 2. veez.

Past Participle.
vëut, vëud, vëu.

Second Class.

VERB ARDOIR OR ARDRE.

Indicative Present.
S. 3. art.

Past Definite.
S. 3. arst.

Past Participle.
ars.

VERB CEINDRE.

Indicative Present.
S. 1. ceing.
3. ceint, chaint.
P. 1. ceignons.

Past Definite.
S. 3. ceinst.

Past Participle.
ceint, ceinct.

VERB CLORE.

Indicative Present.	*Subjunctive Present.*
S. 3. clot.	S. 3. clodet.
P. 2. cluëz.	
Past Definite.	*Past Participle.*
S. 3. clost.	clos.

VERB CREINDRE.

Indicative Present.	*Subjunctive Present.*
S. 1. criem, crien, crieng, criens, crain.	S. 1. criegne.
3. crient.	*Imperative.*
Imperfect.	crains.
S. 1. cremoie.	

VERB DESPIRE.

Indicative Present.	*Past Definite.*
S. 2. despis.	S. 3. despist, despeis.
3. despist.	*Past Participle.*
P. 3. despisent.	despit.

VERB DIRE.

Indicative Present.	*Conditional.*
S. 1. di.	S. 1. diroie, direie.
2. dis, diz.	
3. dit, dict.	*Subjunctive Present.*
P. 1. disons.	S. die.
2. dites, dittes.	
3. dïent.	*Imperfect.*
Past Definite.	S. 1. desisse, deïsse.
S. 1. dis, diz.	3. disist, dissest.
2. disis, deïs.	
3. dist, dit.	*Imperative.*
P. 2. deïstes.	S. 2. di, dis.
3. dirent, distrent.	P. 2. dites, dictes.
Future.	*Past Participle.*
S. 1. dirai, dirrai.	dit, dist, deit.

VERB DUIRE (LAT. DUCERE).

Indicative Present.	*Past Definite.*
S. 3. duit.	S. 3. duist.
P. 1. duisons.	P. 3. duistrent, duisent.

Imperfect.	*Subjunctive Present.*
S. 1. duisoie.	S. 1. duise, duie.

Past Participle.
duit.

VERB ESCRIRE.

Indicative Present.	*Past Definite.*
S. 3. escrit, escript.	S. 3. escrist, escrit.
P. 1. escrivons.	P. 3. escrirent.

Past Participle.
escrit.

VERB FAIRE.

Indicative Present.

S. 1. faz, faç, fais, faiz, fai.
   2. fais, fes, faiz, fez.
   3. fait, fet, feit, fai, faict.
P. 1. faisons, faesmes.
   2. faites, feites, faictes.
   3. font, funt, feent.

Imperfect.

S. 1. faisoie, fesoie.

Past Definite.

S. 1. fis, fiz.
   2. fesis, feïs, fis.
   3. fist, feist, feit, fei.
P. 1. feïmes, feïsmes.
   2. fesistes, feïstes, faïstes, feïtes.
   3. firent, fisent, fisdren.

Pluperfect (Neo-Latin).

S. 3. fisdra, fistdra.

Future.

S. 1. ferai, ferrai, fairai.

Conditional.

S. 1. feroie, fereie, freie.

Subjunctive Present.

S. 1. face, fache.
   3. facet, faz', faice.
P. 2. façoiz.

Imperfect.

S. 1. fesisse, feïsse.
   3. feisis.

Imperative.

S. 2. fai, faz, faiz, fais.

Past Participle.
fait, feit, fet, fat, faict.

VERB FEINDRE.

Indicative Present.   *Past Definite.*

P. 1. feignons.   S. 3. feinst.

Past Participle.

feint, finct, fint, foynt.

VERB FRAINDRE.

Indicative Present.   *Past Participle.*

S. 3. fraint.   frait.
P. 1. fraignons.

VERB JOINDRE.

Indicative Present.   *Past Definite.*

S. 3. joint.   S. 3. joinst.
P. 1. joignons.

Past Participle.

joint, juint.

VERB MANOIR OR MAINDRE.

Indicative Present.   *Subjunctive Present.*

S. 1. maing, main, mains.   S. 1. maigne.
   3. maint, maent.   *Imperfect.*
P. 3. mainent.   S. 1. mainsisse.

Past Definite.

S. 1. mes.   *Imperative.*
   3. mest.   S. 2. main.

Future.   *Present Participle.*

S. 3. maurai, mandrai.   menant.

Past Participle.

mes.

VERB METRE OR MATRE.

Indicative Present.

S. 1. met, metz.
   3. met, mait, mest.
P. 3. metent.

Past Definite.

S. 2. meïs.
   3. mist.
P. 2. meïstes, mistes.
   3. mistrent, mirent, missent.

Subjunctive Present.

S. 1. mete, meche.

Imperfect.

S. 1. meïsse.
   3. meïst.

Past Participle.

mis, mes.

VERB OCCIRRE OR OCIRE.

Indicative Present.

S. 1. oci.
   3. ocit, ochit, ochist.
P. 3. ocïent.

Past Definite.

S. 1. ocis, occis.
   3. occist, ocist.
P. 2. oceïstes.
   3. ocistrent.

Future.

S. 1. ocirrai, ocirai, ochirai.

Subjunctive Present.

S. 1. ocie, ochie.

Imperfect.

S. 3. occisist, oceïst.
P. 1. occisissons.
   3. ocesissent.

Past Participle.

ocis, ochis.

VERB PLAINDRE.

Indicative Present.

S. 1. plain, plaing, pleing, plains.
   2. plains.
P. 1. plaignons.

Past Definite.

S. 3. plainst.

Subjunctive Imperfect.

S. 1. plainsisse.

Past Participle.

plaint.

VERB POINDRE.

Indicative Present.

S. 3. point.
P. 1. poignons.

Past Definite.

S. 3. poinst.

Past Participle.

point.

VERB PRENDRE.

Indicative Present.

S. 1. preing, preng, pren, pran.
  2. prens.
  3. prent.
P. 1. prenons.
  2. prenez.
  3. prendent, prenent,
    prandent.

Imperfect.

S. 1. prenoie.

Past Definite.

S. 1. pris.
  2. presis.
  3. prist, prest, pres,
    prinst, print.
P. 1. preïmes.
  2. preïstes.
  3. pristrent, presdrent,
    prisent, prindrent.

Pluperfect (Neo-Latin).

S. 3. presdre, presdra.

Future.

S. 1. prendrai, prenderai,
    penrai, panrai, prindrai

Subjunctive Present.

S. 1. prenge, preigne,
    praigne, prengue,
    prengne, prende.

Imperfect.

S. 1. presisse, preïsse.
P. 2. prissiez.

Imperative.

S. 2. pren, prens.
P. 2. prennez, prendez,
    pernez.

Past Participle.

pris, prins.

VERB QUERRE OR QUERIR.

Indicative Present.

S. 1. quier, quiers.
  2. quiers.
  3. quiert.
P. 1. querons.
  3. quierent.

Future.

S. 1. querrai.

Subjunctive Present.

S. 1. quiere.
P. 3. quiergent.

VERB QUERRE OR QUERIR—*continued.*

Imperfect.	*Imperfect.*
S. 1. queroie, querroie.	S. 1. quesisse, queïsse.

Past Definite.

S. 1. quis.	*Past Participle.*
3. quist.	
P. 2. queïstes, quistes.	quis.
3. quistrent, quissent.	

VERB RESPONDRE.

Indicative Present.	*Past Definite.*
S. 1. respons.	S. 3. respont.
3. respont, respunt.	*Past Participle.*
	respons.

VERB SËOIR.

Indicative Present.	*Subjunctive Present.*
S. 3. siet.	S. 1. siee.
P. 3. sieent, siedent.	*Imperative.*
Past Definite.	S. 2. sié, siet.
S. 1. sis.	*Present Participle.*
3. sist.	sëaut, sedant.
P. 3. sisdrent, sirent.	

Past Participle.

sis.

VERB SOLDRE.

Indicative Future.	*Imperative.*
S. 1. sorrai.	S. 2. sol.
Subjunctive Present.	*Past Participle.*
S. 1. soille.	sols.

VERB SORDRE.

Indicative Present.	*Present Participle.*
S. 3. sourt, surt.	sourdant, sourjant.
P. 3. surdent.	
Past Definite.	*Past Participle.*
S. 1. sors.	sors, sours.

VERB TAINDRE.

Indicative Present.	*Past Definite.*
S. 1. taing.	S. 3. teinst.
P. 1. taignons.	*Past Participle.*
	taint, teint.

VERB TRAIRE.

Indicative Present.	*Future.*
S. 3. trait, tret.	S. 1. trairai, trerai, trarai.
Past Definite.	*Past Participle.*
S. 3. traist, trais.	trait, tret.

Third Class.

VERB BOIVRE.

Indicative Present.	*Past Definite.*
S. 2. bois.	S. 1. bui.
3. boit.	3. but.
P. 1. bevons.	P. 2. bustes.
3. boivent	3. burent.
Imperfect.	*Future.*
S. 1. bevoie.	S. 1. bevrai, beverai.
3. beuvoit.	*Past Participle.*
	bëut, bëu.

I

VERB CONOISTRE OR CONUISTRE.

Indicative Present.

S. 1. cunuis, connois, quenuis.
   2. congnois.
   3. cunuist, connoist,
      conoit, cognoit.
P. 1. counisçons.
   2. conissiés.
   3. conoissent, quenoissent.

Past Definite.

S. 1. conui, connui.
   3. conut, cunut, counut,
      cunuit, cogneut.
P. 3. conurent, cognurent.

Future.

S. 1. conoistrai.

Imperfect.

S. 1. connissoie.

Subjunctive Imperfect.

S. 1. conëusse.

Past Participle.
conëud, conëu, cogneu.

VERB CORRE. *Cᵘ*

Indicative Present.

S. 3. cort, court, curt, queurt.
P. 3. corent, queurent,
      keurent.

Future.

S. 1. corrai.

Past Definite.

S. 3. curut.
P. 3. corurent.

Subjunctive Present.

S. 1. core, cure, queure.

VERB CROIRE.

Indicative Present.

S. 1. croi, crei, creid, crois.
   2. crois.
   3. croit, creit.
P. 3. croient, creient.

Subjunctive Imperfect.

S. 1. crëusse.

Imperative.

S. 2. croi.
P. 2. creez.

Past Definite.

S.   crui.

Future.

S. 1. crerrai, crerai, cresrai,
      credrai, qerrai.

Past Participle.
crëu.

VERB DEVOIR.

Indicative Present.

S. 1. doi, dois, doibz.
   2. dois, doiz, deiz.
   3. doit, deit.
P. 1. devons, doyens.
   3. doivent, deivent, deent,
      doient.

Past Definite.

S. 3. dut, deubt.
P. 3. durent.

Future.

S. 1. devrai, deverai, debvrai.

Subjunctive Present.

S. 1. doive, deive, doie.

Imperfect.

S. 1. dëusse, deuïsse, doüse.

Past Participle.

deü.

VERB DOLOIR.

Indicative Present.

S. 1. doil, dueil, duel.
   2. dels.
   3. delt.

Past Definite.

P. 3. dolurent.

Future.

S. 1. daurai.

Conditional.

S. 1. dolroie.

Subjunctive Present.

S. 1. doille.

Present Participle.

dolent, dolant, doliant.

Past Participle.

dolu.

VERB ESTOVOIR.

Indicative Present.

S. 3. estuet, estoet, estot.

Past Definite.

S. 3. estut, estot.

Future.

S. 3. estavra, estovra,
      estevra.

Subjunctive Present.

S. 3. estucet, estuce.

Imperfect.

S. 3. estëust.

VERB GESIR.

Indicative Present.	*Subjunctive Present.*
S 1. gis.	S. 1. gise.
3. gist.	*Imperfect.*
P. 1. gisons.	
3. gisent.	S. 1. gëusse.
Past Definite.	*Present Participle.*
P. 3. jut.	gisant.
Future.	*Past Participle.*
S. 1. girrai, girai, gerrai.	gëu, gëut, jut.

VERB LIRE.

Indicative Present.	*Subjunctive Present.*
S. 2. leis.	S. 1. lise.
Past Definite.	*Past Participle.*
S. 2. lëis.	lëu, lut.
3. list.	

VERB MORIR.

Indicative Present.	*Future.*
S. 1. muir.	S. 1. morrai, murrai.
2. muers.	*Subjunctive Present.*
3. muert, meurt, mor.	S. 1. muire, meure.
Past Definite.	*Imperfect.*
S. mourt, mourit.	S. 1. morisse.
P. 3. mururent.	

Past Participle.
mort.

VERB MOVOIR.

Indicative Present.	P. 2. mëustes.
S. 1. mué.	3. murent.
3. muet.	*Future.*
Past Definite.	S. 1. mouverai.
S. 1. mui.	*Past Participle.*
3. mut.	mëu.

VERB PAROIR.

Indicative Present.	*Future.*
S. 3. pert.	S. 3. parra, perra.
Past Definite.	*Subjunctive Present.*
S. 3. parut.	S. 3. paire, pere.

Past Participle.

parëut.

VERB PLAISIR OR PLAIRE.

Indicative Present.	*Subjunctive Present.*
S. 3. plaist, plest, plastz.	S. 3. plaise, pleise, place.
Past Definite.	*Imperfect.*
S. 3. plot.	S. 3. plëust, ploüst.
Future.	*Past Participle.*
S. 3. plaira.	plëu.

VERB POOIR.

Indicative Present.

S. 1. puis, pois.
2. pués, pois, poz, peus.
3. puët, pued, pot, put, peult.
P. 1. poons.
2. poëz, poës, pouëz, povez.
3. podent, poient, puyent, pueent, poënt, peuvent.

Pluperfect (Neo-Latin).

S. 3. pouret

Future.

S. 1. porrai, porai, purrai, purrei, pourrai, porrays.

Subjunctive Present.

S. 1. puisse.
3. puist, puisse.

Imperfect.

S. 1. pooie, povoie, povoys.

Past Definite.

S. 1. poi.
3. pot, pod, peut.
P. 3. porent, pourent, peureut.

Imperfect.

S. 1. pëusse, poüsse, poïsse, peuïsse, puüsse, peüsce.
3. pëust, poüst, podist.

Past Participle.

pëu.

VERB SAVOIR.

Indicative Present.
S. 1. sai, sais, sçay.
   2. ses, seis, sez, sçais.
   3. set, seit, scet.
P. 1. savons.
   3. sevent, seivent.

Past Definite.
S. 1. soi, seu.
   3. sot, sout, sceut. ·
P. 3. sorent, sourent,
     souurent.

Future.
S. 1. savrai, saverai, sarai,
     sçarai.

Subjunctive Present.
S.   sache, sace, saiche.

Imperfect.
S. 1. sëusse, sëuse, sëusce,
     scëusse, sceuïsse.
   3. soust.

Imperative.
P. 2. sachiez, sacez, saivez.

Present Participle.
sachant.

Past Participle.
sëu.

VERB SOLOIR.

Indicative Present.
S. 1. soil, sueil, suel.

S. 3. solt, soelt.
P. 3. suelent.

VERB TAISIR OR TAIRE.

Indicative Present.
S. 3. taist, test.

Past Definite.
S. 3. tout, teut.

Future.
S. 1. tairrai, tairai.

Subjunctive Present.
S. 1. taise, teise.

Imperfect.
S. 3. teust.

Imperative.
S. 2. tais, teis.
P. 2. teisiez.

Past Participle.
tëu.

VERB TOLIR OR TOLDRE.

Indicative Present.
S. 3. tolt, tout, taut.

Subjunctive Present.
S. 1. toylle.

VERB TOLIR OF TOLDRE—*continued.*

Past Definite.

S. 1. toli.
3. tolit, tost.
P. 3. tollirent.

Past Participle.

tolut, tolud, tolu, toleit.

VERB VALOIR.

Indicative Present.

S. 1. vail, vaill.
2. vals.
3. valt, vaut, vault.
P. 3. valent.

Future.

S. 1. vaurai, vaudrai, vauldrai.

Subjunctive Present.

S. 1. vaille.

Present Participle.

vailant.

Past Definite.

S. 1. valui.
3. vallut.

Past Participle.

valu.

VERB VOLOIR.

Indicative Present.

S. 1. voil, vol, vueil, vuel,
    voeil, voeill, voel,
    veul, veuil, veuill,
    veux.
2. vués, vels, vols, veus,
    viaus, viax, veulz,
    veux, veulx, wels.
3. vuet, voelt, velt, veut,
    veult, weult, violt,
    vialt, viaut, volt,
    veolt, welt, wet.
P. 1. volons.
2. volez, vollés, voeilés.
3. vuelent, voelent, vuel-
    lent, volent, volunt,
    veullent,   welent,
    wellent.

Past Definite.

S. 1. vols, voz.
2. volsis.

S. 3. volt, vout, vot, voult,
    volst, vost.
P. 2. volsistes.
3. volrent, vorent, voud-
    rent.

Pluperfect (Neo-Latin).

S. 3. voldret, voldrat.

Future.

S. 1. volrai, vourai, vourrai,
    voldrai, voudrai, vorrai,
    vorai, vaurai.

Subjunctive Present.

S. 1. voille, vueille, voeille,
    veuille.

Imperfect.

S. 1. volsisse, vousisse, vau-
    sisse, vosisse, voulsisse.
3. volxist, vousist, voulust.

Past Participle.

volu.

Mixed Class.

Verb beneïstre.

Indicative Present.	*Subjunctive Present.*
S. 3. beneïst.	S. 1. benie.
Future.	*Past Participle.*
S. 1. beneïstrai.	benëoit, benoit, benoist, benit.

Verb naistre.

Indicative Present.	*Past Definite.*
S. 3. naist.	S. 1. nasqui.
P. 3. nessent.	P. 2. naquistes.

Past Participle.

né.

Verb veincre.

Indicative Present.	*Indicative Imperfect.*
S. 1. vainc.	S. 1. vencoie.
2. vains.	*Past Definite.*
3. vaint.	S. 1. venqui.
S. 1. venquons.	*Future.*
2. venquez.	S. 1. vaincrai.
3. vainquent.	*Past Participle.*
	vencu.

Verb vivre.

Indicative Present.	*Future.*
S. 2. vis.	S. 1. vivrai.
3. vit.	*Subjunctive Imperfect.*
Past Definite.	S. 3. vesquist.
S. 3. visquet.	*Past Participle.*
P. 3. vesquirent.	vescut, vescu.

We should not have been justified in giving a complete conjugation of each of the above Verbs. Still less could

we aim, in an elementary work like this, at putting on
record *all* Verbs entitled to a mention in the three classes.
The student will notice how often an analogical modern
French form has superseded the etymological Old French
form; for instance, the strong Preterite form *ceinst* from
cinxit, has given way to the Modern *ceignit*, which discards
the stem accent, while the old Past Participle *ceint*, cor-
rectly formed from Latin *cínctus*, has been preserved, and
not been succeeded by a neological *ceigni*, as the new Past
Definite would lead one to expect. The following verbs
show in the Modern language the principle of accent
variation.

Mourir, meurt.	tenir, tient.
Mouvoir, meut.	venir, vient.
Pouvoir, peut.	quérir, quiert.
Vouloir, veut.	seoir, sied.
Percevoir, perçoit.	savoir, sait.
Devoir, doit.	avoir, ai.

And their compounds, when such exist.

SECOND PART—SYNTAX

Two main considerations hold sway over this portion of Old French Grammar. The first and principal is the proximity of Old French to Latin; the second, the greater simplicity and flexibility of its construction when compared with Modern French. Latin being synthetic and Modern French analytic, the Syntax of the Old language, standing as it does as a link between the two, shares at first strongly in the constructions of the first, and by degrees shades off into those of the latter. So Old French has hardly a Syntax of its own : the student who reads it with a mind impregnated with the syntactical processes of Latin and of Modern French, will hardly ever be at a loss to understand any construction, and will be able to draw comparisons as he goes along, provided he bears in mind what profound alterations the *Lingua Romana* made in the syntax of literary Latin, and how different from Cicero's Latin was the language used in literature under the emperors and in the early Middle Ages. The following chapters are therefore more especially intended to mark wherein Old French syntax differs from Modern French syntax, and a short chapter on Old Gallicisms, whose meaning and formation are not always very easy to trace, will be added to the Syntax proper.

This is concerned with words and their use, with the position of words in a clause, with the arrangement of clauses in a sentence. Hence three divisions, which we shall take in their order of decreasing generality. The language in its creative process followed an order exactly opposite. We invert this for the sake of dealing first with the least important chapter.

Syntax is, perhaps, of all the fields belonging to the Romance scholar, the one in which he has made least progress. There is great difficulty in generalising into rules syntactical processes whose history embraces, leaving out of account the pre-literary period, about five centuries (from the eleventh to the sixteenth inclusive). A great deal of information, which may be described as of a statistical nature, and without which the grammarian cannot advance to safe systematic conclusions, is still awanting.

Celtic influence practically amounts to nothing (see *Keltische Sprache*, by Ernst Windisch, in Gröber's *Grundriss der Romanischen Philologie*), so far as definite information goes, for our acquaintance with the grammar of the Celtic spoken in Gaul is exceedingly slight.

The influence of the *Lingua Romana* is direct, but it is not much easier to trace, because little of this spoken form of Latin has reached us in the shape of writing (see *die Lateinische Sprache in den Romanischen Ländern*, by Wilhelm Meyer, also in the *Grundriss*).

The comparative grammar of the Romance languages has made little progress since the days of Diez. The third part of his grammar still contains the best historical presentment of French syntax. A. Tobler's *Vermischte Beiträge zur Französischen Grammatik* is the next best work of investigation.

In France there is no dearth of historical grammars dealing with the transformation of Syntax, by Brachet, L. Clédat, F. Brunot, etc. More comprehensive works are those of the late A. Darmesteter and of G. Paris now in course of publication. There is reason to fear that the systematic exposition, promised by the latter, under the title of *Grammaire sommaire de l'ancien Français*, as the second volume of his *Manuel d'ancien Français*, may be long withheld from the public. To such procrastinations are those subjected who will send forth none but perfect work. On the other hand, the publication of A. Darmesteter's *Cours de Grammaire Historique*, is proceeding smoothly. The fourth and last part, treating of the historical syntax, may be expected in 1896.

For the grammar of sixteenth century French, one should consult *Le seizième siècle en France*, by Darmesteter and Hatzfeld. For the seventeenth century, one may use *Französische Syntax des xvii. Jahrhunderts*, by A. Haase.

CHAPTER I

The Arrangement of Clauses in the Period

In a stage of language in which printing is unknown, in which reading and writing, as compared with mere speaking, count for very little, the syntactical order is more than elsewhere a compromise springing up anew in every sentence between emotional utterance and the seeking for an intellectually clear expression. The natural order comes thereby into prominence. The requirements of the sense, and the discretion of the writer are the only check on the abandonment of the so-called logical order, demanding that the principal clause should precede the dependent clause, and that Conjunctions or Relative Pronouns should link themselves immediately to their antecedent. Example of illogical order :—

Que enfant n'ourent, peiset lor en fortment.
(Vie de St. Alexis.)
Mod.: Il leur pesait beaucoup qu'ils n'avaient pas, qu'ils n'eussent pas, de ne pas avoir, d'enfant.

The Modern language, more philosophic, and further removed from the elasticity of Romance and of Latin, has become stricter, especially in the connection of relative clause with principal clause. For instance, sentences like 'le cheval que vous avez est le meilleur,' are compulsory in Modern French, but Old French could proceed otherwise. It could separate Relative Pronouns and Conjunctions from their antecedents and give each clause separately. Ex.:

1. *Cil* sunt montet *ki* le message firent.
(Chanson de Roland.)
Mod.: *Ceux qui* ont porté le message sont montés.
2. *Li chevals* est mieldre *ke* vos aveiz.

Or else it could adhere to the logical order of clause sequence by disregarding that of word sequence. Then an inversion took place in the principal clause, and brought the subject from its proper place to the end of the clause, in order that it might play the part of an immediate antecedent. Ex.:

1. Que maudit soit *il qui* adjourne tels folz.
(Maistre Pathelin.)
Mod.: Maudit soit *celui qui* cite de tels imbéciles.
English: Cursed be *he who* summons such fools.
2. Mult esgarderent Constantinople *cil qui* onques mais ne l'avoient veue. (Villehardoin.)
Mod.: *Ceux qui* n'avaient jamais encore vu Constantinople la regardèrent fort.
3. Est mieldre *li chevals ke* vos aveiz.

In a complex sentence, where dependent clauses and principal clauses are variously interlocked, the order of the clauses and the arrangement of the related terms within each may be determined by the order of natural prominence in the mind of the speaker. Ex.:

> Il n'a si rice home en France, se tu vix sa fille avoir, que tu ne l'aies. (Aucassin et Nicolete.)
> Mod.: Il n'y a pas en France un homme si riche, que tu ne puisses avoir sa fille, si tu le veux.

A double *que* is sometimes found, which, if introduced into the above, would make it run thus: Il n'a si rice home en France, *que* se tu vix sa fille avoir, *que* tu ne l'aies.

Of the Conjunction *que* (derived from the Relative Pronoun), in its primitive Latin *Neuter* sense, there are many examples. It may, then, have a Neuter Pronoun as an antecedent (in the Modern language *ce* or the Impersonal *il*). Ex.:

> *Ceu ke* li Filz venist ne fut mie atorneit senz le consoil de la sainte Triniteit.   (St. Bernard.)
>
> Mod.: *Il* ne fut pas décidé sans l'aveu de la sainte Trinité *que* le Fils viendrait.

Que, as Relative Pronoun, may refer to the same *ce* used as an Indefinite Noun of quantity, and is separable from it. Ex.:

> Avoient laissié en leurs logis *ce de harnas que* ilz avoient.   (Froissard.)
>
> Mod.: Ils avaient laissé dans leur camp *ce qu'* ils avaient en fait de bagages.

The omission of the Demonstrative, which the Modern language demands as antecedent, is frequent. Ex.:

1. Vecy donques que luy demande.   (Maistre Pathelin.)
   Mod.: Voici donc *ce* que je lui demande.

Compare the modern incidental phrases: *qui pis est, que je crois.*

2. Loys XI ... c'estoit le plus humble en parolles et *qui* plus travailloit.   (Ph. de Commines.)
   Mod.: ... et *celui qui* travaillait le plus.
3. *Qui* l'out portet volontiers le nodrit.
                                        (Vie de St. Alexis.)
   Mod.: *Celle qui* l'avait porté l'éleva volontiers.

The sequence of clauses is sometimes redundantly established by means of a Relative Pronoun instead of a Conjunction. Ex.:

> C'est a vous *a qui* je vendy six aulnes.
>   (Maistre Pathelin.)
>
> Mod.: C'est à vous *que* je vendis six aunes.

Examples of faulty or over-concise sequence and of anacoluthon are not rare. Ex.:

1. J'ay veu beaucoup de tromperies en ce monde et *de beaucoup* de serviteurs envers leurs maistres.
                                        (Ph. de Commines.)

Mod. : J'ai vu beaucoup de tromperies en ce monde
et beaucoup de serviteurs *tromper* leurs maîtres.

2. Celluy qui perd vent et alaine,
Son fiel se creve sur son cueur.   (Villon.)
Mod. : *Le* fiel se crève sur le cœur *de celui* qui perd
le souffle et l'haleine.

3. Del ovre *qu'* out si enginee
Sofert tel aise e teu *hachee*
Se merveilla puis mainte gent.   (Chronique.)
Mod. : Bien des gens se sont étonnés depuis de
l'œuvre qu'il avait accomplie, et *de ce qu'* il avait
éprouvé un tel bonheur et une telle mort.

4. Qui donques fust a ichele assamblee,
Et fust en la sale qui tant est longue et lée,
Li rois porta corone qui vëoit l'assamblee,
Diroit que tels leëce ne fu mais demenee.
                                  (Bible de Sapience.)
Mod. : *Si quelqu'un* avait été à cette réunion,
Et s'il avait été dans la salle, qui était très longue
et très large,
Tandis que le roi, qui voyait l'assemblée, portait
sa couronne,
Il aurait dit que jamais on n'avait témoigné telle
allégresse.

The subject of the dependent clause may, by anticipation,
stand as object in the principal clause.   Ex. :
Son compaingnon puet il bien esprouver
Que volentiers il li voldroit donner
La garison.   (Amis et Amiles.)
Mod. : Il peut bien reconnaître *que son compagnon* lui
voudrait volontiers donner sa guérison.

There may be no other sign of subordination than an
inversion in the logical order of the clauses.   Ex. :
Ourent lor vent, laissent corre par mer.   (Alexis.)
Mod. : *Dès qu'ils* eurent le vent favorable, ils prirent
le large.

The meanings of *avant que, depuis que, jusqu' à ce que,* etc.,
as the context may show, spring up from such inversions.

CHAPTER II

THE POSITION OF WORDS IN A CLAUSE

THE logical order, the almost unbroken rule of Modern French, is to begin with the Subject, then come the Verb (or Auxiliary followed by Past Participle), the Attributes, the Direct and Indirect Objects, and lastly the Complements. Old French indulges with the utmost freedom in inversions of every kind. It does so with great literary effect, and not without some syntactical advantages. There is hardly any limit to permissible inversions. A few are compulsory.

Examples of Permissible Inversions:

I. In Compound Tenses the Past Participle may precede the Auxiliary. Ex.:

  1. Toutes fois que *endossé l'aurez.*
    Mod.: Toutes les fois que vous *l'aurez endossé.*
  2. Ainsi que *commandé* t' *avoye.*
    Mod.: Comme je t' *avais commandé.*
  3. Que *maudit soit* il qui adjourne tels folz.

(Maistre Pathelin.)

    Mod.: Qu'il *soit maudit* celui qui. . . .

II. The Direct Object may precede the Subject. Ex.:

  Et *ce bien*, qui n'est pas petit, luy apprint adversité.
(Ph. de Commines.)
  Mod.: Et l'adversité lui apprit *ce bien*. . . .

Usually the precedence of the Object throws the Subject back after the Verb.

In other arrangements they are found side by side before or after the Verb. Ex.:

  Encores faict *dieu grant grace* a ung prince.
(Ph. de Commines.)

III. Subject or Object **may** appear between Past Participle and Auxiliary. Ex. :

1. Tel nurisce *avoit Deus doneit* à sa petite creature.
(St. Bernard.)
Mod. : Dieu avait donné une telle nourrice . . .
2. Et Gormunz *ad l'espee traite.*
(Gormund et Isembart.)
Mod. : Et Gormund a tiré l'épée.

IV. The Attribute may be placed before the Verb, and this, with the subject, may occupy any order that suits the purpose of the writer. Ex. :

1. *Riches hom* fut de grant nobilitet.
(Vie de St. Alexis.)
Mod. : *C'était un homme riche* de haute naissance.
2. Qu'est *il bonhomme* !   (Maistre Pathelin.)

V. The Indirect Object, or terms similarly related to the Verb, may precede the Verb. Ex. :

Par la grant force du soleil il fut fondu.
(Les Cent Nouvelles nouvelles.)

VI. Complements and Adverbs may be found in almost any place, and are often massed before the Verb and Subject. Ex. :

1. Mais *sur tout* luy a servy sa grant largesse.
(Ph. de Commines.)
2. Tere majur *mult* est loinz.   (Ch. de Roland.)
Mod.: La terre plus grande est *bien loin.*
3. En ce son voyage vaqua le bon marchant l'espace de cinq ans.   (Les Cent Nouvelles nouvelles.)
4. Son mary, au bout des diz cinq ans retourné, beaucoup la loa et plus que par avant l'ama.
(*ibidem.*)
5. En nostre presence sur le gravier par la grand force du soleil il fut fondu.   (*ibidem.*)

VII. Inversion was permissible even in groups of two or more words standing to each other in a case-relation. Ex. :

K

1. Aussy m'a elle faict quelquefoys *du plaisir beaucoup.*
(Ph. de Commines.)
2. Mais *des meilleurs* voeil jo retenir *treis.*
(Ch. de Roland.)
Mod.: Mais je veux retenir *trois des meilleurs.*
3. Franc de France repairent *de roi cort.*
Mod.: Les Francs de France retournent *de la cour du roi.*
4. Si passiseiz selon mon pere tor.
Mod.: Si vous passiez devant *la tour de mon père.*

VIII. The order of the negation is often inverted.   Ex.:

1. *Point ne* me trouvai l'omme esgaré.
(Charles d'Orléans.)
2. *Plus ne* t'en dy.   (Villon.)
Mod.: Je ne t'en dis pas davantage.

IX. Adjectives usually precede the Noun, yet they may stand after it, especially with an Article prefixed.   Ex.:

1. Deus biax enfans petis.
2. Un roi rice paiien.
3. France la dulce.
4. Chere Espaigne la bele.
5. Aucassin li biax, li blons, li gentix, li amorous.
6. Un destrier grant et puissant.

X. Infinitives may stand before the Verb that governs them; the Subject or Object of an Infinitive may precede it (against Modern rule), etc.   Ex.:

1. A bon droit *appeler me povoye.*   (Ch. d'Orléans.)
Mod.: A bon droit *je pouvais m'appeler.*
2. Seyez ententif et curieux de tout honneur suyvir.
(Perceforest.)
3. Et si vous sont esguillon *a vostre cheval haster et poindre.*   (*ibidem.*)
Mod.: Voici des éperons *pour presser et piquer votre cheval.*
4. Et comencent *la rive a aprochier.*   (Villehardoin.)

XI. The Subjective Personal Pronoun may be at some distance from its Verb. Ex.:

1. Se *tu* femme *vix* avoir. (Aucass. et Nicolette.)
   Mod.: Si tu veux avoir une femme.
2. *Elle,* qui jeune estoit et en bon point, et qui point n'avait de faute des biens de dieu, *fut* contrainte par son trop demourer de prendre ung lieutenant.
   (Les Cent Nouv. nouv.)

XII. The Objective Personal Pronoun may stand after the Verb, though the Modern tongue may require it to be before the Verb. Ex.:

Ce *poise moi*—que je fac *vos.* (Auc. et Nicol.)
Mod.: Cela *me pèse*—que je *vous fasse.*

Iluec paist *l'om.* (Alexis.)
Mod.: Là, *on le* nourrit.

When the Modern tongue requires the Pronoun after the Verb, it may stand before it in Old French. Ex.:

Si *les* battez;—Or *vous* couvrez!
Mod.: Battez-*les*;—Maintenant couvrez-*vous.*

XIII. The Pronoun of Third person may precede that of Second or First person. Ex.:

1. Nous *le vous* octroyons. (Perceforest.)
   Mod.: Nous *vous l'* accordons.
2. Le dieu souverain *le* me laisse si garder! (*ibidem.*)
   Mod.: Que le Dieu souverain *me* laisse *le* garder ainsi! (*me le* laisse garder).

XIV. Interrogative sentences and Infinitive clauses also show deviations from the Modern order. Ex.:

1. Aves *le me vos* tolue ne emblee? (Auc. et Nicol.)
   Mod.: Me l'avez-vous prise ou enlevée?
2. *Aler vus en* estoet. (Chans de Roland.)
   Mod.: Il faut *vous en* aller.
3. Sa gent *me* commencierent a escrier. (Joinville.)
   Mod.: Ses gens commencèrent à *me* crier.

The Infinitive was felt to be a noun far more than it is

now; hence the practice of connecting the pronoun with the nearest finite verb-form.

XV. The emphasis sought in Modern French by the use of *c'est . . . que* may be obtained by mere position. Ex.:

> Mais *acomblemenz* fuïr nes celes choses ou . . . ta propre volenteiz puet penre deleit. (St. Bernard.)
> Mod.: Mais *c'est* le comble *que* de fuir même les choses auxquelles ton cœur peut se plaire (peut prendre délices).

The Modern language may practically no longer number 'position' among its syntactical resources. The development of the conjunctional and prepositional modes of ordering the sentence has pushed aside the natural or poetic order.

Examples of Compulsory or Regular Inversions.

While we comprised under the preceding head displacements which are merely positions at variance with the Modern order, we now have only properly so-called Inversions to mention. Inversion means the placing of the Subject after the Verb because some other term has taken its proper place at the beginning of the clause.

Inversion is compulsory in parenthetical clauses, as in Modern French.: Ex.:

> Sire, *dist el damoisel*, ainsi me face dieu. (Perceforest.)
> Mod.: Sire, *dit le jeune homme*, que Dieu me rende tel.

It is regular in clauses whose Verb is a 'Verbum dicendi,' that is, a Verb of saying (thinking, perceiving, seeing). Ex.:

> 1. Lors *luy dist le chevalier* au cueur enferré.   (*ibidem.*)
> Mod.: Alors *le chevalier* au cœur bardé de fer *lui dit.*
> 2. Quant *ot li pedre* la clamor de son fil.
>
>   (Vie de St. Alexis.)
> Mod.: Quand *le père entendit* l'appel de son fils.
> 3. *Respond la medre*: jol ferai por mon fil.   (*ibidem.*)
> Mod.: *La mère répond*: Je le ferai pour mon fils.

It is compulsory when the sentence begins with *si*, a favourite Conjunction. Ex.:

> *Si* en face *mes sires* tout sa volonté.
> (Renaut de Montauban.)

Mod.: Que *mon maître en fasse* comme il voudra.

It is regular after Adverbs and adverbial expressions. Ex.:

1. *Encor ai je* ci une bone espee.   (Auc. et Nicol.)
2. *La* perdoient *les plusieurs* force et alaine. (Froissart.)
3. *Le mercredi au soir,* dont la bataille fut a lendemain, s'en vint *Philippe d'Artevelle.* (*ibidem.*)

Hence it follows that if for some rhetorical reason or from any other cause the author does not reserve for the Subject the first place in the clause, it does not keep its place *before* the Verb at all, but follows it by inversion. Though this cannot be laid down as a rule, it is a general practice.

Elliptical and Periphrastic Order.

The kind of ellipsis to which the key, in spoken expression, is easily found in accompanying gesture or in tone of voice, is frequent. It appears most in stereotyped phrases. Ex.:

> Mult grant il fiert.
> Mod.: Il frappe maint grand *coup.*
>
> Or de gaber—or du fuir.
> Mod.: Maintenant *mettons-nous* à blaguer—*c'est le moment de* fuir.

This infinitive with *de*, as a syntactical device, is not yet extinct. Compare *et grenouilles de sauter—et tous de rire.*

Ellipsis of a noun after the definite article gives to the article the force of a substantive. Ex.:

> *Al* David—*l'* autrui—*le* Richard.
> Mod.: *du temps de* David—*le bien d'*autrui—*le champ de* Richard.

An abstract term of an honorific nature sometimes appears in respectful discourse. Ex. :

> Vers les vertus Deu, for *envers Dieu.*
> Pri toe mercit, for *je te prie.*

The Noun *cors,* Mod. *corps,* is a frequent circumlocution of the Personal Pronoun. Ex. :

> Onques nul home fors *vostre cors* n'amai.
> Mod. : Je n'aimai jamais d'autre homme que *vous.*

Periphrastic turns, repetitive phrases, recurrent epithets, expletive adverbs, such as *si, ja,* and *car,* for which there is no room in the close Modern concatenation, and which remind the reader of Herodotus and Homer, characterising as they do a familiarly poetic style, distinguish the Old French clauses.

CHAPTER III

The Use and Meaning of the Parts of Speech

In this department of Syntax the influence of the *Lingua Romana* is more apparent than in the former one. Indeed the Syntax of the Old French Parts of Speech, to be perfect, would require no less than a foregoing Syntax of the *Lingua Romana.* As no such thing exists as yet, comparisons with the practice of classical latinity must be sparingly used, though it is certain that the acquaintance of early French writers with Latin has introduced into their writings an element of latinity which the people lacked, but which it would be idle to overlook as a factor in the shaping of the written tongue.

Also we do not wish to enter here upon a research of the Syntax of Old French as an aim in itself. A running commentary on its practice in literature is what we have in view ; so we shall not refrain from choosing our examples from verse, in which Syntax may be affected by metrical requirements, and we shall draw many of our illustrations from the extracts annexed to this book, so as to give confidence to the student in facing their grammar when translating them.

We shall deal with each Part of Speech in succession, and in the same order as in the 'Accidence' of this book.

I. SYNTAX OF THE ARTICLE

The Articles are less used in Old French than in Modern French. The Definite Article is omitted before Abstract Nouns, as in English; a Noun used partitively has seldom any Article at all, and the Article Indefinite is of more frequent use as a Pronoun than as an Article proper. The Modern rule for the substitution of *de* for *du, de la, des* in certain connections does not exist. Names of countries and of nations are not preceded by the Definite Article, but it stands before Cardinal Numerals. Superlatives may dispense with it. Ex.:

1. A grant peyne povoit endurer *paix.*
(Ph. de Commines.)
2. Et ce bien luy apprint *adversité.* (*ibidem.*)
3. *Ardent desir* de veoir *païs* eschaufa l' atrempé cueur d'un marchant. (Les Cent Nouv. nouv.)
4. Ce qui appartenoit *a* nouveau chevalier. (Perceforest.)
5. Il luy donnoit *argent et estatz.* (Ph. de Commines.)
6. Il se mettoit a mescontenter les gens *par petiz* moyens.
(*ibidem.*)
7. Il chaussa *brays* neufves en ung secret lieu.
(Perceforest.)
8. Trop ad perdut *del* sanc. (Ch. de Roland.)
9. Jo l' en cunquis *Guales Escoce Islande.* (*ibidem.*)
10. Envers *Espagne* turnet sun vis. (*ibidem.*)
11. A remembrer li prist . . . *de dulce* France. (*ibidem.*)
12. A l' *une* main si od sun piz batud. (*ibidem.*)
13. *Les dis* sun grant, *les cinquante* menues. (*ibidem.*)
14. La chievre ahenne *de* froment. (Chronique.)
15. Ele *melz* connaist.
16. La quel d' eles l' aveit *plus* chier.

Mod.: 1. *la* paix; 2. *l'* adversité; 3. *un* ardent désir
. . . *des* pays; 4. à *un* nouveau chevalier; 5. *de l'* argent et
des états; 6. par *de* petits moyens; 7. *des* culottes neuves;
8. perdu *de* sang; 9. *le* pays de Galles, *l'* Ecosse, *l'* Islande;
10. vers *l'* Espagne; 11. *de la* douce France; 12. avec *une*
main; 13. *dix* sont grandes, *cinquante* petites: 14. la chèvre
cultive *du* froment; 15. elle sait *le* mieux; 16. laquelle
d'elles l'aimait *le* plus.

The use of *le*, Definite Article, in expressing fractions,
as against English ' a, one,' accounts for Gallicisms of Old
French, as: *les quatre*, meaning: four out of the five, *les
trois*, three out of the four, etc.

II. SYNTAX OF THE NOUNS

Case and Gender have to be considered under this head.

Case.

In so far as case applies to Adjectives and Pronouns
much that we say now will not be repeated in the next
two chapters.

The Subjective Case is the case in which Subject and
Attribute are put, and Adjectives or Articles relating to
them.

The Objective Case is the case in which the Direct
and Indirect Objects of Verbs are put, and Adjectives and
Articles relating to them.

Prepositions, too, govern the Objective case, and so
does the Old Gallicism *il a* or *a*, for Modern *il y a*, ' there
is,' ' there are.' Ex.:

Subj. case : *Bons* fut *li siecles*, ja mais n' iert si *vailanz.*
Mod.: Le temps était bon, il n' y en aura jamais plus
de si excellent.

Obj. case : Prist *muilier vailant.*
Mod.: Il prit une excellente femme.

Subj. case : Si fut *uns sire* de Rome la citet.
Mod.: Il y avait donc un seigneur de la cité de Rome.

Obj. case : Donc il remembret de *son seinor celeste.*
Mod. : Alors il se souvint de son seigneur céleste.

Subj. case and Obj. case : Puis vait *li enfes l' emperedor* servir.
Mod. : Puis l'enfant va servir l'empereur.

Obj. case : *Enfant* nos donne qui seit a ton talent.
Mod. : Donne-nous un enfant qui soit selon ta volonté.

Subj. case Sing., Obj. case Plur. : Sur *toz ses pers* l'amat li *emperedre.* (Vie de St. Alexis.)
Mod. : L'empereur l'aima plus que tous ses pairs.

Obj. case : *Trois periz at* en nostre sentier. (St. Bernard.)
Mod. : Il y a trois périls dans notre sentier.

Subj. case : *Guenes* oth num. (St. Léger.)
Mod. : Guène il eut pour nom. Il s'appelait Guène.

The synthetic expression of case-relation caused in Genitives and Datives the frequent non-appearance of the Case Prepositions *de* and *a*. Examples :

1. Al *tens Noë* et al *tens Abraham.*
   Mod. : Au temps *de* Noé et au temps *d'*Abraham.

2. Al *comand deu.*
   Mod. : Selon le commandement *de* Dieu.

3. La *chambre son pedre.*
   Mod. : La chambre *de* son père. (Vie de St. Alexis.)

4. Li sanct Lethgier, li Evvrui. (St. Léger.)
   Mod. : Ceux *de* Saint Léger, ceux *d'* Evruin.

5. En la *garde dieu* me commant. (Mauvais Riche.)
   Mod. : A la garde *de* Dieu je me recommande.

6. Chascun en *droit soy* aura assez à faire. (Perceforest.)
   Mod. : Chacun en ce qui le concerne aura assez à faire.

7. Gefreiz d'Anjou, *le rei gunfanunier.* (Ch. de Roland.)
   Mod. : Geoffroi d'Anjou, gonfalonier *du* roi.

8. *Amors Nicolete.*
   Mod. : Amour *pour, envers* N.

9. Ne placet Deu, ne ses seinz, ne ses angles.   (*ibidem.*)
   Mod.: Ne plaise *à* Dieu, ni *à* ses saints, ni *à* ses anges.

10. Ne porrés men pere faire honte.   (Auc. et Nicol.)
    Mod.: Vous ne pourrez faire honte *à* mon père.

11. La *grevance lu roi.*
    Mod.: La persécution *venant du* roi.

Many relations expressed in the Modern language by Prepositions are put appositionally in the Old.   Ex.:

1. Rome la citet.
   Mod.: La cité *de* Rome.

2. Si out nom Alexis.
   Mod.: Ainsi il reçut le nom *d'*Alexis.

3. Mult i a poi femmes.
   Mod.: Il y a bien peu *de* femmes.

4. Averad terme un meis.
   Mod.: Il aura un terme *d'*un mois.

Gender.

The history of French Gender, as related to Latin Gender, is beyond the scope of this book.   In Old French, as might be expected, there is some indecision as to the Gender attaching to some words.   The names of trees, feminine in Latin, are masculine in Old French, beginning with *arbre*, from *arborem*.   Nouns in *-eur* and *-our*, from Latin *-orem*, are feminine, even when they are masculine in the Modern language.   Ex.:

> Mais li amors de l'onme est en el cuer *plantee* dont
>   *ele* ne puet iscir.   (Auc. et Nicol.)
> Mod.: Mais l'amour de l'homme est *planté* dans son
>   cœur, d'où *il* ne peut sortir.

Isolated words, which cannot be classified, are found indifferently in either Gender, others have passed from one Gender to the other within the Old French period, and others again have a Gender in Old French which the Modern tongue has not accepted. Ex.:

> *Li* tors estoit *faëlé.*
> Une crevëure de *la tor.*   (Auc. et Nicol.)
> Mod.: *La* tour était en gradins.
> Une fissure de *la* tour.

These processes involve no syntactical difficulty, and therefore need not be further dwelt upon.

III. SYNTAX OF THE ADJECTIVE

In matter of Case the Adjective follows the Noun; in matter of Gender it is free from the Modern artificialities as to its adverbial value in certain phrases; in matter of Place it is subject to laws that are too vague or too subtle to admit of rapid explanation. The adjective is almost always in its 'natural' position, that is where the speaker or writer, unhampered by an acquired grammatical prejudice, though swayed by traditional usage, unpremeditatingly places it. In matter of agreement, it need not, when qualifying two or more Substantives, agree with any other than the last. Ex.:

> Vous ne devez avoir le pied ne la jambe *endormye,*
>   mais *legere* et *aperte.*   (Perceforest.)

Adjectives which etymologically had no separate feminine termination never took *e,* or, if they did so occasionally, it was an irregularity till towards the end of the Old French period. Ex.:

> 1. Carl repairet od sa *grant* host.   (Ch. de Roland.)
>   Mod.: Charles retournait avec sa *grande* armée.
> 2. Pillars venoient qui portoient *grandes* coutilles.
>   (Froissart.)
>   Mod.: Il venait des pillards qui portaient de *grands* couteaux.

The first example is an instance of early agreement, the second of late agreement.

The distinctions between *fol* and *fou, vieux* and *vieil,* etc., did not rest on a grammatical rule, as they do at present. Ex.:

1. *Bel* nom li metent sulonc cristïentet.

   (Vie de St. Alexis.)

   Mod.: Ils lui donnent un *beau* nom selon les traditions chrétiennes.
2. Un heaulme bon et *bel.*

   Mod.: Un heaume *bel* et **bon,**

   or, un heaume bon et *beau.*

IV. SYNTAX OF THE PERSONAL PRONOUN

The Latin Pronoun Subject did not appear in a connected syntactical period. Old French uses or omits the Pronoun Subject with much liberty. On the whole, as a substitute for one and the same Subject, it is not expressed more than once in a period, while Modern French, with but few exceptions, requires it whenever a Verb is used. Ex.:

1. *Il* portoit ung habillement . . . et sembloit bien prince . . . et tiroit tousjour droict . . . et y avoit d'obeyssance autant que mon seigneur de Charroloys. (Ph. de Commines.)

The *il* here does Pronoun duty for all the ensuing Verbs, *sembloit, tiroit, y avoit.*

2. Le plus sage c'estoit le roy Loys XI . . . et ne s'ennuyoit point a estre refusé . . . mais y continuoit. (Ph. de Commines.)

   Mod.: . . . et *il* ne se rebutait point . . . mais *il* continuait.

In the above period there is no Pronoun Subject at all, the presence of the Subject at the beginning making ambiguity impossible in the absence of any other Subject in the ensuing clauses.

3. Lors *print* son cheval et *saillit* en la selle, et si tost qu'il fut monté le chevalier luy alla mettre au poing ung fort espieu et *dist.* (Perceforest.)

The first two clauses of the above have not even a Pronoun Subject, for the Subject expressed in the preceding period in the text is still understood. A new Subject appears in 'le chevalier,' and, as confusion is impossible, it is not again expressed in the following clause.

4. Croy que le roy n'en delibera. (Ph. de Commines.)
   Mod.: *Je* crois que le roi . . .
5. Toute celle semainne fumes en festes et en quarolles.
   (Joinville.)

   Mod.: . . . *nous* fûmes.

In sentences like the last two, the Pronoun Subject does not appear, because the inflection of the Verb and the context show sufficiently what Pronoun is understood.

The forms *je, tu, il, ils* may stand in places where Modern French demands: *moi, toi, lui, eux.* Ex.:

1. *Je* et mi compaingnon mangames a la Fonteinne
   l'Arcevesque. (Joinville.)
   Mod.: *Moi* et mes compagnons nous mangeâmes . . .
2. C'est *il*, sans autre, vrayement. (Maistre Pathelin.)
   Mod.: C'est *lui*, sans erreur possible.
3. Ce sui *ge*—iest *tu* ce?
   Mod.: C'est *moi*—est-ce *toi*?

The Impersonal *il* may be omitted. Ex.:

Del primier et del secont nos *covient* or parler.
(St. Bernard.)

Mod.: *Il* nous faut maintenant parler du premier et du second.

It is usually omitted in *i a, i avoit*, for Mod. *il y a, il y avait*.

The 'anticipatory' *il*, from Latin *illic*, is most frequent. This *il* points to the Subject placed by inversion after the Verb. The Modern language uses it when it says: *il arrive des soldats*, for *des soldats arrivent*. The co-relative to the anticipatory *il* is, before an Infinitive, the preposition of 'respect' *de*, also used in Modern French in that capacity: IL *arrive* DE *perdre sa fortune*, 'one may happen to lose one's money.' Anticipation of the Object, or of a whole clause viewed as Object, is often expressed by *le*.

An emphatic *il* may stand where *ce, ceci,* or *cela* would be found nowadays. Ex. :

> *Il* sera fait, dit-il.

The Object Pronoun also enjoys freedom from Modern restrictions.

The heavier forms *moi, toi, soi, lui* could take before the Verb places now exclusively reserved for the lighter *me, te, se, le, la*. Ex. :

1. Pour *soy* tirer d'un mauvais pas. (Ph. de Commines.)
2. Pur *mei* losengier le faiseit. (Roman de Brut.)
   Mod. : Elle le faisait pour *me* flatter.
3. *Lei* volt molt honorer. (Vie de St. Alexis.)
   Mod. : Il *la* veut fort honorer, or, to preserve the emphasis of the inversion : *Elle,* il *la* veut fort honorer.

The Feminine *lei,* undistinguishable from the Masculine in the form *li,* stood regularly in connections requiring *elle* in the Modern language. Ex. :

> Ele senti li vielle dormoit qui avoec *li* estoit.
>
> (Auc. et Nicol.)
>
> Mod. : Elle s'assura que la vieille qui était avec *elle* dormait.

L' stands in the Old language for *li,* and therefore for *lui* and *lei,* while it never stands for anything but *le, la* in the Modern. Ex. :

> Un fil lor donet, si *l'*en sourent bon gret.
>
> (Vie de St. Alexis.)
>
> Mod. : Il leur donne un fils, aussi ils *lui* en surent bon gré.

The Accusative Pronoun *le, la* is left to be understood before its dative forms. Ex. :

> . . . Sun sunge lur conta,
> Tut en ordre *lur* dist, si cum il le sunga
> Mod. : Il leur conta son songe,
> Il *le leur* dit tout en ordre . . .

Lor stands even after Prepositions, when *eux* must be used in the Modern tongue. Ex.:

> La generacions esliroient entre *lour* cinquante des plus saiges hommes. (Joinville.)
>
> Mod.: Ceux de la tribu éliraient entre *eux* cinquante des hommes les plus sages.

The regular use of *lor* as Indirect Object to a Verb appears in the following example:—

> Un fil *lor* donet, si l'en sourent bon gret.
>
> Mod.: Il *leur* donne un fils . . .

The non-reflective *lui* and *eux* occasionally take the place of *se*. Ex.:

> 1. Car jamais ne se boutoient avant pour *eulx* faire détruire. (Froissart.)
>
>   Mod.: Car ils ne s'avançaient jamais pour *se* fair tuer.
>
> 2. De *lui* vengier targier ne se volt plus.
>   (Ch. de Roland.)
>
>   Mod.: Il ne veut plus tarder à *se* venger.

The Modern tongue sometimes requires a construction with *lui* or *elle*, where *soi* is regular in the Old. Ex.:

> Ele bien avoit dit a *soi*-meismes. (Roman de Tristan.)
> Mod.: Elle *s'*était bien dit à *elle*-même.

The Personal Pronoun governed by a Preposition is found for a Possessive. Ex.:

> N'ai je plus vaillant que vos veés sor li cors *de mi*.
> Mod.: Je n'ai rien qui vaille, sauf ce que vous voyez sur *mon* corps, sur moi.

The order of Pronouns and their place in the clause, as alluded to in another chapter, may differ from Modern French. Ex.:

> Renart, vous *te tu* confesser?
> Mod.: Renard, veux-*tu te* confesser?
> *Le me* rendez, for rendez-*le-moi*.

While rejecting on the whole the pleonastic Personal

Pronoun of Old French, the Modern language has introduced it in its interrogative word order.   Ex.:

> L'eve del Ebre, *ele* lur est devant.   (Ch. de Roland.)
> Mod.: *L'eau* de l'Ebre *est* devant eux.

But, interrogatively : L'eau de l'Ebre est-*elle* devant eux?
The accented form of the Personal Pronoun was connected with the ordinal numeral in a phrase now archaic. *Lui sisisme* means 'he and five others.'   Voltaire says similarly : *Le roi attaqua* LUI QUATRIÈME, le *roi s'enfuit* LUI ONZIÈME, meaning—the king was the fourth man to attack, the king was the eleventh man who fled.

V. POSSESSIVE ADJECTIVE PRONOUNS

In point of Case these Pronouns are quite regular. Examples of the Objective stand among our examples illustrating the Cases of Nouns.   Here is an example of the Subjective Case :—

> Ele vint a le tor u *ses* amis estoit.   (Auc. et Nicol.)
> Mod.: Elle vint à la tour où était *son* ami.

The Possessive Adjective does not necessarily exclude the Definite Article or another Pronoun as it does in Modern French.   Ex.:

1. En *son* *l'*orteil *del* pié.   (Auc. et Nicol.)
   Mod.: Dans *l'*orteil de *son* pied.
2. En *ce son* premier voyage ;
   Les autres ses freres.   (Les Cent Nouv. nouv.)

The forms *no, vo* and *nostre, vostre* appear promiscuously as Adjectives.   Ex.:

1. Car *vostre* peres me het
   Et trestos *vos* parentés.   (Auc. et Nicol.)
   Mod.: Car *votre* père me hait
   Et toute *votre* parenté.
2. Mais puis que *vostre* volentés est et *vos* bons. (*ibidem.*)
   Mod.: Mais puisque c'est *votre* volonté et *votre* désir.

Lor does not take *s,* being properly speaking a genitive. Ex. :

> Il li rendroient la cité et totes les *lor* choses.
> (Villehardoin.)

The pronominal forms *mien, tien, sien, nostre, vostre, lor* appear, against Modern usage, as Adjectives quite regularly, either with or without an Article. Ex. :

1. Deux berbis *sienes.*   (Chronique.)
2. Ja sui jou *li vostre* amie.   (Auc. et Nicol.)
   Mod. : Assurément je suis *votre* amie.
3. En *meie* foi, sire, fol sumes.   (Rom. de Brut.)
   Mod. : Par *ma* foi, Sire, nous sommes fous.
4. Mahoms ait s'ame par *la soie* pitié.
   (Huon de Bordeaux.)
   Mod. : Que Mahomet ait son âme par un effet de *sa* pitié.

When they were used as Pronouns, the Definite Article, compulsory in Modern French, was easily dispensed with. Ex. :

> *Tiens* suis a durer a tousjours.   (Alain Chartier.)
> Mod. : Je suis *le* tien, or better, *à toi* pour toujours.

The pronominal forms are found as real Nouns, in the same way as in Modern French. Ex. :

> Le mius *del suen* duner volreit a cele que plus
> l'amereit.   (Rom. de Brut.)
> Mod. : Il voudrait donner le meilleur du *sien* (de *son bien*) à celle qui l'aimerait le plus.

The short form too may be used pronominally. Ex. :

> Kar de vus sul ai bien vengiet *les noz.*
> (Chans. de Roland.)
> Mod. : Car sur vous seul j'ai bien vengé *les nôtres.*

VI. DEMONSTRATIVE ADJECTIVE-PRONOUN

The Case-distinctions appear from the following examples :—

L

Subj. case : *Cil* qui mix torble les gués est li plus sire
clamés. (Auc. et Nicol.)

Mod.: *Celui* qui trouble le mieux les guets est proclamé
le plus grand.

Obj. case : Se je ne vos fac ja *cele* teste voler. (*ibidem.*)

Mod. : Si je ne vous fais pas voler *cette* tête.

Obj. case : Vos m'avés tolu la riens en *cest* mont que
je plus amoie. (*ibidem.*)

Mod. : Vous m'avez enlevé la chose que j'aimais le plus
en *ce* monde.

Subj. case : Et *cist* consaus li fu donez. (Joinville.)

Mod. : Et *ce* conseil lui fut donné.

Cestui and *celui*, the first of which is now extinct, at first
Indirect Objects, then Direct Objects, later Subjects and
Pronouns in their own right, are seen in the following
sentences :—

1. Si nous *cestui* assavorons. (St. Bernard.)
   Mod.: Si nous goûtons *à ceci*.
2. Il ne prendrait mie *cestui* plet ne autre. (Villehardoin.)
   Mod.: Il ne prendrait point *cet* engagement ni un autre.
3. Ensi ke *celui* covient loquel ke soit esleire.
   (St. Bernard.)
   Mod. : Tandis qu'à *celui-ci* il incombe de choisir.

Cist and *cil* could be opposed to each other like the
Modern *celui-ci* and *celui-là*.

Cestui-ci, Fem. : *ceste-ci*, was formerly parallel to *celui-ci*,
celle-ci, but is now extinct, except in Neuter, *ceci*. Ex. :

1. Quant ceste-cy si me faudra. (Mauvais Riche.)
   Mod.: Quand *celle-ci* aussi me fera défaut.
2. Quel bee est *ce cy*? (Maistre Pathelin.)

Ce in the Neuter stood where the Modern tongue requires *cela* or *ceci*. Ex. :

1. Quant la royne entendit *ce*, elle print le jouvencel par
   la main. (Perceforest.)
   Mod. : Quand la reine entendit *cela*, elle prit le jeune
   homme par la main.

2. Disoient que tot *c'ere* mals. (Villehardoin.)

Mod.: Ils disaient que tout *cela* était mal.

The Old French practice is preserved in *ce semble, sur ce, ce disant.*

We have already seen the omission of the Demonstrative Pronouns when they are looked for as links in the period. Within clauses the same omission took place. Ex.:

Si n'est assez. (Villon.)

Mod.: Si *ce* n'est assez.

Ce as Direct Object in the Neuter is often understood. Ex.:

1. Voy *que* Solmon escript en son roulet. (Villon.)

Mod.: Vois *ce* que Salomon écrit en son rôle.

2. Vecy doncque *que* luy demande. (Maistre Pathelin.)

Mod.: Voici donc *ce* que je lui demande.

Still it is even now quite right to say: *nous n'avons* QUE *faire de* . . .

The Adjective-Pronouns *icist* and *icil, cist* and *cil,* are translatable by the Modern *ce, cette,* etc., *celui, celle, celui-ci,* etc., according to the connection in which they stand.

One says now: *ce* SONT *mes amis.* Yet at one time one could say: *ce* EST *Renart, Belins et l'asne.*

(Roman de Renart.)

VII. RELATIVE PRONOUN

The form *cui,* an Indirect Object, would have been a valuable legacy from Latin if it had not soon lost its identity. Parallel at first in use and in formation with *cestui* and *celui,* it became confused with the Subject form *qui,* and *qui* itself suffered from the likeness. In consequence *cui* and *qui* are found promiscuously in fundamentally different connections, which in Syntax must be kept apart, though they are undistinguished to all outward appearance.

I. Examples of *Regular* use of Relative Pronoun :—

Subject.: Et li gait *qui* estoit sur le tor les vit venir.

(Auc. et Nicol.)

Mod.: Et le guet *qui* était sur la tour les vit venir.

Direct Object. : Nicolete *que* je tant aim.

(Auc. et Nicol.)

Mod. : Nicolette *que* j'aime tant.

Indirect Object. : *Cui* il meschiet, tuit li mesoffrent.

(Chronique.)

Mod. : *A qui* il arrive malheur, tous le maltraitent.

En *cui* compaingnie je, Jehans sires de Joinville.

(Joinville.)

Mod. : En compagnie *de qui*, moi, Jean, sire de Joinville.

Que in the accented form *quoy* after a Preposition. **Ex.** :
Dieu me doint la grace *perquoy* je puisse devenir tel.

(Perceforest.)

Mod. : Que Dieu me donne la grâce par *laquelle* je pourrai devenir tel.

The Neuter *que.* Ex. :

Ceu *que* comandeit nos est. (St. Bernard.)

Mod. : Ce *qui* nous est commandé.

II. **Examples of *Confused* use of Relative Pronoun.** *Que* as Subject for *qui* :—

Vous me dictes chose *qui* ne soit possible, et *que* a aultres que a vous ne soit advenue.

(Les Cent Nouv. nouv.)

Mod. : Vous ne me dites pas une chose *qui* ne soit possible et *qui* ne soit arrivée à d'autres que vous.

Cui as Direct Object for *que* :—

Les autres roys . . . *cuy* Dex absoyle. (Joinville.)

Mod. : Les autres rois . . . *que* Dieu absolve.

Qui as Direct Object for *que* is a false appearance, *qui* standing then for *cui*.

Qui as Indirect Object for *cui*. This is again a false appearance for the same reason.

III. The Neuter *que* had all the force of the Latin *quod*, and needed no antecedent to lean upon. Ex. :

Je fereie *que* fols. (Ch. de Roland.)

Mod. : Je ferais *ce que* ferait un fou.

The Neuter Interrogative Pronoun, *que, quei, quoy*, in

Indirect speech, is necessarily confused with the corresponding Relative. Ex.:

> Va sçavoir *que* nous pourrons manger.
> (Mauvais Riche.)

> Mod.: Va savoir *ce que* . . .

(Compare with English *what*, Latin *quid* or *id quod*.)

The compulsory Modern French use of the Pronoun *lequel* instead of *qui* in certain connections, is unknown to Old French.

Dont was pronominal, and became an alternative for *de cui*, *de quoy*, very early. Ex.:

> Nos tant de gent i vëons perir, *dont* nos dolor avons.
> (St. Bernard.)

> Mod.: Nous y voyons périr tant de gens, ce *dont* nous sommes affligés.

There is a peculiar elliptic use of *qui* for *si on*, *si il*, of which the following are examples:

> C'est un vain estude *qui* veult . . .
> (quoted by Diez.)

> Mod.: C'est un labeur inutile *si on* veut . . .
> Il faut soingner, *qui* veult vivre.   (Pathelin.)
> Mod.: Il faut travailler, *si l'on* veut vivre.
> Il aurait dure departie de ce, *qui* ne le secourroit.
> (Pathelin.)

> Mod.: Il (le berger Agnelet) aurait peine à se tirer de là, *si on* ne le secourait.
> Les escuz ne verront soleil de l'an qui ne les m'emblera.
> Mod.: Les écus . . . *si on* ne me les prend.

The Pronoun *liquels* that has grown up beside *qui* has none of its peculiarities, and requires no notice of its own. Ex.:

> Li clers rensuï l'autre, *liquex* cuida descendre.
> (Joinville.)

> Mod.: Le prêtre poursuivit l'autre, *lequel* crut descendre.

VIII. INTERROGATIVE PRONOUN

Cui or *qui* stands for *à qui.* Ex. :

Qui fu li vestemens qui me fu aportés ?
Mod. : *A qui* était le vêtement qui me fut apporté.
(Bible de Sapience.)

Qui, the old emphatic Neuter form (*quei, quoi*, from *qued, quid*), still appears in the seventeenth century. Ex. :

Qui vous peut retenir à la campagne ?
(Princesse de Clèves.)

Nineteenth century French :

Qu'y a-t-il *qui* vous retienne . . . ?

There is nothing to distinguish in either Indirect or Direct speech the Interrogative *li quels* from the Relative of the same form. Ex. :

1. Mais primes voleit assaier *la quel* d'eles l'aveit plus chier.   (Rom. de Brut.)
   Mod. : Mais d'abord il voulut éprouver *laquelle* d'elles l'aimait le plus.

2. *Li quels* de vos m'arguërat de pechiet ?   (St. Bernard.)
   Mod. : *Lequel* de vous me convaincra d'un péché ?

IX. INDEFINITE PRONOUNS

Under this name are gathered together words which answer in turn to the description of Nouns, Adjectives and Adverbs, or at least to two of these.

A whole class of them have become in the Modern language almost indissolubly bound up with the negative particle *ne*, and when separated from it, they keep the negative force that so constant a partnership has given them. It is not so in the Old language. When used without the negative *ne*, they have an affirmative meaning of the most emphatic kind.

These Pronouns are *alcun, nuls, riens, persone* (the two

latter are Feminine Nouns in origin and use, rather than Indefinite Pronouns).   Examples :

1. E si *alcons* est apelez de muster fruisser u de
   chambre.   (Lois de Guill. le Conq.)
   Mod. : Et si *quelqu'un* est accusé d'avoir forcé un
   cloître ou une chambre.
2. Or dient *les aucuns*.   (Froissard.)
   Mod. : Alors *quelques-uns* disent.
3. Et se *nus* ne *nule* demande.   (Roman de la Rose.)
   Mod. : Et si *quelqu'un* ou *quelqu'une* demande.
4. Tu *nule rien* ne lur laisses.   (Roman de Brut.)
   Mod. : Tu ne leur laisse aucune *chose*.
5. De *persone* dex cure ne prent s'est *grande* u non.
                                        (Bible de Sapience.)
   Mod. : Dieu ne prend pas garde si *quelqu'un* est grand
   ou non.

The use of *nul*, separated from *ne*, is restricted, by the fact that its etymology involves a negation, to interrogations and to constructions with the Conjunction *si*.   It has then the sense of *quelconque, quiconque*.   In the earliest French documents its Syntax is contradictory for that very reason.

Here is an example of its dative :

Nului ne le porroie dire.
Mod. : Je ne le pourrais dire *à pērsonne*.

The Indefinite Article *un* is a component in several Indefinite Pronouns.   This points to an extensive pronominal use.   The Modern language would use *quelqu'un* or more definitely *celui*, in the following clause :—

Lequel avoit pour premier chambellan *ung* qui depuis
s'est appele monseigneur de Chimay.
                                        (Ph. de Commines.)

Un may stand before an Indefinite Pronoun of which it is a component.   Ex. :

Ensi *c'uns chascuns* de nos preist.   (St. Bernard.)
Mod. : Afin que *chacun* de nous prie.

The Old language has no hesitation in using *un* in the Plural, in the sense of a 'couple,' and of 'several' (*deux, quelques, des*).

> Avoit *unes* grandes joës . . . et *unes* grans narines lees et *unes* grosses levres . . . et *uns* grans dens gaunes et lais. (Auc. et Nicol.)
>
> Mod.: Il avait *de* grandes joues, et *de* grandes narines larges et *de* grosses lèvres et *de* grandes dents jaunes et laides.

Several Indefinite Pronouns and Adjectives are also Adverbs. *Moult, quant, tant,* and *tout* belong to that class. The modern adverbial use of *même* has little warranty in the Middle Ages, and that of *tout* is only partly justified. *Neant*, only a Noun in Modern French, is also an Adverb in the Old language.

Examples of Adverbial use.

1. Nicolete eut faite le loge *mout* bele et *mout* gente.
   (Auc et Nicol.)
   Mod.: Nicolette avait fait la tente *très* belle et *fort* jolie.
2. Corps féminin qui *tant* es tendre. (Villon.)
   Mod.: Corps féminin qui es *si* tendre.
3. Toutes ont dras de soie *tout* a lor volentés.
   (Roman d'Alixandre.)
   Mod.: Elles ont toutes des vêtements de soie *tout à fait* à discrétion.
4. Ensi ke soit li chariteiz de foit *nïant* finte.
   (St. Bernard.)
   Mod.: Afin que la charité soit de foi *non* feinte.

Examples of Pronominal use.

1. Mais ne pur *quant* bele ert et gente. (Rom. de Brut.)
   Mod.: Mais en dépit de *tant* (néanmoins) elle était belle et aimable.
2. *Tant* ai ëu, or ai si poi. (*ibidem.*)
   Mod.: J'ai eu *tellement*, maintenant j'ai si peu.

3. As feluns gendres la tolirent.
   Et Leir de *tute* saisirent. (Rom. de Brut.)
   Mod. : Aux perfides gendres ils la prirent,
        Et mirent Lear en possession de *toute* (la
        contrée).
4. Tost l'as d'*alques* a *neient* mis. (*ibidem.*)
   Mod. : Tu l'as vite réduit de *beaucoup* à *rien.*

Indefinite Pronouns and Adverbs used substantively often omit *de* between Noun and Complement. Ex. :

1. Tant ont *or* et *argent.* (Bible de Sapience.)
   Mod. : Ils ont tant *d'*or et *d'*argent.
2. Ont assés *deniers.* (*ibidem.*)
   Mod. : Ils ont assez *de* deniers.
3. Que vous diroie jou *plus* ?
   Mod. : Que vous dirais-je *de* plus ?

The principal Indefinite Pronouns, which would be better styled Determinative Adjectives and Indefinite Nouns, are : *alcun, altre, chascun, meint, mesme, nul, plusieurs, tant, quant, tel, tout, nesun,* and *alquant.*

Examples as Adjectives.

1. Ne t'en sai dire *altre* mesure. (Rom. de Brut.)
   Mod. : Je ne t'en sais dire *autre* chose.
2. Si m i convient que *chascune* semaynne aille a pleit.
                          (Chronique.)
   Mod. : Il me faut *chaque* semaine aller plaider.
3. Fol sumes que *tel* gent avuns ci atrait.
                          (Rom. de Brut.)
   Mod. : Nous sommes fous d'avoir amené ici de *telles* gens.
4. *Nesune* male choze ne puet laianz entrer.
                        (Rom. d'Alixandre.)
   Mod. : *Aucune* mauvaise chose ne peut entrer dedans.
5. Jo t'aim sur *tute* crïature. (Rom. de Brut.)
   Mod. : Je t'aime plus que *toute* créature.
6. Dicunt *alquant* estrobatour. (Albéric de Besançon.)
   Mod. : *Quelques* troubadours disent.

7. *Tante* confusion.
   Mod.: Une confusion *si grande.*
8. *Quantes* fois.
   Mod.: *Combien de* fois.

Examples as Nouns.

1. Quant *aucuens* se welt ewïer per aventure a un
   altre. (St. Bernard.)
   Mod.: Quand *quelqu'un* veut se rendre égal à un *autre.*
2. Estre sires sor *altrui.* (*ibidem.*)
   Mod.: Etre le maître d'*un autre.*
3. Ensi *c'uns chascuns* de nos preist. (*ibidem.*)
4. Les *mains* sunt vestues de cendés.
   (Rom. d'Alixandre.)
   Mod.: *Beaucoup* d'entre elles sont vêtues de soie.
5. Ala as murs de la vile et lor dist *ce meisme.*
   (Villehardoin.)
   Mod.: Il alla aux murs de la ville et leur dit cela
   même.
6. Nen est *nuls* ki bien ne saichet. (St. Bernard.)
   Mod.: Il n'y en a *pas un* qui ne sache bien.
7. *Les plusiors* sunt vestues d'osterins.
   (Rom. d'Alixandre.)
   Mod.: *La plupart* sont vêtues de pourpre.
8. *Teis* cuide avoir lou cuer mult sain.
   (Ch. de Croisade.)
   Mod.: *Un tel* croit avoir le cœur en bon état.
9. *Toutes* ont dras de soie. (Rom. d'Alixandre.)
10. *Li auquent* dïent qu'ele en estoit fuïe.
    (Auc. et Nicol.)
    Mod.: *Les uns* dirent qu'elle s'était enfuie.

Qui, when it is repeated at the beginning of two, or
several successive clauses, in the sense of Modern *les
uns . . ., les autres . . .*, is an Indefinite Pronoun.

Tout, used adverbially, sometimes takes the sign of the
Plural. That it fitfully takes that of the Feminine arises
from a confusion of *e d'appui* (between sounded *t* and en-

suing consonant) with *e féminin.* (Group of analogy: *tante, quante, souvente, toute.*)

When used to express a whole, it may forego the article and be treated like the distributive *tout,* meaning 'each,' 'every.' Ex.:

> Que *tute terre* sache que li sires est deu de Israel.
> (Livre des Rois.)
> Mod.: Que toute *la* terre sache que le Seigneur est le Dieu d'Israël.

The following are purely adjectives: *quelque, quelconque.* Ex.:

> Ne prengue sur eulx subside, tailles, ne a *quelconque* charge ne les impose. (Christine de Pisan.)
> Mod.: Qu'il ne prenne des subsides sur eux ou des tailles, et qu'il ne leur impose pas une charge *quelconque.*

On is purely a Nominative Noun. Ex.:

> 1. Que durreit *l'um* a celui ki cest Philistien ocireit?
> (Livre des Rois.)
> Mod.: Que donnerait-*on* à celui qui tuerait ce Philistin?
> 2. *L'en* n'y ouoit goutte pour la noise. (Froissart.)
> Mod.: L'*on* n'y entendait rien à cause du bruit.

Here are examples of the use of *el*—

> Encor vous mande rois Karlemaine *el.*
> (Rom. de Rou.)
> Mod.: Le roi Charlemagne vous commande encore *autre chose.*
> Toth per enveia, non *per el.* (St. Léger.)
> Mod.: Tout par envie, et non *autrement.*

A few more partake of the nature of Conjunctions by the addition of a separable *que* that often entails the Subjunctive mood, and are composite expressions which can be reduced to their various elements. These Pronouns are : *quanque, que que ; quel que, quel qui ; qui que ; lequel que, quoi que ; qui qui ; qui qu'onques.* Ex. :

1. De *quanque* me donas soies tu graciës.
   (Rom. d'Alixandre.)
   Mod. : De *tout ce que* tu me donnas, sois remercié.
2. *Kelle que* li sostance soit c'um desiret. (St. Bernard.)
   Mod. : *Quel que* soit le soutien que l'on désire.
3. *Qui que* le tiengne por fol.   (Rom. de Renart.)
   Mod. : *Qui que ce soit qui* le tient pour sot.
4. Celui covient *loquel* ke soit esleire.   (St. Bernard.)
   Mod. : A celui-là il sied de choisir *lequel ce doit être.*
5. *Coi qu'*il aient esté, or ne sont pas dolent.
   (Bible de Sapience.)
   Mod. : *Quoi qu'ils* aient été, ils ne sont pas affligés maintenant.
6. *Que que* Rollenz Guenelon fors fesist.
   (Ch. de Roland.)
   Mod. : *Quoi que* Roland ait fait pour offenser Ganelon.
7. *Ki ki unches* volsissent estre pruveires.
   (Livre des Rois.)
   Mod. : *Ceux, quels qu'ils* fussent, qui voulurent être prêtres.

The Modern *quelque . . . que,* in which *que* is twice put, arose from pleonastic confusion. There is a similar pleonastic use of *que* and *ce* in : *Qu'est-ce que c'est qu'il a dit?* and in all interrogations of that complex kind.

Quant que with the Indicative is Modern *tant que : quant que il pot,* for *tant qu'il put.*

X. SYNTAX OF THE INVARIABLE PARTS OF SPEECH.

For several reasons, especially owing to the difficulty of generalisation, and owing to the idiomatic nature of the constructions in which words forming the material of this chapter are found, it is advisable to throw upon commentaries the burden of disposing of the Syntax of Adverbs, Prepositions, and Conjunctions. For one thing, if once we set aside the large mass of Adverbs which are qualificative, and reserve our attention for those which express general ideas, these run so easily into Conjunctions and Prepositions, to discharge what are called 'relational' functions, that an adherence in Syntax to those time-honoured divisions would be something worse than merely conventional. So we do not attempt it, and we give a place in these pages on Elementary Grammar to such remarks only as are instructive to an intending reader of Old French literature, without trenching on the province of the etymological dictionary.

The change of Adverbs into Prepositions and Conjunctions is often without an outward sign in Old French. The Modern language makes in such cases an extensive use of the Case Prepositions *de* and *à*, and of the elementary Conjunction *que*, a feature that is already visible in the Old language. The Demonstrative *ce*, either reduced to a connective component particle, or as a Neuter Pronoun, plays an important part here. *Jusqu'à ce que* shows this function of *ce* to advantage, and illustrates also the fashion in which adverbial, prepositional, and conjunctional elements may be joined to form French relational phrases.

I. *Ainçois* and *ains*, whose proper sense is equivalent to *avant* and *auparavant*, are found with the meaning of *plus tôt* 'sooner,' 'earlier,' and of *plutôt* 'rather,' and even with a value closely akin to that of *plus* in a comparison. Ex.:

1. Se mal fu *ainz*, or est mult pis.   (Rom. de Brut.)
   Mod.: S' il était mal *avant*, maintenant il est bien pis.
2. Je encherche per quel raison li filz prisist *anceos* char
   que li peires.   (St. Bernard.)
   Mod.: Je recherche pour quelle raison le Fils prit
   chair (s'incarna) *plutôt* que le Père.
3. Et en ceste chose est *anzois* li prelaiz obediens a
   lui k'il ne soit a son prelait.   (*ibidem.*)
   Mod.: Et en cette chose le prélat est *plus* obéissant
   envers lui, qu'il ne l'est envers son prélat.

With *que* the Conjunctions *ainçois que*, *ainz que*, are formed, meaning *avant que*. Ex.:

Mais *ançois* que il fussent d'une lieue aprochié.
                    (Rom. d'Alixandre.)

Mod: Mais *avant qu*'ils se fussent approchés d'une lieue.

Ainçois and *ainz* are Conjunctions without *que*, and have then the same meaning as the Modern *mais*. Ex. :

> Leïr n'aveit mie ublïe cument sa fille l'out amé, *ains* l'out bien suvent ramembré. (Rom. de Brut.)
>
> Mod. : Lear n'avait pas oublié combien sa fille l'avait aimé, *mais* au contraire il se l'était bien souvent rappelé.

The following is an example of prepositional use :

> Ne fut si forz bataille *enceis* ne pois cel tens.
> (Ch. de Roland.)
>
> Mod. : Il n'y eut si rude bataille ni *avant* ni depuis ce temps.

II. *Droit, dreit*, as Adverb, has the same meaning nowadays as formerly. Ex. :

> *Dreit* a Tarson espeiret ariver.   (Vie de St. Alexis.)
> Mod. : Il espéra arriver *droit* à Tarse.

A dreit and *por droit* signify *à bon droit*, English : 'justly.'

As for *endroit*, it appears as Preposition and as Adverb As preposition it is equivalent to the Modern *quant à*. Ex.

> Ju ne paroles mies de ceu assi cum ju *endroit de mi* m'en eschuïsse bien.   (St. Bernard.)
>
> Mod. : Je ne parle nullement de cela comme si *quant à moi (pour ma part)* je m'en gardais bien.

As Adverb, *endroit* often accompanies another Adverb, and emphasises its meaning. Ex. :

> 1. Molt la veïsse volontiers *ore endroites*.
> (Rom. de la Rose.)
>
> Mod : Je la verrais bien volontiers *tout de suite*.
>
> 2. Molt m' anuie certes et grieve
> *Orendroit* que l'aube ne crieve.   (*ibidem.*)
>
> Mod : Certes cela me contrarie et m'afflige beaucoup Que l'aube ne paraisse *tout de suite*.

The Modern Noun *endroit* is derived from that use.

III. The synonymy of Particles of Place deserves our attention. In principle, *ci* or *ycy* expresses the places occupied by the speaker or referred to by him as nearest ; *lu* expresses the place occupied by anybody else or referred to as the remotest. *Illuec* is akin to *la* in meaning. Ex. :

> Le maus que cil avoient, ont *illuecques* laissiés.
> Mod. : Les maux qu'avaient ceux-là, ils les ont laissés *là*.

Ci is the unaccented substitute for the emphatic *ici*. Yet it is not, like the Modern *ci*, used in composition only. Ex. :

> Car *ci* sunt or de present nostre frere. (St. Bernard.)
> Mod. : Car *ici* sont maintenant présents nos frères.

In close connection with *de* or *que*, *ci* assists in the formation of Prepositions. Ex. :

> 1. La nuit le guete *deci* al esclairier. (Aliscans.)
>   Mod : La nuit il le guette *jusqu'à* l'aube.
> 2. Car ne set prince *dessi en* orïant,
>   *Dessi qu'en* Acre ne *des qu'en* Bocidant.
>   (Huon de Bordeaux.)
>   Mod. : Car il ne connaît de prince d'ici en Orient,
>   *D'ici jusqu'à* Acre, ni *jusqu'en* Occident.

Deci appears also in the sense of *désormais, maintenant*. Ex. :

> Deffoons mun barun *deci*. (Marie de France.)
> Mod. : Déterrons mon maître *maintenant*.

Ça (from *ecce hac*) may have the same meaning as *ci*. Ex. :

> Se vils fu la, plus vils sui *ça*. (Rom de Brut.)
> Mod. : Si j'étais humilié là, je le suis encore plus *ici*.

But it conveys properly an idea of motion from one place to another, as suggested by the Latin for both *çà* and *là*. Ex. :

> Par ceu k'il delivrement poient corre et *zai* et *lai*.
> (St. Bernard.)
> Mod. : Par ce qu'ils peuvent courir facilement *çà* et *là*.

Ça, like *ci*, may assist in forming Prepositions and Adverbs. Both may refer to time as well as to place.

IV. *Ja* is a favourite particle with Old French. Its meaning in the Modern Language has been divided between *déjà* and *jamais*. *Ja*, like *si*, is very often expletive and need not be translated, except when it stands for purposes of emphasis. Ex.:

> *Ja* est ço Rollanz ki tant vos soelt amer.
> > (Ch. de Roland.)
> Mod : C'est Roland, *Roland lui-même*, qui vous aime tellement.

Ja refers to the past, or points to a future time. Ex.:

1. *Ja* piéça je mis ton cueur en voye de tout plaisir.
   > (Ch. d'Orléans.)
   Mod. : Il y a *déjà* longtemps que . . .
2. Mais cele le ciel en jura
   Que *ja* od lui ne remanra . . . (Rom. de Brut.)
   Mod. : Mais celle-ci en prit le ciel à témoin,
   Que *désormais* il ne resterait avec lui . . .

With the negation *ne*, *ja* is equivalent to *ne* . . . *plus*, *ne* . . . *jamais, jamais* . . . *ne*, etc. Ex.:

1. *Ne* quier jou *ja* a vo car adeser.
   > (Huon de Bordeaux.)
   Mod. : Je *ne* demande *plus* à toucher votre chair.
2. Il *ne* le vous faut *ja* celer. (Les cent Nouv. nouv.)
   Mod. : Il *ne* faut *pas* vous le celer *plus longtemps*.

There is sometimes an excess of negation. Ex.:

> *Ne ja* . . . *ne* sera recouvrée. (Villehardoin.)
> Mod. : *Jamais* elle *ne* sera recouvrée.

Ja enters in the Conjunction : *ja soit ce que.* Ex.:

> *Ja soit che que* mais ne les vit. (Disciplina Clericalis.)
> Mod. : *Quoique qu'il ne* les vît jamais.

The compound *jamais*, in the Modern tongue as in the Old, conveys an idea of indefiniteness which, according to the context, takes a negative or an affirmative character. Ex.:

Se je *jamais* vos povie aprochier.

(Thibaut de Champagne.)

Mod.: Si *un jour*, si *jamais*, je pouvais m'approcher de vous.

Onques is the positive equivalent of Modern *jamais*. Ex.:
Onques certes plus dolens hom *ne* fu. (*ibidem*.)

Mod.: Certes il *n'*y eut *jamais* un homme plus malheureux.

V. *Mais* in its etymological sense is the same as Modern *plus*, *davantage*, and is generally connected with the negative particle *ne*, *ne* . . . *mais* standing for *ne* . . . *plus*. Ex.:
Nen parlez *mais*, se jo nel vus comant.

(Ch. de Roland.)

Mod.: Ne parlez pas *davantage*, à moins que je ne le vous commande.

It is found in the sense of *désormais*, and with *que* it forms a Preposition and Conjunction. Ex.:
Quant veit li pedre que *mais* n'avrat enfant, *mais que* cel sol. (Vie de St. Alexis.)

Mod.: Quand le père voit que *désormais* il n'aura pas d'enfant, *excepté* celui-là seul.

The phrases *ne mais que*, and *ne mais*, being equivalent to *ne* . . . *pas plus que*, have also the same sense of 'except.' Ex.:
Ja od lui ne remanra *ne mais que* un sul chevalier.

(Rom. de Brut.)

Mod.: Il *ne* restera *plus* avec lui *qu'*un unique chevalier.

Mais with *onques* has the sense of modern *jamais avant*, *jamais encore*. Ex.:

1. Et distrent bien que *onques mes*
   Nul chevalier ne prist tel fes d'armes.

(Fabliau publié par Barbazan.)

2. Donc out tel doel, *unkes mais* n'out si grant.

(Ch. de Roland.)

Mod.: Alors il eut une telle affliction, que *jamais* n'en eut-il une si grande.

M

Ja, with *mais*, and *ne ja jor* properly indicate a future time; Modern: *jamais plus, jamais à l'avenir.* Ex.:

1. *Ja mais* n'ert hum plus volentiers le serve.
   (Ch. de Roland.)
   Mod.: Il n'y aura *jamais plus* un homme qui le serve plus volontiers.
2. De lui vengier *ja mais* ne li iert sez.   (*ibidem.*)
   Mod.: De se venger *jamais* ne lui sera assez; *or*, better, Il ne pourra *jamais* se venger assez.

The use of *mais* as a Conjunction is similar to that of the Modern language and needs no illustration.

VI. The Old sense of *par* is closer to that of Latin *per* than the Modern one. Ex.:

1. *Par* tut sun regne fist mander.   (Rom. de Brut.)
   Mod.: Il fit proclamer *partout dans* son royaume.
2. Rollanz s'en turnet, *par* le camp vait tut suls.
   (Ch. de Roland.)
   Mod.: Roland s'en va, il *parcourt* le champ de bataille tout seul.

Par is therefore equivalent to *à travers, dans toutes les parties de.* With reference to time it means *durant*, and is emphatic. Ex.:

   Par quinze jours, seignour, chele joie dura.
   (Bible de Sapience.)
   Mod.: Cette joie, seigneur, dura *pendant* quinze jours *entiers.*

Par is found in the sense of *après.* Ex.:

   Je le vous desferai l'un *par* l'autre.   (Joinville.)
   Mod.: Je vous en ferai compensation l'un *après* l'autre.

De par has the sense of Modern *de la part de* (and is better traced back to Latin *pars* than to Latin *per*). Ex.:

   Qu'a sun pere Leïr le port
   De par sa fille.   (Rom. de Brut.)
   Mod.: Qu'il le porte à son père Lear
   De la part de sa fille.

There is a particle *par*, often expletive, which Old French is very fond of using, like *très*, as an Adverb of intensity, usually with another Adverb. Ex.:

1. David que deus *par* amat tant. (Vie de St. Alexis.)
   Mod.: David que Dieu aima *tellement*.
2. Tant *par* estoit blance la mescinete. (Auc. et Nicol.)
   Mod.: La jeune fille était *tellement* blanche.

When joined to a Verb, *par* intensifies its idea, like the Modern *achever*, to finish, *parachever*, to finish *completely*.

Tres intensifies in the same way the meaning of an Old French Verb, or of an Adjective—*Oïr*, to hear, *tresoïr*, to hear quite well; *tous*, all, *trestous*, one and all.

VII. *Com*, as a simple temporal or causative Conjunction, presents no difficulty.

In Comparison it is much used instead of Modern *que*. Ex.:

1. Ja mais n'iert tels *com* fut as anceisors.
   (Vie de St. Alexis.)
   Mod.: Il ne sera jamais tel *qu'*il était au temps de nos ancêtres.
2. Ki abbeit sunt si *cum* nos. (St. Bernard.)
   Mod.: Qui sont abbés ainsi *que* nous.
3. Cez choses sunt ateirieies ensi *cum* eles doyent estre. (*ibidem.*)
   Mod.: Ces choses sont arrangées ainsi *qu'*elles doivent l'être.
4. Tant *cum* je t'oi plus en chierté, tant m'ëus tu plus en vilté. (Rom. de Brut.)
   Mod.: Autant *que* je t'ai aimée davantage, autant m'as-tu plus abaissé; *or*, better, plus je t'ai aimée, plus tu m'as abaissé.

Yet *que* is used whenever the second term of the sentence, instead of being comparative, is simply consecutive. Ex.:

Une pucele vint ci, le plus bele riens du monde, *si que* nos quidames que ce fust une fee. (Auc. et Nicol.)
Mod.: Une jeune fille vint ici, la plus belle chose du monde, *si* belle *que* nous crûmes que c'était une fée.

Com may stand for *comment,* both in indirect and direct interrogation.   Ex. :

> Oliviers frere, *cum* le purrum nus faire ?
> (Ch. de Roland.)
>
> Mod. : Frère Olivier, *comment* le pourrons-nous faire ?

It stands also for *combien* and for exclamative *quel, que.* Ex. :

> *Cum* a mal ore,
> *Cum* grant peine me curut sore. . . . (Mystère d'Adam.)
> Mod. : *Combien* pour mon malheur,
>   *Quelle* grande affliction s'abattit sur moi. . . .
>
> *Com* avez or bien dit !   (Launcelot du Lac.)
> Mod. : *Que* vous avez bien parlé maintenant !

Com may be strengthened by the adjunction of *par.* Ex.:

> *Cum par* sunt las !
> Mod. : *Qu'*ils sont *donc* malheureux !

Com with the Subjunctive mood means *comme si.*   Ex. :

> Or crie *com fust* joues.   (Bible de Sapience.)
> Mod. : A présent il crie *comme s'*il était jeune.

VIII. *Si* is the principal Adverb of manner of the Ancient language.   When it has a precise sense it means *ainsi, aussi.*   Ex.:

> 1. Grant aviltance li sembla
>   Que *si* l'aveient fait descendre.   (Rom. de Brut.)
>   Mod. : Cela lui sembla un grand affront
>   Qu'ils l'eussent fait *ainsi* descendre.
> 2. Iloec truvat Engelier le Guascuign
>   Et *si* truvat Anseïs e Sansun.   (Ch. de Roland.)
>   Mod. : Là, il trouva . . .
>   Et *aussi* . . .

Very often it is emphatic only, or even quite expletive; it is then useless, or impossible, to translate it.   It often appears at the beginning of the second term of a sentence in reference to the first, or else it is used to effect the transition from one sentence to another. It can then be translated by *et*. Ex.:

> Bien son tuit conreé, *si* ont assez deniers.
> (Bible de Sapience.)
> Mod. : Ils sont tous bien équipés, *et* ils ont assez de deniers.

The Conjunction *si* is, by its vagueness, adapted to express, or rather to shadow forth, an indefinite number of syntactical ' relations.' It is left to the reader or hearer to understand, in each particular case, what precise relation is intended.

In the Old language an equivalent for *tellement* was sometimes produced by the addition to *si* of the Adverb *faitement*, which was also found after *com*. Ex.:

> Ala tote jour par mi le forest *si faitement* que onques
> n oi noveles de li.   (Auc. et Nicol.)
> Mod. : Il alla tout le jour au milieu de la forêt *de telle façon* que jamais il n'eut de ses nouvelles.

In the same way, *si* or *ausi*, followed by the Past Participle *fait*, became equivalent to *tel, quel*. Ex.:

De *si faite* mort.	*D'ausi fait* mal.
Mod. : de *telle* mort.	Mod. : de *tel* mal.
	<div align="right">(Auc. et Nicol.)</div>

Italian has *così fatto*, and Modern French still uses *fait* in the sense of English *fit*, which may be thence derived.

In Old French *si* could be used absolutely. Ex.:

> Nomeyement or en cest tens ke li malices est *si* enforciez.
> Mod. : Surtout à présent, en ce temps où l'impiété est *très* grande.

Si and *com* often stand beside one another. Ex.:

1. Certes, forz est amors *si cum* morz.   (St. Bernard.)
   Mod. : Certes, l'amour est *aussi* fort *que* la mort.
2. S'il l'aime *si com* il dist.   (Auc. et Nicol.)
   Mod. : S'il l'aime *autant* qu'il dit.

But if no comparison is intended, a translation by *aussi* . . . *que* would be out of place. Ex.:

Si fait Eva sa feme, *si com* lisant trovon.

(Bible de Sapience.)

Mod.: De même fait Eve sa femme, *comme* nous le trouvons en lisant.

In speaking of *si* it is convenient to show how fond Old French was of heaping Adverb upon Adverb, and of seeking energy of expression in the wealth of synonyms expressive of intensity. Ex.:

1. Et *tant* et *si tres bien* le fit. (Les Cent Nouv. nouv.)
2. *Tres fort* esbahy et *moult* esmerveillé. (*ibidem.*)
3. En *trestout tel* etat.

IX. *Neis* is synonymous with the Modern Adverb *même*, but it is usually negative in sense, on account of its etymology. Ex.:

Ni ne murmuret *nes* dons quant celes choses li defaillent. (St. Bernard.)

Mod.: Et il ne murmure *pas même* alors que ces choses lui font défaut.

X. The Case Preposition *a*. This Preposition partakes of the meaning of the Latin *ad* and of the Latin *in*; so it expresses movement towards, or stillness in, a place. A third meaning, without Latin analogy, is that of *a* with verbs governing 'from' in English. Those meanings are all well known to the Modern tongue, though the use of *a* after Verbs expressing movement is not so free nowadays as formerly, *vers* and *pour* having taken over some of the functions fulfilled by the mediæval *a*.

Leaving aside points of similitude, we attach ourselves to the following peculiarities :—

(*a*) *A* expresses possession, material. Ex.:

Les temples *aux* dieux.
Le cueur *au* dit marchant.
Les mains *as* gendres.
Les freins *a* or.

Mod. : Les temples *des* dieux.
Le cœur *du* dit marchand.
Les mains *des* gendres.
Les freins *d'*or.

The possessive relation may be synthetically expressed. Ex. :

Qui *frere sa fame* est.   (Villehardoin.)
Mod. : Qui est le frère *de sa* femme.

(*b*) *A* and *atout* stand for *avec, de,* or *dans*.   Ex. :
Je vous donne a boire *a* mon escuëlle.
(Auc. et Nicol.)
Ce fist ele *a* ses beles mains.
Al dei.
Mod. : Je vous donne à boire *dans* mon écuelle.
Elle fit ceci *avec* ses belles mains.
Du doigt.

(*c*) *A* stands for *selon*.   Ex. :
Vous gardez dedans vous *a* votre pouvoir tous les
enseignements.   (Perceforest.)
Mod. : Vous gardez en vous *selon* votre pouvoir tous
les enseignements.

(*d*) *A* stands for *de*.   Ex. :
Vous me jurerez *a* garder.
Mod. : Vous me jurerez *de* garder.
On ne vey jamais si peu de sang yssir *a* tant de
mors.   (Froissart.)
Mod. : On ne vit jamais si peu de sang sortir *de*
tant de morts.

The Modern language says, in a kindred spirit : ' Il fit
passer la rivière à son armée.'   He made his army cross
the river.

(*e*) *A* stands for *pour* before an Infinitive.   Ex. :
Si vous sont esguillon *a* votre cheval haster et
poindre.
Mod. : Voici des éperons *pour* pousser et piquer
votre cheval.

(*f*) *A* stands for *comme*. Ex.:

Le plus prisié barun *a* seignur avras.
Mod.: Tu auras *comme* seigneur le baron le plus
estimé. (Roman de Brut.)

(*g*) *A* stands for *en*. Ex.:

A sauveté; *a* joie.
A sëure conscïence.
Mod.: *En* sûreté; joyeusement.
En sûreté de conscience.

(*h*) *A* stands for *par*, especially after Passive Verbs.
Ex.:

Sun regne li unt toleit *a* force.
Mod.: Ils lui ont enlevé son royaume *par* force.

(*i*) *A* stands in formulas expressive of time or place
instead of Mod. *pour*, or of Mod. absolute Accusative. Ex.:

E fu pris un parlement *a* l'endemain. (Villehardoin.)
Mod.: Une entrevue fut fixée *pour* le lendemain.
Au jour que je parti de nostre païz. (Joinville.)
Mod.: Le jour où je quittai notre pays.

XI. The Case Preposition *de*. The Modern language
has hardly lost any of the mediæval uses of *de*, it has only
restricted, specified, and systematised them.

The following are somewhat unusual:—

(*a*) *De* stands for *depuis*. Ex.:
Cuit *de* quatre jours.
Mod.: Cuit *depuis* quatre jours.

(*b*) *De* stands for *par* after a Passive Verb. Ex.:
Ço seit dit *de* nul hume vivant.
Mod.: Que cela ne soit dit *par* nul homme vivant.

Also after *faire* governing an Infinitive with passive
force. Ex.:

De saint batesme l'ont fait regenerer. (Alexis.)
Mod.: Ils lui ont donné une nouvelle vie *par* le
saint baptême.

(*c*) *De* stands for *quant à, pour, au sujet de, sur.*   Ex.:

> *De* fiertei resemble un lion.
> Mod.: *Pour* la fierté il ressemble à un lion.

This use is very frequent, and we call this *de* the preposition of 'respect,' because it shows with respect to what, or whom, a statement is made.   It may happen that the statement about the person or thing introduced by *de* is actually left out, and has to be supplied from the context by the imagination of the reader.   Ex.:

> Filz Alexis, *de* ta dolente medre!   (Alexis.)
> Mod.: Fils Alexis, *que je suis en peine de* ta malheureuse mère!

This use gives the key to the puzzling Modern phrases: *on dirait* D'*un fou, ce que c'est que* DE *nous*, meaning: it looks like the doing of a madman, what sorry (grand) folk we are.
Further Old French instances are:

> *Des* morz il cumencet a pluret.   (Ch. de Roland.)
> Mod.: Il commence à pleurer *sur* les morts.

> Bone chose est *de* pais.
> Mod.: *Quant au* pays, c'est une bonne chose.

> *De* vostre mort fust grans damages.
> Mod.: En ce qui concerne votre mort, c'eût été grand dommage.

(*d*) *De* stands for *à.*   Ex.:

> Nés sui *de* Valenciennes.
> Mod.: Je suis né *à* Valenciennes.

> . . . ceste cité, quar ele est *de* crestïens.
>   (Villehardoin.)
> Mod.: cette cité, car elle est *à* des chrétiens.

(*e*) *De* stands for *que* in a Comparison.   Ex.:

> Nostre sente est plus sëure *de* la voie des mariez.
>   (St. Bernard.)
> Mod.: Notre voie est plus sûre *que* celle des mariés.

(*f*) *De* often does not appear at all before an Infinitive when Mod. French requires it.   Ex.:

> Bien soffeist a salveteit *soffrir* pacïemment.
> Mod.: Il suffit pour son salut *de* souffrir patiemment.

XII. *Entre* in the Old language often stands for *parmi* in the New.   Ex.:

> *Entre* les ondes de ceste seule.   (St. Bernard.)
> Mod.: *Parmi* les ondes de cette vie.
> Pria que sa parole fust *entr'* els escoutee.
>   (Bible de Sapience.)
> Mod.: Il demanda que sa parole fut écoutée *au milieu* d'eux.

XIII. In principle, the Conjunction *et*, in the Old language, continues or introduces an affirmation, and the Conjunction *ne* continues or introduces a negation.   Yet there is a use of *ne* appertaining both to its proper function and to that of the affirmative *et*, and best translated by *et* . . . *ne* . . . *pas*; *et*; *ou*; as the case may be.

1. Tous les ochiront n'en remanra un vis.
                             (Bible de Sapience.)
   > Mod.: Ils les tueront tous *et* il *n'*en restera *pas* un vivant.

2. De ce ne vous desdiray ja,
   Ne ne m'en verrez reffuser.   (Mauvais Riche.)
   > Mod.: Sur ce point je ne vous contredirai jamais,
   >   *Et* vous *ne* m'en verrez *pas* refuser.

3. Ce sont toutes tribouilleries que de plaider a folz
   ne a folles.   (Maistre Pathelin.)
   > Mod.: C'est du temps perdu que de plaider pour des fous *et* pour des folles.

4. S'il trovoit mes bués *ne* mes vaces *ne* mes brebis.
                             (Auc. et Nicol.)
   > Mod.: S'il trouvait mes bœufs *ou* mes vaches *ou* mes brebis.

5. Ce il te pueent *ne* tenir *ne* baillier.
                             (Raoul de Cambrai.)
   > Mod.: Ils peuvent *soit* t'accorder, *soit* te refuser cela.

XIV. The Conjunction *que* is often omitted in Old French, whether it be simple or a component in a conjunctive phrase. Yet it may happen that the other component is understood, and *que* alone expressed. Ex. :

1. Je crois le soleil est levé.   (Mauvais Riche.)
   Mod. : Je crois *que* le soleil est levé.
2. Cacha moi de la terre, *que* je n'i poi entrer.
   (Bible de Sapience.)
   Mod. : Il me chassa de la terre, *de sorte que* je n'y puis entrer.

The non-appearance of *que* is often the outcome of that peculiar Syntax which leaves relations unexpressed. Ex. :

Li perfides tam fud cruel,
Lis ols del cap li fait crever.   (St. Léger.)
Mod. : Le perfide fut *si* cruel *qu*'il lui fit crever les yeux de la tête.
Si'st empeiriez, toz bien vait remanent.   (Alexis.)
Mod. : Il s'est *tellement* empiré *que* tout bien va en diminuant.

On the other hand an abnormal Syntax and an excessive use of *que* are not rare.

Que que has the same value as *pendant que*. Ex. :

Que qu'ensi fait son duel la belle.
(Audefroi le Bastart.)
Mod.: *Pendant que* la belle en fait ainsi son deuil.

The Modern *tantôt . . . tantôt, tant de . . . que de, plus . . . plus* have equivalents in the Old language in the shape of *que . . . que; que . . . tant*. Ex. :

1. Mais tant par aventure ala,
   Que sus, *que* jus, *que* cha, *que* la.
   (Guillaume d'Angleterre.)
   Mod. : Mais au hasard il chemina si bien,
   Tantôt en haut, *tantôt* en bas, *d'abord* ici, *puis* là.
2. . . . e altretant en furent nafrez, si que seisante milie des Philistiens en furent *que* morz *que* blesciez.
   (Livre des Rois.)

Mod.: . . . et autant furent blessés, de sorte que d'entre les Philistins il y en eut soixante mille, *tant de* morts *que de* blessés.

3. *Que* plus vieux, *tant* plus sage.

Mod. : *Plus* on est vieux, *plus* on est sage.

This Conjunction is a formative element in a great many Conjunctive phrases and in some Prepositions. Ex. :

Trenchet la teste *d'ici qu'* as denz menuz.
(Ch. de Roland.)

Mod. : Lui tranche la tête *jusqu'*aux dents menues.

Puisque has been preserved in one sense only, that of causative ' since.' It also meant ' after.' Ex. :

On ne devoit nul home occire *puis que* on li avoit donnei a mangier . . . (Joinville.)

Mod.: On ne devait tuer aucun homme *après* qu'on lui avait donné à manger.

Por ce que and *por que* are equivalent to the Modern *parce que* and often to *afin que.* Ex. :

De trois tisons est faite cest sente, *por ceu ke* li piet ne puist glacier. (St. Bernard.)

Mod. : Cette voie est faite de trois poutres *afin que* le pied ne puisse glisser.

The phrases *combien que, comment que, encore que, ja soit ce que,* were equivalent to *quoique.* Ex. :

Si commençay de cueur a souspirer, *combien que* grand bien me faisoit de vëoir France. (Ch. d'Orléans.)

A ce que, meaning *de manière que* ; *dementre que,* meaning *pendant que* ; *tant que* and *jusque* in the sense of *jusqu'à ce que,* are extinct.

XV. *Car* meant at first *donc* as well as *pour cela, c'est pourquoi.* Ex. :

Dïent paien : Sire, *car* le pendés.
(Huon de Bordeaux.)

Mod.: Les païens disent : Sire, pendez-le *donc.*

It is sometimes used idiomatically instead of *que,* and is a frequent expletive.

XVI. *Sinon* was separable into its constituent parts *si* and *non*. (So were *avant* and *que*, etc.) **Ex.** :

> Qu'il ne poïssent mie rentrer, *se* par son commande-
> ment *non*.   (Rom. de Tristan.)
> Mod. : Qu'ils ne puissent pas rentrer, *sinon* avec son
> consentement.

XVII. The preposition *o, ot, od, ab*, from Latin *apud*, instead of *cum*, expressed accompaniment, instrument, Mod. : *avec, de*. Its original sense appears in the following example :

> Primos didrai vos dels honors
> Que il auuret *ab* duos seniors.   (St. Léger.)
> Mod. : Je vous parlerai d'abord des honneurs qu'il
> eut *auprès de* deux seigneurs.

XVIII. *Dens, dans* appeared very late in Old French. It supplanted *dedenz* as a Preposition. The latter became then purely adverbial. There is a peculiar force in the Modern use of *dedans, derrière, dessous, dessus, avec, après*, which tends to bring them near the pronominal adverbs *en* and *y*. **Ex.**:

> Le chien s'enfuit : courez *après*.
> Voilà les soldats : mon frère est-il *avec* ?

Besides *avec, avuec*, from *apud hoc*, the Old language used in that way *poruec* from *pro hoc*, and *senuec* from *sine hoc*. Meanings : therewith, therefore, therewithout.

XI. INTERROGATION AND NEGATION

Little of the liberty of the Old language has survived in the New with respect to these two points.

In Interrogation the Modern language has made a rule of repeating, under certain conditions, the Subject after the Verb in the shape of a Pronoun. One says : Son père est-*il* ici ?—This pleonasm is unknown to the Old language. Ex :

> Est *tout* prest ?   (Mauvais Riche.)
> Mod. : *Tout* est-*il* prêt.

The following constructions in the light of the Modern practice would be irregularities of various kinds :—

1. Pour quoy me dis tant de laidure ?
   Mod. : Pourquoi me dis-*tu* tant de vilaines choses ?
2. Feraz ?
   Mod. : *Le* feras-*tu* ?
3. Pourquoy ne fera ?
   Mod. : Pourquoi ne *le* fera-t-*il* pas ?
4. Et *nus* que calt ?
   Mod. : Et que *nous* importe-t-*il* ?
5. Et *tu* comment le sés ?
   Mod. : Et *toi*, comment le sais-*tu* ?
6. Avez *les vos* oblies ?
   Mod. : *Les* avez-*vous* oubliés ?
7. Aimmes me tu ?
   Mod. : *M'*aimes-*tu* ?
8. N'i a roi ?
   Mod. : N'y a-t-*il un* roi ? *or*, N'y a-t-*il pas de roi* ?

When the Negation appeared in an interrogative sentence the particle *ne* could be omitted.   Ex. :

> Estoit il point vostre aloué ?   (Maistre Pathelin.)
> Mod. : *N'*était-il pas votre employé ?

The negative particle proper is *ne*, its older form is *nen*, and it is found without any of the emphasising Nouns or Adverbs that came to be inseparably associated with it. Ex. :

> Jo *nen* ai ost ki bataille li dunget.   (Ch. de Roland.)
> Mod. : Je *n'*ai *pas* d'armée qui lui livre bataille.

But more usually (with emphasising noun) :

> Mais *nen* est *mies* totevoies sëure del tot.
>
> (St. Bernard.)
>
> Mod. : Mais toutefois elle *n'*est *pas* du tout sûre.
>
> Ne *nen* atroverunt *mies* trop estroite la sente cil
> qui . . .   (*ibidem.*)
> Mod. : Et ils *ne* trouveront *pas* la voie trop étroite,
> ceux qui . . .

Another liberty may be taken. The emphatic additions *pas, point, mie, goutte,* are found by themselves with full negative value.

The same thing happens to adverbial expressions with *ne,* which convey something more than a purely negative idea, such as the combinations : *ne . . . mais, ne . . . plus, ne . . . ja,* etc.

Pas, mie, poinct, goutte are, properly speaking, Nouns which lost their particular meaning (a step, a crumb, a dot, a drop) on being incorporated with the Negation. But it was not so with all Nouns drawn into that service. When Modern French says : *Je m'en soucie comme d'une guigne* (in English : I don't care a fig) the meaning of *guigne,* a tiny sour cherry, is alive in the mind. Similarly Old French said : *il ne prise une cinelle,* he does not care a berry.

The particle *ne* and its auxiliary Adverbs *pas, mie,* etc., need not be separated by the statement they qualify, as the Modern language usually requires. When they are united or when their order is reversed, they become emphatic. Ex. :

> *Ne mies* k'il del tot puist estre senz pechiet.
> (St. Bernard.)
> Mod. : *Non pas* qu'il puisse être tout à fait sans péché.
> *Ne ja mais* ne retornereient.   (Roman de Rou.)
> Mod. : *Jamais* ils ne retourneraient.

After the particle *ne, pour* is a favourite substitute for the Modern *à cause de,* in conformity with the Latin use of *prae.*   Ex. :

> Ele *ne* santi ne mal ne dolor *por* le grant paor qu'ele
>   avoit.   (Auc. et Nicol.)
> Mod. : Elle ne sentit ni mal ni douleur *à cause de* la
>   grande peur qu'elle avait.

Quand même with the Conditional often translates *por* with the Infinitive. Ex. :

> Je nel lairoie, *por* les membres *coper,*
> N'aille . . .   (Amis et Amiles.)
> Mod. : Je ne manquerais, *quand même* on me *couperait*
>   les membres, d'aller . . .

Modern *pour* . . . *que* with the Subjunctive, equivalent to *quoique, quelque* . . . *que, si* . . . *que,* is derived from the use of *por* in negative clauses. Ex.:

Pour bon *qu*'il soit, je ne l'aime point.

As for *ne* after Verbs of fearing, hindering, and doubting —and after similar expressions—the Old language avails itself fully of the freedom which is to some extent still allowed to writers in the New. It may be safely said that the use of *ne* in mediæval literature, though not arbitrary, was far more extended than nowadays. From Romance, *non,* reduced to atonic *nen, ne, n,* and coinciding more or less in Syntax and in form with Latin *ne, nec, neque,* passed into Old French as a very ungrammatical particle. Still, its applications can be accounted for.

XII. OLD GALLICISMS

We can give here only a very superficial survey of a few uncommon uses of the most common words of the language.

I. *Avoir* could enter into a large number of phrases, whose pattern is kept in the modern : *avoir envie, avoir soif,* etc. Examples :

Avoir merveilles	**means**	to become astonished.
avoir chier	„	to love.
avoir vil	„	to despise.

Also, *avoir en chierté, avoir en vilté.*

II. *Estre* is used in numerous idioms. Examples :

Bien *luy fut* advis qu'il fut roy. (Impers. use).
Mod. : Il fut bien de l'opinion qu'il était roi.

Et si *vous sont* esguillon.
Mod. : Et *voici* des éperons *pour vous.*

Ce seroyt grant chose que *de luy.*
Mod. : Il lui arriverait de se distinguer grandement.

Cil est *a* enscombrement, *a* esjoïssement, etc.
Mod. : Celui-là embarrasse, réjouit, etc.

More idiomatic still are :

> *Estre bien de,* meaning *être bien traité par,* and *n'est qui* de ses maux l'allege, for *il n'y a personne qui* le soulage de ses maux.

One finds also *n'est celui qui, n'i a celui qui,* in the same sense.

III. *Faire* appears in a few elliptical phrases : *faire a blasmer* means faire *quelque chose qui soit* à blâmer. Ex. :

> *Font a repenre* cil ki presumptious sunt.
>
> > (St. Bernard.)
>
> Mod. : Ceux qui sont présomptueux *s'exposent à être réprimandés.*
>
> Ne faites a gaber. (Bible de Sapience.)
> Mod. : Ne *donnez pas prise* à la plaisanterie.

Faire que fou means faire *ce que ferait* un fou. Ex. :

> Aganipus *fist que curteis.* (Rom. de Brut.)
> Mod. : Aganipe *se conduisit en* homme courtois.
>
> Mult bel le saluërent et *firent que baron.*
>
> > (Bible de Sapience.)
>
> Mod. : Ils le saluèrent très cordialement et *agirent comme* des gentilshommes.
>
> Il font mult que vilain. (Richard Cœur de Lion.)
> Mod. : Ils se conduisent tout à fait *comme des* manants.

When *faire* stands for another verb, which it frequently does, to avoid repetition, it adopts the grammar of that verb, and is styled *verbe suppléant,* or *verbum vicarium.*

IV. *Tenir, venir,* and *tourner* are used idiomatically with the Preposition *a* followed by a Noun. Ex. :

> *Tenir a* gas ; *tenir a* vil.
> Mod. : Regarder *comme* une plaisanterie ; tenir *pour* vil, or *mépriser.*

N

Il me *vient a* plaisir, *a contraire*, etc.
Mod. : Je trouve agréable, déplaisant, etc.

Vos cliquettes luy *tournent a* deplaisir.
Mod. : Votre crécelle lui cause de l'ennui.

V. Here are a few miscellaneous idioms :

(*a*) with *tenir* :

Elle ne se peut gueres *tenir qu'*elle *ne* demandast.
(Les Cent Nouv. nouv.)
Mod. : Elle ne peut longtemps se retenir de demander.

(*b*) with *aller* :

Il *en yra* ainsi qu'il *en pourra aller*.
(Maistre Pathelin.)
Mod. : Arrive que voudra ; *or*, cela marchera comme
cela pourra.

(*c*) with *peu* :

A *peu qu'*il nel tua.   (Rom. de Brut.)
Mod. : *Il s'en fallut* de peu qu'il ne le tuât; *or*, au
point qu'il faillit le tuer.

Et *par poi que* li ost ne fu tote perdue.
(Villehardoin.)
Mod. : Et *peu s'en fallut que* l'armée ne fût toute
détruite.

(*d*) with *il y a* :

Il n'y a *mais que* de.
Il n'y a *fors* de.
Mod. : Il n'y a plus qu'à, il n'y a qu'à.

(*e*) with Prepositions and Adverbs :

1. Com *ainz* pot ; qui *ains ains*.
Mod. : Le plus tôt qu'il put ; à qui mieux mieux.

2. *Entre* toi *et* mestre Belin.
Mod. : Toi et maître Belin *à vous deux*.

3. Et Ysengrins prent ses sacs *entre* lui et sun chereton.
(Chronique.)
Mod. : *A eux deux* Ysengrin et son charretier prennent
les sacs.

4. Et me manda que se je vousisse que nous loïssiens
une nef *entre li et moy.* (Joinville.)
Mod. : Et il me manda que, si je voulais, nous louerions
un navire *à nous deux.*

5. Elle revint au jardin *entre* li et sa pucielle.
(Empereur Constant.)
Mod. : *Elle et* sa fille suivante revinrent au jardin.

(*f*) with a pronoun :
Il ses cors.
Mod. : *Lui-même,* lui *en personne.*

VI. A certain number of Modern Gallicisms find their
explanation in the Old language. Ex. :

Ysengrins moult bien se deffent,
As denz les mort : *qu'en puet-il mais* ?
(Rom. de Renart.)
Mod. : Ysengrin se défend fort bien,
Il les mord avec ses dents : que peut-il faire
de *plus* ?

N'en pouvoir mais is still often heard, though its sense
can no longer be gathered except by a reference to the
ancient meaning of *mais.*

Aler EN *messagier,* to go as a messenger, explains *traiter*
EN *ami,* se mettre EN *soldat.*

The old verb *demeurer,* to delay, explains *il n'y a pas péril
en la* DEMEURE, to which the Modern meaning of *demeurer*
and *demeure* gives no clue.

Ne pas laisser de, not to fail to, based on a now isolated
meaning of *laisser,* is a common mediæval expression.
Ex. :

Or ne *lairai* nem mete en lor bailie. (Alexis.)
Je *n'attendrai pas plus longtemps* pour me mettre en
leur pouvoir.

XIII. SYNTAX OF THE VERB

The Auxiliary Verbs.

We understand this title in its widest application, in order to include several Verbs whose office is not strictly limited to being Auxiliaries of Tense.

As in the Modern language, some Verbs properly conjugated with *avoir* may take *estre.* They are mostly Intransitive Verbs which may be used transitively. Ex. :

> Ele s'estraint en son mantel . . . tant que cil *furent* passé outre. (Auc. et Nicol.)
> Mod. : Elle s'enveloppa dans son manteau, jusqu'à ce qu'ils *eurent* passé outre.

Examples appear of the opposite process, the substitution of *avoir* for *estre* in some purely Intransitive Verbs; in Reflective Verbs this is not rare. Ex. :

> 1. Tant *s'ont* entrebaisié. (Bible de Sapience.)
> Mod. : Ils *se sont* tellement entre-baisés.
> 2. Trois fois le list, lors *s'a* pasmé. (Floire.)
> Mod. : Il le lut trois fois, alors il *s'est* pâmé.

With that exception *avoir* does in no way differ from its Modern functions, but *estre* may, like 'to be' in English, be joined to the Gerundium (confused with the Present Participle), and thus form a fresh series of tenses, parallel to those which in the Modern language are exclusively simple tenses. Ex :

> Affin qu'elle vous *soit aydant* et *confortant* en tous besoings. (Perceforest.)
> Mod. : Afin qu'elle vous *aide* et vous *réconforte* en tous vos besoins.

But a more faithful translation, conveying the idea of continuity of that Present, would be :

> Afin qu'elle *vous serve de* secours et de consolation dans tous vos besoins.

Several Verbs are put to a similar use. They are *aller*, *devoir, venir, faire*. Ex. :

1. Il *ala atendant*, he was waiting.
2. Ainçoys *l'aloient couvetant*
   Et ses deux jambes delechant.   (Mauvais Riche.)
   Mod. : Mais ils le *caressaient* et lui léchaient les deux jambes.
3. As Engleis *vindrent apreismant*.   (Roman de Rou.)
   Mod. : Ils *s'approchèrent* des Anglais.
4. Si li vent a l'encontre et la *font* bienvaingnant.
                                                (Chronique.)
   Mod. : Ils vont à sa rencontre et lui *souhaitent* la bienvenue.

With an Infinitive, *faire* and (which is no exception to Modern use) *se prendre* or *se mettre* may form expressions of a similar nature. Ex. :

1. Car riens *donner* ne luy *feray*.   (Mauvais Riche.)
   Mod. : Car je ne lui *donnerai* rien.
2. Del solier u il ert *se prent* a avaler.
                                         (Bible de Sapience.)
   Mod. : *Il se met* à descendre de la couche où il était.

Faire, savoir, soloir, voloir, povoir often accompany Infinitives as Intensive Auxiliaries. Ex. :

Mes enfants que je *vols* engendrer. (Amis et Amiles.)
Dou conte Ami que il *pot* tant amer.

Voloir with Infinitive, like Modern *aller*, may express immediate futurity. Ex. :

Occire les *voldra*—il *va* les tuer.

Povoir and *devoir* have largely taken over the functions of the old Subjunctive. Ex. :

Il le *fesist* !—Il *pouvait* (il *aurait dû*) le faire !

In the future, the auxiliary *avoir*, now an inseparable suffix, might be disconnected from its Infinitive.

Faire, still more than in the Modern language, is used to avoid repetition of a Verb. Ex.:

1. Si tu desires . . . poverteit . . . nes ancor plus ardenment ke li gent del seule ne *facent* les richesses.
(St. Bernard.)
Mod.: Si tu ne désires pas même plus ardemment la pauvreté que les gens du monde ne *désirent* les richesses.

2. Et me couvient assez plus qu'il ne *fait* toy.
(Chronique.)
Mod.: Et il me faut beaucoup plus *qu'à toi.*

A, avoit, ot, stand for Modern *il y a, il y avait, il y eut.*

The Conjugation.

Transitive Verbs have become Intransitive and *vice versa*; some Old French Reflective Verbs are no longer so, and some have become Reflective that were not so in Old French. Ex.:

1. La voiz del segnur *crollant le* desert.
(Traduct. des Psaumes.)
Mod.: La voix du Seigneur *ébranlant* le désert.

Croller, now *crouler,* is no longer a Transitive Verb.

2. Mais a grant paingne i peut cil *avaler.*
(Amis et Amiles.)
Mod.: Mais celui-ci y peut à grand peine *descendre.*

Avaler is no longer Intransitive.

3. Je *m'i* cumbaterai.   (Livre des Rois.)
Mod.: *Je me battrai* avec lui.

Combattre is no longer Reflective.

4. Ne demoura c'un poi, a sa fin *en ala.*
(Bible de Sapience.)
Mod.: Il ne tarda que peu, il *s'en* alla à sa fin.

S'en aller is now always Reflective.

5. Rex Chielperings, il *se* fut mors.   (St. Léger.)

Se mourir is no longer in general use.

6. Qui *tei* a *mort.*   (Ch. de Roland.)
  Mod. : Celui qui t'a *tué.*

Mourir is no longer used transitively.

Changes have occurred in the Case or Preposition governed. Ex. :

> Je prie *a* Dieu, is now je prie *Dieu.*
> Il print congé *au* roi, is now il prit congé *du* roi.
> Entendre *a* quelqu'un, has become entendre *quelqu'un.*
> Accorder *a,* is now *s'*accorder *avec.*
> Si *le* vous prions, would now be nous vous *en* prions.

Faire *a* savoir is now faire savoir *à.*

Intransitive verbs, especially those expressing movement, may be followed by an Accusative particularising the general idea of the verb. Ex. :

> Charlemagnes vint *un antif sentier.*
> Mod. : Charlemagne vint *par* un ancien chemin.
> S'en aler *le* trot—s'en aller *au* trot.

The Modern rule that after two Verbs governing different objects, the object must be expressed twice, is not adhered to. Ex. :

> *Dieu* en *rendirent* grâces et loërent forment.
>   (Bible de Sapience.)
> Mod.: Ils en rendirent grâces *à Dieu* et *le* louèrent fort.

When there are several Subjects, agreement with any other than the nearest is unnecessary. Ex. :

1. Ces paroles *oid* Saul e tuz ces de Israel.
                        (Livre des Rois.)
  Mod.: Saül et tous ceux d'Israël *entendirent* ces paroles.

2. Et en *ot* le roy de France et ses gens le premier encontre. (Froissart.)

Mod. : Le roi de France et ses gens en *eurent* le premier choc.

There is much freedom in the handling of Reflective Verbs, whether they be essentially or only accidentally Reflective. Ex. :

1. Sire meies, *saniez* vos mismes. (St. Bernard.)

Mod. : Sire médecin, guérissez-*vous* vous-même.

2. Et li rois Pharao de son siege est levés.

(Bible de Sapience.)

Mod. : Et le roi Pharaon *s'est* levé de son siège.

The Adverb of place *en* is a favourite, often expletive, addition to Verbs expressing change of place. The Modern language has dropped it in many instances as useless, and occasionally has glued it to the Verb, as in *emporter, emmener, enlever, s'enfuir*, etc. Ex. :

1. Venes vos *ent* o moi. (Bible de Sapience.)

Mod.: *Venez* avec moi.

2. Dont *s'en* ist fors Jacob. (*ibidem.*)

Mod.: D'*où* Jacob *se tira.*

3. Joseph l'*en* fit porter. (*ibidem.*)

Mod. : Joseph le fit *emporter.*

4. Qu'entre ses bras l'*en* a levee. (Rom. de Tristan.)

Mod. : Qu'entre ses bras il l'a *enlevée.*

Modern French has many constructions in which the Infinitive, active to all appearance, has the force of a Passive. Here is an example from the Old literature :

Je durrai tun cors *a devorer* a bestes et a oisels.

(Livre des Rois.)

Mod.: Je donnerai ton corps *à dévorer* aux bêtes et aux oiseaux ; *or*, to show the meaning conveyed : Je donnerai ton corps aux bêtes, . . . *pour qu'il soit* dévoré.

These constructions with *à* arise partly from the way in which the *Lingua Romana*, after certain Verbs, modified the

Accusativus cum Infinitivo of Classical Latin (saying *jubeo* AD *te domum ire*, instead of *jubeo te domum ire*), partly from phonetic confusion (*amare* and *amari* both give *amer*), partly from Teutonic analogy and partly from the ease with which the Infinitive could pass from a transitive to an intransitive meaning. This Syntax is not without its ambiguity. *Je fais porter le pain à mon fils* may mean either 'I make my son carry the bread,' or, 'I cause the bread to be carried to my son.' Ex.:

1. Se porpensa de sun frere *a engeignier.*
   (Rom. de Brut.)
   Mod.: Il réfléchit comment il duperait son frère; but literally: Il pensa en soi-même de son frère à *être* trompé.
2. Je le reu, dieu merchi, encor l'ai *a garder.*
   (Bible de Sapience.)
   Mod.: Je le recouvrai, Dieu merci, et je l'ai encore en ma garde; but literally: Je le recouvrai, . . . et je l'ai encore pour *être* gardé.
3. Oï qu'il aloient de Nicolete parlant et qu'il *le mena-çoient a occire.*   (Auc. et Nicol.)
   Mod.: Il entendit qu'ils parlaient de Nicolette et qu'ils *menaçaient de la tuer.*

Old French admits of a freer Plural agreement with collectives grammatically Singular than does Modern French. In this respect (and in many more) it approaches the English practice (often derived from Norman). Ex.

1. Je vueil bien que ma gent *voient* que je ne *les* soustenrai. . . .   (Joinville.)
   Mod.: Je veux que mon monde *voie* bien que je ne *le* soutiendrai.
2. Quant li pueples, qui la *estoit* assemblez, *oy* ce, il se *escrierent* . . . et li *prierent.*   (*ibidem.*)
   Mod.: Quand le peuple, qui était assemblé là, entendit cela, il *s'écria* . . . et le *pria.*

It does not admit of a formal agreement of Verbs with

a purely grammatical *ce*, when the Personal Pronoun is the real Subject. Ex.:

> Se c'*estes* vous ; Mod. : Si *c'est* vous.
> Si n'*estes* vous ; Mod. : Si ce n'*est* vous.

XIV. INFINITIVE AND GERUND

The Modern functions of the Infinitive are derived from more extensive uses in Old French.

The Modern language allows the substitution of an incidental clause with the Infinitive and introduced by a Preposition, for a dependent clause with a finite tense and introduced by a Conjunction. But it allows of this only when the Subject of the dependent clause is of the same person as the Subject, or sometimes as the Object of the principal clause. For instance, we may say Je lui défends *de partir* instead of Je défends *qu'il parte*, but we cannot say Je lui parlerai *avant de partir* in the sense of Je lui parlerai *avant qu'il parte*, though we may well use it to mean Je lui parlerai *avant que je parte*.

The Old language does not acknowledge those restrictions as compulsory, and does not shun the ambiguity resulting from the neglect of them. The context has to be taken into account for a correct interpretation of such sentences.

The Latin construction of the *Accusativus cum Infinitivo* (the putting in the Accusative of the Subject of an Infinitive and thus forming a clause without a finite tense or Conjunction), has survived, especially in translations from Latin, and in writers well versed in the Latin language. Ex.:

> Il covient *ensi vivre celui* ki paistres est, c'um ne puist nule chose repenre en sa vie. (St. Bernard.)
> Mod. : Il sied *que celui* qui est pasteur *vive* de telle sorte qu'on ne puisse rien lui reprocher dans sa vie.

Nevertheless, open constructions of Old French must

occasionally be drawn together in the New language.
Ex. :

> Que nous savons bien *qu'ele est tolue* lui et son pere a
> tort. (Villehardoin.)
> Mod. : Que nous savons bien lui *avoir été enlevée* à tort
> ainsi qu'à son père.

The passage from one construction to another is sometimes ungrammatical. Ex :

> Si m'i convient *que aille* a plait et *estre* en grant
> painne. (Chronique.)
> Mod. : Il me faut *aller* plaider et *être* . . .
> *or*, Il faut *que j'aille* . . . et *que je sois* . . .

It is a proper function of the Modern Infinitive to be a
Verbal Noun. Old French made a very extensive use of
such Infinitives in constructions now obsolete. Ex. :

1. Quant ele a *celui plorer* fini. (Rom. de Tristan.)
   Mod. : Quand elle a fini *de* pleurer celui-ci.
2. Que vos vaut li *dementers*
   Li *plaindres* ne li *plurers*. (Auc. et Nicol.)
   Mod. : A quoi vous servent vos *lamentations*,
   Vos *plaintes* et vos *pleurs*.
3. A la bataille *commencier*.
   Mod. : Au *commencement de* la bataille.
4. Quanque a *estre*.
   Mod. : Tout ce qui a *vie*.

Verbal nouns are masculine.

The Old Infinitive in negative clauses may stand for the
Imperative (as it may nowadays in rules of arithmetic,
cooking receipts, etc.). Ex. :

> De mon fil di moi voir, ne me *mentir* point.
> (Bible de Sapience.)
> Mod. : Dis-moi la vérité sur mon fils, ne me *mens*
> point.

The 'Infinitive of Purpose,' governed by another Verb

without an intervening Preposition, is still more frequent than in Modern French. Ex.:

> *Trovent* Bernart l'archeprestre
> En un fosse les chardons *pestre*. (Roman de Renart.)
> Mod.: . . . . qui était dans un fossé, *pour* y paître les chardons.

The Latin Gerund, closely akin to the Infinitive, was very much like the Present Participle in form. Hence a frequent confusion in French with the Present Participle. In consequence not every verbal form that ends in *-ant* can be legitimately termed a Present Participle.

After Prepositions, for instance, in Latin a Gerund, in French an Infinitive, is expected. Hence when we read *en parlant* beside *pour parler*, we may remove the faulty Present Participle by reading *parlant* as a *Gerund* (for *in parlando*), though elsewhere we must read the Infinitive (*pro parlare*). Gerunds are somewhat frequent in Old French. Ex.:

> Le roy eut, *par* la paix *fesant*, grant coup de la terre
> le conte. (Joinville.)
> Mod.: Le roi, *par* la paix *qu'il fit*, obtint une grande partie des terres du comte.

In the Old language the Gerund, as in Italian and Spanish, is invariable. This distinguishes it from the Present Participle, which is duly declined, as in Latin.

XV. PAST PARTICIPLE

The agreement of Past Participles is a question that has not reached in Modern French a satisfactory issue. The language, insufficiently conscious of what would be correct, and fitful in its practice, has not imposed any natural laws upon the grammarians. A conventional rule of agreement was the ultimate remedy for a chronic uncertainty. No such settlement was possible in Old French, in the absence of an academic body able to raise a standard in the cause of unity and to enforce obedience to it.

But a pretty clear statement can be made of the different ways of treating Past Participles in Old French.

Auxiliary *Estre.*

There is first the Past Participle of Passive Verbs. No difficulty should occur here. Agreement with the Subject is compulsory. Common sense commands it; wherever it is omitted in texts it should be restored and the omission laid down to illiterateness or carelessness on the part of the copyist. Ex. :

> *Nostre sire fut* en la cruiz *nafrez.*

The *z* at the end of *nafrez*, for *ts*, *ds*, contains the *s* characterising the Subject, and this is as it should be.

In Intransitive Verbs and in Reflective Verbs the matter is somewhat different. The necessity of an agreement with the Subject is not quite so obvious. Yet agreement is the almost unbroken rule for Intransitive Verbs at least.

In Reflective Verbs complications arise from the grammatical distinctness and substantial identity of Subject and Object Pronoun. Whether we refer the Past Participle to the one or to the other, the correct agreement in Gender and Number will be obtained, the ' Case,' however, remains unsettled. It can be determined only by a previous choice between the Subject and the Reflective Pronoun. If the Subject be chosen, the Past Participle will be put in the Nominative; if the Reflective Pronoun is preferred, the Past Participle will be put in the Objective case. The former agreement is the prevailing one. Ex. :

1. **Dedanz son lit** *s'est* tost *cochiez.*   (Rom. de Troie.)
   Mod. : Dans son lit il *s'est* bientôt *couché.*
2. **Nicolas** *s'est armés.*   (Rom. d'Alixandre.)
   Mod. : Nicolas *s'est armé.*

Hence it follows that the Modern language, by deciding that the agreement shall take place with the Reflective Pronoun (when it is the Direct Object), has separated itself from the Old.

As to those Verbs conjugated with *estre* and with a Reflective Pronoun as Indirect Object, agreement took place with the Subject without hesitation; the adjunction of a noun as Direct Object could not confuse the issue.

Auxiliary *Avoir*.

Now we come to the question of agreement when the Verb is Transitive and the Auxiliary is *avoir*. Here the relative positions of Auxiliary, Object and Participle, are of some account. In so far as the influence of Latin went, it taught agreement of Past Participle with Direct Object, in gender, number and case, without any exception. When put to the test of reason such a teaching seems unimpeachable. In consequence, both etymology and logic are on the side of an agreement with the Direct Object under all circumstances. Yet the ease with which Old French separated from one another, Auxiliary, Participle and Object, by inserting Complements between them, strengthened a tendency towards viewing Past Participles as Invariable. This was the case mainly when the Object followed the Past Participle, the Auxiliary standing first,—hence the Modern rule based on this order. This was the case also when the Past Participle stood at the beginning of a clause, or when its Object was a Relative Pronoun. In all other arrangements, the balance of evidence, especially in the works of men of culture, is in favour of an agreement. Yet exceptions are so numerous, and so systematic in the literature of the people, that the laying down of a hard and fast rule is out of the question.

Nor is the Modern system defensible from a logical point of view. Agreement should be compulsory in all cases, regardless of position of Object, or else it should be altogether forbidden. In that way, one tendency of the Ancient language would be made absolute at the cost of the other.

Examples of Agreement.

1. Cum *la cena* Jhesus *oc faita*.   (Passion de Christ.)
   Mod. : Quand Jésus eut *fait la cêne*.

2. Lors font les chevaus ensieler,
   Et puis lor *a on amenes.*　　　　　　　　(Perceval.)
   Mod. : Ils font alors seller les chevaux,
   　　　Et puis on *les* leur *a amenés.*
3. Qu'entre ses bras l'en *a levee,*
   Besie l'a e *acolce.*　　　　　　　　(Rom. de Tristan.)
   Mod. : Qu'il *l'a enlevée* dans ses bras,
   　　　Et l'a *baisée* et *embrassée.*
   Li emperere *a prise* sa *herberge.*　　　　(Ch. de Roland.)
   Mod. : L'empereur a *pris* sa débridée.

Examples of Invariability.

1. Judas cum *og mangied la sopa.*　　　(Pass. de Christ.)
   Mod. : Quand Judas *eut mangé la soupe.*
2. Icele nuit *ont grant joie mené.*　　　(Ogier le Danois.)
   Mod. : Cette nuit *ils* ont *donné carrière à une grande
   joie.*
3. Pensez des mals *qu'il od ëu.*　　　　(Rom. de Tristan.)
   Mod. : Pensez aux maux *qu'il a soufferts.*
4. *Caint a l'espee* dont d'or mier est li puing.
   　　　　　　　　　　　　　　　　　(Aliscans.)
   Mod. : *Il a ceint l'épée* dont la poignée est d'or pur.

When the Participle *fait,* or any other, is followed by an Infinitive dependent upon it, instances of agreement and instances of disagreement can be brought forward in numbers fairly equal. Modern grammars forbid the agreement of *fait* in such connections. Ex. :

1. La chose unt tost *faite saveir.*　　　(Rom. de Brut.)
   Mod. : Ils ont bientôt *fait* savoir la chose.
2. Si l'a *faite* vive *enfoïr.*　　　　　　(*ibidem.*)
   Mod. : Il l'a *fait* enfouir vive.

When the Past Participle refers grammatically to two or more Objects, it agrees with the nearest only. Ex. :

Le pié li a et la gambe *embrachie.*　　　(Aliscans.)
Mod. : Il lui *a embrassé* le pied et la jambe.

When the Feminine Complements of negation *riens,*
mies, goute, etc., have their original substantive value, the
Participle may agree with them. Ex.:

   . . . vos n'aves *riens* nule cele nuit *ole.*

(Guill. d'Anglet.)

   Mod.: . . . vous n'avez cette nuit entendu aucune
   chose.

Elliptical constructions need not interfere with the agreement of the Participle. Ex.:

   Ne fu tiex olz vëue, n'assemblee
   Com Desramez ot *fete* e *ajoustee.*   (Guill. d'Orange.)
   Mod.: Jamais armée ne fut vue ni assemblée
       Telle que *celle que* D. avait faite et organisée.

XVI. ABSOLUTE VERBAL CONSTRUCTION

The Ablative Absolute of Latin, occurring in incidental
clauses with a Present or Past Participle, or a Gerund,
remained in Old French in the shape of an absolute accusative with a present or past participle. Ex.:

   Gières *despitiez les estuides* des lettres, *laissie la maison*
       et les choses de son pere, quist l'abit de sainte con-
       versation.   (Li dialoge Gregoire le Pape.)
   Mod.: Aussi, *l'étude* des lettres (*étant*) *méprisée, la*
       maison de son père (*étant*) *abandonnée,* il rechercha
       l'habit du moine.
   Racontanz quatre disciples.   (*ibidem.*)
   Mod.: *D'après le récit de* . . .

In these constructions, the Gerund shows its threefold
nature: noun, verb, adverb. Ex.:

   De mon *vivant*—A son corps *défendant*— Chemin
   faisant—Jouant, dansant, riant, les heures s'écoulent
   —Sur son *séant.*

Old French said also: en mon *dormant*—en un *tenent*—en
son *estant.*

XVII. MOODS AND TENSES

Indicative.

Old French does not shun the Indicative in some of the dependent clauses for which the Modern language prescribes the Subjunctive. Ex.:

1. Vous prie que vous me *tenez* promesse. (Perceforest.)
   Mod. : Je vous prie que vous me *teniez* parole.
2. Il convient que vous me *promettez.* (*ibidem.*)
   Mod.: Il convient que vous me *promettiez.*
3. C'est grand pitié qu'il *convient* que je soye.
   (Ch. d' Orléans.)
   Mod.: C'est grand dommage qu'il *convienne* que je sois.
4. Il faut que nous luy *reboutons.* (Maistre Pathelin.)
   Mod. : Il faut que nous le *remettions* sur la voie.
5. Il ne demoura pas si pou que les dix ans ne *furent* passez ains que sa femme le revist.
   (Les Cent Nouv. nouv.)
   Mod. : Il ne s'absenta pas si peu que dix ans ne *fussent* passés avant que sa femme le revît.

As should be well known, the difference between the Subjunctive and Indicative Moods is grounded in psychology. What the mind conceives as dependent on itself, or proceeding from itself, it puts in the Subjunctive. What it perceives as realised in the outer world, or removed beyond itself, it puts in the Indicative. So, when comparing the respective spheres of Subjunctive and Indicative in Modern French, with that belonging to each in Old French, any difference must arise from a difficulty or divergence in distinguishing matter of thought from matter of fact.

The relation of the past tenses to one another in a historical narrative is less strictly laid down than it is in Modern French. This is shown by some overlapping in the use of the Past Definite and Imperfect on one hand,

of the Pluperfect and Past Anterior on the other hand,
while the Past Indefinite which stands out distinctly
between those two pairs, has not, in spite of its isolation,
escaped confusion.

In principle, as in the Modern tongue, the Old Imperfect is descriptive and the Old Past Definite is historical.
But the Modern conception of what is respectively historical or descriptive does not always tally with the mediæval
view ; and Old French is able to pass with remarkable
rapidity from the historical standpoint to the descriptive,
and *vice-versa.* Ex. :

1. Grans *fu* par les espaules et le viaire *ot* fier.
   (Rom. d'Alixandre.)
   Mod. : Ses épaules *étaient* fortes et il *avait* le visage
   fier.

2. Tiebalt *fu* pleins d'engin e pleins *fu* de feintie.
   A hume ne a feme ne porta amistie.
   (Rom. de Rou.)
   Mod. : Tibolt *était* plein d'esprit et il *était* plein de
   tromperies,
   Il ne *portait* amitié ni aux hommes ni aux
   femmes.

3. La femme al paisant, dementre qu'il *manga,*
   A la charue vint, ...   (*ibidem.*)
   Mod. : La femme du paysan, pendant qu'il *mangeait,*
   Vint à la charrue, . . .

4. Quant la femme Renier sout de veir e oi
   Que Rou *tint* sun seignur. . . .   (*ibidem.*)
   Mod. : Quand la femme de René sut, pour l'avoir vu
   et entendu,
   Que Rou *retenait* son seigneur.

5. Neirs *ert* li tens, ne *fist* pas cler.   (*ibidem.*)
   Mod. : Le temps *était* noir, il ne *faisait* pas clair.

6. Mult par *ert* gros, el monde n'*ot* son per. (Aliscans.)
   Mod. : Il *était* très gros, il n'*avait* pas son pareil au
   monde.

The Past Definite is almost stereotyped in a few for-

mulas frequently used, such as *il eut*, or *il y eut*; or simply
eut, ot, for *il y avait*; *il eut nom*, for *il s'appelait*, etc.

The historical Present is found to alternate with the
Past Definite in the same sentence. Ex.:

> Li perfides tam *fud* cruels,
> Lis ols del cap li *fait* crever.   (Vie de St. Léger.)
> Mod.: Le perfide *fut* si cruel,
>   Qu'il lui *fit* crever les yeux de la tête.
> *Or*, Le perfide *est* si cruel qu'il lui *fait* . . .

The **Past Indefinite** is found instead of the Past Definite.
Ex.:

> Carles li reis, nostre emperere magnes,
> Set anz tuz pleins *ad estet* en Espaigne.
>   (Ch. de Roland.)
> Mod.: Le roi Charles, notre grand empereur,
>   *Fut* en Espagne sept ans entiers.

This is very frequent in poetry: the Past Indefinite is
the epic and lyric past tense. The Pluperfect is often used
with similar effect in the Modern language.

Instead of the Pluperfect we find the Past Definite.
Ex.:

> 1. . . . sun sunge lur conta,
>   Tut en ordre lur dist si cum il le *sunga*.
>   Mod.: Il leur conta son songe,
>   Il le leur dit tout en ordre comme il *l'avait
>   songé*.
> 2. Si vint une novele en l'ost . . . que messire
>   Folques de Nulli . . . *fina* et *morut*.
>   (Villehardoin.)
>   Mod.: Une nouvelle se répandit dans l'armée . . .
>   que Monseigneur Folq. de Nully *avait cessé* de vivre
>   et *était mort*.

Here is an example of the use of the Past Anterior
instead of the Pluperfect:

Nous trouvames que uns forz vent *ot* rompues les cordes.   (Joinville.)

Mod. : Nous trouvâmes qu'un grand vent *avait* rompu les cordes.

In a set historical narrative the tenses may differ from Modern usage in a marked manner.   Ex. :

' David le fulc qu'il *out* en guarde a altre cumandad, e si cume sis peres *l'out cumandé*, al ost s'en alad. Saul lores e li fiz Israel el val de Terebinte *tindrent* les esturs encuntre ces de Philistiim   E David vint a Magala en l'ost ki *aprestez se fud* a bataille ; e ja *fud* la noise levé e li criz · kar Israel *out* ordené ses eschieles de une part, e li Philistien de altre part.   Cume ço oid David, la u li herneis *fud*, laisad ço qu'il *portad*, curut a la bataille e se bien *esteust* a ses freres demandad.   Si cume David nuveles *demandad*, este-vus Goliat ki en *vint* del ost as Philistiens, e si cume einz *l'out fait* devant David *parlad*.'   'Livre des Rois.)

Mod. : David confia a un autre le troupeau qu'il *avait* en garde, et comme son père le lui *avait commandé*, il s'en alla à l'armée.   Saül et les fils d'Israël . . . *tenaient* alors campagne contre les Philistins.   Et David vint à Magala dans l'armée qui *s'était préparée* pour la bataille, et déjà le bruit et les cris *étaient* intenses, car Israël *avait rangé* ses bataillons d'un côté et les Philistins avaient placé les leurs de l'autre.   Quand David entendit cela, il laissa ce qu'il *portait* là où *étaient* les bagages, courut à la bataille et demanda à ses frères si tout *allait* bien. Comme David *demandait* les nouvelles, voilà Goliath qui *vient* de l'armée des Philistins et *parle* devant David comme il *avait fait* auparavant.

To sum up what concerns the tenses of the Indicative : the Past Definite very frequently trenches upon the sphere now strictly reserved for the Imperfect, both Past Definite and Imperfect may be found for the Pluperfect, the Past

Indefinite occupies ground now divided between the Past Definite and the Pluperfect, and the Past Anterior often appeared in places where the Pluperfect only may stand at present.

Subjunctive.

Modern French has not ratified the use of the Subjunctive after some of the Old French Conjunctions which it has inherited, partly because their meaning has been changed, and partly because they have been brought under new rules. Ex. :

1. Et comme ils *fussent* en joyeuses devises.
   (Les cent Nouv. nouv.)
   Mod. : Et comme ils *étaient* en joyeux propos.
2. Frappez sus voz ennemys *tant que* vous *ayez* victoire.
   (Perceforest.)
   Mod. : Frappez sur vos ennemis *jusqu'à ce que* vous ayez victoire.

The Modern construction *tant que vous* AUREZ would altogether miss the meaning of *tant que vous* AYEZ.

After verbs of thinking and perceiving, Modern French admits of the Subjunctive only if they are used interrogatively or negatively. Formerly the Subjunctive was used in affirmative clauses as well. Ex. :

Je *cuidoie* vraiement qu'il se *fust* courrouciez a moi.
(Joinville.)
Mod. : Je croyais vraiment qu'il *s'était* courroucé contre moi.

The Subjunctive in the principal clause was more frequent in Old French than nowadays. It had then generally an 'optative' value, and expresses a desire, a wish, a vow. It may be used optatively in relative clauses. Ex. :

Se le met en la dieu main, qui le *gart* de mort.
(Villehardoin.)
Mod. : Et je le mets en la main de Dieu, que *je prie de* le *garder* du danger de mort.

It often entails in dependent clauses a Subjunctive which the Modern tongue rejects. Ex.:

> Mais tut *seit* fel, chier ne se *vende* primes.
> (Ch. de Roland.)
> Mod.: Félon soit quiconque ne se *vendra* pas cher d'abord.

The Modern language puts in the Indicative hypothetical clauses introduced by *si*, the Old admitted of the Subjunctive. Ex.:

> Li quens Rollanz unkes n'amat cuard . . . ne chevalier, s'il ne *fust* bons vassals. (Ch. de Roland.)
> Mod.: Le comte Roland n'aima jamais un couard . . . ni un chevalier, s'il n'*était* bon vassal.

But the Future of the Indicative is not now allowable. It was in Old French. Ex.:

> Aerde la meie langue as meies jodes *si* mei ne *rememberra* de tei. (Oxford Fr. Psalter.)
> Mod.: Que ma langue adhère à mes joues, *si* je ne me souviens pas de toi.

The Subjunctive often stood in principal clauses where the Conditional has to be put in our days, partly because the optative function of the former has gone over to the latter. Ex.:

> 1. E Deus, dist-il, ici ne *volsisse* estre.
> (Vie de St. Alexis.)
> Mod.: Dieu, dit-il, je *voudrais* ne pas être ici.
> 2. A dont *veïssiés* varlets mettre en oeuvre et cerchier a tous lez. (Froissart.)
> Mod.: Alors vous *auriez vu* les valets se mettre à l'ouvrage et chercher de tous côtés.

It is still possible to build hypothetical statements, provided they be in the Pluperfect, wholly in the Subjunctive, instead of the usual association of the Indicative in dependent clause with the Conditional in the principal clause. Ex.:

S'il eût été mon ami, il *eût* combattu pour moi, instead
 of the commoner
S'il *avait* été mon ami, il *aurait* combattu pour moi.

Old French enjoys the same freedom to a larger extent,
and need show no consistency in using it. Ex. :

1. Si *fusse* ung povre ydiot et folet, au cueur *eusses* de
 t'excuser couleur.   (Villon.)
 Mod.: Si j'*étais* un pauvre idiot et un fou, tu *aurais*
  un prétexte de t'excuser auprès du cœur.
2. . . Qui od lui *fust*
 Et aprés lui sun regne *ëust*,
 S'il le *poeient* delivrer.   (Rom. de Brut.)
 Mod. : Qui *serait* avec lui
 Et qui *aurait* son royaume après lui,
 S'ils *pouvaient* le délivrer.

The sequence of tenses may be wrong from the Modern
standpoint, or the Syntax may be at variance with Modern
rules on Indirect oration; also the hypothesis underlying a
statement may not be expressed. Ex. :

1. Ichil qui la *fust* donc a chel assenblement
 Et del pere et del fil *veït* l'embrachement,
 S'il *ëust* jëuné trois jours en un tenent,
 Sachies que de mengier ne li *presist* talent.
       (Bible de Sapience.)
 Mod. : Celui qui *aurait été* à cette rencontre
 Et qui *aurait vu* l'embrassement du père et du fils,
 Même s'il *avait jeûné* trois jours de suite,
 Sachez que l'envie de manger ne l'*aurait* pas *pris*.
2. Deist lur ce que il voldreit,
 Et tut *fust fait* que il direit,
 Tant que sun regne li *rendist*,
 Et en s'enur le *restablist*.   (Rom. de Brut.)
 Mod. : Qu'il leur dît ce qu'il voudrait,
 Et tout ce qu'il dirait *serait fait*,
 Jusqu'à ce qu'il lui *aurait rendu* son royaume,
 Et qu'il l'*aurait rétabli* en son honneur.

3. . . . qui li souslevoient sa vestëure ansi com ce *fuissent* nois gauges, et estoit graille parmi les flans, qu'en vos dex mains le *pëusciés* enclorre.

(Auc. et Nicol.)

Mod. : . . . qui lui soulevaient ses vêtements comme si *ç'avaient été* des noisettes, et elle était si mince à la taille que vous *auriez pu* la tenir dans vos deux mains.

Notice that in the examples collected above, Modern and Ancient grammar are at variance, not only about the Moods, but also about the Tenses. Thus it is seen that the strict modal and temporal relations established in the Modern language between Verb of principal clause and Verb of dependent clause are of a less inflexible character in the Old language.

The Conditional stands occasionally where a Future is expected. Ex. :

On m'a fait honte, je l'*amenderais* quant je porrais.

(Chronique.)

Mod. : On m'a insulté, j'y *mettrai* ordre quand je pourrai.

To sum up, it remains to contrast in point of theory the Subjunctive with those forms of the Indicative which are currently called the Conditional Mood, and to dwell at the same time on the relations in which the tenses of the Subjunctive stand to one another.

In the case of unreal hypothesis, the Old language began by using the Imperfect of the Subjunctive in both clauses. In a later, but still early, period, the Future Imperfect appeared in the principal clause along with the Subjunctive Imperfect in the Conditional clause. From the twelfth century, the Imperfect of the Indicative takes the place of the Imperfect Subjunctive in the Conditional clause. Yet the two earlier modes remain in existence. Hence the three types, for a time co-existent : *jo venisse se jo pëusse, jo vendreie se jo pëusse, jo vendreie se jo pooie,* to which a fourth type may also be added : *jo venisse, se jo pooie.*

The above applies to unreal hypothesis placed in present or future time as related to the subject.

When the unreal hypothesis stood to the subject in the relation of past time, the Old language, here again, began by using the Imperfect of its Subjunctive, but with the value of a Pluperfect which it had in Latin. Later, it substituted, in both clauses, its Pluperfect for the earlier Imperfect, saying then *jo fusse venu, se jo eüsse pëu.* The third stage was marked by the appearance of the modern association je *serais venu, si j'avais pu,* beside which the construction of the second stage *je fusse venu, si j'eusse pu,* still exists within limits.

CHAPTER IV

OLD FRENCH SPELLING

OLD French diphthongs have become monophthongs. Though still written with two vowel signs, they are now pronounced as a single vowel-sound. For instance *ai,* now sounded *è* and *é,* was pronounced *a-i* in two distinct articulations forming one syllable. *Au* was not always equivalent to *o,* but was pronounced *a-u,* or rather *a-ou,* Latin *u* being in sound what we represent now by *ou.* In the same way *eu* was *e-ou, ou* was *o-ou.* Subject to such variations in the course of ages, we can draw up, for convenience in reading and in using vocabularies or glossaries, the following imperfect table of equivalence in spelling :—

Vowels.

The same word may be spelt with

ei, oi, ai, e, eei, eoi	for Mod.			*ai, oi.*
al	stands for Mod.			*au.*
el, iau	„	„	„	*eau, eu.*
o, u, ou, eu	„	„	„	*eu.*
oe, ue, eo	„	„	„	*eu.*

u, o, ol, and	stands for Mod.			*ou.*
oi	„	„	„	*ui.*
ui	„	„	„	*oi.*
ai	„	„	„	*a.*
ié	„	„	„	*é.*
eu, ou	„	„	„	*u.*
u	„	„	„	*o.*
y	„	„	„	*i.*
i	„	„	„	*y.*

Consonants.

as, os, is, us	stand for Mod.			*â, ô, î, û.*
ax, ex, ox	„	„	„	*aux, eux, oux.*
es	„	„	„	*é, ê.*
et final	„	„	„	*é.*
ill final	„	„	„	*il.*
us final	„	„	„	*ux.*
c, k	„	„	„	*ch.*
g	„	„	„	*j.*
k	„	„	„	*qu.*
k, qu	„	„	„	*c* hard.
c	„	„	„	*ss.*
w	„	„	„	*g* hard.
ngn	„	„	„	*gn.*
x	„	„	„	*s, x.*
z	„	„	„	*s, x.*
s	„	„	„	*z.*

Old French consonants are liable to be doubled in the Modern language and *vice versa*.

The revival of Latin and Greek scholarship in the fifteenth century brought about the re-appearance of Latin letters which had been phonetically altered in the previous periods of organic growth. These letters are parasitic, and most of them have since been ejected.

For instance, in the spelling *faict* for *fait*, from *factus*, the *c* of the Latin re-appears though previously absorbed in the monophthong *ai*.

Elision is far less taken advantage of than in the Modern language. Ex.:

Aussi tost en leur presence *que en* leur absence.
(Ph. de Commines.)
Mod.: Autant en leur présence *qu'en* leur absence.

Yet Vowels are elided in Old French which can on no account be omitted in the Modern tongue, often because the latter has lost an alternative form in *e*, used by the former. Ex.:

1. Aller ne puis *n'* avant *n'* arrière.
   Mod.: Je ne puis aller *ni* en avant, *ni* en arrière.
2. Il n'y a beste ne oiseau *qu'en* son jargon ne chante ou crye.
   Mod.: Il n'y a ni bête ni oiseau *qui en* son jargon ne chante ou ne crie.

The Old language says *ne . . . ne* beside *ni . . . ni* and *que* beside *qui*.

L appended to the preceding word stands for *le*; Ex.: *rendrel*.

S is appended in the same way, for *se*.

Old French does not absolutely require the so-called 'euphonic *t*.' Ex.:

1. Te *faudra il* ces maulx attendre. (Villon.)
   Mod.: Te *faudra-t-il* attendre ces maux.
2. Mangüe il ?
   Mod.: Mange-t-il ?

CHAPTER V

OLD FRENCH VERSIFICATION.

FRENCH mediæval verse-making rests on three principles.

1. The number of syllables is strictly limited in each line. The more usual lines are the lines of ten syllables,

of twelve syllables, and of eight syllables.   When once it
is clear which of those metres the poet has adopted, any
deficiency or excess in the number of syllables is a fault.
The so-called *e* mute may be a sounding vowel, or may
not.

2. The tonic accent resting on the last sounding syllable
of each word is used to break the monotony of the line,
and to bring about rests in certain places.   In the decasyllabic line the rest, or cesura, is after the fourth sounding syllable, in the dodecasyllabic line (the Alexandrine)
it is after the sixth syllable.   Verses are thus broken at
regular intervals, breaks in the grammatical structure
generally fall in with the break in the metre; the sounding syllable immediately preceding the break receives an
emphatic tonic stress, to which are subordinated the minor
accents of the other words in a harmony, the subtlety and
infinite variety of which almost completely baffle the
foreign ear.

3. The tonic stress and the final rest, which would, as a
matter of course, accompany the last sounding syllable of
each line, are diversified from the tone and from the rest
at the cesura (the break in the body of the line), by the
assonance that turns the last vowel into a ringing note,
and throws it into harmony with any number of preceding
or following lines.

Modern French has both spoilt and improved this
beautiful and simple conception of poetry.

It has replaced assonance by rhyme; it has forbidden the
clashing of vowels between word and word; it forbids at
the cesura syllables that are breathed, though not sounded,
unless it can get rid of them by elision, and it has en-
cumbered the primitive design with byzantine niceties.

Here is an example of Old French verse, and an indication of the manner in which such lines may be taken to
pieces.

The line is the decasyllabic line, used in heroic and epic
poetry, and the extracts are from the Chanson de Roland.

We begin by showing the cesura, the assonance, and the
counting of the sounding syllables.

E is a sounding vowel, unless it be deliberately elided, or dropped at the cesura.

1. Rollanz s'en turnet, | par le camp vait tut suls |

  Cercet les vals | e si cercet les munz |

  Iloec truvat | et Ivorie e Ivun |

  Truvat Gerin, | Gerer sun cumpaignun |

  Iloec truvat | Engeler le Guascun.

2. Ço dit Rollanz | 'bel cumpainz Oliver, |

  Vos fustes fils | al bon cunte Reiner, |

  Ki tint la marche | de Genes desur mer, |

  Pur hanste freindre | e pur escuz pecier |

  E pur osberc | e rompre e desmailler |

  En nule terre | n' ot meillur chevaler.' |

Students will notice the regularity of the cesura after the fourth syllable, the break in grammatical structure at the same place, which allows the voice to rise and then to subside a little longer than when words are closely bound up by the sense, thus enabling the fifth *e*-syllable, which often follows the tonic fourth, to be lost in the pause without breaking the metre for the ear; lastly, the same phenomena repeated at the end of the line, but crowned by the assonance which one single vowel held in common with the preceding or following line is sufficient to produce.

As for the rise and fall of the voice as it passes over the toneless syllables, along the tonic and semi-tonic vowels of the line, it will be seen in the following notation.

It must be remembered that the rise at the cesura and at the end of the line is the most marked, and reacts upon the strength and place of the others; also that monosyllabic words are tonic, unless in a place or function compelling tonelessness.

The figures mark the strong tones, and those on vowels written in italics are the strongest.

      1   2   1   2

1. Rollanz s'en *tur*net, par le camp vait tut *suls*,

      1   2   1   2

   Cercet les *vals* e si cercet les m*unz*;

      1   2   1   2

   Iloec truv*at* et Ivorie et Iv*un*,

      1   2   1   ½   2

   Truvat Ger*in*, Gerer sun cumpaig*nun*,

      1   2 ½ 1   2

   Iloec truv*at* Engeler le Guas*cun*

      1   2 ½ 1   2

   E si truv*at* Berenger e Ot*un*,

      1   2 ½ 1   2

   Iloec truv*at* Anseïs e Sans*un*,

      1   2   1   ½ 2

   Truvat Ger*ard* le veill de Russill*un*;

      1   2   1   2

   Par un e *un* les ad pris le bar*un*,

     ½   2   1   2   3

   Al arcev*es*que en est venuz a*tut*,

      1   2   1   2

   Sis mist en r*eng* dedevant ses gen*uilz*.

      1   2   1   2

2. Ço dit Roll*anz*, 'bels cumpainz Oliv*er*,

      1   2   1   2

   Vos fustes f*ilz* al bon cunte Rein*er*

      1   2   1   2

   Ki tint la m*ar*che de Genes desur *mer*;

      1   2   1   2   3

   Pur hanste fr*ein*dre e pur escuz peci*er*

      1   2   1   ½ 2

   E pur osb*erc* e rompre e desmail*ler*,

     ½   2   1   ½ 2

   Pur orgoill*os* et veintre e esma*ier*

      1   2   1   ½ 2

   E pur proz*do*mes tenir e conseil*ler*

      1   2   1   ½ 2

   E pur glut*uns* e veintre e esma*ier*

      1   2   1   2

   En nule *terre* n'ot meillor cheval*er*.'

The Alexandrine's twelve syllables are counted as follows (the extract is taken from the poem that gave its name to that line: le Roman d'Alixandre):

```
 1  2 3 4  5  6      1     2  3   4    5   6
```
En icele forest, | dont vos m'oëz conter, |
```
 1 2 3  4 5   6      1   2   3    4    5  6
```
Nesune male choze | ne puet laianz entrer. |
```
 1  2  3   4 5   6       1 2  3    4   5  6
```
Li home ne les bestes | n'i ozent converser, |
```
 1   2   3 4 5   6      1  2   3    4   5  6
```
Onques en nesun tans | ne vit hom yverner, |
```
 1   2    3   4    5     6     1 2 3  4  5 6
```
Ne trop froit ne trop chaut | ne neger ne geler. |
```
 1  2 3 4    5  6      1    2   3    4  5  6
```
Ce conte l'escripture | que hom n'i doit entrer, |
```
 1 2   3  4   5 6     1  2   3     4   5 6
```
Se il nen at talent | de conquerre ou d'amer. |
```
 1  2 3 4   5   6      1  2   3     4 5 6
```
Les deuesses d'amors | i doivent habiter, |
```
 1   2   3   4 5  6    1 2  3  4   5    6
```
Car c'est lor paradix | ou el doivent entrer, |
```
 1  2   3   4 5 6      1  2 34  5  6
```
Li rois de Macedoine | en a oï parler |
```
 1  2   3    4    5    6      1   2    3   4  5   6
```
Qui cercha les merveilles | dou mont et de la mer. |

Notice the seventh odd syllable at the cesura, and in
the seventh line the full value of *e* before a word beginning
with a vowel.

Final *e* is elided, that is to say, silent in pronunciation,
only when the poet requires this for the metre. As for
the 'hiatus,' or clashing of vowels, so much feared by the
Moderns from an affectation out of keeping with the genius
of the language, it is no more forbidden than is a syllabic
mute *e* following upon a vowel in the line.

Example of treatment of *e*.

```
 1  2    3  4    1  2   3     4  5 6
```
Ma bonn*e* epee | *que ai* ceint*e au* coté.

Example of Hiatus.

```
 1  2  3  4    1  2   3    4   5 6
```
Jusqu'*a un* an | aurons France saisie.

Example of Metrical e Mute.

```
 1 2    3  4    1  2  34  5     6
```
Devant Marsile | il s'ecri*e* moult haut.

As visible from the line headed 'Example of Hiatus,' it is quite legitimate to have, at the end of the line, a supernumerary mute syllable, as we have seen at the cesura.

The lines in the specimens forming the third part of this book are correct. Should any appear short, it will be because the reader in counting the syllables elides vowels which the poet has not so elided. If any line appears long, it will be because the reader pronounces as two syllables what the poet intended to be a diphthong, or that he fails to elide where the poet intends elision to take place. Final *t* or *-nt* after *e* mute, need not prevent elision.

THIRD BOOK

SPECIMENS AND GLOSSARY

PETITE CHRESTOMATHIE DE L'ANCIEN FRANÇAIS

Students are recommended to begin their reading with the last
Specimen, and to take the others in backward order

PREMIÈRE PARTIE

PROSE

Fragment d'un Sermon de St. Bernard

(12ème *siècle*)

Uns sermons communs

Granz est ceste mers, chier frere, et molt large, c'est
ceste presente vie ke molt est amere et molt plaine de
granz ondes, ou trois manieres de gent puyent solement
trespesseir, ensi k' il delivreit en soient, et chascuns en sa
maniere. Troi homme sunt : Noë, Daniel et Job. Li 5
primiers de cez trois trespesset a neif, li seconz per pont et
li tierz per weit. Cist troi homme signifient trois ordenes
ki sunt en sainte eglise. Noë conduist l'arche per mei lo
peril del duluve, en cui je reconois apermenmes la forme
de ceos qui sainte eglise ont a governeir. Daniel, qui 10
apeleiz est bers de desiers, ki abstinens fut et chastes, il
est li ordenes des penanz et des continanz ki entendent
solement a deu. Et Job, ki droituriers despensiers fut de
la sustance de cest munde, signifiet lo feaule peule qui est
en mariaige, a cuy il loist bien avoir eu possession les 15
choses terrienes. Del primier et del secont nos covient
or parler, car ci sunt or de present nostre frere, et ki
abbeit sunt si cum nos, ki sunt del nombre des prelaiz ; et
si sunt assi ci li moine ki sunt de l'ordene des penanz dont
nos mismes, qui abbeit sommes, ne nos doyens mies osteir, 20
si nos per aventure, qui jai nen avignet, nen avons dons
oblieit nostre profession por la grace de nostre office. Lo

227

tierz ordene, c'est de ceos ki en marïaige sunt, trescorrai ju
or briément, si cum ceos qui tant nen apartienent mies a
25 nos cum li altre. C'est cil ordenes ki a weit trespesset
ceste grant meir ; et cist ordenes est molt penevous et
perillous, et ki vait per molt longe voie, si cum cil ki nule
sente ne quierent ne nule adrece. En ceu appert bien ke
molt est perillouse lor voie, ke nos tant de gent i vëons
30 perir, dont nos dolor avons, et ke nos si poc i vëons de
ceos ki ensi trespessent cum mestiers seroit ; car molt est
griés chose d'eschuïr l'abysme des vices et les fossés des
criminals pechiez entre les ondes de cest seule, nomeyement or en cest tens ke li malices est si enforciez. Mais
35 li ordenes des continenz trespesset a pont, et nen est nuls
ki bien ne saichet ke ceste voie ne soit plus briés et plus
legiere et plus sëure. Mais ju larai or ester lo los, et si
materai avant les periz ki sunt en ceste voie ; car ceu valt
molt miez et si est plus utle chose. Droite est voirement,
40 chier frere, nostre sente et plus sëure de la voie des marïez ;
mais nen est mies totevoies sëure del tot. Trois periz at
en nostre sentier ; ou quant ancuens se welt ewïer per
aventure a un altre, ou quant il welt ayere raleir, ou esteir
el pont. Nule de cez trois choses ne puet soffrir li estrece
45 del pont et li estroite voie ke moinet a vie. Fuyons, chier
frere, lo peril de tenzon, ensi c'uns chascuns de nos preist
ensemble le prophete ke li piez d'orgoil ne nos vignet, car
lai chaürent cil ki font malvestiet. De celuy qui la main
at mis a la charrue et aprés se retornet ayere, est certe
50 chose qu'il apermenmes trabuchet et ke li mers cuevret son
chief. Cil mismes ki ester welt, ancor ne lacet il mies la
voie, cel covient il totevoies chaor per ceu qu'il ne welt esploitier, car cil ki aprés vont lo bottent et trabuchent.
Estroite est li voie, et cil qui esteir welt est a enscombre-
55 ment a ceos qui welent aleir avant et ki desirent esploitier.
De ceu est ceu ke li altre l'arguënt et reprennent et dïent
k'il soffrir ne puient la perece de sa tevor, cuy il assi cum
per uns awillons destraignent et bottent assi cum a lor
mains, ensi ke celui covient loquel ke soit esleire, c'est ou
60 esploitier ou del tot defaillir. Ne nos covient donkes mies
resteir et molt moens nos covient ancor rewardeir ayere

Map 229

ou nos ewïer as altres; mais mestiers nos est ke nos corriens et ke nos nos hastiens en tote humiliteit, ke cil ne
soit ancune fïeye trop eslonziez de nos qui fors est issuz si
cum giganz por corre la voye.   Si nos cestui assavorons et 65
nos adés lo mattons davant l'eswart de nostre cuer, dons
corrons nos ligierement et tost trait per son odour.   Ne
nen atroverunt mies trop estroite la sente del pont cil qui
par lei vorront corre.   De trois tisons est faite ceste sente,
por ceu ke li piet de ceos ki a lei se vorront apoier ne 70
puist glacier en la vie.   Li primiers est li poine del cors,
li seconz li povertez de la sostance del munde, li tierz li
obedïence d'umiliteit, car per maintes tribulatïons nos
covient entrer el regne de deu; et cil ki welent devenir
riche chieent ens temptatïons et el laz del dïaule; 75
et cil ki de deu se departit per inobedïence, repairet senz
dotte per obedïence a lui.   Et por ceu covient il ke cez
trois choses soyent ajointes ensemble, car li poine del cors
ne puet estre estaule entre les richesces, ne li obedïence
senz la poine ne puet mies estre ligierement discrete, et li 80
poverteiz en deleit ne puet estre estaule ne glorïouse.
Mais eswarde si tu perfeitement nen es delivreiz des periz
de ceste meir, quant cez choses sunt ateirïeies ensi cum
eles doyent estre, c'est lo cuvise de la char, et lo covise des
oylz et l'orgoil de vie.   Et dons seront eles a droit 85
ateirïeies si tu en la poine eschuïs l'impacïence, en la poverteit lo cuvise et en l'obedïence ta propre volenteit;
car cil qui murmurarent perirent per les serpenz, et cil qui
welent estre riche, il ne dist mies cil qui sunt riche, mais
cil kel welent estre, chieent el laz del dïaule. 90

FRAGMENT DU CHEVALIER À LA CHARRETTE, PAR MAP

(12ème siècle)

Atant son venu li chevalier jusqu'au pont: lors com-
mencent à plorer toz durement tuit ensemble.   Et Lanceloz lor demande porquoi il plorent et font tel duel ?   Et il

dient que c'est por l'amor de lui, que trop est perillox li
5 ponz.   Atant esgarde Lanceloz l'ève de çà et de là : si
voit que ele est noire et coranz.   Si avint que sa véue
torna devers la cité, si vit la tor où la raïne estoit as fenes-
tres.   Lanceloz demande quel vile c'est là ?—' Sire, font-il,
c'est le leus où la raïne est.'   Si li noment la cité.   Et li
10 lor dit : ' Or n'aiez garde de moi, que ge dout mains le pont
que ge onques mès ne fis, nè il n'est pas si périlleux d'assez
comme ge cuidoie.   Mès moult a de là outre bele tor, et
s'il m'i voloient hébergier il m'i auroient encor ennuit à
hoste.'   Lors descent et les conforte toz moult dure-
15 ment, et lor dit que il soient ausinc tout asséur comme
il est.

Il li lacent les pans de son hauberc ensenble et li cousent
à gros fil de fer qu'il avoient aporté, et ses manches méees-
mes li cousent dedenz ses mains, et les piez desoz ; et a
20 bone poiz chaude li ont péez les manicles et tant d'espès
comme il ot entre les cuisses.   Et ce fu por miaux tenir
contre le trenchant de l'espée.

Quant il orent Lancelot atorné et bien et bel si lor prie
que il s'en aillent.   Et il s'en vont, et le font naigier outre
25 l'ève, et il enmainent son cheval.   Et il vient à la planche
droit : puis esgarde vers la tor où la raïne estoit en prison,
si li encline.   Après fet le signe de la verroie croiz enmi
son vis, et met son escu derriers son dos, qu'il ne li nuise.
Lors se met desor la planche en chevauchons, si se traïne
30 par desus, si armez comme il estoit, car il ne li faut ne
hauberc ne espée ne chauces ne heaume ne escu.   Et cil
de la tor qui le véoient en sont tuit esbahï, ne il n'i a nul
ne nule qui saiche veroiement qui il est ; mès qu'il voient
qu'il traïne pardesus l'espée trenchant à la force des braz
35 et à l'enpaignement des genouz ; si ne remaint pas por les
filz de fer que des piez et des mains et des genous ne saille
li sanz.   Mès por cel péril de l'espée qui trenche et por
l'ève noire et bruiant et parfonde ne remaint que plus ne
resgart vers la tor que vers l'ève, ne plaie ne angoisse
40 qu'il ait ne prise naient ; car se il a cele tor pooit venir il
garroit tot maintenant de ses max.   Tant s'est hertiez et
traïnez qu'il est venuz jus qu'à terre.

LES AMBASSADEURS DES CROISÉS À VENISE, PAR GEOFFROY DE VILLEHARDOIN (1150-1213)

Li dux de Venise qui ot nom Henris Dandole, et ere
mult sages et mult prouz, si les honora mult, et il, et les
autres gens, et les virent mult volentiers; et quand ils
baillerent les lettres lor seignors, si se merveillerent mult
por quel affaire il erent venus en la terre. Les lettres **5**
erent de creance; et distrent li contes que autant les creist
en come lor cors, et tenroient fait ce que cis six feroient.
Et li dux lor respont: 'Seignors, je ai veues vos lettres,
bien avons queneu que vostre seignor sont li plus haut
home qui soient sans corone, et il nos mandent que nos **10**
creons ce que vos nos direz, et tenons ferme ce que vos
ferez. Or dites ce que vos plaira.'—Et li message respondirent: 'Sire, nos volons que vos aiez vostre conseil; et
devant vostre conseil nos vos dirons ce que nostre seignor
vos mandent, demain se il vos plaist.'—Et li duch lor **15**
respont que il lor requeroit respit al quart jor; et adonc
aroit son conseil ensemble, et porroient dire ce que il re-
queroient.

Il attendirent tres ci quart jor que il lor ot mis; il
entrerent el palais qui mult ere riches et biax, et troverent **20**
li duc et son conseil en une chambre: et distrent lor message en tel maniere: 'Sire, nos somes a toi venu de par
les hals barons de France qui ont pris le signe de la croiz
por la honte Jesu-Christ vengier, et por Jerusalem conquerre, se Diex le voelt soffrir. Et porce que il savent **25**
que nule genz n'ont si grant pooir come vos et la vostre
gent, vos prient por Dieux que vos aiez pitié de la terre
d'oltremer, et de la honte Jesu-Christ vengier, comment
ils puissent avoir navie et estoire.—En quel maniere? fait
li dux.—En totes les manieres, font li message, que vos lor **30**
saurez loer ne conseiller que il faire ne soffrir puissent.—
Certes, fait li dux, grant chose nos ont requise, et bien
semble que il béent à haut affaire; et nos vos en respon-
drons d'ici à huit jorz; et ne vos merveillez mie se li

35 termes est lons, car il convient mult penser à si grant
chose.'

Al termes que li dux lor mist, il revinrent el palais.
Totes les paroles qui là furent dites et retraites ne vos
puis mie reconter; mais la fin de la parole fut tels: 'Sei-
40 gnors, fait li dux, nos vos dirons ce que nos avons pris à
conseil, se nos y poons metre nostre grant conseil et le
commun de la terre que il ottroit, et vos vos conseilleroiz
se vos le pourroiz faire ne soffrir. Nos ferons vuissiers à
passer quatre mil et cinq cent chevaus, et neuf mille
45 escuyers, et ès nés quatre mil et cinq cent chevaliers, et
ving mille serjans à pié; et à toz ces chevaus et ces genz
iert telx la convenance que ils porteront viande a nuef mois.
Tant vos feromes al mains, en tel forme que on donra por
le cheval quatre mars et por li home deux; et totes ces
50 convenances que nos vos devisons, nos tendrons por un an,
dès le jor que nos departirons del port de Venise à faire le
servise Dieu et la chrestienté, en quelque leu que ce soit.
La somme de cest avoir qui ici est devant nommé, si monte
quatre-ving-cinq mille mars. Et tant feromes al mains que
55 nos metteromes cinquante galées par l'amour de Dieu, par
tel convenance que, tant com nostre compaignie durera, de
totes conquestes que nos feromes par mer ou par terre, la
moitié en aurons, et vos l'autre. Or, si vos conseillez, se
vos le porroiz faire ne soffrir.'

60   Li messages s'en vont et distrent que ils parleroient
ensemble et lor en respondront lendemain. Conseillerent
soi et parlerent ensemble celle nuit, et si s'accorderent al
faire; et lendemain vindrent devant le duc et distrent:
'Sire, nos sommes prest d'asseurer ceste convenance.' Et
65 li dux dist qu'il en parleroit à la soe gent, et ce que il tro-
veroit, il le lor feroit savoir. Lendemain al tierz jor,
manda li dux, qui mult ere sages et proz, son grant conseil,
et li conseilx ere de quarante homes des plus sages de la
terre. Par son sens et engin, que il avoit mult cler et
70 mult bon, les mist en ce que il loerent et volrent. Ensi
les mist, puis cent, puis deux cent, puis mil, tant que tuit le
creanterent et loerent. Puis en assembla ensemble bien dix
mil en la chapelle de Saint-Marc, la plus belle qui soit, et si

lor dist, que il oïssent messe del Saint-Esperit, et priassent
Dieu que il les conseillast de la requeste as messages que 75
il lor avoient faite, et il si firent mult volentiers.

Quant la messe fu dite, li dux manda par les messages, et
que ils requissent à tot le pueple humblement que il volsissent que celle convenance fust faite. Li messages vindrent
el mostier. Mult furent esgardé de mainte gent qui ne les 80
avoient ainsi mais veuz. Joffroy de Ville-Hardoin li
mareschaus de Champaigne monstra la parole por l'accort;
et par la volenté as autres messages lor dist: 'Seignor, li
barons de France li plus halt et li plus poestez nos ont à
vos envoiez; si vos crient merci, que il vos preigne pitiez 85
de Hierusalem qui est en servage des Turcs, que vos por
Dieu voilliez lor compaigner à la honte Jesu-Christ vengier; et por ce vos y ont eslis qui il sevent que nulles gens
n'ont si grant pooir, qui sor mer soient, come vos et la
vostre genz, et nos commanderent que nos vos enchaissiens 90
as piez, et que nos n'en leveissiens desque vos ariez otroyé
que vos ariez pitié de la Terre-Sainte d'outremer.'

Maintenant li six message s'agenoillerent à lor piez mult
plorant; et li dux et tuit li autre s'escrierent tuit à une
voix, et tendant lor mains en halt, et distrent: 'Nos 95
l'otroions, nos l'otroions!' Enki ot si grant bruit et si
grant noise, que il sembla que terre fondist.

SIÉGE DE GADRES, PAR LE MÊME AUTEUR

La velle de la saint Martin vindrent devant Gadres en
Esclavonie, si virent la cité fermee de halz murs et de
haltes torz, et pour noiant demandissiés plus bele ne plus
fort ne plus riche. Et quant li pelerin la virent, il se merveillerent mult et distrent li uns a l'autre 'coment porroit 5
estre prise tel vile par force, se diex meismes nel fait?'
Les premieres nés vindrent devant la vile et aëncrerent et
atendirent les autres et al matin fist mult bel jor et mult
cler, et vinrent les galies totes et li huissier et les autres
nés qui estoient arrieres, et pristrent le port par force et 10

rompirent la chaaine qui mult ere forz et bien atornee, et
descendirent a terre, si que li porz fu entr'aus et la vile.
Lor veïssiez maint chevalier et maint serjant issir des nés
et maint bon destrier traire des huissiers et maint riche
15 tref et maint pavellon.

Einsinc se loja l'oz et fu Gadres assegie le jor de la saint
Martin.   A cele foiz ne furent mie venu tuit li baron, car
encor n'ere mie venuz li marchis de Montferrat qui ere
remés arriere por afaire que il avoit.   Estiennes del Perche
20 fu remés malades en Venise et Mahis de Monmorenci, et
quant il furent gari, si s'en vint Mahis de Monmorenci
aprés l'ost a Gadrez ; mes Estienes del Perche ne le fist
mie si bien, quar il guerpi l'ost et s'en ala en Puille
sejorner.   Avec lui s'en ala Rotrox de Montfort et Ives de
25 la Ille et maint autre, qui mult en furent blasmé, et passerent au passage de marz en Surie.

L'endemain de la saint Martin issirent de cels de Gadres
et vindrent parler le duc de Venise que ere en son paveillon.   Et li distrent que il li rendroient la cité et totes les
30 lor choses sals lor cors en sa merci.   Et li dus dist qu'il
n'en prendroit mie cestui plet ne autre, se par le conseil
non as contes et as barons, et qu'il en iroit a els parler.

Endementiers que il ala parler as contes et as barons,
icele partie dont vos avez oï arrieres, qui voloient l'ost
35 depecier, parlerent as messages et lor distrent 'por quoi
volez vos rendre vostre cité ?   Li pelerin ne vos assaldront
mie ne d'aus n'avez vos garde, se vos vos poëz defendre
des Venisïens, dont estes vos quites.'   Et ensi pristrent un
d'aus meïsmes qui avoit non Robert de Bove, qui ala as
40 murs de la vile et lor dist ce meïsmes.   Ensi entrerent li
message en la vile et fu li plais remés.   Li dus de Venise
com il vint as contes et as barons, si lor dist 'seignor, ensi
voelent cil de la dedanz rendre la cité sals lors cors a ma
merci, ne je ne prendroie cestui plait ne autre se per voz
45 conseill non' et li baron li respondirent 'sire, nos vos loons
que vos le preigniez et si le vos priön.'   Et il dist que il
le feroit.   Et il s'en tornerent tuit ensemble al paveillon
le duc por le plait prendre, et troverent que li message s'en
furent alé par le conseil a cels qui voloient l'ost depecier.

E dont se dreça uns abes de Vals de l'ordre de Cistials, et 50
lor dist 'seignor, je vos deffent de par l'apostoile de Rome
que vos ne assailliez ceste cité, quar ele est de crestiens et
vos iestes pelerin.' Et quant ce oï li dus, si en fu mult
iriez et destroiz et dist as contes et as barons 'seignor, je
avoie de ceste vile plait a ma volonté, et vostre gent le 55
m'ont tolu et vos m'aviez convent que vos le m'aideriez a
conquerre, et je vos semoing que vos le façoiz.'

Maintenant li conte et li baron parlerent ensemble et cil
qui a la lor partie se tenoient, et distrent 'mult ont fait grant
oltrage cil qui ont cest plait desfet, et il ne fu onques jorz que 60
il ne meïssent paine a cest ost depecier ; or somes nos honi,
se nos ne l'aidons a prendre.' Et il vienent al duc et li
dïent 'sire, nos le vos aiderons a prendre por mal de cels
qui destorné l'ont.' Ensi fu li consels pris ; et al matin
alerent logier devant les portes de la vile, et si drecierent 65
lor perrieres et lor mangonials et lor autres engins dont il
avoient assez ; et devers la mer drecierent les eschieles
sors les nés. Lor commencierent a la vile a geter les
pieres as murz et as tors. Ensi dura cil asals bien par v
jors et lor si mistrent lors trenchëors a une tour, et cil 70
commencierent a trenchier le mur. Et quant cil dedenz
virent ce, si quistrent plait tot atretel com il l'avoient
refusé par le conseil a cels qui l'ost voloient depecier.

TRAITS DE LA VIE DE SAINT LOUIS, PAR JOINVILLE
(1224-1317)

Ce saint home ama Dieu de tout son cuer et ensuivi ses
œuvres ; et y apparut en ce que, aussi comme Dieu morut
pour l'amour que il avoit en son peuple, mist-il son cors en
avanture par pluseurs foiz pour l'amour que il avoit a son
peuple, et s'en feust bien soufers, se il voulsist, si comme 5
vous orrez ci-après. L'amour qu'il avoit à son peuple
parut à ce qu'il dit à son ainsné filz en une moult grant
maladie que il ot à Fonteinne-Bliaut : 'Biau filz, fist-il, je
te pri que tu te faces amer au peuple de ton royaume ; car

10 vraiement je ameraie miex que un Escot venist d'Escosse
et gouvernast le peuple du royaume bien et loialment, que
tu le gouvernasses mal apertement.' Le saint roy ama
tant vérité que neis aus Sarrazins ne voult-il pas mentir
de ce que il leur avoit en convenant. . . .

15 De la bouche fu-il si sobre, que onques jour de ma vie
je ne li oy deviser nulles viandes, aussi comme maint
richez hommes font ; ainçois manjoit pacientment ce que
ses queus li appareilloient et mettoit on devant li. En ses
paroles fu-il attrempez ; car onques jour de ma vie je ne li

20 oy mal dire de nullui, ne onques ne lui oy nommer le
dyable, lequel nous est bien espandu par le royaume : ce
que je croy que ne plait mie à Dieu. Son vin trempoit
par mesure, selonc ce qu'il véoit que le vin le pooit soufrir.
Il me demanda en Cypre pourquoy je ne metoie de l'yaue

25 en mon vin, et je li diz que ce me fesoient les phisiciens,
qui me disoient que j'avoie une grosse teste et une froide
fourcelle, et que je n'en avoie pooir de enyvrer. Et il me
dist que il me decevoient ; car, se je ne l'apprenoie en ma
joenesce, et je le vouloie temprer en ma vieillesce, les

30 goutes et les maladies de fourcelle me prenroient, que
jamez n'auroie santé ; et se je bevoie le vin tout pur en ma
vieillesce, je m'enyvreroie touz les soirs ; et ce estoit trop
laide chose de vaillant home de soy enyvrer. . . .

Il m'apela une foiz et me dist : ' Je n'ose parler à vous
35 pour le soutil senz dont vous estes, de chose qui touche à
Dieu ; et pour ce ai-je appelé ces frères qui ci sont, que je
vous weil faire une demande.' La demande fu tele :
'Seneschal, fist-il, quel chose est Dieu ?' Et je le diz :
'Sire, ce est si bone chose que meilleur ne peut estre.—

40 Vraiement, fist-il, c'est bien respondu que ceste response
que vous avez faite : est escripte en cest livre que je tieing
en ma main. Or vous demandé-je, fist-il, lequel vous
ameriés miex, ou que vous feussiés mesiaus, ou que vous
eussiés fait un pechié mortel ?' Et je, qui onques ne li

45 menti, li respondi que je en ameraie miex avoir fait trente,
que estre mesiaus. Et quand les frères s'en furent partis,
il m'appela tout seul, et me fist seoir à ses piez, et me dist :
'Comment me deistes-vous hier ce ?' Et je li diz que

encore li disoie-je, et il me dit : ʻVous deistes comme
hastis musarz, car nulle si laide mezelerie n'est comme 50
d'estre en pechié mortel, pour ce que l'ame qui est en
pechié mortel est semblable au dyable : par quoy nulle si
laide mezelerie ne peut estre . . .ʼ

Il me demanda si je lavoie les piez aux povres le jour
du grant jeudi : ʻSire, dis-je, en maleur ! les piez de ces 55
vilains ne laverai-je jà.   Vraiement, fist-il, ce fu mal dit ;
car vous ne devez mie avoir en desdaing ce que Dieu fist
pour nostre enseignement.   Si vous pri-je pour l'amour de
Dieu, premier, et pour l'amour de moy, que vous les acous-
tumez à laver . . .ʼ   60

Maintes foiz avint que en esté il se alloit seoir au boiz
de Vinciennes après sa messe, et se acostoioit à un chesne
et nous fesoit seoir entour li ; et touz ceulz qui avoient
afaire venoient parler à li, sanz destourbier de huissier ne
d'autre.   Et lors il leur demandoit de sa bouche : ʻA-yl 65
ci nullui qui ait partie ?ʼ   Et cil se levoient qui partie
avoient, et lors il disoit : ʻTaisiéz-vous touz, et en vous
deliverra l'un après l'autre.ʼ   Et lors il appeloit monseigneur
Pierre de Fonteinnes et monseigneur Geffroy de Villete, et
disoit à l'un d'eulz : ʻDelivrez-moy ceste partie.ʼ   Et quand 70
il véoit aucune chose à amender en la parole de ceulz qui
parloient pour luy, ou en la parolle de ceulz qui parloient
pour autrui, il-meismes l'amendoit de sa bouche . . .

Il me conta que il ot une grant desputaison de clers et
de Juis ou moustier de Clygni.   Là ot un chevalier à qui 75
l'abbé avoit donné le pain léens pour Dieu, et requist à
l'abbé que il li lessast dire la première parole ; et en li
otria à peinne.   Et lors il se leva et s'apuia sus sa croce,
et dit que l'en li feist venir le plus grant clerc, et le plus
grant mestre des Juis ; et si firent-il ; et li fist une demande 80
qui fu tele : ʻMestre, fist le chevalier, je vous demande se
vous créez que la Vierge Marie, qui Dieu porta en ses flans et
en ses bras, enfantast vierge, et que elle soit mère de Dieu.ʼ
Et le Juif respondi que de tout ce ne créoit-il riens.   Et le
chevalier li respondi que moult avoit fait que fol, quand il 85
ne la créoit ne ne l'amoit, et estoit entré en son moustier
et en sa meson.   ʻEt vraiement, fist le chevalier, vous le

comparrez.' Et lors il hauça sa potence et feri le Juif lès
l'oye et le porta par terre. Et les Juis tournèrent en fuie
90 et enportèrent leur mestre tout blecié; et ainsi demoura
la desputaison. Lors vint l'abbé au chevalier, et li dist
que il avoit fait grant folie. Et le chevalier dit que encore
avoit-il fait greingneur folie, d'assembler tele desputaison;
car avant que la desputaison feust menée à fin, avoit-il
95 céans grant foison de bons crestiens, qui s'en feussent parti
touz mescréanz, par ce que il n'eussent mie bien entendu
les Juis. 'Aussi vous di-je, fist li roys, que nulz, se il
n'est très-bon clerc, ne doit desputer à eulz; mès l'omme
lay, quant il ot mes-dire de la lay crestienne, ne doit pas
100 desfendre la lay crestienne, ne mais de l'espée, de quoy il
doit donner parmi le ventre dedens, tant comme elle y
y peut entrer . . .'
    Je le revi une autre foiz à Paris, là où touz les prelaz
de France le mandèrent que il vouloient parler à li, et le
105 roy ala ou palaiz pour eulz oïr. Et là estoit l'evesque Gui
d'Ausserre, qui fu fuiz monseigneur Guillaume de Mello,
et dit au roy pour touz les prelaz en tel manière: 'Sire, ces
seigneurs qui ci sont, arcevesques, evesques, m'ont dit que je
vous deisse que la crestienté se perit entre vos mains.' Le
110 roy se seigna et dist: 'Or me dites comment ce est.—Sire,
fist-il, c'est pour ce que en prise si pou les excommenie-
mens hui et le jour, que avant se lessent les gens mourir
excommeniés, que il se facent absodre, et ne veulent faire
satisfaccion à l'Esglise. Si vous requièrent, sire, pour
115 Dieu et pour ce que faire le devez, que vous commandez à
vos prevoz et à vos baillifz que touz ceulz qui se souffer-
ront escommeniez an et jour, que en les contreingne par
la prise de leur biens à ce que ils se facent absoudre.' A
ce respondi le roys que il leur commanderoit volentiers de
120 touz ceulz dont en le feroit certain que il eussent tort. Et
l'evesque dit que il ne le feroient à nul feur, que il li des-
viassent la court de leur cause. Et le roy li dist que il ne
le feroit autrement; car ce seroit contre Dieu et contre
raison, se il contreignoit la gent à eulz absoudre, quand
125 les clercs leur feroient tort. 'Et de ce, fist le roy, vous en
doins-je un exemple du conte de Bretaigne, qui a plaidé

sept ans aus prelaz de Bretaingne tout excommenié; et
tant a esploitié que l'apostole les a condempnez touz. Dont
se je eusse contraint le conte de Bretaingne la première
année de li faire absoudre, je me feusse meffait envers 130
Dieu et vers li.' Et lors se soufrirent les prelaz; ne
onques puis n'en oy parler que demande feust faite des
choses desus dites.

Aventure sur Mer, par le même auteur

Au mois d'aoust entrames en nos neis a la Roche de
Marseille: a celle journee que nous entrames en nos neis,
fist l'on ouvrir la porte de la nef, et mist l'on touz nos
chevaus ens, que nous deviens mener outre mer; et puis
reclost l'on la porte et l'enboucha l'on bien, aussi comme   5
l'on naye un tonnel, pour ce que, quant la neis est en la
grant mer, toute la porte est en l'yaue.   Quant li cheval
furent ens, nostre maistres notonniers escrïa a ses notonniers qui estoient ou bec de la nef et lour dist 'est aree
vostre besoingne?' et il respondirent 'oïl, sire, vieingnent 10
avant clerc et li provere.'   Maintenant que il furent venu,
il lour escrïa 'chantez de par dieu'; et il s'escrïerent tuit a
une voiz '*veni creator spiritus.*' Et il escrïa a ses notonniers
'faites voile de par dieu'; et il si firent.   Et en brief tens
li venz se feri ou voile et nous ot tolu la vëue de la terre, 15
que nous ne veïsmes que ciel et yaue: et chascun jour
nous esloigna li venz des païs ou nous avions estei neiz.
Et ces choses vous moustre je que cil est bien fol hardis,
qui se ose mettre en tel peril atout autrui chatel ou en
pechié mortel; car l'on se dort le soir la ou on ne set se   20
l'on se trouvera ou font de la mer au matin.

En la mer nous avint une fiere merveille, que nous
trouvames une montaigne toute ronde qui estoit devant
Barbarie.   Nous la trouvames entour l'eure de vespres et
najames tout le soir, et cuidames bien avoir fait plus de 25
cinquante lieues, et lendemain nous nous trouvames devant
icelle meïsmes montaigne; et ainsi nous avint par dous
foiz ou par trois.   Quant li marinnier virent ce, il furent

tuit esbahi et nous distrent que nos neis estoient en grant
30 peril : car nous estiens devant la terre aus Sarrazins de
Barbarie. Lors nous dist uns preudom prestres que on
appeloit doyen de Malrut, car il n'ot onques persecucïon
en paroisse, ne par defaut d'yaue ne de trop pluie ne
d'autre, que aussi tost comme il avoit fait trois processïons
35 par trois samedis, que diex et sa mere ne le delivrassent.
Samedis estoit : nous feïsmes la premiere processïon entour
les dous maz de la nef, je meïsmes m'i fiz porter par les
braz, pour ce que je estoie grief malades. Onques puis
nous ne veïsmes la montaigne, et venimes en Cypre le
40 tiers samedi.

Fragment d'Aucassin et Nicolette

(13ème *siècle*)

Aucassins fu mis en prison si com vos avés oï et
entendu, et Nicolete fu d'autre part en le canbre. Ce fu el
tans d'esté, el mois de mai, que li jor sont caut, lonc et
cler, et les nuis coies et series. Nicolete jut une nuit en
5 son lit, si vit la lune luire cler par une fenestre, et si oï le
lorseilnol center en garding, se li sovint d'Aucassin sen
ami qu'ele tant amoit. Ele se comença a porpenser del
conte Garin de Biaucaire qui de mort le haoit ; si se pensa
qu'ele ne remanroit plus ilec, que s'ele estoit acusee et li
10 quens Garins le savoit, il le feroit de male mort morir.
Ele senti que li vielle dormoit qui aveuc li estoit. Ele se
leva, si vesti un blïaut de drap de soie que ele avoit mout
bon ; si prist dras de lit et touailes, si noua l'un a l'autre,
si fist une corde si longe come ele pot, si le noua au piler
15 de le fenestre, si s'avala contreval el gardin, et prist se
vesture a l'une main devant et a l'autre deriere ; si s'escorça
por le rousee qu'ele vit grande sor l'erbe, si s'en ala aval
le gardin. Ele avoit les caviaus blons et menus recercelés,
et les ex vairs et rïans, et le face traitice et le nés haut et
20 bien assis, et les levretes vremelletes plus que n'est cerisse
ne rose el tans d'esté, et les dens blans et menus, et avoit

les mameletes dures qui li souslevoient sa vestëure ausi con
se fuissent II nois gauges, et estoit graille parmi les flans,
qu'en vos dex mains le pëusciés enclorre; et les flors des
margerites, qu'ele ronpoit as ortex de ses piés, qui li 25
gissoient sor le menuisse du pié par deseure, estoient
droites noires avers ses piés et ses ganbes, tant par estoit
blance la mescinete. Ele vint au postiç; si le deffrema,
si s'en isci par mi les rues de Biaucaire par devers l'onbre,
car la lune luisoit mout clere, et erra tant qu'ele vint a le 30
tor u ses amis estoit. Li tors estoit faëlé de lius en lius,
et ele se quatist delés l'un des pilers. Si s'estraint en son
mantel, si mist sen cief par mi une crevëure de la tor qui
vielle estoit et anciienne, si oï Aucassin qui la dedens
plouroit et fasoit mot grant dol et regretoit se douce amie 35
que tant amoit. Et quant ele l'ot assés escouté, si
comença a dire.

DÉLIVRANCE DE CALAIS, PAR FROISSART (1337-1410)

Après le departement du roy de France et de son ost du
mont de Sangates ceulx de Calais veirent bien que leur
secour estoit failly, dont ilz estoient en si grant douleur et
destresse que le plus fort se povoit a peine soustenir. Lors
ilz prierent tant monseigneur Iehan de Vienne leur cappi- 5
taine quil monta aux carneaulx des murs de la ville : et fist
signe a ceulx de dehors quil vouloit parler a eulx. Quant
le roy d'Angleterre ouyt ces nouvelles il y envoya monseigneur Gaultier de Manny et messire Basset. Quant ilz
furent la monseigneur Iehan de Vienne leur dist : Chiers 10
seigneurs vous estes moult vaillans chevaliers en fait darmes
et scavez que le roy de France que nous tenons a seigneur
nous a ceans envoyés, et commanda que nous gardissions
ceste ville et chastel si que blasme nen eussions et luy nul
dommaige, nous en avons fait nostre povoir. Or est nostre 15
secours failly et nous si estrains que nous navons de quoy
vivre, si nous conviendra tous mourir ou enrager de famine
si le gentil roy vostre seigneur na mercy de nous. Laquelle

Q

chose luy vueillez prier en pitié et quil nous vueille laisser
20 aller tout ainsi que nous sommes, et vueille prendre la ville
et le chastel et tout lavoir qui est dedans, si en trouvera
assez.   A ce respondit messire Gaultier de Manny et dist.
Iehan nous scavons partie de lintencion monseigneur le roy,
car il nous la dit.   Saichez que ce nest mye son entente que
25 vous en puissiez aller ainsi, ains est son intencion que vous
mettez tous a sa pure voulente, ou pour ranconner ceulx
quil luy plaira, ou pour faire mourir, car ceulx de Calais
luy ont tant fait de contrarietez et de despitz, le sien ont
fait despendre et grant foison de ses gens mourir que cest
30 ung nombre.   Monseigneur Iehan de Vienne dist.   Ce seroit
trop dure chose pour nous.   Nous sommes ceans ung petit
de chevaliers et escuyers qui loyaulment avons servy le roy
de France nostre souverain sire, si comme vous feriez le
vostre en pareil semblable cas.   Et avons endure maint
35 mal et mesaise.   Mais aincois souffrerons encores plus de
peine que oncques gens darmes ne souffrirent la pareille
que nous consentissions que le plus petit garcon de la ville
eust autre mal que le plus grant de nous, mais nous vous
prions que par vostre humilite veuillez aller par devers le
40 roy dAngleterre et luy prier quil ait pitie de nous ; si ferez
courtoisie, car nous esperons en luy tant de gentillesse que
a la grace de Dieu son propos se changera.   Monseigneur
Gaultier et monseigneur Basset retournerent devers le roy
et lui recorderent ce que dit est.   Et le roy dist quil navoit
45 voulente de faire autrement, fors quilz se rendissent simplement a son vouloir, messire Gaultier dist, monseigneur vous
pourrez bien avoir tort, car vous nous donnez tres mauvais
exemple.   Si vous nous envoyes en aucune de vos forteresses
nous nirons mye si voulentiers si vous faictes ces gens
50 mettre a mort, car ainsi feroit on de nous par semblable cas.
Les parolles aiderent a soustenir plusieurs barons qui la
estoient.   Si dist le roy dAngleterre.   Seigneurs ie ne
vueil mye estre tout seul contre vous tous, sire Gaultier
vous direz au cappitaine de Calais que la plus grant grace
55 quil pourra trouver en moy, cest quilz se partent de la
ville six des plus notables bourgeois les chiefz tous nudz
et tous deschaussez les hars au col et les clefz de la ville et

du chastel eu leurs mains et de ceulx ie feray a ma voulente,
et le remanant ie prendrai a mercy.

A tant revint monseigneur Gaultier a monseigneur Iehan 60
qui l'attendoit sur les murs, si luy dist tout ce quil avoit
peu faire au roy. Je vous prie dist monseigneur Iehan quil
vous plaise cy demourer tant que iaye tout cestuy affaire
remonstre a la communaulte de la ville, car ilz mont cy
envoye, et a eulx en tient, ce mest advis, den respondre. 65
Lors messire Iehan vint au marche, et fist sonner la cloche,
si assemblerent tantost en la halle hommes et femmes de
la ville. Si leur fist messire Iehan rapport des parolles ci
devant recitees et leur dist bien que autrement ne povoit
estre et sur ce eussent advis et briefve responce. Lors 70
commencerent a plorer toutes manieres de gens et a demener
lel dueil quil nest si dur cueur qui les veist quil nen eust
pitié. Et mesmement messire Iehan et lermoioit tendrement. Apres se leva le plus riche bourgeois de la ville que
on appeloit messire Eustace de sainct Pierre lequel dist 75
devant tous. Seigneurs grans et petits grand meschief
seroit de laisser mourir ung tel peuple qui cy est par
famine ou autrement quant on y peut trouver aucun moyen
et feroit grant aulmosne et grace envers nostre Seigneur
qui de tel meschief les pourroit garder. Jay endroit moy 80
si grant esperance davoir pardon envers nostre Seigneur se
ie meurs pour ce peuple sauver que ie vueil estre le premier.
Quant sire Eustace eut ce dit chascun le alla odorer de pitie
et plusieurs se gettoient a ses piedz en pleurs et en profons
soupirs. Secondement ung autre tres honneste bourgeois 85
et de grant affaire se leva et dist quil feroit compaignie a
son compere sire Eustace, si appelloit on cestuy sire Iehan
d'Aire. Après se leva Iaques de Visant qui estoit moult
riche de meubles et de heritaiges et dist quil tiendroit compaignie a ses deux cousins, Ainsi fit Pierre Visant son 90
frere, et puis le Vme et le VIe, lesquelz se atournerent ainsi
que le roy avoit dit. Et adonc monseigneur Iehan monta
sur une petite hacquenee, car a grant malaise pouvoit il
aller a pied, et les mena devers la porte. Lors fut grant
dueil des hommes, des femmes, des enfans, des larmes et 95
souspirs. Et ainsi vindrent iusques a la porte que messire

Iehan fit ouvrir, et se fist enclorre dehors avecques les six
bourgeois entre les portes et les barrieres. Si dist a monseigneur Gaultier de Manny qui le attendoit la. Je vous
100 delivre comme cappitaine de Calais par le consentement
du povre peuple de ceste ville ces six bourgeois. Et ie
vous iure que ce sont et estoient au iourdhuy les plus hon-
norables et notables de corps, de chevance et de bourgeoisie
de la ville de Calais. Si vous prie gentil sire que vous
105 vueillez prier le roy pour eulx quilz ne meurent pas. Je
ne scais dist messire Gaultier que monseigneur le roy en
vouldra faire, mais ien feray mon povoir. Lors fut la
barriere ouverte, si allerent ces six bourgeois devers le
palais du roy et messire Iehan rentra en la ville. Quant
110 messire Gaultier eut presente ces six bourgeois au roy ilz
sagenouillerent et dirent a joinctes mains. Gentil sire roy
veez nous icy six qui avons este bourgeois de Calais et
grans marchans, si vous apportons les clefz de la ville et
du chastel et nous mettons en vostre pure voulente pour
115 sauver le remanent du peuple de Calais qui a souffert moult
de griefz. Si vueillez avoir pitie et mercy de nous par
vostre haulte noblesse. Lors plorerent de pitie les contes,
barons, chevaliers et autres qui illec estoient assemblez a
grant nombre. Le roy regarda sur eulx tres despitement.
120 Car moult hayoit le peuple de Calais pour les grans contrarietez et dommaiges que le temps passe sur mer luy
avoient fait, si commanda que on leur trenchast les testes.
Tous prioient au roy si acertes quilz povoient quil en
voullist avoir mercy, mais il ny vouloit entendre. Lors
125 messire Gaultier de Manny dist. Haa gentil sire vueillez
refrener vostre couraige, vous avez la renommee de souve-
raine noblesse. Or ne vueillez faire chose par quoy elle
soit amendrie ne que on puisse parler sur vous en nulle
vilennie; toutes gens diroient que ce seroit cruaulte si vous
130 faisiez mourir si honnestes bourgeois qui de leur voulente
se sont mis en vostre mercy pour les autres sauver. Adonc
grigna le roy et dist, soit fait venir le couppe teste, ceulx
de Calais ont fait mourir tant de mes hommes que il convient ceulx cy mourir aussi. Adonc la royne qui estoit
135 moult enceinte se mist a genoulz en plorant et dist. Ha

gentil sire puis que ie repassay la mer en grant peril ie ne
vous ay riens requis. Or vous prie humblement en don
que pour le filz saincte Marie et pour lamour de moy vous
vueillez auoir de ces six hommes mercy. Le roy la regarda
et se teut une piece, puis dist, ha dame ie aymasse mieulx 140
que vous fussiez autre part que cy, vous me priez si acertes
que ie ne vous puis esconduire, si les vous donne a vostre
plaisir. Lors la royne amena ces six bourgeois en sa
chambre, si leur fist oster les chevestres dentour le col, et
les fist revestir et disner tout a leur aise, puis donna a 145
chascun six nobles et les fist conduire hors de lost a
sauvete.

BATAILLE DE COURTRAI, PAR LE MÊME AUTEUR

Je fuis adont infourmé par le seigneur d'Estonnevort, et
me dist que il vey, et aussi firent plusieurs, quant l'oriflambe fut desploiee et la bruïne se cheÿ, ung blanc coulon
voller et faire plusieurs volz par dessus la baniere du roy;
et quant il eut assez volé, et que on se deubt combatre et 5
assambler aux ennemis, il se print a séoir sur l'une des
bannieres du roy; dont on tint ce a grant signiffïance de
bien. Or approchierent les Flamens et commenchierent a
jetter et a traire de bombardes et de canons et de gros
quarreaulx empenez d'arain; ainsi se commença la bataille. 10
Et en ot le roy de France et ses gens le premier encontre,
qui leur fut moult dur; car ces Flamens, qui descendoient
orgueilleusement et de grant voulenté, venoient roit et dur,
et boutoient en venant de l'espaule et de la poitrine ainsi
comme senglers tous foursenez, et estoient si fort entre- 15
lachiés tous ensemble qu'on ne les povoit ouvrir ne desrompre. La fuirent du costé des François par le trait des
canons, des bombardes et des arbalestres premierement
mort: le seigneur de Waurin, baneret, Morelet de Halwin
et Jacques d'Erc. Et adont fut la bataille du roy reculee; 20
mais l'avantgarde et l'arrieregarde a deux lez passerent
oultre et enclouïrent ces Flamens, et les misrent a l'estroit.

Je vous diray comment sur ces deux eles gens d'armes les
commencierent a pousser de leurs roides lances a longs fers
25 et durs de Bourdeaulx, qui leur passoient ces cottes de
maille tout oultre et les perchoient en char ; dont ceulx qui
estoient attains et navrez de ces fers se restraindoient pour
eschiever les horïons : car jamais ou amender le peuïssent
ne se boutoient avant pour eulx faire destruire. La les
30 misrent ces gens d'armes a tel destroit qu'ilz ne se sçavoient
ne povoient aidier ne ravoir leurs bras ne leurs planchons
pour ferir ne eulz deffendre. La perdoient les plusieurs
force et alaine, et la tresbuchoient l'un sur l'autre, et se
estindoient et moroient sans coup ferir. La fut Phelippe
35 d'Artevelle encloz et pousé de glaive et abatu, et gens de
Gand qui l'amoient et gardoient grant plenté atterrez
entour luy. Quant le page dudit Phelippe vey la mesad-
venture venir sur les leurs, il estoit bien monté sur bon
coursier, si se party et laissa son maistre, car il ne le
40 pouvoit aidier ; et retourna vers Courtray pour revenir a
Gand.

(A)insi fut faitte et assamblee celle bataille ; et lors que
des deux costez les Flamens furent astrains et encloz, ilz
ne passerent plus avant, car ilz ne se povoient aidier.
45 Adont se remist la bataille du roy en vigeur, qui avoit de
commencement ung petit branslé. La entendoient gens
d'armes a abatre Flamens en grant nombre, et avoient les
plusieurs haches acerees, dont ilz rompoient ces bachinets
et eschervelloient testes ; et les aucuns plommees, dont ilz
50 donnoient si grans horrïons, qu'ilz les abatoient a terre.
A paines estoient Flamens chëuz, quant pillars venoient
qui entre les gens d'armes se boutoient et portoient grandes
coutilles, dont ilz les partuoient ; ne nulle pitié n'en avoient
non plus que se ce fuissent chiens. La estoit le clicquetis
55 sur ces bacinets si grant et si hault, d'espees, de haches, et
de plommees, que l'en n'y ouoit goutte pour la noise. Et
onÿ dire que, se tous les heaumiers de Paris et de Broux-
elles estoient ensemble, leur mestier faisant, ilz n'euïssent
pas fait si grant noise comme faisoient les combatans et
60 les ferans sur ces testes et sur ces bachinets. La ne s'es-
pargnoient point chevalliers ne escuïers, ainchois mettoient

la main a l'euvre par grant voulenté, et plus les ungs que les autres ; si en y ot aucuns qui s'avancerent et bouterent en la presse trop avant ; car ilz y furent encloz et estains, et par especïal messire Loÿs de Cousant, ung chevallier de 65 Berry, et messire Fleton de Revel, filz au seigneur de Revel ; mais encoires en y eut des autres, dont ce fut dommage : mais si grosse bataille, dont celle la fut, ou tant avoit de pueple, ne se povoit parfurnir et au mieulx venir pour les victorïens, que elle ne couste grandement. Car 70 jennes chevalliers et escuïers qui desirent les armes se avancent voulentiers pour leur honneur et pour acquerre loënge ; et la presse estoit la si grande et le dangier si perilleux pour ceulx qui estoient enclos ou abatus, que se on n'avoit trop bonne ayde, on ne se povoit relever. Par 75 ce party y eut des François mors et estains aucuns ; mais plenté ne fut ce mie ; car quant il venoit a point, ilz aidoient l'un l'autre. La eut ung molt grant nombre de Flamens occis, dont les tas des mors estoient haulx et longs ou la bataille avoit esté ; on ne vey jamais si peu de 80 sang yssir a tant de mors.

Quant les Flamens qui estoient derriere veirent que ceulx devant fondoient et chëoient l'un sus l'autre et que ilz estoient tous desconfis, ilz s'esbahirent et jetterent leurs plançons par terre et leurs armures et se misrent a la 85 fuitte vers Courtray et ailleurs. Ilz n'avoient cure que pour eulx mettre a sauveté. Et Franchois et Bretons aprés, quy les chassoient en fossez et en buissons, en aunois et en marés et bruieres, cy dix, cy vingt, cy trente, et la les recombatoient de rechief, et la les occïoient, se ilz 90 n'estoient les plus fors. Si en y ent ung moult grant nombre de mors en la chace entre le lieu de la bataille et Courtray, ou ilz se retraioient a saulf garant. Ceste bataille advint sur le Mont d'Or entre Courtray et Rosebeque en l'an de grace nostre seigneur, mil iij^c iiij^{xx}. et II., le jeudi 95 devant le samedi de l'advent, le xxvij^e. jour de novembre, et estoit pour lors le roy Charles de France ou xiiij^e. an de son ëage.

LES DERNIERS JOURS DE LOUIS XI., PAR PHILIPPE DE COMMINES (1447-1509)

Quelques cinq ou six mois devant cette mort, il avoit suspicion de tous hommes, et specialement de tous ceux qui
estoient dignes d'avoir authorité. Il avoit crainte de son
fils, et le faisoit estroitement garder : ne nul homme ne le
5 voyoit, ne parloit à luy, sinon par son commandement.   Il
avoit doute à la fin de sa fille, et de son gendre, à present
Duc de *Bourbon,* et vouloit sçavoir quelles gens entroyent
au *Plessis* quand et eux.   A la fin, rompit un conseil, que
le Duc de *Bourbon,* son gendre, tenoit leans par son com-
10 mandement.   A l'heure que sondit gendre, et le Comte de
Dunois revinrent de remener l'Ambassade, qui estoit venuë
aux nopces du Roy son fils, et de la Reyne, à *Amboise,* et
qu'ils retournerent au *Plessis,* et entrerent beaucoup de gens
avec eux, ledit Seigneur qui fort faisoit garder les portes,
15 estant en le galerie, qui regarde en la cour dudit *Plessis,*
fit appeler un de ses Capitaines des Gardes, et luy commanda
aller taster aux gens des Seigneurs dessus dits, voir s'ils
n'avoyent point de Brigandines sous leurs robes, et qu'il le
fit comme en devisant eux, sans trop en faire de semblant.
20 Or regardez pour avoir fait beaucoup vivre des gens en suspicion et crainte sous luy, s'il en estoit bien payé, et de quelles
gens il pouvoit avoir seureté, puis que de son fils, fille, et
gendre il avoit suspicion. Je ne dis point pour luy seulement
mais pour tous autres Seigneurs, qui desirent estre craints,
25 jamais ne se sentent de la revanche, jusques à la vieillesse :
car pour la penitence ils craignent tout homme.   Et
quelle douleur estoit à ce Roy d'avoir cette peur et ces
passions ?
Il avoit son Medecin, appelé maistre Jacques *Coctier,* à
30 qui en cinq mois il donna cinquante quatre mille Escus con-
tans (qui estoit à la raison de dix mil escus pour mois, et
quatre mille par dessus) et l'Evesché d'*Amiens* pour son
neveu, et autres offices et terres pour luy, et pour ses amis.
Ledit Medecin luy estoit si tres-rude que l'on ne diroit point
35 à un valet les outrageuses et rudes parolles, qu'il luy disoit,

et si le craignoit tant ledit Seigneur, qu'il ne l'eut osé envoyer hors d'avec luy, et si s'en plaignoit à ceux à qui il en
parloit, mais il ne l'eut osé changer, comme il faisoit tous
autres serviteurs, pource que ledit Medecin luy disoit
audacieusement ces mots : *Je sçay bien qu'un matin vous* 40
m'envoyerez comme vous faites d'autres : mais (par un grand
serment qu'il juroit) *vous ne vivrez point huict jours après.*
Ces mot l'espouvantoit fort, et tant qu'après ne le faisoit
que flater, et luy donner, qui luy estoit un grand Purgatoire
en ce monde, veu la grande obeïssance qu'il avoit euë de 45
tant de gens de bien, et de grands hommes.

Il est vray qu'il avoit fait de rigoureuses prisons, commes
cages de fer, et autres de bois, couvertes de pates de fer par
le dehors, et par le dedans, avec terribles fermures de
quelques huict pieds de large, de la hauteur d'un homme, et 50
un pied plus.   Le premier qui les devisa, fut l'Evesque de
Verdun, qui en la premiere qui fut faite, fut mis incontinent,
et y a couché quatorze ans.   Plusieurs depuis l'ont maudit,
et moy aussi, qui en ay tasté, sous le Roy de present, huict
mois.   Autrefois avoit fait faire à des *Allemans* des fers 55
tres-pesans et terribles, pour mettre aux pieds, et y estoit
un anneau, pour mettre au pied, fort malaisé à ouvrir,
comme à un Carquan, la chaine grosse et pesante, et une
grosse boule de fer au bout, beaucoup plus pesante que
n'estoit de raison, et les appeloit-l'on *les Fillettes du Roy.* 60
Toutesfois j'ay veu beaucoup de gens de bien prisonniers les
avoir aux pieds, qui depuis en sont saillis à grand honneur,
et qui depuis ont eu de grands bien de luy . . .

Ledit Seigneur, vers la fin de ses jours, fit clorre, tout à
l'entour, sa maison du *Plessis-lez-Tours,* de gros barreaux de 65
fer, en forme de grosses grilles, et aux quatre coins de sa
maison, quatre moineaux de fer, bons, grands, et espais.
Lesdites grilles estoient contre le mur, du costé de la place,
de l'autre part du fossé : car il estoit à fonds de cuve, et y
fit mettre plusieurs broches de fer, massonnées au dedans le 70
mur, qui avoient chacune trois ou quatre points, et les fit
mettre fort près l'une de l'autre.   Et davantage ordonna
dix Arbalestriers, dedans lesdits fossés, pour tirer à ceux
qui en approcheroient, avant que la porte fut ouverte, et

75 entendoit qu'ils couchassent ausdits fossez, et se retirassent
aus dits moineaux de fer. Il entendoit bien que cette
fortification ne suffisoit pas contre grand nombre de gens,
ne contre une armée : mais de cela il n'avoit point de peur,
seulement craignoit-il que quelque Seigneur, ou plusieurs,
80 ne fissent une entreprise de prendre la place de nuict, demy
par amour, et demy par force, avec quelque peu d'intelligence, et que ceux-là prissent l'authorité, et le fissent vivre
comme homme sans sens, et indigne de gouverner. La
porte du *Plessis* ne s'ouvroit, qu'il ne fut huict heures du
85 matin, ny ne baissoit on le pont jusques à ladite heure, et
lors y entroient les Officiers, et les Capitaines des gardes
mettoient les portiers ordinaires ; et puis ordonnoient leur
guet d'Archers, tant à la porte que parmy la cour, comme
en une place de frontiere estroitement gardée : et n'y en-
90 troit nul que par le guichet, et que ce ne fut du sceu du
Roy, excepté quelque Maistre-d'hostel, et gens de cette
sorte, qui n'alloient point devers luy. Est-il donques possi- ↙
ble de tenir un Roy pour le garder, plus honnestement, et
en plus estroite prison, que luy mesmes se tenoit ? Les
95 cages où il avoit tenu les autres, avoient quelques huict
pieds en carré, et luy qui estoit si grand Roy, avoit une
petite cour de Chasteau à se pourmener, encore n'y venoit-
il gueres : mais se tenoit en la galerie, sans partir de là,
sinon par les chambres, et alloit à la messe, sans passer par
100 ladite cour. Voudroit-l'on dire que ce Roy ne souffrit pas
aussi bien que les autres ? qui ainsi s'enfermoit, qui se
faisoit garder, qui estoit ainsi en peur de ses enfans, et de
tous ses prochains parens, et qui changeoit et muoit de jour
en jour ses serviteurs qu'il avoit nourris, et qui ne tenoient
105 bien ne honneur que de luy, tellement qu'en nul d'eux ne
s'osoit fier, et s'enchainoit ainsi de si estranges chaines et clos-
tures. Si le lieu estoit plus grand que d'une prison commune,
aussi estoit-il plus grand que prisonniers communs.
. . . . De nostre Roy
110 j'ay esperance (comme j'ay dit) que nostre Seigneur ait eu
misericorde de luy, et aussi aura-il des autres, s'il luy plaist.
Mais à parler naturellement (comme homme qui n'a aucune
literature, mais quelque peu d'expérience et sens naturel)

n'eut-il point mieux valu à eux, et à tous autres Princes, et
hommes de moyen estat, qui ont vescu sous ces Grands, et 115
vivront sous ceux qui regnent, eslire le moyen chemin en
ces choses ?   C'est à sçavoir moins se soucier, et moins se
travailler, et entreprendre moins de choses, et plus craindre
d'offenser Dieu, et à persecuter le peuple, et leurs voisins,
et par tant de voyes cruelles, que j'ay assez déclarées par 120
cydevant, et prendre des aises et plaisirs honnestes ?
Leurs vies en seroient plus longues.   Les maladies en
viendroient plus tard, et leur mort en seroit plus regrettée,
et de plus de gens, et moins desirée, et auroient moins à
douter la mort.   125

Fragment du Curial d'Alain Chartier

(15ème *siècle*)

La court, affin que tu l'entendes, est ung couvent de gens
qui soubz faintise du bien commun sont assemblez pour
eulx interrompre ; car il n'y a gueres de gens qui ne ven-
dent, achaptent ou eschangent aucunes foiz leurs rentes ou
leurs propres vestemens ; car entre nous de la court nous   5
sommes marchans affectez qui achaptons les autres gens, et
autresfoiz pour leur argent nous leur vendons nostre hu-
manité precïeuse.   Nous leur vendons et achaptons autruy
par flaterie ou par corrupcïons ; mais nous sçavons tres bien
vendre nous mesmes a ceulx qui ont de nous a faire.   Com-   10
bien donc y peus tu acquerir qui es certain sans doubte et
sans peril ? veulx tu aller a la court vendre ou perdre ce bien
de vertu, que tu as acquis hors d'icelle court ?   Certes, frere,
tu demandes ce que tu deusses reffuser, tu te fies en ce dont
tu te deusses deffier et fiches ton esperance en ce que te tire   15
a peril.   Et se tu y viens, la court te servira de tant de
mensonges controverses d'une part, et de l'autre de tant
de charges que tu auras dedans toy mesmes bataille con-
tinuëlle et soussiz angoisseux, et pour certain homme n'est
qui pourra bonnement dire que ceste vie fust bieneuree qui   20

par tant de tempestes est achatee et en tant de contrarïetez
esprouvee.

Et si tu me demandes que c'est de vie curïale, je te re-
spons frere, que c'est une pouvre richesse, une habondance
25 miserable, une haultesse qui chiet, ung estat non estable,
ainsi comme ung pillier tremblant, et une mortelle vie; et
ainsi peut estre appellee de ceulz qui sont amoureuz de
saincte liberté.

Fuiez, hommes vertüeuz, fuiez et vous tenez loing d'icelle
30 assemblee, se vous voulez bien et seurement vivre sur le
rivage, en nous regardant noier de nostre gré mesmes, et
nostre aveuglement mesprisez, qui ne peut ou ne veult
congnoistre nostre pouvre meschief.

DEUXIÈME PARTIE

POESIE

———◆———

Vie de Saint Alexis

(11ème *siècle*)

Bons fut li secles al tens ancïenor,
quer feit i ert e justise et amor,
si ert credance, dont or n'i at nul prot;
tot est mudez, perdude at sa color,
ja mais n'iert tels com fut as anceisors. 5
 Al tens Noë et al tens Abraham
et al David que deus par amat tant
bons fut li siecles, ja mais n'iert si vailanz :
vielz est e frailes, tot s'en vait declinant;
si'st empeiriez, tot bien vait remanant. 10
 Puis icel tens que deus nos vint salver,
nostre anceisor ourent cristïentet;
si fut uns sire de Rome la citet,
riches hom fut de grant nobilitet;
por çol vos di d'un son fil voil parler. 15
 Eufemïens (ensi out nom li pedre)
cons fut de Rome dels mielz qui donc i erent;
sor toz ses pers l'amat li emperedre,
donc prist muilier vailant et honorede
des mielz gentils de tote la contrede. 20
 Puis converserent ensemble longement.
que enfant n'ourent, peiset lor en fortment;
deu en apelent andui parfitement;
' e reis celestes, par ton comandement
enfant nos done qui seit a ton talent.' 25

Tant li preierent par grant humilitet,
que la muilier donat feconditet :
un fil lor donet, si l'en sourent bon gret.
de saint batesme l'ont fait regenerer,
bel nom li metent sulonc cristïentet.   30

    Fud baptiziez, si out nom Alexis.
qui l'out portet volentiers le nodrit.
puis li bons pedre ad escole le mist ;
tant aprist letres que bien en fut guarniz.
puis vait il enfes l'emperedor servir.   35

    Quant veit li pedre que mais n'avrat enfant
mais que cel sol que il par amat tant,
donc se porpenset del siecle ad en avant :
or volt que prenget muilier a son vivant;
donc li achatet filie d'un noble franc.   40

    Fut la pulcele de molt halt parentet,
filie ad un comte de Rome la citet ;
n'at plus enfant, lei volt molt honorer.
ensemble en vont li dui pedre parler ;
lor dous enfanz volent faire asembler.   45

    Noment le terme de lor asemblement :
quant vint al faire, donc le font gentement.
danz Alexis l'esposet belement,
mais de cel plait ne volsist il nïent :
de tot en tot ad a deu son talent.   50

    Quant li jorz passet et il fut anuitiet,
ço dist li pedre 'filz, quer t'en vai colchier
avoc ta spose, al comand deu del ciel.'
ne volst li enfes son pedre corocier,
vint en la chambre od sa gentil muilier.   55

    Com veit le lit, esguardat la pulcele,
donc li remembret de son seinor celeste
que plus at chier que tot aveir terrestre :
'e deus,' dist il, 'com forz pechiez m'apresset !
s'or ne m'en fui, molt criem que ne t'en perde.'   60

    Quant en la chambre furent tot sol remés,
danz Alexis la prist ad apeler ;
la mortel vide li prist molt a blasmer,
de la celeste li mostret veritet ;
mais lui ert tart qued il s'en fust alez.   65

'Oz mei, pulcele, celui tien ad espos
qui nos redenst de son sanc precïos,
en icest siecle nen at parfite amor;
la vide est fraile, n'i at durable honor;
ceste ledice revert a grant tristor.'   70
    Quant sa raison li at tote mostrede,
puis li comandet les renges de s'espede
et un anel dont il l'out esposede.
donc en eist fors de la chambre son
    pedre:
en mie nuit s'en fuit de la contrede.   75
    Donc vint edrant dreitement a la mer:
la nef est preste ou il deveit entrer;
donet son pris et enz est aloëz.
drecent lor sigle, laisent corre par mer;
la pristrent terre ou deus lor volst doner.   80
    Dreit a Lalice, une citet molt bele,
iloc arivet sainement la nacele:
donc en eisit danz Alexis a terre;
mais jo ne sai com longes i converset.
ou que il seit de deu servir ne cesset.   85
    D'iloc alat en Alsis la citet
por une imagene dont il odit parler,
qued angele firent par comandement deu
el nom la virgene qui portat salvetet,
sainte Marie qui portat damne deu.   90
    Tot son aveir qu'od sei en out portet
tot le depart que riens ne l'en remest;
larges almosnes par Alsis la citet
donet as povres ou qu'il les pot trover:
por nul aveir ne volt estre encombrez.   95
    Quant son aveir lor at tot departit,
entre les povres s'asist danz Alexis:
receut l'almosne quant deus la li tramist;
tant en retint dont son cors pot guarir;
se lui'n remaint, sil rent as poverins.   100
    Or revendrai al pedre et a la medre
et a la spose qui sole fut remese.
quant il ço sourent qued il fuïz s'en eret,

ço fut granz dols qued il en demenerent,
e granz deplainz par tote la contrede.   105
    Co dist li pedre ' chiers filz, com t'ai perdut ! '
respont la medre ' lasse, qu' est devenuz ? '
ço dist la spose ' pechiez le m'at tolut.
amis, bels sire, si poi vos ai oüt !
or sui si graime que ne puis estre plus.'   110
    Donc prent li pedre de ses meilors serjanz,
par moltes terres fait querre son enfant :
jusqu'en Alsis en vindrent dui edrant ;
iloc troverent dan Alexis sedant,
mais n'enconurent son vis ne son semblant.   115
    Si at li enfes sa tendre charn mudede
nel reconurent li dui serjant son pedre :
a lui medisme ont l'almosne donede ;
il la receut come li altre fredre ;
nel reconurent, sempres s'en retornerent.   120
    Nel reconurent ne ne l'ont enterciet.
danz Alexis en lodet deu del ciel,
d'icez sos sers cui il est almosniers :
il fut lor sire, or est lor provendiers ;
ne vos sai dire com il s'en firet liez.   125
    Cil s'en repairent a Rome la citet,
noncent al pedre que nel pourent trover ;
s'il fut dolenz ne l'estot demander.
la bone medre s'en prist a dementer
et son chier fil sovent a regreter.   130
    ' Filz Alexis, por quei t' portat ta medre ?
tu m'iés fuïz, dolente en sui remese.
ne sai le leu ne ne sai la contrede
ou t'alge querre ; tote en sui esguarede :
ja mais n'ierc liede, chiers filz, ne n'iert tes pedre.' 135
    Vint en la chambre pleine de marrement ;
si la desperet que n'i remest nïent ;
n'i laissat palie ne nëul ornement.
a tel tristor atornat son talent,
onc puis cel di nes contint liedement.   140
    ' Chambre,' dist ele, ' ja mais n'estras parede,
ne ja ledice n'iert en tei demenede.'

si l'at destruite com s'hom l'oüst predede;
sas i fait pendre e cinces deramedes :
sa grant honor a grant dol at tornede.   145
    Del dol s'asist la medre jus a terre,
si fist la spose dan Alexis acertes :
'dame,' dist ele, 'jo ai fait si grant perte !
ore vivrai en guise de tortrele :
quant n'ai ton fil, ensembl'ot tei voil estre.'   150
    Respont la medre 's'od mei te vols tenir,
sit guarderai por amor Alexis.
ja n'avras mal dont te puisse guarir.
plainons ensemble le dol de nostre ami,
tu del seinor, jol ferai por mon fil.'   155
    Ne pot estre altre, mettent el consirrer ;
mais la dolor ne podent oblider.
danz Alexis en Alsis la citet
sert son seinor par bone volentet :
ses enemis nel pot onc enganer.   160
    Dis e set anz, n'en fut nïent a dire,
penat son cors el damne deu servise :
por amistet ne d'ami ne d'amie,
ne por honors qui lui fussent tramises,
n'en volt torner tant com il ad a vivre.   165
    Quant tot son cor en at si atornet
que ja son voil n'istrat de la citet,
deus fist l'imagene por soe amor parler
al servitor qui serveit al alter ;
ço li comandet 'apele l'home deu.'   170
    Ço dist l'imagene 'fai l'home deu venir
en cest monstier, quer il l'at deservit,
et il est dignes d'entrer en paradis,'
cil vait, sil quiert, mais il nel set choisir,
icel saint home de cui l'imagene dist.   175
    Revint li costre a l'imagene el monstier ;
'certes,' dis il, 'ne sai cui entercier.'
respont l'imagene 'ço'st cil qui lez l'hus siet ;
pres est de deu e del regne del ciel ;
par nule guise ne s'en volt esloinier.'   180
    Cil vait, sil quiert, fait l'el monstier venir.

R

es vos l'esemple par trestot le païs
que cele imagene parlat por Alexis;
trestuit l'honorent li grant e li petit,
e tuit le preient que d'els aiet mercit.   185
    Quant il ço veit quel volent honorer,
'certes,' dist il, 'n'i ai mais ad ester;
d'iceste honor nem revoil encombrer.'
en mie nuit s'en fuit de la citet,
dreit a Lalice rejoint li ses edrers.   190
    Danz Alexis entrat en une nef;
ourent lor vent, laissent corre par mer:
dreit a Tarson espeiret ariver,
mais ne pot estre, ailors l'estot aler:
tot dreit a Rome les portet li orez.   195
    Ad un des porz qui plus est pres de Rome,
iloc arivet la nef a cel saint home.
quant veit son regne, durement se redotet
de ses parenz, qued il nel reconoissent
e de l'honor del siecle ne l'encombrent.   200
    'E deus,' dist il, 'bels reis qui tot governes,
se tei ploüst ici ne volsisse estre.
s'or me conoissent mi parent d'este terre,
il me prendront par pri ou par podéste:
se jos en creid, il me trairont a perte.   205
    Mais en por hoc mes pedre me desirret,
si fait ma medre plus que femme qui vivet
avoc ma spose que jo lor ai guerpide.
or ne lairai nem mete en lor bailie:
nem conoistront, tanz jors at que nem virent.'   210
    Eist de la nef e vait edrant a Rome:
vait par les rues dont il ja bien fut cointes,
altre puis altre, mais son pedre i encontret.
ensemble od lui grant masse de ses homes:
sil reconut, par son dreit nom le nomet: 215
    'Eufemïens, bels sire, riches hom,
quer me herberge por deu en ta maison:
soz ton degret me fai un grabaton
empor ton fil dont tu as tel dolor:
tot sui enferms, sim pais por soe amor.'   220

Quant ot li pedre la clamor de son fil,
plorent si oil, ne s'en pot astenir:
'por amor deu e por mon chier ami,
tot te dorrai, bons hom, quant que m'as
    quis.
lit et hostel e pain e charn e vin.   225
   'E deus,' dist il, 'quer oüsse un serjant
quil me guardast: jo l'en fereie franc.'
un en i out qui sempres vint avant:
'es me,' dist il, 'quil guard par ton comand:
por toe amor en soferrai l'ahan.'   230
   Cil le menat endreit soz le degret,
fait li son lit ou il pot reposer;
tot li amanvet quant que bosoinz li ert.
vers son seinor ne s'en volt mesaler;
par nule guise ne l'en pot hom blasmer.   235
   Sovent le virent e li pedre e la medre
e la pulcele qued il out esposede:
par nule guise onques ne l'aviserent:
n'il ne lor dist, n'il ne li demanderent,
quels hom esteit ne de quel terre il eret.   240
   Soventes feiz les veit grant dol mener
e de lor oilz molt tendrement plorer,
et tot por lui, onques nïent por el:
il les esguardet, si met el consirrer;
n'at soin quel veient, si est a deu tornez.   245
   Soz le degret ou gist sor une nate,
la le paist l'hom del relief de la table:
a grant povérte deduit son grant barnage.
ço ne volt il que sa medre le sachet:
plus aimet deu que trestot son lignage.   250
   De la vïande qui del herberc li vient
tant en retient dont son cors en sostient;
se lui 'n remaint, sil rent as almosniers;
n'en fait musgode por son cors engraissier,
mais as plus povres le donet a mangier.   255
   En sainte eglise converse volentiers;
chascune feste se fait acomungier.
sainte escriture ço ert ses conseillers:

del deu servise le rovet esforcier ;
par nule guise ne s'en volt esloinier.   **260**
    Soz le degret ou il gist e converset,
iloc deduit liedement sa povérte.
li serf son pedre qui la maisniede servent
lor lavedures li getent sor la teste :
ne s'en corocet ned il nes en apelet.   **265**
    Tuit l'escharnissent, sil tienent por bricon :
l'egue li getent, si moilent son linçol ;
ne s'en corocet rienz cil saintismes hom,
ainz preiet deu qued il le lor pardoinst
par sa mercit, quer ne sevent que font.   **270**
    Iloc converset eisi dis e set ans ;
nel reconut nuls ses apartenanz,
ne nëuls hom ne sout les sos ahanz,
fors sol li liz ou il a gëut tant :
ne pot muder ne seit aparissant.   **275**
    Trente quatre ans at si son cors penct.
deus son servise li volt guerredoner.
molt li engrieget la soe enfermetet ;
or set il bien qued il s'en deit aler ;
cel son serjant ad a sei apelet :   **280**
    'Quier mei, bels fredre, et enque e parchamin
et une penne, ço pri toe mercit.'
cil li aportet, receit les Alexis :
de sei medisme tote la chartre escrist,
com s'en alat e com il s'en revint.   **285**
    Tres sei la tint, ne la volt demostrer,
nel reconoissent usque il s'en seit alez.
parfitement s'ad a deu comandet ;
sa fin aproismet, ses cors est agravez ;
de tot en tot recesset del parler.   **290**
    Li bons serjanz quil serveit volentiers
il le nonçat son pedre Eufemiien,
soef l'apelet, si li at conscilliet :
'Sire,' dist il, 'morz est tes provendiers,
e ço sai dire qu'il fut bons crestiiens.   **295**
Molt longement ai ot lui converset :
de nule chose certes nel sai blasmer,

⊖ ço m'est vis que ço est li om Deu.'
toz sols s'en est Eufemiiens tornez,
vint a son fil ou gist soz son degret. 300
Quant ot li pedre ço que dit at la chartre,
ad ambes mains deront sa blanche barbe:
'E! filz,' dist il, 'com doloros message!
vis atendeie qued a mei repaidrasses,
par Deu mercit que tum reconfortasses. 305
Filz Alexis, de ta dolente medre!
tantes dolors at por tei enduredes,
e tantes fains e tantes seiz passedes,
e tantes lairmes por le tuen cors ploredes!
cist duels l'avrat encui par acorede. 310
    O filz, cui ierent mes granz ereditez,
mes larges terres dont jo aveie assez,
mi grant palais en Rome la citet?
empor tei, filz, m'en esteie penez:
puis mon deces en fusses onorez. 315
    Blanc ai le chief e la barbe ai chanude:
ma grant onor aveie retenude
empor tei, filz, mais n'en aveies cure,
si grand dolor ui m'est apareüde!
filz, la toe aneme seit el ciel assolude! 320
    Tei covenist helme e bronie a porter,
espede ceindre come toi altre per,
ta grant maisniede doüsses governer,
le gonfanon l'emperedor porter,
com fist tes pedre e li tuens parentez.' 325
    De la dolor que demenat li pedre
grant fut la noise, si l'entendit la medre.
la vint corant com feme forsenede,
batant ses palmes, cridant, eschavelede;
veit mort son fil, a terre chiet pasmede. 330
    Qui donc li vit son grand duel demener,
son piz debattre e son cors degeter,
ses crins detraire e son vis maiseler,
e son mort fil baisier et acoler,
n'i out si dur ne l'estoüst plorer. 335

MORT DE ROLAND. FRAGMENT DE LA CHANSON DE ROLAND

(11ème *siècle*)

De ço cui calt? se fuiz s'en est Marsilies,
remés i est sis uncles l'algalifes,
qui tint Kartagene, Alferne, Garmalie,
e Ethïope, une terre maldite ;
la neire gent en ad en sa baillie,   5
granz unt les nes e lees les orilles,
e sunt ensemble plus de cinquante milie.
icil chevalchent fierement e a ire,
puis si escrïent l'enseigne paienisme.
ço dist Rollanz 'ci recevrums martirie,   10
e or sai ben n'avuns guaires a vivre ;
mais tut seit fel ki chier nes vende primes !
ferez, seignur, des espees furbies,
si calengiez e voz morz e voz vies,
que dulce France par nus ne seit hunie   15
quant en cest camp vendrat Carles misire,
de Sarrazins verrat tel discipline,
cuntre un des noz en truverat morz quinze,
ne laisserat que nus de beneïsse'.   Aoi.
   Quant Rollanz veit la cuntredite gent,   20
ki plus sunt neir que nen est arremenz,
ne n'unt de blanc ne mais que sul les denz,
ço dist li quens ' or sai jo veirement
que hoi murrum par le mien escïent.
ferez, Franceis, car jol vus recumant.'   25
dist Oliviers 'dehait ait li plus lenz !'
a icest mot Franceis se fierent enz.
   Quant paien virent que Franceis i out poi,
entr' els en unt e orgoill e cunfort;
dist l'uns al altre 'li emperere ad tort.'   30
li algalifes sist sur un ceval sor,
brochet le bien des esperuns a or ;
fiert Olivier deriere en mi le dos,

le blanc osberc li ad desclos el cors,
par mi le piz sun espiet li mist fors ;   35
e dit aprés ' un colp avez pris fort.
Carles li magnes mar vus laissat as porz ;
tort nus ad fait, nen est dreiz qu'il s'en lot,
kar de vus sul ai bien vengiet les noz.'
   Oliviers sent que a mort est feruz,   40
de lui vengier targier ne se volt plus,
tient Halteclere, dunt li aciers fut bruns,
fiert l'algalife sur l'elme a or agut,
e flurs e pierres en acraventet jus,
trenchet la teste d'ici qu'as denz menuz,   45
brandist sun colp, si l'a mort abatut :
e dist aprés ' paiens, mal aies tu !
iço ne di Karles i ait perdut ;
ne a muillier ne a dame qu'as vëud
n'en vanteras el regne dunt tu fus   50
vaillant denier que m'i aies tolut
ne fait damage ne de mei ne d'altrui.'
aprés escrïet Rolland qu'il li aiut.   Aoi.
   Oliviers sent qu'il est a mort nafrez,
de lui vengier ja mais ne li iert sez ;   55
de Halteclere maint grant i ad duuet,
en la grant presse or i fiert cume ber,
trenchet cez hanstes e cez escuz buclers,
e piez e puinz, espalles e costez.
ki lui veïst Sarrazins desmembrer,   60
un mort sur altre a la terre geter,
de bon vassal li poüst remembrer.
l'enseigne Carle n'i volt mie ublïer,
Munjoie escrïet e haltement e cler.
Rollant apellet, sun ami e sun per,   65
' sire cumpaign, a mei car vus justez.
a grant dulur ermes hoi desevret.'
li uns vers l'altre cumencet a plurer.   Aoi.
   Rollanz reguardet Olivier al visage ;
teinz fut e pers, desculurez e pales,   70
li sancs tuz clers par mi le cors li raiet,
encuntre terre en chieent les esclaces.

'deus,' dist li quens, 'or ne sai jo que face.
sire cumpainz, mar fut vostre barnages!
ja mais n'iert hum ki tun cors cuntrevaillet.   **75**
e! France dulce, cum hoi remendras guaste
de bons vassals, cunfundue e desfaite!
li emperere en avrat grant damage.'
a icest mot sur sun cheval se pasmet.   Aoi.
As vus Rollant sur sun cheval pasmet,   **80**
e Olivier ki est a mort nafrez.
tant ad sainiet, li oil li sunt trublet,
ne luinz ne pres ne poet vedeir si cler
que reconuisset nisun hume mortel.
sun cumpaignun, cum il l'at encuntret,   **85**
sil fiert amunt sur l'elme a or gemet,
tut li detrenchet d'ici que al nasel,
mais en la teste ne l'ad mie adeset.
a icel colp l'ad Rollanz reguardet,
si li demandet dulcement e suëf   **90**
'sire cumpain, faites le vus de gred?
ja est ço Rollanz ki tant vos soelt amer;
par nule guise ne m'avez desfiet.'
dist Oliviers 'or vus oi jo parler;
jo ne vus vei: veied vus damnedeus!   **95**
ferut vus ai: car le me pardunez.'
Rollanz respunt 'jo n'ai nient de mel;
jol vus parduins ici e devant deu.'
a icel mot l'uns al altre ad clinet;
par tel amur as les vus desevrez.   **100**
Oliviers sent que la mort mult l'anguisset.
ambdui li oil en la teste li turnent,
l'oïe pert e la vëue tute;
descent a piet, a la terre se culchet,
d'ures en altres si reclaimet sa culpe,   **105**
cuntre le ciel ambesdous ses mains juintes,
si prïet deu que pareïs li dunget,
e beneïst Karlun e France dulce,
sun cumpaignum Rollant desur tuz humes.
falt li li coers, li helmes li embrunchet,   **110**
trestuz li cors a la terre li justet;

morz est li quens, que plus ne se demuret.
Rollanz li ber le pluret, sil duluset ;
jamais en terre n'orrez plus dolent hume.
Li quens Rollanz quant mort vit sun ami 115
gesir adenz, cuntre orïent sun vis,
ne poet muër ne plurt e ne suspirt,
mult dulcement a regreter le prist :
'sire cumpaigu, tant mar fustes hardiz !
ensemble avum estet e anz e dis, 120
nem fesis mal ne jo nel te forsfis.
quant tu iés morz, dulur est que jo vif.'
a icest mot se pasmet li marchis
sur son ceval qu'um claimet Veillantif.
afermez est a ses estreus d'or fin ; 125
quel part qu'il alt, ne poet mie chaïr.
Ainz que Rollanz se seit apercëuz,
de pasmeisuns guariz ne revenuz,
mult granz damages li est aparëuz :
mort sunt Franceis, tuz les i ad perdut, 130
senz l'arcevesque e senz Gualtier del Hum.
repairiez est de la muntaigne jus,
a cels d'Espaigne mult s'i est cumbatuz,
mort sunt si hume, sis unt paien vencut ;
voeillet o nun, desuz cez vals s'en fuit 135
e si reclaimet Rollant qu'il li aiut :
'e ! gentilz queus, vaillanz hum, u iés tu ?
unkes nen oi poür la u tu fus.
ço est Gualtiers ki cunquist Maëlgut,
li niés Droün al vieill e al canut ; 140
pur vasselage suleie estre tis druz.
ma hanste est fraite e perciez mis escuz,
e mis osbercs desmailliez e rumpuz,
par mi le cors ot lances sui feruz ;
sempres murrai, mais chier me sui venduz.' 145
a icel mot l'at Rollanz entendut,
le cheval brochet, si vint puignant vers lui. Aoi.
'Sire Gualtier,' ço dist li quens Rollanz,
'bataille as faite par le mien essïent,
vus devez estre vassals e combatanz. 150

mil chevaliers ne menastes vaillanz ?
n'erent a mei, per ço les vus demant,
rendez les mei, que besuign m'en a grant.'
respunt Gualtiers ' n'en verreiz un vivant ;
laissiez les ai en le dulurus camp.   155
de Sarrazins nus i truvames tant,
Turs et Ermines, Chaninés e Persanz,
de cels de Bal les meillurs cumbatanz
sur lur chevals arabiz e curanz.
une bataille avum faite si grant,   160
n'i ait paien que devers nus s'en vant ;
seissante milie en remest mort sanglant.
iloec avuns perduz trestuz noz Francs.
vengiez nus sumes as noz acerins branz.
de mun osberc m'en sunt rumput li pan,   165
plaies ai multes as costez et as flancs,
de tutes parz m'ist fores li clers sancs ;
trestuz li cors me va enfeblïanz,
sempres murrai par le mien essïent.
jo sui vostre hum, si vus tien a garant,   170
ne m'en blasmez, se jo m'en vai fuiant,
mais or m'aiez a tut vostre vivant.'
　　Rollanz ad doel, si fut maltalentifs,
en la grant presse cumencet a ferir,
de cels d'Espaigne en ad getet morz vint,   175
e Gualtiers sis e l'arcevesques cinc.
dïent paien ' feluns humes ad ci :
guardez, seignur, que il n'en algent vif.
tut par seit fel ki nes vait envaïr
e recrëanz ki les lerrat guarir.'   180
dunc recumencent e le hu e le cri,
de tutes parz les revunt envaïr.　　Aoi.
　　Li quens Rollanz fut mult nobles guerriers,
Gualtiers del Hum est bien bons chevaliers,
li arcevesques pruzdum e essaiez :   185
li uns ne volt l'altre nïent laissier.
en la grant presse i fierent as paiens.
mil sarrazin i descendent a piet,
e a cheval sunt quarante millier.

mien escïentre nes osent aproismïer; 190
il lancent lur e lances e espiez,
wigres e darz e museraz e algiers.
as premiers colps i unt ocis Gualtier,
Turpin de Reins tut sun escut perciet,
quasset sun elme, si l'unt nafret el chief 195
e sun osberc rumput e desmailliet,
par mi le cors nafret de quatre espiez;
dedesus lui ocïent sun destrier.
or est granz doels quant l'arcevesques chiet. Aoi.
   Turpins de Reins quant se sent abatut, 200
de quatre espiez par mi le cors ferut,
isnelement li ber resaillit sus;
Rollant reguardet, puis si li est curuz
e dist un mot 'ne sui mie vencuz;
ja bons vassals nen iert vifs recrëuz.' 205
il trait Almace, s'espee d'acier brun,
en la grant presse mil colps i fiert e plus;
puis ce dist Carles qu'il n'en espargnat nul,
tels quatre cenz i troevet entur lui,
alquanz nafrez, alquanz par mi feruz, 210
si out d'icels ki les chiefs unt perdut:
ço dit la geste e cil ki el camp fut,
li ber sainz Gilies pur cui deus fait vertuz
e fist la chartre el mustier de Loün;
qui tant ne set ne l'ad prud entendut. 215
   Li quens Rollanz gentement se cumbat;
mais le cors ad tressuët e mult chalt,
en la teste ad e dulur e grant mal,
rut ad le temple pur ço que il cornat;
mais saveir volt se Charles i vendrat, 220
trait l'olifan, fieblement le sunat.
li emperere s'estut, si l'escultat.
'seignur,' dist il, 'mult malement nus vait:
Rollanz mis niés hoi cest jur nus defalt,
jo oi al corner que guaires ne vivrat. 225
ki estre i voelt, isnelement chevalzt!
sunez voz graisles tant que en cest ost ad!'
seissante milie en i cornent si halt,

bruient li munt e respundent li val.
paien l'entendent, nel tindrent mie en gab ;   230
dit l'uns al altre ' Karlun avrum nus ja.'   Aoi.
   Dïent paien ' l'emperere repairet,
de cels de France odum suner les graisles ;
se Carles vient, de nus i avrat perte.
se Rollanz vit, nostre guerre novellet.   235
perdud avuns Espaigne nostre terre.'
tel quatre cent s'en asemblent a helmes
e des meillurs ki el camp quient estre,
a Rollant rendent un estur fort e pesme :
or ad li quens endreit sei sez que faire.   Aoi.   240
   Li quens Rollanz quant il les veit venir,
tant se fait forz e fiers e maneviz,
ne lur lerrat tant cum il serat vifs.
siet el cheval qu'um claimet Veillantif,
brochet le bien des esperuns d'or fin,   245
en la grant presse les vait tuz envaïr,
ensembl' od lui l'arcevesques Turpins.
dist l'uns al altre ' ça vus traiez, amis !
de cels de France les corns avuns oït ;
Carles repairet li reis poësteïfs.'   250
   Li quens Rollanz unkes n'amat cuard
ne orguillus ne hume de male part
ne chevalier, s'il ne fust bons vassals.
e l'arcevesque Turpin en apelat :
' sire, a pied estes, e jo sui a ceval ;   255
pur vostre amur ici prendrai estal,
ensemble avruns e le bien e le mal,
ne vus lerrai pur nul hume de car ;
encui rendrunt a paiens cest asalt
li colp d'Almace e cil de Durendal.   260
dist l'arcevesques ' fel seit ki n'i ferrat.
Carles repairet ki bien nus vengerat.'
   Dïent paien ' si mare fumes net !
cum pesmes jurz nus est hoi ajurnez !
perdut avum noz seignurs e noz pers.   265
Carles repairet od sa grant ost, li ber,
de cels de France odum les graisles clers,

grant est la noise de Munjoie escrïer.
li quens Rollanz est de tant grant fiertet,
ja n'iert vencuz pur nul hume carnel;   270
lançuns a lui, puis sil laissums ester.'
e il si firent darz e wigres assez,
espiez e lances e museraz enpennez;
l'escut Rollant unt frait e estroët
e sun osberc rumput e desmailet,   275
mais enz el cors nel unt mie adeset;
Veillantif unt en trente lius nafret,
desuz le cunte si li unt mort getet.
paien s'en fuient, puis sil laissent ester;
li quens Rollanz a pied i est remés. Aoi.   280
    Paien s'en fuient curuçus e iriet,
envers Espaigne tendent del espleitier.
li quens Rollanz nes ad dunc encalciez,
perdut i ad Veillantif sun destrier:
voeillet o nun, remés i est a piet.   285
al arcevesque Turpin alat aidier,
sun elme ad or li deslaçat del chief,
si li tolit le blanc osberc legier,
e sun blialt li ad tut detrenchiet,
e ses granz plaies des pans li ad lïet,   290
cuntre sun piz puis si l'ad enbraciet,
sur l'erbe vert puis l'at suëf culchiet;
mult dulcement li ad Rollanz preiet:
'e, gentilz hum, car me dunez cungiet!
noz cumpaignuns, que oümes tant chiers,   295
or sunt il mort, nes i devuns laissier;
joes voeill aler e querre e entercier,
dedevant vus juster e enrengier.'
dist l'arcevesques 'alez e repairiez.
cist camps est vostre, la mercit deu, e miens.' 300
    Rollanz s'en turnet, par le camp vait tut suls,
cercet les vals e si cercet les munz;
iloec truvat e Ivorie et Ivun,
truvat Gerin, Gerier sun cumpaignun,
iloec truvat Engelier le Guascuign   305
e si truvat Berengier e Otun,

iloec truvat Anseïs e Sansun,
truvat Gerard le vieill de Russillun :
par un e un les ad pris li baruns,
al arcevesque en est venuz atut, 310
sis mist en reng dedevant ses genuilz.
li arcevesques ne poet muër n'en plurt,
lievet sa main, fait sa beneïçun ;
aprés ad dit 'mare fustes, seignur !
tutes voz anmes ait deus li glorïus ! 315
en pareïs les mete en saintes flurs !
la meie mort me rent si anguissus,
ja ne verrai le riche empereür.'

   Rollanz s'en turnet, le camp vait recercier
desuz un pin e foillut e ramier 320
sun cumpaignun ad truvet Olivier,
cuntre sun piz estreit l'ad enbraciet.
si cum il poet al arcevesque en vient,
sur un escut l'ad as altres culchiet ;
e l'arcevesques l'ad asols e seigniet. 325
idunc agrieget li doels e la pitiet.
ço dit Rollanz 'bels cumpainz Olivier,
vus fustes filz al bon cunte Reinier,
ki tint la marche de Genes e Rivier :
por hanste fraindre, pur escuz peceier 330
e pur osberc rumpre e desmaillier
pur orguillus e veintre e esmaier
e pur pruzdumes tenir e conseillier
[e pur glutuns e veintre e esmaier]
en nule terre n'out meillur chevalier.' 335

   Li quens Rollanz, quant il veit morz ses pers
e Olivier, qu'il tant poeit amer,
tendrur en out, cumencet a plurer,
en sun visage fut mult desculurez.
si grant doel out que mais ne pout ester, 340
voeillet o nun, a terre chiet pasmez.
dis l'arcevesques 'tant mare fustes, ber.'

   Li arcevesques quant vit pasmer Rollant,
dunc out tel doel, unkes mais n'out si grant :
tendit sa main, si ad pris l'olifan. 345

en Rencesvals ad une ewe curant;
aler i volt, si'n durrat a Rollant.
tant s'esforçat qu'il se mist en estant,
sun petit pas s'en turnet cancelant,
il est si fiebles qu'il ne poet en avant,   350
nen ad vertut, trop ad perdut del sanc.
ainz que um alast un sul arpent de camp,
falt li li coers, si est chaeiz avant:
la sue mort le vait mult anguissant.

    Li quens Rollanz revient de pasmeisuns,   355
sur piez se drecet, mais il ad grant dulur;
guardet aval e si guardet amunt:
sur l'erbe vert, ultre ses cumpaignuns,
la veit gesir le nobilie barun,
ço est l'arcevesques que deus mist en sun num;   360
claimet sa culpe, si reguardet amunt,
cuntre le ciel amsdous ses mains ad juint,
si prïet deu que pareïs li duinst.
morz est Turpins li guerreiers Charlun.
par granz batailles e par mult bels sermuns   365
cuntre païens fut tuz tens campïuns.
deus li otreit seinte beneïçun! Aoi.

    Quant Rollanz vit l'arcevesque qu'est morz,
senz Olivier une mais n'out si grant dol,
e dist un mot qui destrenche le cor: 370
'Carles de France chevalche cum il pot;
en Rencesvals damage i at des noz:
li reis Marsilies ad tant perdut de s'ost,
cuntre un des noz ad bien quarante morz.'

    Li quens Rollanz veit l'arcevesque a terre,   375
defors sun cors veit gesir la buëlle,
desuz le frunt li buillit la cervelle.
desur sun piz, entre les dous furcelles,
cruisiedes ad ses blanches mains, les belles.
forment le plaint a la lei de sa terre.   380
'e, gentilz hum, chevaliers de bon aire,
hoi te cumant al glorïus celeste:
ja mais n'ert hum plus volentiers le serve.
des les apostles ne fut unc tel prophete

pur lei tenir e pur humes atraire.   385
ja la vostre anme nen ait doel ne surfaite!
de pareïs li seit la porte uverte!'
   Ço sent Rollanz que la mort li est pres,
par les oreilles fors li ist li cervels;
de ses pers prïet a deu que les apelt   390
e pois de lui al angle Gabrïel.
prist l'olifan, que reproce n'en ait,
e Durendal s'espee en l'altre main.
plus qu'arbaleste ne poet traire un quarrel
devers Espaigne en vait en un guarait,   395
en sum un tertre, desuz dous arbres bels,
quatre perruns i ad de marbre faiz:
sur l'erbe vert la est caeiz envers,
si s'est pasmez, kar la mort li est pres.
   Halt sunt li pui e mult halt sunt li arbre.   400
quatre perruns i ad luisanz de marbre;
sur l'erbe vert li quens Rollanz se pasmet.
uns sarrazins tute veie l'esguardet,
si se feinst mort, si gist entre les altres,
del sanc luat sun cors e sun visage.   405
met sei en piez e de curre se hastet:
bels fut e forz e de grant vasselage,
par sun orguill cumencet mortel rage,
Rollant saisit e sun cors e ses armes,
e dist un mot 'vencuz est li niés Carle;   410
iceste espee porterai en Arabe.'
prist l'en sun pung, Rollant tirad la barbe:
en cel tirer li quens s'aperçut alques.
   Ço sent Rollanz que s'espee li tolt.
uvrit les oilz, si li ad dit un mot: 415
'mien escïentre tu n'iés mie des noz.
tient l'olifan, que unkes perdre ne volt,
sil fiert en l'elme ki gemmez fut a or,
fruisset l'acier e la teste e les os,
amsdous les oilz del chief li ad mis fors,   420
jus a ses piez si l'ad tresturnet mort.
aprés li dit 'culvert, cum fus si os
que me saisis ne a dreit ne a tort?

ne l'orrat hum ne t'en tienget pur fol.
fenduz en est mis olifans el gros,   425
ça jus en est li cristals e li ors.'
   Ço sent Rollanz le vëue a perdue,
met sei sur piez, quanqu'il poet s'esvertüet;
en sun visage sa culur ad perdue.
tint Durendal s'espee tute nue.   430
dedevant lui ad une pierre brune:
dis colps i fiert par doel e par rancune,
cruist li aciers, ne fraint ne ne s'esgruignet.
e dist li quens 'sancte Marie, aïue!
e, Durendal, bone, si mare fustes!   435
quant jo n'ai prud, de vus nen ai mais cure!
tantes batailles en camp en ai vencues
e tantes terres larges escumbatues,
que Carles tient, ki la barbe ad canue.
ne vos ait hum ki pur altre s'en fuiet!   440
mult bons vassals vus ad lung tens tenue,
jamais n'iert tels en France l'asolue.'
   Rollanz ferit el perrun de Sartainie;
cruist li aciers ne briset ne n'esgraniet.
quant il ço vit que n'en pout mie fraindre,   445
a sei meïsme la cumencet a plaindre.
'e, Durendal, cum iés e clere e blanche!
cuntre soleill si reluis e reflambes!
Carles esteit es vals de Morïanie,
quant deus del ciel li mandat par sun angle   450
qu'il te dunast a un cunte cataigne;
dunc la me ceinst li gentilz reis, li magnes.
jo l'en cunquis e Anjou e Bretaigne,
si l'en cunquis e Peitou e le Maine,
jo l'en cunquis Normendie la franche,   455
si l'en cunquis Provence e Equitaigne
e Lumbardie e trestute Romaine,
jo l'en cunquis Baiviere et tute Flandres
e Buguerie e trestute Puillanie,
Custentinnoble dunt il out la fiance,   460
e en Saisunie fait om ço qu'il demandet;
jo l'en cunquis Guales Escoce Islande;

e Engleterre, que il teneit sa cambre;
cunquis l'en ai païs e terres tantes
que Carles tient, ki ad la barbe blanche. 465
pur ceste espee ai dulur e pesance :
miez voeill murir qu'entre paiens remaigne,
damnes deus pere, n'en laissier hunir France ! '
    Rollanz ferit en une pierre bise ;
plus en abat que jo ne vus sai dire. 470
l'espee cruist, ne fruisset ne ne brise,
cuntre le ciel amunt est resortie.
quant veit li quens que ne la fraindrat mie,
mult dulcement la plainst a sei meïsme :
' e, Durendal, cum iés belle e saintisme ! 475
en l'orie punt asez i ad reliques :
la dent saint Pierre e del sanc saint Basilie
e des chevels mun seignur saint Denise,
del vestement i ad sainte Marie.
il nen est dreiz que paien te baillisent, 480
de chrestïens devez estre servie.
ne vus ait hum ki facet cuardie !
mult larges terres de vus avrai cunquises
que Carles tient, ki la barbe ad flurie ;
li empereres en est e ber e riches.' 485
    Ço sent Rollanz que la mort le tresprent,
devers la teste sur le quer li descent ;
desuz un pin i est alez curant,
sur l'erbe vert s'i est culchiez adenz.
desuz lui met s'espee e l'olifant, 490
turnat sa teste vers la paiene gent :
pur ço l'at fait que il voelt veirement
que Carles dïet e trestute sa gent,
li gentilz quens qu'il fut morz cunquerant.
claimet sa culpe e menut e suvent, 495
pur ses pecchiez deu purofrid lu guant.   Aoi.
    Ço sent Rollanz de sun tens n'i ad plus,
devers Espaigne gist en un pui agut ;
a l'une main si ad sun piz batud :
' deus, meie culpe vers les tues vertuz 500
de mes pecchiez, des granz e des menuz,

que jo ai fait des l'ure que nez fui
tresqu'a cest jur que ci sui consoüz.'
sun destre guant en ad vers deu tendut;
angle del ciel i descendent a lui.   Aoi.   505
   Li quenz Rollanz se jut desuz un pin,
envers Espaigne en ad turnet sun vis,
de plusurs choses a remembrer li prist:
de tantes terres cume li bers cunquist,
de dulce France, des humes de sun lign,   510
de Carlemagne, sun seignur, kil nurrit.
ne poet muër n'en plurt e ne suspirt.
mais lui meïsme ne volt metre en ubli,
claimet sa culpe, si prïet deu mercit:
' veire paterne, ki unkes ne mentis,   515
saint Lazarun de mort resurrexis
e Danïel des lïuns guaresis,
guaris de mei l'anme de tuz perilz
pur les pecchiez que en ma vie fis.'
sun destre guant a deu en purofrit,   520
sainz Gabrïels de sa main li ad pris.
desur sun braz teneit le chief enclin,
juintes ses mains est alez a sa fin.
deus li tramist sun angle cherubin
e saint Michiel de la mer del peril,   525
ensemble od els sainz Gabrïels i vint:
l'anme del cunte portent en pareïs.

LA BELE EREMBORS.   ROMANCE

(12ème siècle)

   Quant vient en mai, que l'on dit as lons jors,
que Franc de France repairent de roi cort,
Reynauz repaire devant el premier front.
si s'en passa lez lo mes Arembor,
ainz n'en dengna le chief drecier a mont.   5
e Raynaut, amis!
   Bele Erembors a la fenestre au jor
sor ses genolz tient paile de color;

voit Frans de France qui repairent de cort
et voit Raynaut devant el premier front :　　　　10
en haut parole, si a dit sa raison.
e Raynaut, amis !
　'Amis Raynaut, j'ai ja vëu cel jor,
se passisoiz selon mon pere tor,
dolanz fussiez, se ne parlasse a vos.'　　　　15
'jal mesfaïstes, fille d'emperëor,
autrui amastes, si oblïastes nos.'
e Raynaut, amis !
　'Sire Raynaut, je m'en escondirai :
a cent puceles sor sainz vos jurerai,　　　　20
a trente dames que avuec moi menrai,
c'onques nul home fors vostre cors n'amai.
prennez l'emmende et je vos baiserai.'
e Raynaut, amis !
　Li cuens Raynauz en monta lo degré　　　　25
gros par espaules, greles par lo baudré ;
blonde ot le poil, menu, recercelé :
en nule terre n'ot si biau bacheler.
voit l'Erembors, si comence a plorer.
e Raynaut, amis !　　　　30
　Li cuens Raynauz est montez en la tor,
si s'est assis en un lit point a flors,
dejoste lui se siet bele Erembors :

.　　　.　　　.　　　.　　　.　　　.　　　.　　　.

lors recomencent lor premieres amors.
e Raynaut, amis !　　　　35

Guérison d'Amis.　Fragment d'Amis et Amiles

(12ème *siècle*)

　Li cuens l'entent, si conmence a plorer,
ne sot que faire, ne pot un mot sonner.
moult li est dur et au cuer trop amer
de ses dous fiuls que il ot engendrez ;
cum les porra ocirre et afolei !　　　　5

se gens le sevent, nus nel porroit tenser,
c'on nel fëist et panre et vergonder.
mais d'autre part se prant a porpanser
dou conte Ami que il pot tant amer,
que lui meïsmes en lairoit afoler, 10
ne por riens nulle ne le porroit vëer,
quant ses compains puet santé recouvrer.
c'est moult grant chose d'omme mort restorer
et si est maus des dous anfans tuër,
nus n'en porroit le pechié pardonner 15
fors dex de glorie qui se laissa pener.
' dex,' dist Amiles, ' qui tout as a sauver,
cist hom si mist son cors por moi tanser
en la bataille dou traïtor Hardré.
quant je li puis de moi santé donner 20
de mes anfans que je vols engendrer,
de moi sont il, por voir le puis conter,
l'ore soit bonne que dex les fist former,
quant mes compains en puet ce recouvrer
que hom qui vive ne li porroit donner 25
fors dex de glorie qui tout a a sauver :
je nel lairoie por les membres coper
ne por tout l'or c'on me sëust donner,
qu'a mes dous fiz n'aille les chiés coper
por Ami faire aïe. 30
Amis compains, puet ce iestre vertez
que vos a moi ci devisé avez,
de mes dous fiz seres resvigourez
quant vos seroiz dou sanc d'euls dous lavez?
li vostres dis n'en sera trespassez.' 35
lors ist Amiles trestouz abandonnez
hors de la chambre, en la sale est entrez.
ceuls qui i furent en a trestoz gietez
serjans, vaslés et chevaliers menbrez,
n'i remest hom qui de mere soit nés. 40
les huis ferma, si les a bien barrez,
les chambres cerche environ de toz lez,
que aucuns hom ne fust laienz remés.
quant voit qu'il est laienz bien esseulez,

c'or porra faire toutes ses volentez,　　45
s'espee prent et un bacin doré,
dedens la chambre s'en est moult tost alez
ou li anfant gisoient lez a lez.
dormans les treuve bras a bras acolez,
n'ot dous si biax desci en Duresté.　　50
moult doucement les avoit resgardez,
tel paor a que chëuz est pasmez,
chiet lui l'espee et li bacins dorez.
quant se redresce, si dist com cuens menbrez
' chaitis, que porrai faire ? '　　55
　Li cuens Amiles fu forment esperduz,
a la terre est envers pasmez chëuz,
li bacins chiet et li brans d'acier nus.
quant se redresce, dist com hom percëuz :
' ahi,' dist il, ' chaitis ! com mar i fuz,　　60
quant tes anfans avras les chiés toluz !
mais ne m'en chaut quant cil iert secorrus,
qui est des gens en grant vilté tenus
et conme mors est il amentëuz ;
mais or venra en vie.'　　65
　Li cuens Amiles un petit s'atarja,
vers les anfans pas por pas en ala,
dormans les treuve, moult par les resgarda,
s'espee lieve, ocirre les voldra ;
mais de ferir un petit se tarja.　　70
li ainznés freres de l'effroi s'esveilla
que li cuens mainne qui en la chambre entra.
l'anfes se torne, son pere ravisa,
s'espee voit, moult grant paor en a.
son pere apelle, si l'en arraisona :　　75
' biax sire peres, por deu qui tout forma,
que volez faire ? nel me celez vos ja.
ainz mais nus peres tel chose ne pensa.'
' biaux sire fiuls, ocirre vos voil ja
et le tien frere qui delez toi esta ;　　80
car mes compains Amis qui moult m'ama,
dou sanc de vos li siens cors garistra,
que gietez est dou siecle.'

' Biax tres douz peres,' dist l'anfes erramment.
' quant vos compains avra garissement,   85
se de nos sans a sor soi lavement,
nos sommes vostre de vostre engenrement,
fair en poëz del tout a vo talent.
or nos copez les chiés isnellement ;
car dex de glorie nos avra en present,   90
en paradis en irommes chantant
et proierommes Jhesu cui tout apent
que dou pechié vos face tensement,
vos et Ami, vostre compaingnon gent,
mais nostre mere, la bele Belissant,   95
nos saluëz por deu omnipotent.'
li cuens l'oït, moult grans pitiés l'en prent
que touz pasmez a la terre s'estent.
quant se redresce, si reprinst hardement.
or orroiz ja merveilles, bonne gent,   100
qui tex n'oïstes en tout vostre vivant.
li cuens Amiles vint vers le lit esrant,
hauce l'espee, li fiuls le col estent.
or est merveilles se li cuers ne li ment
la teste cope li peres son anfant,   105
le sanc reciut el cler bacin d'argent :
a poi ne chiet a terre.
    Quant ot ocis li cuens son fil premier
et li sans fu coulez el bacin chier,
la teste couche delez le col arrier,   110
puis vint a l'autre, hauce le brant d'acier,
le chief li tranche tres par mi le colier,
le sanc reciut el cler bacin d'or mier,
et quant l'ot tout, si mist la teste arrier.
les dous anfans couvri d'un tapis chier,   115
hors de la chambre ist li cuens sans targier,
moult par a fait les huis bien verroillier.
au conte Ami vint Amiles arrier,
qui el lit jut malades.
    Au conte Ami est Amiles venus,   120
qui jut malades entre les ars volus.
le bacin tint plain de sanc et de jus.

dou sanc ses fiuls cui il avoit toluz
les chiés des cors et copez par desus.
Amis le voit, moult en est esperduz.   125
or se demente et dist 'las ! tant mar fuz,
que tu venis en terre.'
    Quaut Amis voit le sanc el bacin cler,
sachiez de voir, n'i ot qu'espoënter.
atant ez vos dant Amile le ber,   130
son compaingnon en prinst a apeller :
'biaus sire Ami, or poëz bien lever,
se par tel chose puet vostre cors saner
et dex de glorie vos weult santé donner
de mes dous fiuls que je ai decolez :   135
ne plaing je nul, foi que doi saint Omer.'
Amis se lieve, si conmence a plorer.
son compaingnon puet il bien esprouver
que volentiers il li voldroit donner
sa garison, s'il la pooit trouver.   140
une grant cuve fait Amile aporter,
son compaingnon a fait dedens entrer ;
mais a grant paingne i puet cil avaler,
tant fort estoit malades.
    Or fu Amis en la cuve en parfont.   145
li cuens Amiles tint le bacin rëont,
dou rouge sanc li a froté le front,
les iex, la bouche, les membres qu'el cors
    sont,
jambes et ventre et le cors contremont,
piés, cuisses, mains, les espaules amout,   150
dou sanc par tout le touche.
    Amiles fu et preudoni et gentis.
son compaingnon, qui ot a non Amis.
lave dou sanc et la bouche et le vis.
moult puet bien croire que il est ses amis,   155
quant ses dous fiuls a si por lui ocis.
oiez, seignor, com ouvra Jhesucris.
si com il touche le sanc el front Ami,
li chiet la roiffe dont il estoit sozprius,
les mains garissent, li ventres et li pis.   160

quant or le voit Amiles ses amis,
deu en rent graces, le roi de paradis,
et ses sains et ses saintes.

Le Monocère. Fragment du Bestiaire de Philippe de Thaun

(12ᵉᵐᵉ *siecle*)

Monosceros est beste,
un corn ad en la teste,
pur çeo ad si a nun.
de buc ele ad façun.
par pucele est prise,   5
or oëz en quel guise.
quant hom le volt cacer
et prendre et enginner,
si vent hom al forest
u sis repaires est;   10
la met une pucele
hors de sein sa mamele,
e par odurement
monosceros la sent:
dunc vent a la pucele,   15
si baiset sa mamele,
en sun devant se dort,
issi vent a sa mort;
li hom survent atant,
ki l'ocit en dormant,   20
u trestut vif le prent,
si fait puis sun talent.
grant chose signefie,
ne larei nel vus die.
    Monosceros griu est,   25
en franceis un-corn est:
beste de tel baillie
Jhesu Crist signefie;

un deu est e serat
e fud e parmaindrat;　　　　　　　　　　30
en la virgine se mist,
e pur hom charn i prist,
e pur virginited,
pur mustrer casteed,
a virgine se parut　　　　　　　　　　　35
e virgine le conceut.
virgine est e serat
e tuz jurz parmaindrat.
ores oëz brefment
le signefïement.　　　　　　　　　　　40
　　Ceste beste en verté
nus signefie dé;
la virgine signefie,
sacez, sancte Marie;
par sa mamele entent　　　　　　　　　45
sancte eglise ensement;
e puis par le baiser
çeo deit signefïer,
que hom quant il se dort
en semblance est de mort:　　　　　　50
dés cum home dormi,
ki en cruiz mort sufri,
ert sa destructïun
nostre redemptïun,
e sun traveillement　　　　　　　　　55
nostre reposement.
si deceut dés dïable
par semblant cuvenable;
anme e cors sunt un,
issi fud dés et hum,　　　　　　　　　60
e içeo signefie
beste de tel baillie.

Le Roi Lear et ses Filles. Fragment du Roman de Brut

(12ème siècle)

Quant Leïr alques afebli,
cume li hoem qui envieilli,
cumença sei a purpenser
de ses treis filles marïer :
ce dist qu'il les marïereit   5
et sun regne lur partireit ;
mais primes voleit assaier
la quel d'eles l'aveit plus chier.
le mius del suen duner volreit
a cele qui plus l'amereit.   10
cascune apela sainglement
et l'aisnee premierement :
'fille,' fait il, 'jo voil saveir
cument tu m'aimes, di m'en veir.'
Gonorille li a juré   15
del ciel tute la deïté
(multe par fu pleine de boisdie)
qu'ele l'aime miels que sa vie.
'fille,' fait il, ' bien m'as amé :
bien te sera guerreduné,   20
car prisié as miels ma viellece
que ta vie ne ta joenece.
tu en avras tel guerredun
que tut le plus prisié barun,
que tu en mun regne esliras,   25
se jo puis, a seignur avras,
et ma terre te partirai :
la tierce part t'en liverrai.'
puis demanda o Ragaü :
'dis, fille, cumbien m'aimes tu ?'   30
et Ragaü out entendu
cume sa suer out respondu,
a cui ses peres tel gré sout
de ce que si forment l'amout :

gré revolt aveir ensement,   35
si li a dit 'certainement
jo t'aim sur tute crïature,
ne t'en sai dire altre mesure,'
'mult a ci,' dist il, 'grant amur,
ne te sai demander graignur;   40
jo te redunrai bon seignur
et la tierce part de m'enur.'
   Adunt apela Cordeïlle
qui esteit sa plus joesne fille.
pur ce que il l'aveit plus chiere   45
que Ragaü ne la premiere
quida que ele cunëust
que plus chier des altres l'ëust.
Cordeïlle out bien escuté
et bien out en sun cuer noté   50
cument ses dous sorurs parloënt,
cument lur pere losengoënt;
a sun pere se vout gaber
et en gabant li vout munstrer
que ses filles le blandisseient   55
et de losenge le serveient.
quant Leir a raisun la mist
cume les altres, el li dist
'qui a nule fille qui die
a sun pere par presumtie   60
qu'ele l'aint plus que ele deit,
ne sai que plus grant amurs seit
cel entre enfant et entre pere
et entre enfant et entre mere;
mes pere es et jo aim tant tei   65
cume jo mun pere amer dei.
et pur tei faire plus certain,
tant as, tant vals et jo tant
     t'ain.'
a tant se tout, plus ne vout dire.
li pere fu de si grant ire,   70
de maltalant devint tuz pers;
la parole prist en travers,

ce quida qu'el l'escarnisist
u ne deignast u ne volsist
u par vilté de lui laissast 75
a recunuistre qu'il l'amast
si cume ses sorurs l'amoënt
qui de tel amur s'afichoënt.
'en despit,' dist il, 'ëu m'as
qui ne volsis ne ne deignas 80
respundre cume tes sorurs :
a eles dous dunrai seignurs
e tut mun regne en mariage
e tut l'avrunt en eritage.
cascune en avra la meitié 85
et tu n'en avras ja plain pié
ne ja par mei n'avras seignur
ne de tute ma terre un dur.
jo te cherisseie et amoe
plus que nul' altre, si quidoe 90
que tu plus des altres m'amasses,
et ce fust dreiz se tu deignasses ;
mais tu m'as rejehi afrunt
que tu m'aimes meins qu'els ne
    funt.
tant cum jo t'oi plus en chierté, 95
tant m'ëus tu plus en vilté.
jamais n'avras joie del mien
ne ja ne m'iert bel de tun bien.'
la fille ne sout que respundre,
d'ire et de hunte quida fundre, 100
ne pout a sun pere estriver
ne il ne la vout escuter.
cum il ains pout n'i demura :
les dous ainsnees maria.
mariee fu bien cascune, 105
al duc de Cornüaille l'une
et al rei d'Escoce l'ainsnee.
si fu la cose purparlee
que après lui la terre avreient
et entr'els dous la partireient. 110

Cordëille qui fu li mendre
n'en pout el faire fors atendre,
ne jo ne sai qu'ele feïst.
li reis bien ne li promist
ne il, tant fu fel, ne sufri   115
que en sa terre ëust mari.
la meschine fu anguissuse
et mult marie et mult huntuse
plus pur ce qu'a tort la haeit
que pur le pru qu'ele en perdeit.   120
la pucele fu mult dolente,
mais ne pur quant bele ert et gente.
de li esteit grant reparlance.
Aganipus uns reis de France
oï Cordeïlle numer,   125
et qu'ele esteit a marïer.
briés et messages enveia
al lei Leïr, si li manda
que sa fille a muillier voleit,
enveiast li, il la prendreit.   130
    Leïr n'aveit mie ublïé
cument sa fille l'out amé,
ains l'out bien suvent ramenbré;
et al rei de France a mandé
que tut sun regne a devisé   135
et a ses dous filles duné,
la meitié a la primeraine
et l'altre aprés a la meiaine;
mais se sa fille li plaiseit,
il li dunreit, plus n'i prendreit.   140
cil quida qui l'out demandee
que pur chierté li fust veee;
de tant l'a il plus desiree,
qu'a merveille li ert loëe.
al rei Leïr de rechief mande   145
que nul aveir ne li demande,
mais sul sa fille li otreit
Cordeïlle, si li enveit.
et Leïr la li otreia:
ultre la mer li enveia   150

sa fille et ses dras sulement,
n'i out altre aparellement.
puis fu dame de tute France
et reine de grant puissance.
cil qui ses sorurs ourent prises,   155
cui les terres furent pramises,
n'i volrent mie tant sufrir
a la terre prendre et saisir,
que li suire s'en demeïst
et li de gré lur guerpeïst.   160
tant l'unt guerreié et destreit
que sun regne li unt toleit
li dus de Cornüaille a force
et Malglamis li reis d'Escoce.
tut lur a li suire laissié;   165
mais il li unt apareillié
que li uns d'els l'avra od sei,
si li trovera sun cunrei
a lui et a ses escuiiers
et a cinquante chevaliers,   170
que il alt henureement
quel part que il avra talent.
le regne unt cil ainsi saisi
et entr'els dous par mi parti,
que Leïr a lur offre pris,   175
si s'est del regne tuz demis.
Malglamis out od sei Leïr:
de primes le fist bien servir,
mais tost fu li curz empiriee
et la livraisuns retailliee;   180
primes faillirent a lur duns,
puis perdirent lur livraisuns.
Gonorille fu trop avere
et grant escar tint de sun pere
qui si grant maisniee teneit   185
et nule cose n'en faiseit.
mult li pesout del costement.
a sun seignur diseit suvent
'que deit ceste assemblee d'umes?
en meie fei, sire, fol sumes   190

que tel gent avuns ci atrait.
ne set mes peres qu'il se fait.
il est entrez en fole rute,
ja est viels hoem et si redute.
huniz seit qui mais l'en cresra   195
ne qui tel gent pur lui paistra.
li suen sergant as nuz estrivent
et li lur les nostres esquivent.
qui poreit sufrir si grant presse ?
il est fols et sa gent perverse :   200
ja n'avra hum gré qui le sert ;
qui plus i met, et plus i pert.
mult est fols qui tel gent cunreie :
trop en i a, tieguent lur veie.
mes peres est sei cinquantisme,   205
desormais seit sei qarantisme
ensemble od nus, u il s'en alt
atut sun pueple, et nus que calt ?'
mult i a poi femme sans visse
et sans racine d'avarisse.   210
tant a la dame amonesté
et tant a sun seignur parlé,
de cinquante le mist a trente,
de vint li retailla sa rente.
et li pere ce desdeigna :   215
grant aviltance li sembla
qui si l'aveient fait descendre.
alez est a sun altre gendre
Hennin, qui Ragaü aveit
et qui en Escoce maneit.   220
mais n'i out mie un an esté
quant il l'ourent mis en vilté :
se mal fu ainz, or est mult pis,
de trente humes l'unt mis a dis,
puis le mistrent de dis a cinc.   225
' caitif mei,' dist il, ' mar i vinc :
se vils fui la, plus vils sui ça.'
a Gonorille s'en ala.
ce quida qu'ele s'amendast
et cume pere l'enurast.   230

mais cele le ciel en jura
que ja od lui ne remanra
ne mais que un sul chevalier.
al pere l'estut otreiier :
dunt se cumence a cuntrister   235
et en sun cuer a purpenser
les biens que il aveit ëuz,
mais or les aveit tuz perduz.
'las mei,' dist il, ' trop ai vesqu
quant jo ai cel mal tens vëu.   240
tant ai ëu, or ai si poi.
u est alé quanque jo oi ?
fortune, trop par es muable,
tu ne puez estre un jur estable,
nus ne se deit en tei fïer :   245
tant fais ta roe fort turner.
mult as tost ta culur muëe,
tost es chaeite, tost levee.
cui tu vués de bun oil veeir
tost l'as munté en grant aveir ;   250
et des que tu turnes tun vis,
tost l'as d'alques a neient mis.
tost as un vilain halt levé
et un rei em plus bas turné :
cuntes, reis, dus, quant tu vués,   255
      plaisses
que tu nule rien ne lur laisses.
tant cum jo fui riches manenz,
tant oi jo amis et parenz ;
et des que jo, las ! apovri,
serganz, amis, parenz perdi.   260
jo n'ai si bon apartenant
qui d'amur me face semblant.
bien me dist veir ma joene fille,
que jo blamoe, Cordeïlle,
qui me dist, tant cum jo avreie,   265
tant amez et prisiez sereie.
n'entendi mie la parole,
ains la haï e tinc pur fole.

T

tant cum jo oi et tant valui
et tant amez et prisiez fui;   270
tant truvai jo qui me blandi
et qui voluntiers me servi:
pur mun aveir me blandisseient,
or se desturnent, s'il me veient.
bien me dist Cordeïlle veir,   275
mais jo nel soi aparceveir.
ne l'aparçui ne l'entendi,
ains la blamai et la haï
et de ma terre la chaçai
que nule rien ne li dunai.   280
or me sunt mes filles faillies
qui lors esteient mes amies,
qui m'amoënt sur tute rien
tant cum jo oi alques de bien.
or m'estuet cele aler requerre   285
que jo chaçai en altre terre.
mais jo cument la requerrai
qui de mun regne la chaçai?
et nun purquant saveir irai
se jo nul bien i truverai.   290
ja meins ne pis ne me fera
que les ainsnees m'unt fait ça.
ele dist que tant m'amereit
cume sun pere amer deveit,
que li dui jo plus demander?   295
dëust mei ele plus amer?
qui altre amur me prometeit,
pur mei losengier le faiseit.'
    Leïr forment se dementa
et lungement se purpensa: 300
puis vint as nés, en France ala,
a un port en Chaus ariva.
la reïne a tant demandee
qu'assez li fu prés enditee.
defors la cité s'arestut,   305
que hoem ne femme nel connut.
un escuiier a enveiié
qui a la reïne a nuncié

que ses peres a li veneit
et par besuing li requereit. 310
tut en ordre li a cunté
cument ses filles l'unt jeté.
Cordeïlle cum fille fist :
aveir que ele aveit grant prist,
a l'escuiier a tut livré, 315
si li a en cunseil ruvé
qu'a sun pere Leïr le port
de par sa fille et sel cunfort
et od l'aveir tut a celé
alt a chastel u a cité 320
et bien se face apareillier,
paistre, vestir, laver, baignier ;
de roials vestimens s'aturt
et a grant enur se sujurt ;
quarante chevaliers retiegne 325
de maisniee, qui od lui viegne :
aprés ce face al rei saveir
qu'il viegne sa fille veeir.
quant cil out l'aveir recoilli
et sun cumandement oï, 330
a sun seignur porta nuveles
qui li furent bones et beles.
a une altre cité turnerent,
ostel pristrent, bien s'aturnerent.
quant Leïr fu bien sujurnez, 335
baigniez, vestuz et aturnez
et maisniee out bien conreee,
bien vestie et bien aturnee,
al rei manda a lui veneit
et sa fille veeir voleit. 340
il reis meïsme par noblece
et la reïne a grant leece
sunt bien luing cuntre lui alé
et volentiers l'unt enuré.
il reis l'a mult bel recëu 345
qui unques ne l'aveit vëu.
par tut sun regne fist mander
et a ses humes cumander

que sun suire trestut servissent
et sun cumandement feïssent;   350
deïst lur ce que il voldreit,
et tut fust fait que il direit,
tant que sun regne li rendist
et en s'enur le restablist.

Aganipus fist que curteis: 355
assembler fist tuz les Franceis,
par lur los et par lur aïe
apareilla mult grant navie.
avuec sun suire l'enveia
em Bretaigne, si li livra   360
Cordeïlle qui od lui fust
et aprés lui sun regne ëust,
s'il le poeient delivrer
et des mains as gendres oster.
cil ourent la mer tost passee   365
et unt la terre delivree:
as feluns gendres la tolirent
et Leïr de tute saisirent.
Leïr a puis treis ans vesqu
et tut le regne em pais tenu   370
et a ses amis a rendu
ce que il aveient perdu;
et aprés les treis ans morut.
en Leecestre, u li cors jut,
Cordeïlle l'enseveli   375
en la crute el temple Jani.

Hector et Andromaque. Fragment du Roman de Troie

(12ᵉᵐᵉ siècle)

Andromacha apelloit l'om
la feme Hector par son droit nom,
gente dame de haut parage,
franche, cortoise, proz et sage.

molt ert lëaus vers son seignor 5
e molt l'ama de grant amor.
de lui avoit dous beaux enfans;
li ainz nez n'avoit qe cinc ans.
Laümedon out nom li uns, 10
qi ne fu laiz ne noirs ne bruns,
mes genz e blanz e blonz e beaus
e flors sor autres damoiseaus.
l'autres out nom, ce dit l'escriz,
Asternantes, mes molt petiz 15
ert li enfens e alaitanz :
n'avoit encor mie trois ans.
   Oiez com fait demostrement :
icelle nuit demainement
qe la trive fu definee
dut bien la dame estre esgaree. 20
si fu elle, jel sai de voir.
li deu li ont fet a savoir
per signes et per visïons
e per interpretacïons
son grant domage e sa dolor. 25
la nuit ainz qe venist le jor
out elle assez paine sofferte.
mes de ce fu sëure e certe,
se Hector s'en ist a la bataille,
ocis i estera sanz faille : 30
ja ne porra del camp eissir,
cel jor li convendra morir.
la dame sout la destinee
qi la nuit li fu demostree.
s'elle out de son seignor dotance, 35
crieme et paor et esmaiance,
ce ne fu mie de merveille.
a li meïsme se conseille.
   'Sire,' fet el, 'mostrer vos voil
la merveille dont je me doil, 40
qe par un poi li cuers de moi
(tel paor ai et tel esfroi,),
ne me desment et ne me faut.
li soverain et li plus haut

le m'ont mostré qe je vos die 45
q'a la bataille n'alez mie.
par moi vos en font deffiance
et merveillouse demonstrance :
n'en vendrïez jamés ariere,
c'om ne vos aportast en biere. 50
ne voelent pas les deïtez
ne les devines poëstez
qe i ailliez, mostré me l'ont.
tel desfïance vos en font
qe vos n'issïez al estor, 55
car vos morrïez sanz retor ;
e quant il vos en font devié,
n'i irez pas senz lor congié.
si mel creez, je vos di bien,
garder devez sor tote rien 60
qe n'enfraigniez lor volunté
ne rien qi soit contre lor gré.'
　　Hector vers la dame s'iraist
qi ce li dist, pas ne li plaist
la parole q'a entendue. 65
ireement l'a respondue :
'desor,' fet il, 'sai je e voi
ne dot de rien ne nel mescroi
q'en vos n'a senz ne escïent.
trop avez pris grant hardement, 70
q'itel chose m'avez nonciee,
se la folie avez songiee ;
si la me venez raconter
et chalongier e deveer
q'armes ne port ne ne m'en isse ! 75
mes ce n'iert ja tant cum je puisse,
qe vers les culverz ne contende
e qe je d'elz ne me defende
qi mon lignaje m'ont ocis
e ci assegiez et assis. 80
se li felon, li deputeire
ooient dire ne retreire
e li baron de ceste vile,
dont il i a plus de dous mile,

qe de songe, se le songiez, 85
fusse si pris ne eslongniez
d'armes porter ne fors eissir,
com me poroie plus honir?
ne voille dex qe ce m'aviegne
qe por ice mort dot ne criegne. 90
n'eu parlez mais, car sachiez bien,
je n'en feroie nule rien.'
    Andromacha plore et sospire.
si grant duel a et si grant ire
qe la colors q'el' out vermeille, 95
teinst e palist, n'est pas merveille,
e par un poi le senz ne pert.
au roi Priant mande en apert
q'il li deviet et le detiegne,
qe lais domages n'en aviegne : 100

  .   .   .   .   .   .

    Des qe ce vit Hector e sout
qe ses peres li devëout
q'il n'i alast a celle foiz,
enragiez fu e si destroiz
qe par un poi n'a molt laidi 105
celle qi ce li a basti.
lui e s'amor a toz jors pert,
qant ce a dit a descovert
sor son devié, sor sa manace :
jamés n'iert jors q'il ne la hace, 110
e parun poi q'il ne la fiert.
ses armes li demande, e qiert
isnelement senz demorance
qe plus ne fera atardance.
    La dame les out destornees, 115
mes a force sont raportees.
son hauberc vest isnelement.
Andromacha el paviment
par maintes foiz estut pasmer,
qant elle vit son cors armer. 120
molt fait grant duel et angoissous ;
le jor redote perillous.

molt li prie qe il remaigne
e qe son corage refraigne.
merci li crie molt sovent;   125
ne li vaut rien, qant ce entent,
qe n'i pora merci trover
ne por braire ne por crïer,
e voit qe por nulle maniere,
por dit, por fait ne por proiiere   130
ne le pora plus retenir,
si a les dames fait venir,
sa mere e ses belles serors.
o criz, o lermes e o plors
l'ont deproiié e conjuré   135
e en maint senz amonesté
q'il ne s'en isse e q'il n'i aille.
n'i a proiiere qi rien vaille,
ne lor monte ne lor vaut rien.
'fiz,' fait la mere, ' or sai ge   140
          bien
qe tu n'as mais cure de moi
ne de ta fame ne dou roi,
qi noz volontez contrediz.
bien devroies croire noz diz,
beauz douz amis, ne nos gerpir.   145
com porïons senz toi garir ?
fiz, chiers amis, qe ferions
se ton cors perdu avïons ?
n'i a celui ne s'oceïst
e cui li cuers ja ne partist.   150
car remanez, beauz amis chiers :
creez les diz de cez moilliers.'
qi donc veïst a com grant peine
Polixena e dame Heleine
se metoient al detenir !   155
mes rien ne vaut, car retenir
nel pueent pas por nulle rien ;
ce lor afie et jure bien.
tant est iriez ne set qe face :
Andromacha het e menace.   160

Quant elle voit qe nëant iert,
o ses dous poinz granz cous se fiert,
fier duel demaine e fier martire,
ses cheveus trait e ront e tire.
bien resemble feme desvee :   165
tote enragiee, eschevelee,
e trestote fors de son sen
court por son fil Asternaten.
des euz plore molt tendrement,
entre ses braz l'encharge e prent.   170
vint el palés atot arieres,
o il chauçoit ses genoillieres.
as piez li met e si li dit
'sire, por cest enfant petit,
qe tu engendras de ta char,   175
te pri nel tiegnes a eschar
ce qe je t'ai dit e nuncié.
aies de cest enfant pitié :
jamés des euz ne te verra.
s'ui assenbles a ceuz de la,   180
hui est ta mort, hui est ta fins.
de toi remandra orfenins.
cruëlz de cuer, lous enragiez,
par qoi ne vos en prent pitiez ?
par qoi volez si tost morir ?   185
par qoi volez si tost guerpir
et moi e li e vostre pere
e voz serors e vostre mere ?
par qoi nos laisseroiz perir ?
coment porrons sens vos gerir ?   190
lasse, com male destinee !'
a icest mot chaï pasmee
a cas desus le paviment.
celle l'en lieve isnelement
qi estrange duel en demeine :   195
c'est sa seroge, dame Heleine.

Fragment du Chevalier à la Charrette, par Chrestien de Troyes

(12ème *siècle*)

Le droit chemin vont cheminant,
Tant qui li jors vet déclinant,
Et vienent au pon de l'espée
Après none, vers la vesprée.
Au pié del' pont, qui molt est max,   5
Sont descendu de lor chevax,
Et voient l'ève félenesse
Noire et bruiant, roide et espesse,
Tant leide et tant espoantable
Com se fust li fluns au déable :   10
Et tant périlleuse et parfonde
Qu'il n'est riens nule an tot le monde
S'ele i chéoit, ne fust alée
Ausi com an la mer betée.
Et li ponz qui est an travers   15
Estoit de toz autres divers,
Qu'ainz tex ne fu ne jamès n'iert.
Einz ne fu, qui voir m'an requiert,
Si max pont ne si male planche :
D'une espée forbie et blanche   20
Estoit li ponz sor l'ève froide.
Mès l'espée estoit forz et roide,
Et avoit deus lances de lonc.
De chasque part ot uns grant tronc
Où l'espée estoit cloffichiée.   25
Jà nus ne dot que il i chiée,
Porce que ele brist ne ploit.
Si ne sanble-il pas qui la voit
Qu'ele puisse grant fès porter.
Ce feisoit molt desconforter   30
Les deus chevaliers qui estoient
Avoec le tierz, que il cuidoient

Que dui lyon ou dui liepart
Au chief del pont de l'autre part
Fussent lié à un perron.   35
L'ève et li ponz et li lyon
Les metent an itel fréor
Que il tranblent tuit de péor.

.   .   .   .

Cil ne li sèvent plus que dire,
Mès de pitié plore et sopire   40
Li uns et li autres molt fort.
Et cil de trespasser le gort
Au mialz que il set s'aparoille,
Et fet molt estrange mervoille,
Que ses piez désire et ses mains.   45
N'iert mie toz antiers ne sains
Quant de l'autre part iert venuz.
Bien s'iert sor l'espée tenuz,
Qui plus estoit tranchanz que fauz,
As mains nues et si deschauz   50
Que il ne s'est lessiez an pié
Souler ne chauce n'avanpié.
De ce guères ne s'esmaioit
S'ès mains et ès piez se plaioit;
Mialz se voloit-il mahaignier   55
Que chéoir el pont et baignier
An l'ève dont jamès n'issist.
A la grant dolor con li sist
S'an passe outre et à grant destrece:
Mains et genolz et piez se blece.   60
Mès tot le rasoage et sainne
Amors qui le conduist et mainne:
Si li estoit à sofrir dolz.
A mains, à piez et à genolz
Fet tant que de l'autre part vient.   65

ALIXANDRE ET LA FOREST DES PUCELES. FRAGMENT
DU ROMAN D'ALIXANDRE

(12^{cme} *siècle*)

Moult fu biaus li vregiers et gente la praële :
moult souëf i flairoient et radise et canele,
garingaus et encens, chitouaus de Tudele.
ens en mi liu del pré ot une fontainele,
li ruisiaus estoit clers et blanque li gravele.   5
a rouge or espagnois passast on la praële.
de fin or tresjeté i ot une ymagele,
sor deus piés de crestal, qui ne ciet ne cancele,
qui reçoit le conduit qui vient par la ruële.
el vregier lor avint une mervelle bele,   10
que desus cescun arbre avoit une pucele :
il nen i avoit nule sergante ne ancele,
mais toutes d'un parage, cascune ert damoisele.
le cors orent bien fait, petite la mamele,
les ious vairs et rïans et la color novele.   15
plus ert espris d'amor ki voit la damoisele
que s'il ëust le cuer bruï d'une estincele.
a Alixandre ont dit li viellart le novele.
quant li rois l'a oïe, joians li fu et bele.
quanques i a alé, ne prise une cinele,   20
s'il ne les voit de prés : les II viellars apele :
' conduisiés moi cest ost de lés ceste vaucele,
que dusqu'en la forest n'ert ostee ma scle.'

En icele forest, dont vos m'oëz conter,
nesune male choze ne puet laians entrer.   25
li home ne les bestes n'i ozent converser,
onques en nesun tans ne vit hon yverner
ne trop froit ne trop chaut ne neger ne geler.
ce conte l'escripture pue hom n'i doit entrer,
si il nen at talent de conquerre ou d'amer.   30
les deuesses d'amors i doivent habiter,
car c'est lor paradix ou el doivent entrer.
li rois de Macedoine en a oï parler,
qui cercha les merveilles dou mont et de la mer,

et ce fist il meïsmes enz ou fons avaler   35
en un vessel de voirre, ce ne puet hon fausser,
qu'il fist faire il meïsmes fort et rëont et cler
et enclorre de fer qu'il ne pëust quasser,
s'il l'estëust a roche ou aillors ahurter,
et si que il poet bien par mi outre esgarder,   40
por vëoir les poissons tornoier et joster
et faire lor agaiz et sovent cembeler.
et quant il vint a terre, nou mist a oublïer :
la prist la sapïence dou mont a conquester
et faire ses agaiz et sa gent ordener   45
et conduire les oz et sagement mener,
car ce fust toz li mieudres qui ainz pëust monter
en cheval por conquerre ne de lance joster,
li gentiz et li larges et li prex por doner.
la forest des puceles ot oï deviser.   50
cil qui tot volt conquerre i ot talent d'aler :
souz ciel n'a home en terre qui l'en pëust torner.

FRAGMENT DU ROMAN DE RENART

(12ᵉᵐᵉ siècle)

Si conme Renart fist peschier a Ysengrin les anguiles

Ce fu un poi devant Noël
que l'en metoit bacons en sel,
li ciex fu clers et estelez,
et li vivier fu si gelez
ou Ysengrin devoit peschier,   5
qu'on pooit par desus treschier,
fors tant c'un pertuis i avoit,
qui des vilains faiz i estoit,
ou il menoient lor atoivre
chascune nuit juër et boivre :   10
un seel i estoit laissiez.
la vint Renarz toz eslaissez

et son compere apela.
'sire,' fait il, 'traiiez vos ça :
ci est la plenté des poissons   15
et li engins ou nos peschons
les anguiles et les barbiaus
et autres poissons bons et biaus.'
dist Ysengrins 'sire Renart,
or le prenez de l'une part,   20
sel me laciez bien a la qeue.'
Renarz le prent et si li neue
entor la qeue au miex qu'il puet.
'frere,' fait il, ' or vos estuet
moul sagement a maintenir   25
por les poissons avant venir.'
lors s'est en un buisson fichiez :
si mist son groing entre ses piez
tant que il voie que il face.
et Ysengrins est seur la glace   30
et li sëaus en la fontaine
plains de glaçons a bone estraine.
l'aive conmence a englacier
et li sëaus a enlacier
qui a la qeue fu noëz :   35
de glaçons fu bien serondez.
la qeue est en l'aive gelee
et en la glace seelee.

LES MEDECINS. FRAGMENT DE LA BIBLE GUIOT

(13ème siècle)

Des fisicïens me merveil :
de lor huevre et de lor conseil
rai ge certes mont grant merveille
nule vie ne s'apareille
a la lor, trop par est diverse   5
et sor totes autres perverse.

bien les nomme li communs nons,
mais je ne cuit qu'i ne soit hons
qui ne les doie mont douter.
il ne voudroient ja trover   10
nul home sanz aucun mehaing.
maint oingnement font e maint baing
ou il n'a ne senz ne raison.
cil eschape d'orde prison
qui de lor mains puet eschaper.   15
sevent bien mentir et guiler
et faire noble contenance,
tout ont trové fors la crëance
que les genz n'ont lor fait a bien.
tiex mil se font fisicïen   20
qui n'en sevent voir nes que gié.
li plus maistre en sont mont chargié
de grant onnui, n'il n'est mestiers
dont il soit tant de mençongiers.
il ocïent mont de la gent :   25
ja n'ont ne ami ne parent
que il volsissent trover sain ;
de ce resont il trop vilain.
mont a d'ordure en ces lïens.
qui en main as fisicïens   30
se met, fols est.   il m'ont ëu
entre lor mains : onques ne fu,
ce cuit, nule plus orde vie.
je n'aim mie lor compaignie,
si m'aït dex, qant je sui sains :   35
honiz est qui chiet en lor mains.
par foi, qant je malades fui,
moi covint soffrir lor ennui.

MARIE DE FRANCE

(13ème siècle)

FABLES

I

Dou leu et de l'aingniel

Ce dist dou leu e dou aignel,
qui beveient a un rossel :
li lox a la sorse beveit
e li aigniaus aval esteit.
irieement parla li lus   5
ki mult esteit cuntralïus ;
par mautalent palla a lui :
‘ tu m’as,’ dist, ‘ fet grant anui.’
li aignez li ad respundu
‘ sire, eh quei ? ’ ‘ dunc ne veis tu ?   10
tu m’as ci ceste aigue tourblee :
n’en puis beivre ma saolee.
autresi m’en irai, ce crei,
cum jeo ving, tut murant de sei.’
li aignelez adunc respunt   15
‘ sire, ja bevez vus amunt :
de vus me vient kankes j’ai beu.’
‘ qoi,’ fist li lox, ‘ maldis me tu ? ’
l’aigneus respunt ‘ n’en ai voleir.’
li lous li dit ‘ jeo sai de veir,   20
ce meïsme me fist tes pere
a ceste surce u od lui ere,
or ad sis meis, si cum jeo crei.’
‘ qu’en retraiez,’ feit il, ‘ sor mei ?
n’ere pas nez, si cum jeo cuit.’   25
‘ e cei pur ce,’ li lus a dit :
‘ ja me fais tu ore cuntraire
e chose ke tu ne deiz faire.’
dunc prist li lox l’engnel petit,
as denz l’estrangle, si l’ocit.   30

Moralité.

Ci funt li riche robëur,
li vesconte e li jugëur,
de ceus k'il unt en lur justise.
fausse aqoison par cuveitise
truevent assez pur eus cunfundre. 35
suvent les funt as plaiz semundre,
la char lur tolent e la pel,
si cum li lox fist a l'ainguel.

II

LA MORS ET LI BOSQUILLON

Tant de loin que de prez n'est laide
La mors.   La clamoit a son ayde 40
Tosjors, ung povre bosquillon
Que n'ot chevance ne sillon :
'Que ne viens, disoit, o ma mie,
'Finir ma dolorouse vie !'
Tant brama qu'advint; et de voix 45
Terrible : ' Que veux-tu ?—Ce bois
Que m'aydiez a carguer, Madame !'
Peur et labeur n'ont mesme game.

THIBAULT DE CHAMPAGNE.   CHANSON D'AMOUR

(13ème *siècle*)

Contre le tens qui desbrise
Yvers, et revient este,
Et la mauvis se desguise,
Qui de lonc tens n'a chante
Ferai chanson.   Car a gre 5
Me vient que j'aie en pense
Amor, qui en moi s'est mise.
Bien m'a droit son dart gete.

U

Douce dame, de franchise,
N'ai je point en vos trove :   10
S'ele ne s'i est puis mise
Que je ne vos esgarde,
Trop avez vers moi fierte.
Mais ce fait vostre biaute,
Ou il n'i a pas de devise,   15
Tant en i a grand plante.

En moi n'a point d'astenance
Que je puisse aillors penser,
Fors que la, ou conoissance
Ne merci ne puis trover.   20
Bien fui fait por li amer ;
Car ne m'en puis saoler.
Et quant plus aurai cheance,
Plus la me convendra douter.

D'une riens sui en doutance,   25
Que je ne puis plus celer,
Qu'en li n'ait un po d'enfance.
Ce me fait deconforter,
Que s'a moi a bon penser
Ne l'ose ele desmontrer.   30
Si feist qu'a sa semblance
Le poisse deviner.

Des que je li fis priere
Et la pris a esgarder,
Me fist amors la lumiere   35
Des iels par le cuer passer.
Cil conduit me fait grever :
Dont je ne me soi garder :
Ne ne puet torner arriere
Mon cuer ; miex voudroit crever.   40

Dame, a vos m'estuet clamer,
Et que merci vos requiere.
Diex m'i laist pitie trover !

Li Fabliaus des Perdris

(13ème *siècle*)

Por ce que fabliaus dire sueil,
en lieu de fable dire vueil
une aventure qui est vraie,
d'un vilain qui delés sa haie
prist deus pertris par aventure.   5
en l'atorner mist moult sa cure :
sa fame les fist au feu metre.
ele s'en sot bien entremetre :
le feu a fait, la haste atorne.
et li vilains tantost s'en torne,   10
por le prestre s'en va corant.
mais au revenir targa tant
que cuites furent les pertris.
la dame a le haste jus mis,
s'en pinça une pelëure,   15
quar moult ama la lechëure,
quant diex li dona a avoir.
ne bëoit pas a grant avoir,
mais a tos ses bons acomplir.
l'une pertris cort envaïr ;   20
andeus les eles en menjue.
puis est alee en mi la rue
savoir se ses sires venoit.
quant ele venir ne le voit,
tantost arriere s'en retorne,   25
et le remanant tel atorne,
mal du morsel qui ramainsist.
adonc s'apenssa et si dist
que l'autre encore mengera.
moult tres bien set qu'ele dira,   30
s'on li demande que devindrent.
ele dira que li chat vindrent,
quant ele les ot arrier traites ;
tost li orent des mains retraites,

et chascuns la seue en porta.   35
ainsi, ce dist, eschapera.
puis va en mi la rue ester,
por son mari abeveter;
et quant ele nel voit venir,
la langue li prist a fremir   40
sus la pertris qu'ele ot laissie.
ja ert toute vive enragie,
s'encor n'en a un petitet.
le col en trait tout souavet,
si le menja par grant douçor.   45
ses dois en leche tout entor.
'lasse,' fait ele, 'que ferai,
se tout menjue, que dirai?
et coment le porrai lassier?
j'en ai moult tres grant desirrier.   50
or aviegne qu'avenir puet,
quar toute mengier le m'estuet.'
    Tant dura cele demoree
que la dame fu saoulee,
et li vilains ne targa mie: 55
a l'ostel vint, en haut s'escrie
'diva, sont cuites les pertris?'
'sire,' dist ele, 'ainçois va pis,
quar mengies les a li chas.'
li vilains saut isnel le pas,   60
seure li cort comme enragiés.
ja li ëust les iex sachiés,
quant ele crie 'c'est gas, c'est gas.
fuiiés,' fait ele, 'Sathanas!
couvertes sont por tenir chaudes.'   65
'ja vous chantasse putes laudes,'
fait il, 'foi que je doi saint Ladre.
or ça mon bon hanap de madre
et ma plus bele blanche nape.
si l'estenderai sus ma chape   70
sous cele treille en cel praël.'
'mais vous prenés vostre coutel
qui grant mestier a d'aguisier:
si le faites un pou trenchier

a cele pierre en cele cort.'   75
li vilains se despoille et cort,
le coutel tout nu en sa main.
a tant es vos le chapelain
qui leens venoit por mengier.
a la dame vint sans targier,   80
si l'acole moult doucement.
et cele li dist simplement :
'sire,' dist el, 'fuiiés, fuiiés !
ja ne serai ou vous soiiés
honis ne malmis de vo cors.   85
mes sires est alés la fors
por son grant coutel aguisier,
et dist qu'il vous voudra trenchier
les coilles, s'il vous puet tenir.'
'de dieu te puist il souvenir,'   90
dist li prestres, 'qu'est que tu dis ?
nous devons mengier deus pertris
que tes sires prist hui matin.'
cele li dist 'par saint Martin,
ceens n'a pertris ne oisel.   95
de vo mengier me seroit bel
et moi peseroit de vo mal.
mais ore esgardés la aval,
comme il aguise son coutel.'
'jel voi,' dist il, 'par mon chapel,   100
je cuit bien que tu as voir dit.'
leens demora moult petit,
ains s'en fuï grant alëure.
et cele crie a bone ëure
'venés vous en, sire Gombaut.'   105
'qu'as tu,' dist il, 'se diex te saut ?'
'que j'ai ? tout a tens le savrés ;
mais se tost corre ne pöés,
perte i avrés si com je croi,
quar par la foi que je vous doi,   110
li prestre en porte vos pertris.'
li preudom fu tos aatis,
le coutel en porte en sa main,
s'en cort aprés le chapelain :

quant il le vit, se li escrie   115
'ainsi nes en porterés mie.'
puis s'escrie a grans alenees
'bien les en portés eschaufees.
ça les lerrés : se vous ataing,
vous seriés mauvais compaing,   120
se vous les mangiiés sens moi.'
li prestre esgarde derrier soi
et voit acorre le vilain.
quant voit le coutel en sa main,
mors cuide estre, se il l'ataint.   125
de tost corre pas ne se faint,
et li vilains penssoit de corre,
qui les pertris cuidoit rescorre ;
mais li prestres de grant randon
s'est enfermés en sa maison.   130

A l'ostel li vilains retorne,
et lors sa feme en araisone :
'diva,' fait il, 'et quar me dis
comment tu perdis les pertris ? '
cele li dist 'se diex m'aït,   135
tantost que li prestres me vit,
si me prïa, se tant l'amasse,
que je les pertris li monstrasse,
quar moult volentiers les verroit ;
et je le menai la tout droit   140
ou je les avoie couvertes.
il ot tantost les mains ouvertes,
si les prist et si s'en fuï.
mais je gueres ne le sivi,
ains le vous fis moult tost savoir.'   145
cil respont 'bien pués dire voir :
or le laissons a itant estre.'
ainsi fu engingniés le prestre
et Gombaus qui les pertris prist.
par exemple cis fabliaus dist :   150
fame est faite por decevoir.
mençonge fait devenir voir

et voir fait devenir mençonge.
cil n'i vout metre plus d'alonge
qui fist cest fablel et ces dis.   155
ci faut li fabliaus des pertris.

FRAGMENTS DU ROMAN DE LA ROSE PAR GUILLAUME DE LORRIS

(13ᵉᵐᵉ *siècle*)

I

Promenade Matinale

En iceli tens déliteus,
Que tote riens d'amer s'esfroie,
Sonjai une nuit que j'estoie.
Ce m'iert avis en mon dormant,
Qu'il estoit matin durement;   5
De mon lit tantost me levai,
Chauçai-moi et mes mains lavai.
Lors trais une aguille d'argent
D'un aguiller mignot et gent,
Si pris l aguille à enfiler.   10
Hors de vile oi talent d'aler,
Por oïr des oisiaus les sons
Qui chantoient par ces boissons
En icele saison novele;
Cousant mes manches à videle,   15
M'en alai tot seus esbatant,
Et les oiselés escoutant,
Qui de chanter moult s'engoissoient
Par ces vergiers qui florissoient,
Jolis, gais et pleins de léesce.   20
Vers une rivière m'adresce
Que j'oï près d'ilecques bruire,
Car ne me soi aillors déduire

Plus bel que sus cele rivière.
D'un tertre qui près d'iluec iere   25
Descendoit l'iaue grant et roide,
Clere, bruiant et aussi froide
Comme puiz, ou comme fonta ne,
Et estoit poi mendre de Saine,
Mès qu'ele iere plus espandue.   30
Onques mès n'avoie véue
Tele iaue qui si bien coroit :
Moult m'abelissoit et séoit
A regarder le leu plaisant.
De l'iaue clere et reluisant   35
Mon vis rafreschi et lavai.
Si vi tot covert et pavé
Le fons de l'iaue de gravele ;
La praérie grant de bele
Très au pié de l'iaue batoit.   40
Clere et serie et bele estoit
La matinée et atemprée :
Lors m'en alai parmi la prée
Contreval l'iaue esbanoiant.
Tot le rivage costoiant.   45

II

Portrait de l'Hypocrisie

Une ymage ot emprès escrite,
Qui sembloit bien estre ypocrite,
Papelardie ert apelée.
C'est cele qui en recelée,
Quant nus ne s'en puet prendre garde,   50
De nul mal faire ne se tarde.
El fait dehors le marmiteus,
Si a le vis simple et piteus,
Et semble sainte créature ;
Mais sous ciel n'a male aventure   55
Qu'ele ne pense en son corage.
Moult la ressembloit bien l'ymage

Qui faite fu à sa semblance,
Qu'el fu de simple contenance;
Et si fu chaucie et vestue   60
Tout ainsinc cum fame rendue.
En sa main un sautier tenoit,
Et sachiés que moult se penoit
De faire à Dieu prières faintes,
Et d'appeler et sains et saintes.   65
El ne fu gaie ne jolive,
Ains fu par semblant ententive
Du tout à bonnes ovres faire;
Et si avoit vestu la haire.
Et sachiés que n'iere pas grasse.   70
De jeuner sembloit estre lasse,
S'avoit la color pale et morte.
A li et as siens ert la porte
Dévéée de Paradis;
Car icel gent si font lor vis   75
Amegrir, ce dit l'Evangile,
Por avoir loz parmi la vile,
Et por un poi de gloire vaine,
Qui lor toldra Dieu et son raine.

PASTOURELLE

(13*ème siècle*)

De Saint Quentin a Cambrai
Chevalchoie l'autre jour;
Les un boisson esgardai,
Touse i vi de bel atour.
La colour   5
Ot freche com rose en mai.
De cuer gai
Chantant la trovai
Ceste chansonnete
    'En non deu, j'ai bel ami,   10
    Cointe et joli,
    Tant soie je brunete.'

Vers la pastoure tornai
Quant la vi en son destour;
Hautement la saluai   15
Et di 'deus vos doinst bon jour
Et honour.
Celle ke ci trove ai,
Sens delai
Ses amis serai.'   20
Dont dist la doucete
    'En non deu, j'ai bel ami,
    Cointe et joli,
    Tant soie je brunete.'

Deles li seoir alai   25
Et li priai de s'amour,
Celle dist ' Je n'amerai
Vos ne autrui par nul tour,
Sens pastour,
Robin, ke fiencie l'ai.   30
Joie en ai,
Si en chanterai
Ceste chansonnete
    'En non deu, j'ai bel ami,
    Cointe et joli,   35
    Tant soie je brunete.'

CHASTEL-NOBLE.   FRAGMENT DE CLEOMADES, PAR
ADENET LE ROI

(13ème *siècle*)

Cleomades vit un chast
encoste un plain, tres fort et bel,
ou il ot mainte bele tour.
bos et rivieres vit entour,
vignes et praieries grans.   5
mult fu li chastiaus bien sëans.
la façon dou castel deïsse,
mais je dont mult que ne meïsse

trop longement au deviser :
pour ce m'en voel briément passer.   10
    Du chastel vous dirai le non :
miols sëant ne vit ainc nus hom,
lors l'apieloit on Chastel-noble.
n'ot tel dusque en Constantinoble,
ne de la dusque en Osterice   15
n'ot plus bel, plus fort ne plus rice.
carmans a cel point i estoit
que Cleomadés vint la droit.
forment li sambloit li chastiaus
de toutes pars riches et biaus.   20
    Cleomadés lors s'avisa
que viers le chastel se trera.
bien pensoit qu'en tel liu manoient
gent qui de grant afaire estoient.
che fu si qu'apriés l'ajournee   25
mult faisoit bele matinee,
car mais estoit nouviaus entrés :
c'est uns tans ki mult est amés
et de toutes gens conjoïs ;
pour çou a non mais li jolis.   30
une tres grant tour haute et forte
avoit asés priés de la porte,
ki estoit couverte de plon,
plate deseure, car adon
les faisoit on ensi couvrir   35
pour engins et pour assallir.
    Cleomadés a avisee
la tour ki estoit haute et lee ;
lors pense qu'il s'arestera
sor cele tour tant qu'il savra,   40
se il peut, a certainité
quel païs c'est en verité.
lors a son cheval adrechié
viers la tour de marbre entaillié.
les chevilletes si tourna   45
que droit sour la tour aresta.
si coiement s'est avalés
que sour aighe coie vait nés.

RUSTEBEUF

(13ème *siècle*)

I

Fragment du Mariage Rustebeuf

En l'an de l'incarnacïon,
VIII jors aprés la nascïon
Jhesu qui soufri passïon,
en l'an soissante,
qu'arbres n'a foïlle, oisel ne chante,   5
fis je toute la rien dolante
qui de cuer m'aime :
nis li musarz musart me claime.
or puis filer, qu'il me faut traime ;
mult ai a faire.   10
deus ne fist home tant de pute aire,
tant li aie fait de contraire
ne de martire,
s'il en mon martire se mire,
qui ne doie de bon cuer dire   15
'je te claim cuite.'
envoier un home en Egypte,
ceste dolor est plus petite
que n'est la moie ;
je n'en puis mais se je m'esmoie.   20
l'en dit que fous qui ne foloie
pert sa saison ;
sui je marïez sanz raison ?
or n'ai ne borde ne maison.
encor plus fort :   25
por plus doner de reconfort
a ceus qui me heent de mort,
tel fame ai prise
que nus fors moi n'aime ne prise.
et s'estoit povre et entreprise   30
quant je la pris,

a ci mariage de pris,
c'or sui povres et entrepris
ausi comme ele,
et si n'est pas gente ne bele.   35
cinquante anz a en s'escuële,
s'est maigre et seche :
n'ai pas paor qu'ele me treche.
despuis que fu nez en la greche
deus de Marie,   40
ne fu mais tele espouserie.
je sui toz plains d'envoiserie :
bien pert a l'uevre.

II

Le Testament de l'Ane

L'evesques si de li s'aprouche
Que parleir i pout bouche a bouche,   45
Et li prestres lieve la chiere.
Qui lors n'out pas monnoie chiere
Desoz sa chape tint l'argent :
Ne l'ozat montreir par la gent.
En concillant conta son conte :   50
'Sire, ci n'afiert plus lonc conte :
Mes asnes at lonc tans vescu ;
Mout avoie en li boen escu,
Il m'at servi, et volontiers,
Moult loiaument XX. ans entiers,   55
Se je soie de Dieu assoux
Chacun an gaaingnoit XX. sols,
Tant qu'il ot espargnié XX. livres.
Pour ce qu'il soit d'enfer delivres
Les vos laisse en son testament,'   60
Et dist l'evesques : 'Diex l'ament,
Et si li pardoint ses mesfais
Et toz les pechiez qu'il at fais !'

CHANSONNETTE, PAR ADANS DE LA HALLE
(13ᵉᵐᵉ *siècle*)

Diex !
Comment porroie
Trouver voie
D'aler a chelui
Cui amiete je sui ?   5
Chainturelle, va-i
   En lieu de mi ;
Car tu fus sieue aussi,
si m'en conquerra miex.
Mais comment serai sans ti ?   10
   Dieus !
Chainturelle, mar vous vi ;
Au deschaindre m'ochies ;
De mes grietés a vous me confortoie,
Quant je vous sentoie,   15
   Ai mi !
A ! le saveur de mon ami.
Ne pour quant d'autres en ai,
A cleus d'argent et de soie,
   Pour men user.   20
Mais lasse ! comment porroie
   Sans cheli durer
   Qui me tient en joie ?

Canchonnete, chelui proie
   Qui le m'envoya,   25
Puis que jou ne puis aler la.
   Qu'il en viengne a moi,
   Chi droit,
   A jour failli,
Pour faire tous ses boins,   30
   Et il m'orra,
Quant il ert joins,
Canter a haute vois :
Par chi va la mignotise,
Par chi ou je vois.   35

FRAGMENT DU ROMAN DE LA ROSE, PAR JEHAN DE MEUNG

(13ème et 14ème siècle)

Comment le traistre Faulx-Semblant
Si va les cueurs des gens emblant,
Pour ses vestemens noirs et gris,
Et pour son viz pasle amaisgris.
'Trop sai bien mes habiz changier,   5
Pendre l'un, et l'autre estrangier.
Or sui chevaliers, or sui moines,
Or sui prélas, or sui chanoines,
Or sui clers, autre ore sui prestres,
Or sui desciples, or sui mestres,   10
Or chastelains, or forestiers :
Briément, ge sui de tous mestiers.
Or resui princes, or sui pages,
Or sai parler trestous langages ;
Autre ore sui viex et chenus,   15
Or resui jones devenus.
Or sui Robers, or sui Robins,
Or cordeliers, or jacobins.
Si pren por sivre ma compaigne
Qui me solace et acompaigne   20
(C'est dame Astenance-Contrainte),
Autre desguiséure mainte,
Si cum il li vient à plesir
Por acomplir le sien désir.
Autre ore vest robe de fame ;   25
Or sui damoisele, or sui dame,
Autre ore sui religieuse,
Or sui rendue, or sui prieuse,
Or sui nonain, or sui abesse,
Or sui novice, or sui professe ;   30
Et vois par toutes régions
Cerchant toutes religions.
Mès de religion, sans faille,
G'en pren le grain et laiz la paille ;

Por gens avugler i abit ;   35
Ge n'en quier, sans plus, que l'abit.
Que vous diroie? en itel guise
Cum il me plaist ge me desguise;
Moult sunt en moi mués li vers,
Moult sunt li faiz aux diz divers.   40
Si fais chéoir dedans mes piéges
Le monde par mes priviléges ;
Ge puis confesser et asoldre
(Ce ne me puet nus prélas toldre)
Toutes gens où que ge les truisse ;   45
Ne sai prélat nul qui ce puisse,
Fors l'apostole solement
Qui fist cest establissement
Tout en la faveur de nostre ordre.

BALLADE, PAR JEHANNOT DE LESCUREL.

(14ème siècle)

Amour, voules-vous acorder
Que je muire pour bien amer?
Vo vouloir m'esteut agreer ;
Mourir ne puis plus doucement;
    Vraiement,   5
Amours, faciez voustre talent.

Trop de malfés porte endurer
Pour celi que j'aim sanz fausser.
N'est pas par li, au voir parler,
Ains est par mauparliere gent.   10
    Loiaument,
Amours, faciez voustre talent.

Dous amis, plus ne puis durer
Quant ne puis ne n'os regarder
Vostre dous vis, riant et cler.   15
Mort, alegez mon grief torment;
    Ou, briefment,
Amours, faciez voustre talent.

CHANSON BALLADÉE, PAR GUILLAUME MACHAUT

(14ᵉᵐᵉ *siècle*)

Onques si bonne journée
 Ne fu adjournee,
Com quant je me departi
De ma dame desiree
 A qui j'ay donnee   5
M'amour, et le cuer de mi.

Car la manne descendi
 Et douceur aussi,
Par quoi m'ame saoulee
Fu dou fruit de dous ottri,   10
 Que Pite cueilli
En sa face coulouree.
La fu bien l'onnour gardee
 De la renommee
De son cointe corps joli,   15
Qu'onques villeine pensee
 Ne fu engendree
Ne nee entre moy et li.
Onques si bonne journee, etc.

Souffisance m'enrichi   20
 Et Plaisance si
Qu'onques creature nee
N'ot le cuer si assevi,
 Ne mains de sousci,
Ne joie si affinee.   25
Car la deesse honnouree
 Qui fait l'assemblee
D'amours, d'amie et d'ami,
Coppa le chief de s'espee
 Qui est bien tempree,   30
A Dangier, mon anemi.
Onques si bonne journee, etc.

x

Ma dame l'enseveli,
　　Et Amours par fi
Que sa mort fust tost plouree.　　　　　35
N'onques Honneur ne souffri
　　(Dont je l'en merci)
Que messe li fu chantée.
Sa charongne trainee
　　Fu sans demouree　　　　　　　40
En un lieu dont on dit : fi !
S'en fu ma joie doublee,
　　Quant Honneur l'entree
Ot dou tresor de merci.
Onques si bonne journee, etc.　　　　　45

VIRELAI, PAR EUSTACHE DESCHAMPS

(14ème siècle)

Sui-je, sui-je, sui-je belle ?
Il me semble, a mon avis,
Que j'ay beau front et doulz viz,
Et la bouche vermeilette ;
Dictes moy se je sui belle.　　　　　5

J'ay vers yeulx, petit sourcis,
Le chief blont, le nez traitis,
Ront menton, blanche gorgette ;
Sui-je, sui-je, sui-je belle ?

J'ay dur sain et hault assis,　　　　　10
Lons bras, gresles doys aussis,
Et, par le faulx, sui greslette ;
Dictes moy se je sui belle.

J'ay piez rondes et petiz,
Bien chaussans, et biaux habis,　　　　15
Je sui gaye et foliette ;
Dictes moy se je sui belle.

J'ay mantiaux fourrez de gris,
J'ay chapiaux, j'ay biaux proffis,
Et d'argent mainte espinglette;   20
Sui-je, sui-je, sui-je belle?

J'ay draps de soye, et tabis,
J'ay draps d'or, et blanc et bis,
J'ay mainte bonne chosette;
Dictes moy se je sui belle.   25

Que quinze ans n'ay, je vous dis;
Moult est mes tresors jolys,
S'en garderay la clavette;
Sui-je, sui-je, sui-je belle?

Bien devra estre hardis   30
Cilz, qui sera mes amis,
Qui ora tel damoiselle;
Dictes moy se je sui belle.

Et par dieu, je li plevis,
Que tres loyal, se je vis,   35
Li seray, si ne chancelle;
Sui-je, sui-je, sui-je belle?

Se courtois est et gentilz,
Vaillains, apers, bien apris,
Il gaignera sa querelle;   40
Dictes moy se je sui belle.

C'est uns mondains paradiz
Que d'avoir dame toudiz,
Ainsi fresche, ainsi nouvelle;
Sui-je, sui-je, sui-je belle?   45

Entre vous, acouardiz,
Pensez a ce que je diz;
Cy fine ma chansonnelle;
Sui-je, sui-je, sui-je belle?

BALLADE, PAR ALAIN CHARTIER

(15ᵉᵐᵉ *siècle*)

O folz des folz, et les folz mortelz hommes
Qui vous fiez tant es biens de fortune,
En celle terre, es pays ou nous sommes,
Y avez-vous de chose propre aucune ?
Vous n'y avez chose vostre nes-une,   5
Fors les beaulx dons de grace et de nature.
Se Fortune donc, par cas d'adventure
Vous toult les biens que vostres vous tenez,
Tort ne vous fait, aincois vous fait droicture,
Car vous n'aviez riens quant vous fustes nez.   10

Ne laissez plus le dormir a grans sommes
En vostre lict, par nuict obscure et brune,
Pour acquester richesses a grans sommes.
Ne convoitez chose dessoubz la lune,
Ne de Paris jusques a Pampelune,   15
Fors ce qui fault, sans plus, a creature
Pour recouvrer sa simple nourriture.
Souffise vous d'estre bien renommez,
Et d'emporter bon loz en sepulture :
Car vous n'aviez riens quant vous fustes nez.   20

Les joyeulx fruictz des arbres, et les pommes,
Au temps que fut toute chose commune,
Le beau miel, les glandes et les gommes
Souffisoient bien a chascun et chascune :
Et pour ce fut sans noise et sans rancune.   25
Soyez contens des chaulx et des froidures,
Et me prenez Fortune doulce et seure.
Pour vos pertes, griefve dueil n'en menez,
Fors a raison, a point, et a mesure,
Car vous n'aviez riens quant vous fustes nez.   30

Se Fortune vous fait aucune injure,
C'est de son droit, ja ne l'en reprenez,
Et perdissiez jusques a la vesture :
Car vous n'aviez riens quant vous fustes nez.

RONDEL, PAR CHARLES D'ORLÉANS

(15ème *siècle*)

Le temps a laissié son manteau
de vent, de froidure et de pluye,
et s'est vestu de broderye,
de soleil luyant, cler et beau.
    Il n'y a beste ne oiseau   5
qu' en son jargon ne chante ou crye.
le temps a laissié son manteau
de vent, de froidure et de pluye.
    Riviere, fontaine et ruisseau
portent en livree jolie   10
gouttes d'argent d'orfavrerie ;
chascun s'abille de nouveau.
le temps a laissié son manteau.

FRAGMENT DE MAISTRE PATHELIN

(15ème *siècle*)

Path. ce bergier ne peut nullement
    respondre aux fais que l'on propose,
    s'il n'a du conseil ; et il n'ose
    ou il ne scet en demander.
    s'il vous plaisoit moy commander   5
    que je fusse a luy, j' y seroye.
Juge. avecques luy ? je cuideroye
    que ce fust trestoute froidure :
    c'est peu d'acquest. *Path.* mais je vous jure
    qu'aussi je n'en veuil rien avoir :   10
    pour dieu soit. or je voys sçavoir
    au pauvret qu'il voudra me dire,
    et s'il me sçaura point instruire
    pour respondre aux fais de partie.
    il auroit dure departie   15
    de ce, qui ne le secourroit.
    vien ça, mon amy. qui pourroit

trouver ? entens. *Berg.* bee. *Path.* quel bee, dea !
par le sainct sang que dieu crëa,
es tu fol ? dy moy ton affaire.   20
Berg. bee. *Path.* bee ! oys tu tes brebis braire ?
c'est pour ton prouffit : entens y.
Berg. bee. *Path.* et dy ouÿ ou nenny,
c'est bien faict. dy tousjours, feras ?
Bèrg. bee. *Path.* plus haut, tu t'en trouveras   25
en grans depens, ou je m'en doubte.
Berg. bee. *Path.* or est plus fol cil qui boute
tel fol naturel en procés.
ha, sire, envoyez l'en a ses
brebis : il est fol de nature.   30
Drapp. est il fol ? sainct sauveur d'Esture !
il est plus saige que vous n'estes.
Path. envoyez le garder ses bestes,
sans jour que jamais ne retourne.
que maudit soit il qui adjourne   35
tels folz que ne fault adjourner.
Drapp. et l'en fera l'en retourner
avant que je puisse estre ouÿ ?
Path. m'aist dieu, puis qu'il est foul, ouÿ.
pour quoy ne fera ? *Drapp.* he dea, sire,   40
au moins laissez moy avant dire
et faire mes conclusïons.
ce ne sont pas abusïons
que je vous dy ne mocqueries.
Juge. ce sont toutes tribouilleries   45
que de plaider a folz ne a folles.
escoutez, a moins de parolles
la court n'en sera plus tenue.
Drapp. s'en iront ilz saus retenue
de plus revenir ? *Juge.* et quoy doncques ?   50
Path. revenir ? vous ne veistes oncques
plus fol en faict ne en response :
et cil ne vault pas mieulx une once.
tous deux sont folz et sans cervelle :
par saincte Marie la belle,   55
eux deux n'en ont pas un quarat.

Fragment du Mistere de la Passion

(15ème *siècle*)

Ici deschargent Jesus de la croix.

Simon. or avant donc, puis que ainsi va.
 je ferai vostre voulenté ;
 mais il me poise en verité
 de la honte que vous me faictes.
 o Jesus, de tous les prophettes   5
 le plus sainct et le plus begnin,
 vous venés a piteuse fin,
 veue vostre vie vertüeuse,
 quant vostre croix dure et honteuse
 pour vostre mort fault que je porte.   10
 se c'est a tort, je m'en rapporte
 a ceulx qui vous ont forjugé.
   Ici chargent la croix a Simon.
Nembroth. Messeigneurs, il est bien chargé ;
 cheminons, depeschons la voie.   15
Salmanazar. j'ai grant desir que je le voie
 fiché en ce hault tabernacle,
 a sçavoir s'il fera miracle,
 quant il sera cloué dessus.
Jeroboam. seigneurs, hastés moi ce Jesus   20
 et ces deux larrons aux coustés.
 s'ilz ne vuellent, si les battez
 si bien qu'il n'y ait que redire.
Claquedent. a cela ne tiendra pas, sire.
 nous en ferons nostre povoir.   25
 Ici porte Simon une partie de la croix et
  Jesus l'autre et le battent les sergens.
Dieu le pere. Pitié doit tout cueur esmouvoir
 a lamenter piteusement
 le martyre et le gref tourment   30
 que Jesus, mon chier filz, endure.
 il porte detresse tant dure,
 que, puis que le monde dura,
 homme si dure n'endura,

laquelle ne peult plus durer   35
sans la mort honteuse endurer,
et n'aura son sainct corps duree
tant qu'il n'ait la mort enduree,
il appert, car plus va durant,
et plus est tourment endurant,   40
sans quelque confort qui l'alege.
si convient que la mort abrege
et de l'executer s'apreste,
pour satiffaire a la requeste
de dame Justice severe,   45
qui pour requeste ne prïere
ne veult rien de ses drois quitter.
Michel, allés donc conforter
en ceste amere passïon
mon filz, plain de dilectïon,   50
qui veult dure mort en gré prendre
et va sa doulce chair estandre
ou puissant arbre de la croix.
Sainct Michel. pere du ciel et roi des rois,
humblement a chere assimplie   55
sera parfaicte et acomplie
vostre voulenté juste et bonne.
 Ici descendent les anges de paradis.

TROISIÈME PARTIE

GLOSSAIRE

LES mots vieux-français cités et traduits dans la partie grammaticale de cet ouvrage et ceux dont la forme et le sens se trouvent dans les dictionnaires modernes ont été exclus de ce glossaire.

Les mots dont la traduction anglaise est donnée dans l'index ne figurent pas toujours dans le glossaire.

Les principales abréviations sont :—

abs.	pour	absolu	interj.	pour	interjection
adj.	,,	adjectif	intr.	,,	intransitif
adv.	,,	adverbe	lat.	,,	latin
cf.	,,	comparez	n.	,,	nominatif
dim.	,,	diminutif	part.	,,	participe
f.	,,	féminin	prép.	,,	préposition
fig.	,,	figuré	prés.	,,	présent
génit.	,,	génitif	réfl.	,,	réfléchi
imp.	,,	impersonnel	subs.	,,	substantif
int.	,,	intensif	v.	,,	voir

A, *prép.*, *à, avec, auprès de, comme, de, en, par, selon, sur;* a son vivant, *pendant sa vie;* ad en avant, *à venir;* a or, *en or*

a, ha, *interj.*

aatir, *irriter*

abaier, *aboyer*

abandoner,-onner, *abandonner; part. troublé*

abatre, abbatre, *abattre*

abb- *cf.* ab-

abbes, abes, abbeit, abé, *abbé*

abesse, *abbesse*

abelir, *plaire, amuser*

abeveter, *guetter*

abiller, *habiller*

abisme, abysme, abit, *abîme*

abit *v.* habit *et* habiter

abregier, abb- *abréger, faire vite*

absoudre, *cf.* asoldre

abusîon, *tromperie, faussetés*

acc- *cf.* ac-

acerin, *d'acier*

acertes, *certes, instamment*

achater, acater, acheter, achapter, *acheter, procurer, subir*

acheter *v.* achater

acier, acer, achier, *acier*

acoler, acoller, *prendre au cou, embrasser*

acomenïer, acomungier, acumunïer, *communier*

329

acompaignier, *accompagner*
acomplir, acumplir, *accomplir*
acomungier *v.* acomenïer
acorder, acc-, *accorder*
acorer, *affliger*
acorre, *accourir*
acort, acc-, *accord*
acoster, *réfl.* *s'approcher, accoster*
acostoier, acostoyer, *appuyer*
acostumer, acoust-, acust-, *avoir l'habitude,prendre l'habitude*
acouardi, acouw-, *timide, poltron*
acoustumer *v.* acostumer
acqu- *v.* aqu-
acquest, *profit, gain*
acquester, *gagner, profiter*
acraventer, -anter, *abattre*
act- *v.* at-
acuser, *accuser*
ad *v.* avoir
ad, *prép. (cf.* a)
adenz, adens, *prosterné*
adés, adez, *aussitôt, toujours*
adeser, *toucher*
adj- *v.* aj-
adm- *v.* am-
adonc, adon, adons, adont, adunc, adonques, *alors*
adorer, odorer, *témoigner du respect, supplier, adorer*
adoucir, adoulcir, *adoucir*
adrece, -esce, -esse, *direction, but*
adrecier, adrechier, adressier, *adresser, tourner ; réfl. s'adresser, se tourner vers*
adv- *cf.* av-
adversaire, adversarie, *adversaire*
aëncrer, *ancrer*
afaire, afere, affaire, *affaire, état, importance*
afeblier, -ir, affoiblir, *affaiblir*
aferir, aff-, *convenir*
afermer, aff-, afirmer, *affermir, affirmer*
aff- *cf.* af-
affecté, *passionné, dominé par les passions*
affiné, *délicat*
afichier, aficer, *affirmer ; réfl. s'obstiner*
afïer, *affirmer, assurer*
afiert *v.* aferir

afin, affin, *afin que*
afiner, *terminer*
afirmer *v.* afermer
afoler, *maltraiter, tuer*
afrunt, *en face*
agait, agayt, *artifice, embûche, jeux*
agenoillier, -er, ajenollier, -ellier, *réfl. s'agenouiller*
agraver, *contrister*
agreer, *plaire*
agregier, agrieger, *devenir plus grave*
agu, -ut, *aigu, pointu*
aguille, *aiguille*
aguiller, *étui à aiguilles*
aguillon, awillon, *aiguillon*
aguisier, *aiguiser*
ahan, *douleur, peine, fatigue*
ahi, aï, *hélas*
ahurter, *heurter*
aïde, aïe, ayde, aiue, aiudha, *aide, taxe, impôt*
aidier, -er, ayder, edier, aiuër, *aider*
aïe *v.* aïde
aige, aighe *v.* aigue
aignel, -eus, -ez, -iaus, agnel, -ial, -eaulx, aingniel, anel, engnel, *agneau*
aigue, aige, aighe, aive, ague, awe, egue, eve, ewe, iave, yaue, eave, eaue, *eau*
aillors, aillours, ailleurs, ailors, *ailleurs*
aim *v.* amer
aimmi, *malheur à moi*
ainc, einc, anc, hauc, ainques, ain, *jamais*
ainçois, ainsois, ainchois, ansçois, anceys, anchois, ançois, ansois, anzois, einçois, einzois, enchois, *avant, auparavant, plutôt, mais*
ains, ainz, einz, ans, anz, anç, *prép. avant ; adv. mais, plutôt, auparavant ; com a., le plus tôt que ; com ainz peut…ne=le moins possible ; ainz que, aussitôt que*
ains, ainz, einz, *jamais*
ainsi, -sy, -sint *v.* ensi

ainsné, -és, -eit, eînznez, -és, aisné, ainné, *aîné*

aiut *v.* amer

air, *air ;* aire, *tempérament, disposition, caractère ;* de bon aire, *excellent*

aise, eise, *aise, occasion, plaisir ; adj. commode, joyeux*

aisselle, -ele, esselle, -ele, asele, *aisselle*

aïst, aïft *v.* aidier

aiue, aiudha, aiuër *v.* aïde, aidier

aive *v.* aigue

ajoindre, adj-, *unir*

ajorner, -ourner, -urner, adjourner, *commencer à faire jour, porter envie à, citer en justice, assigner*

ajournee, *point du jour, aube*

ajurner *v.* ajorner

al- *cf.* au-

al = *à le*

alaine, aleine, *haleine*

alaitier, aleter, *allaiter, teter*

alc- *v.* auc-

alc *v.* auques

alegier, aleger, aligier, alleger, *alléger, décharger*

aleine *v.* alaine *et* alener

alenee, *haleine, souffle*

alener, *pressentir*

aler, aleir, aller, *aller, mourir*

aleure, *pas, train, allure*

algalife, *calife*

algier, *dard*

aliance, -ence, *alliance*

all- *cf.* al-

almosnier, *qui reçoit l'aumône*

aloër, alouer, *loger, installer, louer, employer*

alonge, *allongement, suite*

alqu- *v.* auqu-

alt *v.* aler

alt *v.* haut

alt- *v.* aut-

alter *v.* autel

amaisgrir, **amegrir**, *devenir, maigre, maigrir.*

amanver, *présenter*

amasser, *amasser, s'amasser*

ambedeus, ambedous *v.* andui

ame, anima, aneme, anma, ainrme, arme, *âme*

amende, em-, emm-, *amende excuse*

amender, -eir, amander, *amender, réparer, faire mieux, éviter, faire grâce ; réfl. s'améliorer*

amendrir, *diminuer, amoindrir*

ament *v.* amender

amentevoir, *nommer, appeler*

amer, ameir, aymer, amert, *aimer ; subs. l'état d'aimer*

ami, amin, amy, *ami, amant, parent*

amie, amye, *amie, amante*

amïete, -ette, *amante*

amisté, -ié, -et, -ei, amité, -iê, *amitié, amour*

amonester, adm-, *conseiller, exciter*

amont, -unt, *en haut, en amont*

amor, -our, -ur, *amour*

an *v.* en, hom

an- *v.* en-

an, *an, année*

anc- *cf.* enc-

anceisor *v.* ancessor

ancele, -elle, *servante*

ancessor, anceisor, ancissier, ancestre, auch-, *ancien, ancêtre*

ancïen, anciien, encïen, *ancien ;* ancïenor, *génit. des anciens*

ancuens *v.* aucuens

ancui, ancoi, encui, *encore ce jour, aujourd'hui même*

and- *cf.* end-

andui, -eus, ambdui, ansdous, amsdous, ambedous, -eus, ambedui, ambesdous, amedui, -ous, -eus, *tous deux*

anel *v.* aignel

anel *n.* aniaus, *anneau*

aneme *v.* ame

anemi *v.* enemi

angle, angele, angret, *ange*

anglois, -oiz, englois, *anglais, Anglais*

angoisse, anguisse, *angoisse, souffrance*

angoissier, -uissier, angoixer, *presser, tourmenter ; s'engoissier s'effrayer de, s'efforcer de*

angoissos, -ous, eus, -eux, anguissus, *plein d'angoisses, tour-
mentant, triste, pressé*
anguile, angille, *anguille*
ans *v.* ains
ant- *cf.* ent-
antan, *l'an passé, autrefois*
anui *v.* enui
anuit, enuit, *cette* nuit, *aujour-
d'hui à la nuit*
anuitier, *faire nuit*
anz *v.* ains, enz
aoi, *interj.*
apareillier, -er, -ellier, -illier,
oillier, appareillier, *appareiller,
préparer, garnir, égaler, se comparer à*
aparellement, *appareil*
aparicion, *apparition*
aparoillier *v.* apareillier
aparoir, app-, *apparaître, se montrer, être évident ;* aparissant,
présent
apartenir, app-, *appartenir ;* part.
prés. *parent, relation*
apeler, apeller, apieler, appeller,
*appeler, invoquer, nommer,
aborder, accuser*
apendre, *dépendre, convenir*
apenser, *réfl.* penser, *réfléchir*
apercevoir, -chevoir, -sevoir,
-çoivre, aparcevoir, -çoivre,
*apercevoir, reconnaître, épier ;
réfl.* reprendre ses sens
apermeunes, *sur-le-champ*
apert, app-, appart, *évident,
adroit, prêt ;* en apert, *ouvertement, publiquement*
apertement, app-, -appar-, *ouvertement, clairement, adroitement*
apieler *v.* apeler
apoier, -oiier, -uier, *appuyer*
aporter, *apporter*
apostle, apostre, *apôtre*
apostoile, -olie, *pape*
apostole *v.* apostoile
apostume, *enflure, abcès*
apovrir, *s'appauvrir*
app- *cf.* ap-
aprendre, app-, *apprendre ;* part.
apris, *instruit, élevé*
aprés, apriés, *prép.* après

apresser, *presser, poursuivre*
aprester, *préparer*
aprochier, -cher, -cer, aprucer,
aprouchier, *approcher*
aproismier, apreismier, aprismer,
approcher, s'approcher
apuier *v.* apoier
aquerre, acquerre, acquerir,
acquérir
aquiter, acuiter, *acquitter, s'acquitter, absoudre*
aqoison *v.* ocoison
ar- *v.* arr-
arabler, *tirer à soi, s'emparer
de*
arabi, arrabi, *arabe, cheval barbe*
arain, *airain*
arbalastier, arbalestrier, *arbalé-
trier*
arc, *n.* ars, arc, arcade
arcevesque, *archevêque*
arche, *l'arche de Noé*
areer, *préparer, faire*
arester *v.* arrester
argent, argant, arjant, *argent*
arguër, *accuser, blâmer*
arier, -iere, arrier, -iere, arere,
erere, arrieres, ayere, *arrière,
auparavant ; équivaut souvent
au préfixe* re- *qui distingue
retirer de* tirer, *retourner de*
tourner, *etc.*
ariver, arr-, *arriver*
arpent, *arpent*
arr- *cf.* ar-
arraisonner, araisoner, *adresser
la parole, apostropher*
arrement, *encre*
arrester, ar-, *occuper, s'arrêter*
ars, *incendie*
as = *à les, avec les*
as *v.* avoir
as, *voici ;* as vus, *vous voyez*
as- *cf.* ass-
asne, *dim.* asnel, *âne*
asoldre, *absoudre ;* part. asolu,
saint
assaier *v.* essaier
assaillir, -alir, ess-, asaillir, -alir,
assaillir, attaquer
assaut, assalt, asalt, *assaut, atta-
que*

assavorer, assavoreir, -ourer, goûter, apprécier le goût de

assegier, as-, assiéger

assemblee, assam-, union, armée, rassemblement

assemblement, assam-, union, rencontre

assembler, -enbler, -ambler, anler, asembler, -anler, essambleir, intr. et réfl. assembler, marier, s'assembler, combattre, assaillir, grouper, réunir, s'unir

assëoir, as-, assëir, asseoir, arrêter, assiéger ; part. assis, formé

assëur, sûr, confiant, assuré

assëurer, as-, assurer, rassurer, confirmer

assevir, toucher ; part. satisfait, contenté

assez, -az, -es, asez, -eiz, -és, assez, beaucoup

assi v. ausi

assimpli, simple

assoux v. asoldre

astenance, abstinence, empire sur soi

astenir, réfl. s'abstenir

astraindre, presser

astronomien, astrologue

ataing v. ateindre

atant, alors, à présent

atardance, retard

atarder, atargier, -ger, -jer, arrêter, réfl. tarder

ateindre, at-, attaindre, atteindre

ateirier v. atirier

atemprer, atremper, tempérer, modérer, accorder

atendre, att-, act-, atandre, attendre

atirier, ateirier, ranger, arranger

atoivre, bétail

ator, atour, att-, actour, appareil, atour, manière, apparence

atorner, -eir, atourner, -urner, tourner, appliquer, disposer, employer, préparer, arranger, habiller, équiper, apprêter

atot, atut, avec, avec eux, etc.

atraire, att-, attirer

atretel v. autretel

atrover, trouver

att- cf. at-

atterrer, jeter à terre, renverser

aturner v. atorner

auctorité, auth-, at-, autorité

aucuens, alqu-, anc-, aucun, ancaulc-, alcon, aucun, quelqu'un

aumosne, alm-, alsm-, aumône, pitié, œuvre pie

aunois, aulnaie, bois d'aunes

auquant, alqu-, quelqu'un

auques, alqu-, aukes, un peu

ausi, aussi, ausinc, assi, ossi, aussy, aussi ; assi cum, comme, ausi com an, jusque dans

ausino v. ausi

autel, alter, autel

autheur, auteur

authorité v. auctorité

autre, al-, aultre, auter, alter, abs. autrui, al-, altri, aultruy, autre, autrement

autrement, al-, aul-, autrement

autresfoiz, quelquefois

autresi, -ssi, altresi, de même, aussi

autretel, pareil, semblable

autrui v. autre

aval, en bas, bas

avaler, descendre, baisser, avaler, tomber

avancier, -cer, avancer, s'avancer

avanpié, avant-pied

avant, avan, prép. et adv., avant, en avant, devant ; ad en avant, à venir ; avant venir, s'approcher

avanture v. aventure

avarisse, avrice, avarice

aveir v. avoir

avenir, adv-, advenir, arriver, parvenir, convenir

aventure, adv-, avant-, hasard, sort, occasion, événement inopiné

aver, avare

aver v. avoir

avers, à côté de, en comparaison avec

aviegne, avignet v. avenir

aviltance, avilissement, abaissement

avis, adv-, adviz, *avis, croyance, opinion*

aviser, adv-, *voir, reconnaître, annoncer, instruire; réfl. réfléchir, se résoudre, parvenir à la connaissance, remarquer*

avoc, -oec, -ec, -euc, -uec, avenques, avecques, ovecques, ovec, ove, *avec, en même temps*

avoir, -oir, er, haveir, aroir; a, *il a, il y a;* avoir a deu son talent, *s'être consacré à Dieu; subst. avoir, richesse, bien, prix;* avoir a nom, *se nommer;* doner a avoir, *donner les moyens*

avrez *v.* avoir

avrice *v.* avarisse

avugler, *aveugler*

awillon *v.* aguillon

ay- *cf.* ai-

ayeul, *aïeul*

ayere *v.* arier

a-yl, *y a-t-il*

Bacheler, -ier, baceler, *jeune homme, garçon, (pauvre) chevalier*

bacin, bassin, *bassin*

bacinet, bachinet, *sorte de casque*

bacon, *jambon*

baignier, -er, bagnier, *baigner*

bailleur, *celui qui donne, qui fournit, qui commande*

baillie, bailie, *pouvoir*

baillier, ballier, *donner, gouverner, avoir en puissance, joindre*

baillif, *gouverneur, préfet, bailli*

baillir, *gouverner, traiter, posséder*

baing, *bain*

baisier, -er, -xier, baisar, -air, besier, *baiser*

baissier, bessier, basser, *baisser*

ban, *ban*

banc, *n.* bans, *banc*

bandement, *action de bander; adv. hardiment*

baptisier, -zier, batisier, *baptiser*

barbel, *pl.* barbiaus, *barbeau*

barnage, -aje, *assemblée des barons, noblesse, vaillance, opulence*

baron, -un, *nom.* ber, bers, *homme, mari, courageux, homme courageux, noble guerrier, vassal;* bers de desiers, *homme d'aspiration*

barre, barriere, *barrière*

bastir, *bâtir, préparer*

bataille, bataille, *bataille*, **bataillon**, *troupe*

bater, *descendre, toucher*

batesme *v.* bautesme

batre, *battre*

baudré, *ceinture*

bautesme, batesme, **baptême**

baverie, *bavarderie*

beaus, beax, beaulx *v.* bel

beauté, biauté, biaultcit, *beauté*

bec, *proue*

bee, *le bêlement des brebis*

beër, baër, *attendre, aspirer à, bayer*

begnin, *bénin*

beivre *v.* boivre

bel, bel-z, beau-s, ax, -aulx, bial, -au, -aus, -ax, -aux, -eulx, *beau, agréable, cher;* il m'est bel de, *je me plais à; adv.* bien

belement, bell-, biel-, benl-, *doucement, gentiment, noblement, correctement*

ben *v.* bien

beneichon, -çun, -son, *bénédiction*

beneïr, beneïstre, benir, *bénir*

ber *v.* baron

berbiz, -is, brebis, -iz, *brebis*

bergier, bergiere, *berger, bergère*

bers *v.* baron

besoigne, -oingne, -ongne, *besoin, affaire, occupation*

besoin, -oing, -oign, uign, bosoinz, *besoin*

beste, *bête, bétail*

beter, *coaguler, figer,* **geler**

beveient *v.* boivre

bial, -au, -ax *v.* bel

biauté *v.* beauté

bible, *livre, volume,* **Bible**

bien, ben, beyn, beem, *bien; subst.* bien, *fortune, vaillance, bonne intention;* avoir a bien, *aimer, apprécier*

bienëuré, benëurez, bonuré, bieneureux, *heureux*
biere, *bière*
bis, biz, *noirâtre, brun*
bise, *vent du nord ; biche*
blamer *v.* blasmer
blanc *f.* blance, blanque, *blanc*
blandir, *flatter, caresser*
blasmer, blamer, *blâmer, accuser, condamner*
blastengier, *faire des reproches*
blecier, -chier, -scier, -sser, *blesser*
blesme, *blême*
blïalt, bliaut, *étoffe de soie et d'or*
blonde, blont, *dimin.* blondet, *blond*
bobant, beubant, *pompe, éclat*
boche, boce, bouche, bouce, buche, *bouche*
boillir, buillir, *bouillir, sourdre*
boin *v.* bon
bois, boiz, bos, *bois*
boisdie *v.* boisie
boisie, boisdie, *félonie*
boisson, *boisson*
boisson *v.* buisson
boivre, bevre, beivre, boire, beuvre, *boire*
bon, buon, boen, boin, buen, *bon, séant, vaillant ; subst. volonté, plaisir, souhait*
bonement, -ant, boin-, bonn-, *franchement, volontiers, bien, justement*
borde, bordete, *petite maison, ferme*
borgois, borjoiz, bourgois, bour-goys, *bourgeois*
borse, borce, bourse, *bourse*
bos *v.* bois
boschage, bocage, boscatge, *bo-cage*
bosoin *v.* besoin
bosquillon, *bûcheron*
boter, bouter, botter, buter, *pousser, frapper, mettre, bour-rer, se rendre ; boter en procès, citer en justice ; réfl. pénétrer, se cacher*
bouce, bouche *v.* boche

boucler, bucler, *bouclier, à boucle, muni d'une boucle*
bourgois, bourse *v.* borgois, borse.
bouter *v.* boter
braire, *crier, brailler*
bramer, *crier, bramer*
brandir, *branler, brandir ;* bran-dir un colp, *donner un coup de sabre*
bransler, *branler*
brant, branc, *n.* branz, brans, *épée, sabre*
bras, braz, braç, *bras*
brebis, -iz *v.* berbis, -iz
brie, *vaurien*
brief, bref, *n.* briés, *bref, court*
brief, *n.* briés, *lettre*
briément, -ant, brefment, *brième-ment, bref*
brigandine, *espèce d'armure*
brisier, -er, *briser, se briser*
broche, *pieu pointu*
brochier, *éperonner*
broderye, brouderie, *broderie*
bronie, broigne, *cuirasse*
brudler, brusler, *brûler*
bruine, broïne, *pluie fine, brouil-lard*
bruïr, *brûler*
bruire, *faire un bruit, donner un écho, murmurer*
bruit, bruyt, *bruit*
brunete, *jolie fille brune*
brusler *v.* brudler
buc, *bouc*
bucler *v.* boucler
buëlle, *les entrailles*
Buguerie, *Bulgarie*
buillir *v.* boillir
buillon, *engeance*
buisson, buison, *buisson*
burel, bureaux, *bure, étoffe com-mune*

C.=q-, qu-, k-
ça, cha, sa, sai, zai, *ici ;* en ça, *depuis lors ;* ça, *voici*
cachier *v.* chacier
caeiz *v.* chaoir
çaiens, chaiens, *ici dedans*
caitif *v.* chaitif
calengier *v.* chalongier

calt *v.* chaloir
cam- *cf.* cham-
campaigne, *campagne*
can- *cf.* chan-
canele, *cannelle*
cant- *v.* chant-
canut *v.* chenu
cap- *cf.* chap-
car, kar, quar, quer, *car, donc, comment, pourquoi ;* quer t'en vai, *va donc*
car- *cf.* char-
carguer *v.* chargier
carman, *charmant*
carneaulx, *créneaux*
carnel, *charnel*
cas, cas, *affaire ;* a cas, *à terre*
casser, quasser, quaissier, *briser, se briser*
casteëd, *chasteté*
cataigne, *chef*
caut *v.* chaut
cauteleux, *rusé, insidieux*
caval *v.* cheval
caver, *creuser*
cavians *v.* chevel
cëanz, cëanz *v.* ceenz
ceenz, ceens, cëanz, cëans, sëans (*cf.* çaiens), *ici dedans*
cei, *cela*
ceindre, çaindre, ch-, seindre, *ceindre*
ceinture, cain-, chain-, seinc-, ceyntur, *ceinture*
cel, ciel, sel, *ce, celui*
cel *v.* ciel
celer, cheler, celler, *celer, cacher ;* a, en celé, *en cachette*
celeste, *céleste, maître des cieux*
celui, cheluy, celi, cheli, *ce, celui*
cembeler, *combattre*
cendal, -el, cendés, *demi-soie*
cenele, cinele, *cenelle, fruit de l'églantier*
ceo, ceu, çou, chou, cio, *cela, ceci, ce ;* de ceu est ceu ke, *ainsi il arrive que ;* che fu si, *il arriva*
cerchier, cercher, sercher, cercer, *chercher, examiner*
cerf, cierf, serf, *n.* cers, *cerf*
cerise, ser-, cerisse, *cerise*

cert, chert, *certain, sûr ;* cert, certe, -es, a certes, acertes, *certainement*
certain, ch-, certen, *certain, sûr, fidèle*
certainité, *certitude*
cervel, cervele, -elle, *cerveau, cervelle*
cescun *v.* chascun
cest, chest, cestui, chestui, *ce, celui*
cev- *v.* chev-
chaaine, chaainne, cheene, chaïne, chainne, chaynne, *chaîne*
chacier, chaicier, chascer, chasser, cacier, cacer, cachier, qacier, *chasser, poursuivre, conduire*
chaïne, chainne *v.* chaaine
chainture *v.* ceinture
chainturelle, *petite ceinture*
chair *v.* char
chaïr *v.* chaoir
chaitif, caitif, chetif, *n.* -is, *chétif, malheureux ;* caitif mei, *malheureux que je suis*
chalce, chausse, *chausse*
chaloir, caloir, challoir, *importer*
chalongier, calengier, chaillenger, *demander, provoquer, défendre, vendre cher*
chalt *v.* chaut
chambre, c-, caubre, *chambre, palais, domaine particulier*
champ, camp, *n.* chans, -nz, cans, *champ, champ de bataille, campagne*
champïon, -un, campïon, -un, *champion*
chanbre *v.* chambre
chanceler, -eller, canceler, *chanceler*
chançon, c-, canchon, *chanson*
chançonete, chansonnette, chansonnelle, *chansonnette*
changier, -er, cangier, -er, jang-, chaingier, *changer*
chanoine, can-, *chanoine*
chanson *v.* chançon
chant, cant, kant, *chant*
chanter, -eir, canter, kanter, center, *chanter*

chanu *v.* chenu

chaoïr, chaair, chaor, chaïr, caoïr, caïr, cader, chëoir, cheïr, cheder, caioïr, këoir, *tomber*, *tourner*, *arriver*

chape, cape, *manteau*

chapel, -iel, -ial, capel, *n.* capiax, chappeaulx, capeaulx, *chapeau*, *couronne*

chapelain, *prêtre officiant*

chapele, -elle, *chapelle*

chapial, -iel *v.* chapel

char, -rn, chair, car, -rn, *chair*

charete, car-, charrete, -ette, *charrette*

chargier, charger, cargier, carcer, carguer, *charger*, *se mettre sur le dos*, *confier*

charn *v.* char

charoingne, -ongne, -uigne, ca-daïre

chartre, cartre, chatre, *prison*

chartre, *charte*, *lettre*, *histoire*, *chronique*

chascun, cas-, chau-, ches-, ces-, *chacun*

chaste, *pur*, *chaste*

chastel, -eau, *n.* -iaus, -iax, *château*

chastelain, *châtelain*

chastré, *rendu impuissant*

chat, *n.* chas, *chat*

chauce *v.* chalce

chaucier, -sser, calcier, cauchier, -cier, *chausser*; *part.* chaussant, *élégant* (en parlant du pied)

chaulx, *chaleur*, *chaud*

chaürent *v.* chaoir

chaus, *Caux, en Normandie*

chaut, -lt, chalt, caut, calt, *chaud*

che- *cf.* ce-

cheance, *chance*, *fortune*, *succès*

cheder *v.* chaoir

chela, *cela*

chelui *v.* celui

chemin, cemin, *chemin*

chenu, ke-, que-, canu, -ut, *gris*, *blanchi*

chëoir *v.* chaoir

cher *v.* chier

chere *v.* chiere

cherir, chierir, *chérir*

cherté, chierté, *charité, amour*

cherubin, cer-, *chérubin*

chesne, chasne, *chêne*

cheval, ceval, caval, chival, *n.* (et *pl.*) chevax, -aux, -aulx, cevaus, -ax, *cheval*

chevalchier, -cier *v.* chevauchier

chevalier, -aler, -allier, -elier, cevalier, cavalleyr, *chevalier*, *cavalier*

chevance, *possession, subsistance*

chevauchier, chevachier, chevalcier, chevalchier, chevalcer, cevaucer, *aller à cheval*

chevauchons, en, *à cheval, à califourchon*

chevel, -eus, -ous, -eulx, chavol, caviaus, quevel, *cheveu*

chevestre, *licol, lien*

chevillete, *chevillette*

chëy *v.* chaoir

chi *v.* ci

chiche, *avare*

chief, chef, cief, kief, quief, queu, cheue, *n.* chiés, ciés, *tête, chef, bout*

chier, cher, cier, *cher, de haut prix, précieux*

chiere, chere, ciere, *visage, mine, accueil*

chierté *v.* cherté

chiés *v.* chief

chiet *v.* chaoir

chitouaus, *sorte d'épices*

choisir, chosir, cuesir, jausir, coisir, *apercevoir, découvrir, voir, choisir*

chose, -sse, -ze, -sce, cose, cosa, kose, cause, *chose, cause, créature*

chosete, -tte, *petite chose, affiquet*

chosir *v.* choisir

ci, chi, si, cy, *ici*

cie- *cf.* ce-

cief *v.* chief

ciel, cel, chiel, ciex, cieulx, chiex, chieus, *ciel*

ciel *v.* cel

cil, chil, *ce, celui*

cinc, chinc, *cinq*

ciuce, *tapis*

cinele *v.* cenele

cinquantisme, *cinquantième*

cist, cis *v.* cest

cité, -et, -eit, chité, cyté, ciptat,
  ciutat, cit, chis, chit, ciu, *cité,
  ville*

clai- *v.* cla-

clamer, *prs.* claim, cleim, *nommer,
  appeler, proclamer, réclamer,
  prétendre,* clamer cuite, *tenir
  quitte, absoudre*

clamor, -our, *appel, plainte*

claré, -et, *boisson composée de vin
  et de miel*

clavette, *petite clef*

clef, *n.* cles, *clef*

cler, cleir, *clair, brillant*

clerc, clers, *homme d'église,
  savant*

cleu *n.* clou

cleufichier, cloffichier, *clouer*

clicquetis, *cliquetis, bruit métal-
  lique*

cliner, *s'incliner*

clore, *fermer, enfermer*

closture, *clôture*

clou, cleu, *clou*

clouër, *clouer*

ço *v.* ceo

coardie, cuardie, *lâcheté*

coart, couart, cuard, -art, cou-
  wart, coarz, *couard, lâche*

coer, coeur, *v.* cuer

coi, coit, coy, quoi, *paisible, tranquille*

coiement, *tranquillement, doucement*

coiffe, *coiffe, coup sur la tête*

coille, *testicule*

cointe, *instruit, prudent, gracieux,
  paré*

col, cou, *cou*

çol=ço le

colchier, colcier *v.* couchier

coler, couler, *couler, glisser*

colier, *cou*

collet, cou, *collet*

color, -our, -ur, -coulor, -our,
  -eur, culur, *couleur*

colorer, cou-, *colorer*

colp, cols *v.* coup

colur *v.* color

com, cum, con, cun, come, cume,
  comme, conme, coume, *comme,
  comment,* que (*après le com-
  par.*), *comme si, combien,
  lorsque, quand ;* com fait, *quel*

comandement, cum-, comm-,
  commandement

comander, comm-, conm-, cum- ;
  comender, comm-, *commander,
  confier*

comant, comm-, comand, cum-,
  comm-, *commandement*

comant *v.* coment

combatre, cum-, *combattre*

combien, cum-, *combien ;* c. que,
  de quelque manière que, quoique

come *v.* com

comencier, -cer, -sier, -chier,
  cu- ; cumancer, cumm-, commencier, -chier, -cer, *commencer*

coment, -ant, comment, -ant,
  coument, cu-, *comment*

commun, *commun ;* le commun,
  l'ensemble, la masse

communaulté, commune, *com-
  munauté*

compaigne, -eigne, compannie,
  compagnie, compagne

compaignie, -agnie, conpaignnie,
  -agnie, cumpaignie, *compagnie,
  association*

compaignier, *tenir compagnie à*

compaignon, conpagnon, cumpaignun, *n.* compains, con-
  pains, cumpains, -aigns, *compagnon, ami*

comparer *v.* comperer

compere, conp-, *compère*

comperer, -arer, conperer, *acheter,
  payer, expier, comparer*

composer, *imposer, pressurer*

compte, compter *v.* conte, conter

con *v.* com

concillier, conciller *v.* conseillier

conclusion, *conclusion, résolution*

condempner, *condamner*

conduire, -ure, *conduire*

conduit, *canal, conduite*

conestable, conn-, cun-, *conné-
  table*

confesser, *réfl. confesser*
confondre, cunfundre, *confondre, ruiner*
confort, cun-, *consolation, secours*
conforter, cun-, *consoler, encourager, soulager*
congié, -gé, -giet, cungé, -et, -iet, cumgiet, *congé, permission*
conjoïr, *féliciter, saluer, accueillir bien*
conn- *cf.* con-
connoissance, cogn-, conissance, *connaissance, accueil*
conoistre, cou-, conn-, cogn-, congu-, que- ; conistre, cou-, cu- ; conuistre, cu- ; conustre, *connaître, reconnaître, avouer*
conquerre, cun-, *conquérir, gagner, vaincre, arrêter*
conquester, *gagner, vaincre*
conreer, -eër, -aër, -oier, *équiper, préparer, arranger, entretenir*
conroi, cunrei, *équipage, troupe, entretien*
cons *v.* conte
conseil, -eyl, -el, -iel, -oil, -eus, cunseil, -eull, *conseil, conduite, décision, en cunseil, secrètement*
conseillier, -er, -oillier, cunseillier, concillier, *conseiller, consulter, faire confidence*
conseilier, -ellier, -illier, cunseillier ; *conseiller, être d'avis ;* se conseiler, *délibérer ;* se conseiler a, *tenir conseil avec*
consevre, *atteindre*
consirrer, *souci, pensée, méditation, résignation ;* metre en consirrer, *se résigner*
consoüz, *frappé à mort*
conte, cunte, comte, compte, *nom.* coens, cuens, quens, cons, *comte*
conte, compte, *conte, compte*
conté, *comté*
contendre, *combattre ;* contendre vers, *se mesurer avec*
contenir, se c., *se contenir, se conduire ; subst. maintien*
contens, *contention, contestation*
conter, cunter, *conter, dire, affirmer*

continent, -ant, *continent, modéré*
contraint, *forcé*
contraire, cuntraire, *adj. et subst.,* contraire, contrariété
contre, contra, cuntre, *prép. et adv.* contre, vers, au contraire
contredire, *contredire, refuser ; part. maudit*
contree, -ede, cuntree, *contrée*
contremont, *en haut*
contreval, *à bas, en bas de, en aval de*
contrevaloir, *équivaloir à*
contrister, cun-, *attrister*
controvers, *contradictoire*
convenance, cov-, *convenence, convenance, traité, accord, promesse*
convenir, couv-, cov-, *s'assembler, convenir, promettre, falloir ;* il covient, *il sied, il faut*
convent *v.* convenir
convent, couvent, cov-, cuv-, *réunion, condition, promesse*
converser, *habiter, séjourner, avoir commerce avec*
coper *v.* couper
coquart, *sot, niais*
cor *v.* cuer
cor, corn, *corne, cor*
corage, -aige, courage, -aige, corrage, *cœur, volonté, intention, courage, ardeur, colère*
corait *v.* corre
corbineur, *rapace, exacteur*
corde, *corde*
cordelier, *moine franciscain*
corn *v.* cor
corner, *jouer du cor, son du cor*
coroceus, curuçus, *courroucé, attristé*
corocier, -ecier, -echier, -ucier, -oucier, correcier, -oucier, courocier, -oucier, ouchier-, -ecier, -echier, -cier, courroucer, curucer, -ecier, -echier, -cier, *courroucer, attrister*
coroie, corroie, *ceinture*
corone, coronet, couronne, couronne, *tonsure*
corre, courre, curre, courir, *courir*
corriens *v.* corre

corroie *v.* coroie

corroi *v.* conroi

corruption, -cïon, *corruption*

cors, corz, corps, *corps, personne ;* come lor cors, *comme eux-mêmes*

cort, court, curt, *n.* corz, cors, cour, *train de maison, tribunal*

cort, court, *court, bref*

cortois, courtois, curteis, *courtois, gentilhomme*

cose *v.* chose

coste, *côte*

costé, -eit, cousté, *n.* costez, *côté,* côte

costement, *dépense*

coster, *coûter*

costoier, *suivre la côte, côtoyer*

costre, *sacristain*

cote, cotte, cute, *long habit, tunique*

cou *v.* ceo

couchier, -er, colchier, -cier, culchier, cochier, cuchier, *coucher*

coul- *v.* col-.

couldre, *coudre*

coulon, colomb, *pigeon*

coup, colp, cop, *n.* cols, cos, cous, coux, *coup, coup de sabre*

coupe, colpe, colped, culpe, couppe, *faute*

couper, colper, cauper, coper, *couper, trancher*

couppe teste, *bourreau*

cour- *cf.* cor-

courir *v.* corre

court, *ressort, juridiction, droit de juger*

courtoisie, *acte de gentilhomme, courtoisie*

cous- *cf.* cos-

coutel, cutel, *couteau*

coutille, *poignard*

cuov- *cf.* cov-

couvent *v.* convent

couverte, *couverture*

cov- *cf.* conv-

covert *v.* covrir

covise, cu-, *convoitise, désir*

covoitise, conv-, couv-; cuveitise, *désir, avarice*

covrir, cuvrir, couvrir, cubrir, *couvrir, cacher, garantir*

cras, gras, *gras*

crëance, -che, credance, croyance, *créance, foi, notion*

crëanter, *promettre, approuver*

crëature, crïat-, crïauture, *créature*

credance *v.* crëance

creer, crïer, *créer*

creindre, crendre, criendre, *craindre,* cremir, *craindre*

creire, creidre *v.* croire

cressier, *engraisser, nourrir*

crestïenté, chrest-, cristïentet, *chrétienté, christianisme*

crever, *crever, percer, se briser*

crevëure, *crevasse, fissure*

cri, *n.* criz, cris, *cri*

crieme, criem, *crainte*

criendre *v.* creindre

crïer *v.* creer

crïer, cryer, crider, *crier, appeler, proclamer*

criminal, -el, *criminel*

cristal, crestal, *n.* -iaus, *cristal*

croce, *béquille*

croire, creire, creidre, *croire*

croisier, -er, cruisier, creusier, *croiser*

croiz, -s, -x, crox, cruiz, -uz, creus, *croix*

cruël, -eus, -ex, -aux, *cruel*

cruisier *v.* croisier

cruisir, *craquer, grincer*

crute, *crypte, caveau*

cu- *cf.* co-

cueillir, cuillir, cuellir, quellir, coillir, ceuillir, cuiedre, *cueillir, recevoir*

cuens *v.* conte

cuer, coer, coeur, cueur, quer, quor, cor, *cœur, volonté*

cui *v.* qui

cuidier, -er, quider, *penser, croire*

cuire, quire, coire, *cuire, brûler, causer une douleur cuisante*

cuit *v.* cuidier

cuite *v.* quite

cuivert, cuvert, culvert, *perfide, traître, lâche*

culcher *v.* couchier

culpe *v.* coupe
culur *v.* color
culvert *v.* cuivert
cum- *cf.* com-
cumgiet *v.* congié
cun- *cf.* con-
cunfundre *v.* confondre
cuntralïus, *querelleur*
cur- *cf.* cor-
cure, qure, *soin, souci*
curer, *guérir*
curial, *de la cour*
curuçus *v.* coroceus
cuveitise, *convoitise*
cuvenable, *convenable*
cuy *v.* qui
cy *v.* ci

Damage, -aige, domage, -aje,
  -aige, dommage, -aige, *dom-*
  mage, tort
dame, damme, *dame, femme,*
  maîtresse
dame-, damle-, damne-deus (*cf.*
  deus), *dieu*
damoisel, -oysel, -oiseau,-oyseau,
  n. -oisiaus, -ax, *jeune gentil-*
  homme, écuyer
damoisele, -elle, -zelle, demoi-
  sele, *jeune fille de noble famille ;*
  cf. donselle
dampner, damner, *damner*
dangier, *principe de puissance,*
  d'autorité, plaisir, opposition,
  manque, danger
dant, *n.* danz, dans, dam, *sei-*
  gneur, maître
dart, *dard*
davant, devant, de avant, davan,
  prép. et adv., devant, avant ;
  subs. la face, le devant
davantage, *de plus, en outre*
de, *prép., quant à, pour, au sujet de*
dé, *n.* dez, *dé*
dé *v.* deus
dea, dia, *vraiment*
debatre, *frapper*
debteur, *débiteur*
débuer, *nettoyer*
debvoir *v.* devoir
deces, *mort, décès*

decevoir, dech-, desc- ; deçoivre,
  dez-, *décevoir*
deci, desci, *jusque, désormais*
declarer, *expliquer*
decliner, *s'incliner*
decoler, *décoller, décapiter*
deconforter *v.* des-
dedenz, -ens, dedanz, -ans, *prép.*
  et adv., dans, dedans
dedesoz, -sus, *sous*
dedesus, *dessus*
dedevant, *devant*
deduire, *conduire, passer, réjouir,*
  s'amuser, réduire à, abaisser,
  supporter
defaillir, deff-, *manquer, être*
  perdu, faillir, faire défaut ;
  part. perdu
defendre, deff-, desf- ; desfandre,
  défendre, garantir, faire défense
deff- *cf.* def-
deffermer, defremer, deff-, desf-,
  ouvrir
deffiance, desf-, *défense*
deffier, def-, desf-, *défier*
definer, *finir, mettre fin à*
defors, *prép. et adv., dehors, hors*
degeter, *tordre*
degré, -et, *degré, escalier*
dehait, dehet, dahet, *déplaisir,*
  honte
dei *v.* doi
deignier, -er, deinguier, daignier,
  deiner, deyner, degner, daigner,
  approuver
deisse *v.* dire
deïté, *divinité, déité*
deiz *v.* devoir
dejoste, dejuste, *à côté de*
del *v.* duel
deleit, delit, *joie, délice*
deleiteus, deliteus, *délicieux,*
  joyeux
delez, -és, dalez, -és, *à côté de*
delit- *cf.* deleit-
delivre, *délivré, prompt*
delivrer, *délivrer, juger ; réfl. se*
  dépêcher
deluge, deluve, diluvie, duluve,
  déluge, destruction
demaine, -eine, -enie, *propriété ;*
  adj. propre

demainement, *même, justement*

demander, *demander, chercher*

demant, *demande*

demener, *mener, conduire, faire;* demener ledice, doel, *montrer de la joie, de la douleur; réfl. se tenir*

dementer, *plaindre, se démener comme un insensé, se lamenter*

dementres, demantres, *pendant que,* en tant dementres com, *tandis que*

demetre, *réfl. se démettre*

demi, -y, dimi, *demi; cf.* mi

demonstrer *v.* demostrer

demorance, -ourance, *délai*

demore, -eure, -ure, *demeure*

demoree, *demeure, retard, délai*

demorer, -ourer, -urer, *demeurer, tarder, durer, en rester; réfl. séjourner, s'attarder*

demostrance, demon-, *indication*

demostrement, *manifestation, démonstration, prédiction*

demostrer, -oustrer, -ustrer, -onstrer, desmonstrer, *démontrer, indiquer, faire voir, annoncer*

demou- demu- *v.* demo-

demy *v.* demi

denier, dener, *denier, argent*

dent, *dent*

departement, *départ, séparation*

departie, *séparation;* avoir dure departie de, *se tirer avec peine de*

departir, *séparer, partager, partir*

depecier, *diviser, détruire*

depens, *dépense, perte*

depescher, *dépêcher;* depescher la voie, *se hâter*

deplaint, *plainte*

depoiller *v.* despoiller

deprïer, -oier, -oiier, -eier, *prier avec instance*

deputaire, -eire, *de mauvais naturel, de bas étage*

deramer, -ar, *déchirer*

derompre, *arracher*

derrier, -iere, -iers, -eres, deriere, -ere, -iers, *prép. et adv., derrière*

des *v.* deus

des, *prép. dès, depuis*

desarmer, *désarmer*

desboursement, *déboursement*

desbriser, *se briser, prendre fin cesser d'être*

descendre, dec-, dex-, dess-, dessandre, *descendre, descendre de cheval, abaisser*

deschaindre, *détacher la ceinture*

descharger, *décharger*

deschaucier, desc-, *déchausser*

deschaus, *déchaussé*

desci *v.* deci

desciple *v.* disciple

desclore, *ouvrir, percer, expliquer*

descoloré, -culurez, *décoloré*

desconfire, *détruire, vaincre*

desconforter, *décourager, perdre courage*

desconseillié, -illié, -eiliet, *sans conseil*

descovrir, -ouvrir, -uvrir, *découvrir;* a descovert, *ouvertement*

descu- *v.* desco-

desdeigner, *dédaigner*

desdein, -ng, *dédain*

deseivre *v.* desevrer

deservir, dess-, *mériter, récompenser*

deseur, deseure *v.* desor, desore

desevrer, desc-, dess-, *séparer, distinguer, partir*

desfaire, deff-, desfere, *détruire, ruiner, tuer; réfl. se débarrasser*

desfïance, *défi, défense*

desguiser, *déguiser, orner*

desguiséure, *déguisement*

desier, -ir, *désir, aspiration*

desirer, -irrer, *désirer*

desirer, *déchirer*

desirier, desirr-, *désir*

desirrer, -ier, *v.* desirer, -ier

deslacier, *délier*

desloial, -oyal, *nom.* -oiaus, *perfide*

desmaillier, *rompre les mailles*

desmembrer, *démembrer*

desmentir, *démentir, faire défaut*

desmontrer *v.* demostrer

desor, desore, desour, deseur, deseure, desur, desure, *prép. et adv., sur, dessus, là-dessus* desoz, -os, -ouz, -ous, -oubz, -uz, dessoubz, *prép. et adv.*, *sous, dessous*

desparer, *déparer, rendre laid*

despartir, *départir*

despendre, *délier*

despendre, *dépenser, distribuer*

despense, *dépens*

despensier, *dépensier, qui dépense*

desperer, *désespérer, mettre au désespoir*

desperet *v.* desparer

despit, *dédain*

despitement, *avec dépit, dédaigneusement ;* subs. *mépris*

desplaisance, *déplaisir*

desploiier, *déployer ∽*

despoillier, -er, -ouiller, depoiller, *dépouiller ;* se despoiller, *ôter son habit*

despuis, *depuis*

desputer, *discuter, se quereller*

desputoison, desputaison, *dispute, discussion, débat*

desque, *jusqu'à ce que*

desrompre, *rompre, séparer*

dessoubz *v.* desoz

destin, destinee, destinnee, *destin*

destor, -our, *détour, sentier*

destorner, *détourner, déconseiller, cacher*

destourber, *empêcher ; subs. empêchement*

destraindre, *serrer, forcer, tourmenter*

destre, dextre, *droit*

destrenchier, *déchirer*

destresse, detr-, *misère*

destrier, -er, *cheval, cheval de bataille*

destroit, -ait, *serré, tourmenté, fâcheux, en détresse ; v.* destraindre

destroit, *détroit, malheur, détresse*

destruction, -un, *destruction*

destruire, *détruire, démanteler*

desur *v.* desor

desus, dessus, *prép. et adv.*, *sur, dessus*

desus, desuz *v.* desoz

desver, derver, *rendre fou, extravaguer, perdre la raison*

desvïer, desvoier, *dérouter, tromper, abandonner*

detenir, *retenir*

detraire, *arracher*

detrenchier, -anchier, -ancier, *couper*

deuësse, diuësse, deesse, *déesse*

deus, deux, deu, dieus, dieux, diu, dex, diex, dix, des, deo, *dieu*

deus, deux *v.* duel

deus, deux *v.* dui

deus or, *désormais*

devant *v.* davant

deveee, *défense*

deveer, *défendre, interdire, empêcher*

devenir, div-, *devenir, venir*

devers, *vers, devers, du côté de, envers, auprès de, à partir de*

devié, *défense*

devier, *s'en aller*

devise, *division, limite, partage*

deviser, *partager, arranger, proposer, commander, inventer, décider, raconter, s'entretenir avec, parler de ;* subs. *récit*

devoir, debvoir, *devoir, vouloir dire*

dex *v.* deus, dis, dui

dexendre *v.* descendre

di *v.* dis

dïable, dïaule, dëable, dy-, *diable*

dïaule *v.* dïable

dict *v.* dit

dïet *v.* dire

diex *v.* deus

diffame, *honte*

diffremer, differmer *v.* deffermer

desf- *cf.* def-, deff-

dilection, *affection, dévouement*

dire, dir, *dire, nommer, raconter*

dis *v.* dit

dis, diz, dix, dex, *dix*

disciple, desc-, *disciple*

discipline, *châtiment, exécution*

disconfort, *découragement, chagrin*

discret, *raisonnable*

disner, *dîner*

dist *v.* dire

dit, dict, *mot, parole, interprétation*

diva *va dire, dis donc, fi*

divers, *différent, incertain*
dobler, doubler, *doubler, accompagner*
doctrine, *doctrine, information*
doel *v.* duel
doi, dei, doit, *n.* dois, doiz, *doigt*
doie *v.* devoir
doinst *v.* doner
dol *v.* duel
dolcement *v.* doucement
doloir, dou-, *faire mal, souffrir, plaindre ; réfl. se plaindre, s'attrister ; part.* dolent, -ant, -iant, *attristé, misérable*
dolor, -our-, -ur, -eur, dulor, -ur, doulour, -eur, *douleur*
doloros, -eus, -eux, dolereus, dulurus, *douloureux, misérable*
doloser, dolouser, doulouser, duluser, *plaindre, regretter, souffrir ; réfl. s'attrister*
dolur *v.* dolor
dolz *v.* dous
domage, -aje, -aige, dommage, -aige *v.* damage
don, *don, présent*
donc, -cq₁, -t, -s, dunc, -t, don, dom, donques, -kes, -cques, dumques, -cques, *donc, alors*
doner, doneir, douner, duner, donner, *donner*
dongier *v.* dangier
donselle, domnizelle, *demoiselle ; cf.* damoisele
dont *v.* donc
dont, dons, dunt, dom, dunc, *dont ; adv. d' où, de ce que*
dot *v.* doter
dotance, dout-, doubt-; doutanche, dutance, *doute, crainte, peur*
doter, dout-, doubt-, dut-, *douter, avoir peur, redouter ; s'en douter, se tromper*
dotte, doute, doubte, dute, *doute, crainte, peur*
dou, *du*
dou- *cf.* do-
doubt- *v.* dot-
doucement, dolc-, dulc-, douch-, doulc- ; *doucemant, doucement*
doucet, *doux, gentil*

douçor, dous-, dolç-, doç-; douçour, dous-, douch-, ; douceur, *douceur, plaisir*
dous *v.* dui
dous, -z, -ch, -x -ç, -sç, -lz,- lx, dolz, dols, doz, -x, -ch, duç, dulç, *f.* dousse, dolce, dolcelt, *doux*
dout- *v.* dot-
doy *v.* doi
doyens *v.* devoir
drap, *n.* dras, *drap, habit, linceul*
drecier, drechier, drescier, dresser, *dresser, élever, diriger*
dreit *v.* droit
dresser *v.* drecier
droit, -eit, -eyt, -oict, *droit, bon, juste, véritable ; adv.* tout à fait, *directement ;* a droit, *convenablement ; subst.* droit, justice ; ne a droit ne a tort, *déloyalement*
droitement, dreit-, *droitement, justement*
droiture, dreit-, droict-, *droit, justice*
droiturier, dreit-, droict-, *droit, juste, brave*
dru, -ut, *fém.* drue, *homme de confiance, ami, amant, amante*
dru, *serré*
duc, duch, *n.* dux, dus, *duc*
duel, doel, dol, del, duol, doueil, dueil, *n.* deus, deux, diax, *douleur, peine ;* plainons le dol de, *lamentons-nous de la perte de*
dui, deus, dex, deux, dous, *deux*
dul- *cf.* dol-
dulce *v.* dous
duluve *v.* deluge
dun- *v.* don-
dur, *largeur de main*
duree, *durée, étendue, immortalité*
durement, *beaucoup, bien, fort*
durer, *durer, s'étendre, supporter, vivre*
durrai, etc. *v.* doner
durté, duresté, *dureté*
dusque, desque, deske, dusques, *jusque ;* desque, *depuis que*
dux, dus *v.* duc
dy *v.* dire

E *v.* en; et
e, *interj.*
ëage, *âge*
edre, *lierre*
edrer *v.* errer
efforcier, -cer, -chier, esforcier,
  -cer, *forcer, serrer, renforcer ;*
  esforcier de, *se consacrer à ;*
  réfl. s'efforcer
effreer, efferer, effraër, esfraër,
  -cer; effroier, esfreder, *effrayer ;*
  réfl. avoir peur, s'efforcer
effroi, -oy, esfroi, *effroi, peur, bruit*
effroier *v.* effreer
eglise, -ze, iglise, ygl-, *église*
egue *v.* aigue
eh, *interj.*
eisi *v.* ensi
eisir, eissir *v.* issir
el, enl = en, *prép. avec l'article le*
el, *autre chose*
ele, *aile*
elme *v.* helme
embler, enbl-, ambl-, *ôter, voler,*
  dérober ; réfl. s'échapper
embracier, -cer, embracier, en-
  braissier, *embrasser, embrasser*
embrunchier, *se baisser, s'affaisser,*
  tomber en avant
emende, emmende *v.* amende
emmener, enm-, anm-, enmainer,
  emmener
empeindre, -aindre, *frapper*
empené, -nné, *empenné*
empereör, -ëur, -edor, enperadur,
  -atour, *n.* emperedre, -ere, -aire,
  empereur
empescher, -ier, *embarrasser*
empirier, -er, enpirer, empeirier,
  empirer, détériorer, maltraiter
empor, *pour, pour l' amour de*
emporter, enp-, anp-, *emporter ;*
  réfl. s'en aller
emprés, -ez, enprés, *prép. et adv.,*
  auprès, après
en *v.* home
en, enn, an, e, in, *en, dans ;* en ce
  que, *au point que*
en, an, ent, ant, int, em, *en*
enb- *cf.* emb-
enboucher, *boucher, fermer*
enc- *cf.* ench-

enchaïner, encaïner, *enchaîner*
enchaissier *v.* enchaucier
enchalcer *v.* enchaucier
enchargier, encar-, enchair-,
  charger, recommander, soulever
enchaucier, enchalcer, encaucer,
  encalcer, enchaissier, *pour-*
  suivre ; enchaissier as piez, *se*
  jeter aux pieds de
enclin, *incliné, baissé, penché*
enclore, -orre, -odre, *enfermer,*
  engloutir, entourer
enclouïrent *v.* enclore
encombrer, encumbrer, ancom-
  breir, *embarrasser, arrêter*
enconoistre, *reconnaître*
encontre, anc- ; encuntre, in-
  contra, *prép. et adv. contre, vers,*
  encontre ; subst. rencontre, choc
encontrer, -untrer, anc-, *rencontrer*
encor, anc-, encore, -es, -oires,
  ancore, *encore, même si*
encoste, *à côté de*
encui *v.* ancui
encum- *cf.* encom-
encun- *v.* encon-
endemain, and-, l'end-, lendemain, *lendemain*
endementres, andementre, endementiers, -antiers, endemen-
  tieres, *pendant ce temps-là ;* e.
  que, *pendant que*
enditer, *indiquer*
endroit, -eit, androit, *prép. et*
  adv., quant à, pour, vers ;
  endreit sei, *pour son compte ;*
  endroit moi, *pour ma part ;*
  justement, directement ; subst.
  manière
endurer, -eir, andurer, *durer,*
  endurer, souffrir, subir
enemi, an- ; inimi, ennemi, -my,
  ennemi, diable
eneslepas, isnelepas, *sur-le-champ*
enfance, *enfance, simplicité, timi-*
  dité
enfant, anf-, amf- ; *n.* infans,
  enfes, emf-, anf-, enfens, *en-*
  fant
enfeblïer, *s'affaiblir*
enfens *v.* enfant
enfer, emf-, inf-, ynf-, *enfer*

enferm, *malade*

enfermeté, -et, inf-; anfermetet, enfirmitas, *infirmité, maladie*

enfiler, *filer, enfiler*

enforcier, -er, *renforcer, donner des forces*

enfraindre, *enfreindre*

enganer, *tromper, circonvenir*

engendrer, -nrer, -rrer, *engendrer*

engenrement, *génération, naissance, action d'engendrer*

engien, -in, *esprit, habileté, ruse, tromperie, recherche, embûches, machine de guerre, instrument de pêche*

engignier, -ingnier, **-inner**, *tromper, surprendre*

englacier, *se glacer, se geler*

engoissier *v.* angoissier

engraissier, -er, *engraisser*

engreger, *empirer*

engregier *v.* agregier

enki *v.* enqui

enlacier, *enlacer, s'attacher à*

enluminer, *éclairer, illuminer*

enmi, *au milieu de*

enn- *cf.* en-

enp- *cf.* emp-

enpaignement, *action de se pousser*

enque, *encre*

enquerre, an-, *enquérir, chercher, demander*

enqui, *là, alors*

enragier, *enrager, être tourmenté, être en fureur*

enrengier, *ranger*

enrichir, *enrichir, s'enrichir*

ens *v.* enz

enscombrement, *empêchement*

enseigne, -egne, -engne, -aingne, -enna, -igne, *anseigne, signe, miracle, cri de guerre, drapeau, renseignement*

enseignement, ans-, *enseignement, éducation*

enseignier, -eigner, -egnier, -nignier, -ignier, -eynar, anseignier, -aimier, *enseigner, apprendre, indiquer*

ensemble, -amble, -auble, -anle, ansemble, -amble, *ensembles, -amble, ensembles, avec*

ensement, -ant, ansiment, *de même*

ensevelir, ensepv-, *ensevelir*

ensi, ansi, einsi, ainsi, -sy, eisi, aysi, issi, isi, ensine, -int, einsinc, -int, ainsinc, *ainsi*

ensuivre, ensuivir, enss-, ensevre, *suivre, poursuivre, s'appliquer à*

entaillier, *entailler, sculpter, tailler*

entendement, *intelligence*

entendre, -andre, ant-, *entendre, écouter, comprendre, être informé, songer, viser*

entente, *attention, but, avis, interprétation, intrigues*

ententif, *n.* -is, *attentif*

entercier, -er, *reconnaître, inviter*

entier, enter, antier, entir, *entier, intègre, irréprochable*

entor, -our, -ur, antor, *prép. et adv., environ, autour*

entree, *entrée, commencement*

entrelachier, *intrelacer*

entremetre, *réfl. s'entremettre, donner des soins, se charger de*

entreprendre, *entreprendre, surprendre, étonner, embarrasser, tourmenter*

entrepris, *embarrassé, gêné*

entreprise, -inse, *entreprise, expédition, tentative*

entrer, an-; intrar, -er, *entrer, commencer*

entur *v.* entor

enui, enn-, ennuy, anui, -it, *ennui, souci, chagrin, contrariété, dégoût*

enuit *v.* anuit

enur *v.* honor

enurer *v.* honorer

envaier *v.* envoier

envaïr, *envahir, assaillir, attaquer, entamer*

enveia *v.* envie

envers, *vers, envers, contre; en comparaison de, de la part de*

envers, *sur le dos, à la renverse*

envie, *envie, désir*

envieillir, *vieillir*

environ, anv-, av-; aveyron, evi-rum, *prép. et adv.*, *autour, environ*

envoier, -oïier, -oyer, -eier, -aier, -ïer, anvoier, -eer, entveier, *envoyer*

envoiserie, *ruse*

euz, ens, ans, *prép. et adv.*, *dans, dedans*

Equitaigne, *Aquitaine*

erbage, erbe *v.* herbage, herbe

ere *v.* estre

ermes *v.* estre

erranment, erramment, esr-; erroment, *sur-le-champ, aussitôt*

errant, esr-, *sur-le-champ; cf.* errer

errer, edrar, -er, *marcher, agir; subs. marche, voyage*

ert *v.* estre

es = en les

es *v.* eneslepas

es, ez, es vos, eykevos, *voici, voilà*; es me, *me voici*

esample *v.* exemple

esbaïr, -hir, *étonner, effrayer*

esbanoier, -oïier, -ïer, *amuser, distraire*

esbatre, *amuser, s'ébattre*

escabin, *échevin*

escarn- *v.* escharn-

eschanger, *échanger*

eschaper, -pper, escaper, *échapper*

eschar, escar, -rn, *moquerie, dérision*

escharnir, esc-, *railler, se moquer*

escharpe, *écharpe*

eschaufer, esc-, *échauffer, s'échauffer*

eschavelé, eschev-, *écheAvelé*

escherveler, *faire sortir la cervelle*

eschiele, *échelle*

eschiver, -ever, -iever, -uïr, eskiver, esquiver, *éviter, fuir*

escïent, -ant, essïent, -ant, encïant, ensïant, *escient, sens, connaissance; a e., p. e., sciemment, certainement, à ma connaissance*

escïentre, *escient*

esclace, *goutte*

escole, *école*

escondire, escun-, *excuser, refuser*

escorchier, -cier, *écorcher*

escorcier, -cer, escourcier, *écourter, retrousser*

escouter, -olter, -ulter, -oter, -uter, eskolter, ascoter, *écouter*

escoutteste, *juge*

escrïer, -ider, *crier, appeler, pousser*

escript *v.* escrit

escripture *v.* escriture

escrire, *écrire*

escrit, escript, *écrit, document, manuscrit*

escriture, escripture, *écriture, écrit, source*

escu, -ut, -ud, *nom.* -uz, -us, *bouclier, écu, profit, gain*

escuële, -elle, *écuelle*

escuellir, esquellir, esqueldre, -keudre, *cueillir, apercevoir, regarder, commencer*

escuïer, -uïier, -uyer, -ueyr, esquïer, *écuyer*

esculter *v.* escouter

escumbatre, *gagner par combat*

escumenïer, excommenier, *excommunier*

escumer, *écumer*

escundire *v.* escondire

escuser, exc-, *excuser, absoudre*

escut *v.* escu

esemple *v.* ex-

esf- *cf.* eff-

esgarder, esgu-, æsw-, *regarder, considérer*

esgarer, esgu-, *égarer, bouleverser*

esgart, *conseil, regard, contemplation*

esgranier, *rompre*

esgrugnier, -uner, *rompre*

esguarder, esguarer *v.* esgarder, esgarer

eslaissier, -er, *réfl. s'élancer; part. passé, plein d'entrain*

esleire *v.* eslire

eslire, esleire, *élire, choisir*

eslonger, -guer, -gier, -zier, esluignier, esloinier, *éloigner*

esmaiance, *émoi*

esmaier, -aiier, -oier, *faire perdre courage, épouranter*

esmouvoir, *émouvoir, commencer, partir*

espagnois, *espagnol*

espalde, -alle *v.* espaule

espandre, *épandre, répandre*

espargnier, *épargner, ménager*

espartir, *disperser*

espaule, -aulle, -alle, -alde, *épaule*

especial, *particulier;* par esp., *en particulier*

espee, -ede, -aa, spee, spede, *épée*

espeiret *v.* esperer

esperdu, *éperdu*

esperer, *espérer, attendre*

esperite, espir, *esprit*

esperon, -un, *éperon*

espés, espais, *épais, fort*

espés, espace, *intervalle*

espïer, *épier*

espiet, -ié, -ieu, *épieu, lance*

espinglette, *petite épingle*

esploitier, -er, -eiter, -oicter, *faire, agir, marcher, se hâter, réussir, avancer;* subs. del esploitier, *à la hâte*

espoantable, *épouvantable*

espoënter, espouoanter, *épouvanter*

espos, *époux*

esposer, *exposer*

espouse, espeuse, spose, *épouse*

espouser, -oser, -user, *épouser, fiancer*

espouserie, *mariage, noces*

esprover, -ouver, *éprouver, s'assurer, reconnaître, vérifier*

esquiver *v.* eschiver

esranment *v.* erranment

esrant *v.* errant

essaier, -aiier, -oier, assaier, asaier, *essayer, éprouver*

essele, -elle *v.* aisselle

essemple *v.* exemple

esseulé, *isolé, seul*

essïent *v.* esc-

essoine, essoyne, exoine, *réserve, excuse, récompense*

est, *ce*

esta *v.* ester

estable, *étable*

estable, -aule, *stable, durable*

establir, -aulir, *établir*

establissement, *établissement*

estaindre, -indre, -ignre, *éteindre, tuer*

estal, *place, position*

estandre *v.* estendre

estane, estan, *étang*

estat, *état, pompe*

estaule, -ir *v.* estable, -ir

este *v.* ist

esté, ested, *été*

estelé, *étoilé*

estendre, -andre, *étendre*

ester, esteir, ster, *se tenir debout, se tenir, rester, être, arriver;* réfl. *s'arrêter;* se mettre en estant, *se dresser sur ses pieds*

estëut *v.* estovoir

estincele, -elle, *étincelle*

estoie *v.* ester

estoire, ist-, yst-, *histoire, vivres, flotte*

estor, -our, -ur, *combat*

estorse, *entorse, foulure, détour, coup, extorsion*

estot *v.* estovoir

estovoir, -ouvoir, -evoir, -avoir, *falloir, convenir, être nécessaire;* subst. *nécessité*

estraindre *v.* estreindre

estraine, -rine, *étrenne, don, provision, charge*

estrange, *étrange, extraordinaire*

estrangier, *écarter, repousser*

estrangler, *étrangler*

estras, *vestibule*

estre, iestre, *être, rester, demeurer, naître, appartenir;* subst. *être, état, condition, vie, nature, domicile*

estrece, *étroitesse*

estreindre, -aindre, estrandre, *étreindre, serrer, presser*

estreit *v.* estroit

estrenne, *chance, fortune, hasard*

estrenne *v.* estraine

estreu, -ieu, estrief, -ier, *étrier*

estriver, *discuter avec, se quereller*

estroër, *trouer*

estroit, -eit, ait, *étroit, serré; adv.*
  étroitement ; mettre a l'estroit,
  serrer de près
estroitemant, estroictement,
  étroitement
estuier, *conserver*
estur *v.* estor
estut *v.* estovoir, ester
esveillier, -ellier, -eler, *éveiller,*
  s'éveiller
esvertuer, *réfl. s'évertuer*
eswarder, eswart *v.* esgarder,
  esgart
et, e, *et*
euls, eulz *v.* il *et* oil
eure *v.* hore
üre, bone-e., *bonheur*
üst *v.* avoir
eux *v.* il
eux *v.* oil
eve *v.* aigue
evesque, ebisque, *évêque*
evesquet, veskié, *évêché*
ewe *v.* aigue
ewïer, *égaler*
ex *v.* oil
excommeniement, *excommunica-*
  tion
excuser *v.* escuser
executer, *exécuter*
exemple, ess- ; example, es-,
  exemple, miracle
experïence, *expérience*
extrace, *naissance*
eykevos *v.* es
ez *v.* es

Fable, *fable, mensonge*
fablel, *n.* -iaus, *petit conte, fabliau*
face, fache, *face, visage*
faciez *v.* faire
façon, -un, faisson, fasson, fason,
  face, forme, façon, manière
  d'être, style
faëlé, *flanqué de piliers, garni de*
  colonnes
faille, *faute ;* avoir f., *manquer*
faillir, falir, *manquer de, faillir,*
  faire une faute, faire défaut,
  falloir, finir ; part. pass. faux,
  perfide ; a jour failli, *à la chute*
  du jour

faindre *v.* feindre
faintement, -aut, *en feignant, en*
  dissimulant
faintise *v.* feintise
faintis, faintif, *dissimulé, lâche*
faire, feire, fere, fayr, *faire, dire,*
  être, arriver ; faire ne souffrir,
  accepter, se contenter de ; se f.
  fort, *présumer ;* se faire liez,
  être content ; si, com fait, *tel*
  quel; subs. action ; avoir a faire
  de, *avoir besoin de*
fais, fes, *fardeau, charge, poids,*
  travail ; a un f., *en masse, tout*
  à coup
fait, fet, faict, faiz, *fait, action,*
  affaire ; fait de partie, *accusa-*
  tion
fame *v.* feme
fauls, faulx, fauz *v.* faus
faulte *v.* faute
faus, fax, fals, fauc, faux, *faux,*
  taille
fausser, -ser, -ceir, *tromper, man-*
  quer à sa parole, rompre, dé-
  clarer faux
faut *v.* faillir
faute, faulte, *faute*
fëaule *v.* feel
feconditet, *fécondité*
fedeil, fedel *v.* feel
feel, fedel, fedeil, fidel, -eil,
  fëaule, *fidèle, loyal*
feindre, faindre, *feindre, hésiter,*
  simuler
feintise, fain-, *dissimulation, pré-*
  texte
feit, feist *v.* faire
feit *v.* foi
feiz *v.* foiz
fel, *obl.* felon, -un, *cruel, perfide ;*
  subst. scélérat, traître
fel *v.* fiel
félenesse, *adj. fém. méchante,*
  cruelle
felonie, -enie, -unie, -uunie,
  félonie, perfidie
feme, fame, femme, famme,
  femne, fenme, *femme ;* fame
  rendue, *une religieuse*
fendre, fandre, *fendre, se fendre*
fenestre, *fenêtre*

fer, fier, *fer*
ferir, *frapper, lancer, combattre ;*
   réfl. se jeter
ferm, ferme, *n.* ferms, fers, *ferme*
fermer, *fermer, attacher, enchaîner*
fermure, *prison, serrure*
ferrer, *ferrer*
fes *v.* fais
feste, *fête*
fet *v.* foi *et* fait
feu, fou, fu, *feu, foyer*
feu, *feu, décédé*
feuer, *presser*
feur, fuer, *prix*
fi *v.* faire
fi, fis, *certain*
fïance, *serment de fidélité, pro-*
   messe, confiance
fïancier, fiencier, *promettre, en-*
   gager sa foi
fichier, -er, *ficher, clouer, placer ;*
   réfl. se cacher
fidel, fideil *v.* feel
fieblement, *faiblement*
fieblet, fieble, *faible*
fiel, fel, *fiel*
fiencier *v.* fia-
fier, *réfl. avec en, se confier*
fier, fer, *fier, farouche, fort,*
   étonnant
fier *v.* fer
fierement, *fièrement, fortement*
fiert *v.* ferir
fierté, -et, *fierté*
fieye *v.* foïe
fil, *n.* fils, filz, fius, fiuls, fix, fiz,
   fis, fieus, fiex, fuiz, *fils*
fil, *n.* fis, *fil*
fille, fillie, filie, *fille*
fils, filz *v.* fil
fin, *fin, limite,* mort, intention,
   arrêt
finablement, *enfin*
finer, -eir, *finir*
firent *v.* ferir
firet *v.* faire
fisicien, *médecin*
fist *v.* faire
fiuls, fiul, fix, *v.* fil
flairier, *fleurer, sentir bon*
flanc, *n.* flans, *flanc*
flater, *flatter*

flor, *gracieux, vigoureux*
flor, flour, fleur, flur, *fleur, farine,*
   ornement
florir, flourir, fleurir, flurir,
   fleurir ; part. flori, fluri, fleuri,
   fleuri, *blanc*
flum, flun, *fleuve*
flur, flurir *v.* flor, florir
foi, fei, fai, foy, foit, feit, fet,
   fiet, fied, fid, *n.* foiz, foyz, *foi,*
   promesse ; foi que, *par la foi*
   que
foïe, feiee, foiee, fïeye, fïede, *fois*
foille *v.* fueille
foilli, foillut, foillu, *feuillu*
foison, fuison, *abondance*
foiz, feiz, faiz, fois, foys, *fois*
fol, *n.* fols, fous, fox, fos, *fou*
foliet, foldtre, folichon
foloier, *intr. et réfl., faire des*
   folies, agir en fou, s'égarer
fond, fons, *fond ;* a fonds de cuve,
   qui n'a pas de talus
fonder, *fonder, tomber, s'écrouler*
fondre, fundre, *fondre, détruire,*
   se fondre
fons *v.* fond
fons, fontaine, -ainne, -einne,
   -ene, funteine, *fontaine, source*
fontainele, -enele, -enelle, *petite*
   fontaine
for *v.* fors
forbir, fur-, *polir*
force, *force, besoin, quantité ;* a
   force, *forcément, par force*
force, *ciseau*
forcelle, fourcele, -chele, furcelle,
   poitrine, estomac ; plur. côtés
   de la poitrine, poumons
forest, *n.* forés, *forêt*
forestier, *étranger, brigand*
forfaire, four-, fors-, forfeïre;
   -ere, *forfaire, mal agir envers*
   quelqu'un,   nuire,   pécher,
   offenser, faillir, détruire ; part.
   pass., coupable, condamné
forjugier, *juger à tort, condamner*
forme, fourme, *forme, manière,*
   condition, emblème, symbole ;
   en tel forme, *à condition que*
forment, fortment, -en, fortement, *beaucoup, bien, fort*

forment *v.* froment
forrer, fourrer, *fourrer, doubler*
fors, for, foers, fores, forz, *prép.
et adv.* hors, dehors ; issir fors,
sortir ; fors que, *excepté, excepté
que ;* metre fors, *faire sortir ;*
fors tant, *sauf cependant*
fors, *peut-être*
forsené, four-, *insensé, affolé*
forsfaire *v.* forfaire
forsîait, furfait, *faute*
fort, *n.* forz, fors, *fort*
fortement, fortment *v.* forment
fortune, *sort, fortune*
fosse, *fossé, fosse, trou*
fou *v.* feu
fou, *hêtre*
four- *cf.* for-
fraile, *frêle*
fraindre, freindre, *rompre, br*ᵢₛ
fraite, frete, *ouverture, brèche*
franc, *libre, noble, sincère*
franc, *franc*
franceis *v.*françois
franchise, *privilège, liberté, franchise, noble conduite*
françois, -ceis, *français*
fremïer, *trembler*
fremir, -yr, *frémir, frémir d'envie*
freor, fraour, *frayeur*
frere, freire, -edre, -adre, -adra,
frère, ami
fres, *f.* fresce,-sche, *frais, nouveau*
froidure, *fig. perte de temps*
froissier, fruissier, -er, froisier,
briser, forcer
froit, *froid*
froment, forment, *froment*
front, frunt, *front, rang*
froter, froster, *frotter*
fruissier *v.* froissier
fruit, frut, fruict, fruyt,*fruit*
fruitaige, *fruit*
fueille, fuelle, foille, fuille,*feuille*
fui *v.* estre
fuie, *fuite*
fuille *v.* fueille
fuïr, fugir, foïr, fouyr, *fuir*
fuite, fuitte, *fuite*
fuiz *v.* fil
fulc, folc, *troupeau de bétail,
multitude*

fundre *v.* fondre
funt *v.* faire
fur, *cf.* for-, four-
fust, *n.* fuz, *bois, arbre*
fuste, *bateau, barque*

Gaaignier, -agnier, -ëgnier, gai-
gnier, -gner, -ngner, gagner,
gangner, *gagner*
gab, *n.* gas, *plaisanterie, dérision*
gaber, *plaisanter, se moquer ;* se
gaber a, *se moquer de*
gai, gay, *gai*
gaimenter, guerm-, guementer,
intr. et réfl., plaindre, lamenter
gaires, gu-, w-, gueres, -e, *beaucoup*
gait, guet, gaite, *sentinelle, garde*
galie, galée, *navire*
gambe, ganbe *v.* jambe
game, *gamme, voix, signe*
gant, guant *n.* uuanz, *gant*
garant, *protecteur, seigneur*
garçon, -chon, *n.* gars, garz,
garçon, serviteur, fou
garde, gu-, *garde, crainte, attention, protection*
garder, gairder, guarder, warder, *garder, faire attention,
attendre, regarder, préserver,
prendre garde ;* ne gardent
l'hore que=*en un clin d'œil ;
réfl.* se garder, se pourvoir, se
douter
gardin, -ing *v.* jardin
garingaus, *sorte d'épice*
garir, guarir, gerir, guerir, warir,
*préserver, maintenir en vie,
garantir, sauver, guérir,
échapper, être guéri*
garison, gua-, guairison, *sûreté,
guérison, provision*
garissement, *guérison*
garnir, guarnir, *armer, munir,
garnir, pourvoir, douer*
garoit *v.* garir
gas *v.* gab et gast
gast, guast, *n.* gas, *inculte, gâté,
dépouillé*
gaster, *dévaster, prodiguer*
gauge nois, *noix étrangère*
gay *v.* gai

ge, gié, *je*

geme, gemme, **jame**, *gemme, pierre précieuse*

gemet, jesmé, *n.* gemez, jemez, *orné de gemmes*

genoilliere, *genouillère*

genol, -uil, jenol, junuclu, *n.* genous, *genou*

gens, giens, gienz, *rien*

gent, *gent, les gens, peuple, famille, homme*

gent, jant, gensz, *gracieux, beau*

gentement, *joliment, bravement, poliment, comme il faut, selon les formes*

gentil, jentil, jantil, *n.* gentis, -ius, -ix, *noble, gracieux, aimable*

gentillece, -esce, -esse, *gentillesse, noblesse, grâce*

gerir *v.* garir

germain, *cousin*

gerpir *v.* guerpir

gesir, *être couché, se coucher;* gist a, *dépend de*

geste, *récit, chronique*

geter *v.* jeter

gié *v.* ge

giendre, gemir, -yr, *gémir*

giens *v.* gens

gieser, *dard*

giganz *v.* jaiant

glacïer, -eier, *glisser*

glaive, glague, gladi, *glaive*

glande, *gland*

glorie, *gloire, ciel*

glorïous, -us, -eus, -eulx, *glorieux;* al glorïus, *à Dieu*

gloton, glouton, glutun, *n.* gloz, glos, glous, gluz, *glouton, brigand*

gorge, gorgette, *gorge*

gort, *golfe, gouffre, mer*

gote, goute, goulte, *goutte, rien*

governance, *gouvernement, puissance*

governer, gou-, gu-; governeir, *gouverner, diriger*

grabaton, *grabat*

grace, grasse, *grâce, qualité*

graignor, greignour, -eur, gregneur, gringnor, grenour, *n.* graindre, *plus grand*

graile, -lle, -sle, grasle, grele, *grêle, mince, svelte*

graile *v.* graisle

graim, *n.* gram, *fâché, triste*

graisle, graile, graille, *sorte de cor, trompe*

grant, grand, **granz**, *grand, nombreux;* maint grant, *maint grand coup,* grant jeudi, *jeudi de Pâques; adv. beaucoup, fort*

gras *v.* cras

gravele, *gravier, sable*

gré, gret, gred, greit, *gré, grâce, volonté, remerciement;* en gré prendre, *agréer;* a gré venir, *faire plaisir; adv. volontiers;* de gré, *exprès*

grec, greu, grieu, griu, *grec*

greche, crece, *crèche*

gred *v.* gré

gref *v.* grief

gregneur, greigneur, -our, -ur, *v.* graignor

grele, gresle *v.* graile

greslette, *dim. de* graile

gret *v.* gré

grevance, *peine, chagrin*

grever, -eir, *grever, peiner, fâcher, être désagréable, être ennuyé, souffrir*

grief, gref, *n.* griés, grez, *pénible, difficile, dangereux, grave*

grieté, *peine, souffrance, chagrin*

grigner, *grincer, ricaner*

gris, *gris; subst. fourrure, petit-gris*

griu *v.* grec

groing, *groin*

gros, *épais, grossier;* el gros, *par le milieu*

gua- *cf.* ga-

guarait, *guéret, champ*

gué, guet, weit, *n.* guez, *gué*

gueredoner *v.* guerredoner

gueres *v.* gaires

guermenter *v.* gaimenter

guerpide *v.* guerpir

guerpir, gerpir, gurpir, gulpir, *abandonner*

guerredoner, guer-, guerreduner, *récompenser*

guerreier, *guerrier*

guerreier *v.* guerroier
guerroier, guer-, *faire la guerre,*
  combattre, presser
guet *v.* gait *et* gué
guigner, *faire signe, regarder ;*
  parer, se parer
guiler, giler, ghiler, *tromper*
guise, vise, *manière*
guisne, *guigne*

Ha, haa, *interj. cf.* a
habit, abit, *habit*
habiter, abiter, *habiter ;* l abit,
  j'y habite
hace *v.* haïr
hache, hace, *hache*
haie, haye, *clôture, haie*
haïr, haÿr, *haïr, accabler de*
  reproches
haire, *chemise de crin*
hait, *joie, plaisir*
halme *v.* helme
halt *v.* haut
hanap, *coupe*
hanste, hante, *bois de lance*
hardement, -ant, *hardiesse*
hardi, -y, *n.* -iz, -is, *courageux*
hart, hairt, *hart, corde*
haste, *broche*
haste, *hâte*
haster, hester, *hâter, presser*
hastif, *n.* -is, *prompt, irré-*
  fléchi
hauberc, hal-, au- ; haubert,
  hal- ; osberc, *cotte de maille*
haucier, halcier, haulcer, hausser, *hausser, avancer, élever*
haultesse, *élévation, hauteur*
haut, hals, halt, alt, hault, *pl.*
  haulx, *haut*
hautement, halt-, ault-, *haut*
haye *v.* haie
hé *v.* het
heaulme *v.* helme
heaumier, *fabricant de casques,*
  armurier
heent *v.* haïr
helme, el-, hal-, hiau-, heaulme,
  heaume, casque
henureement, *honorablement*
herbage, erbage, *prairie*
herbe, erbe, *herbe*

herbegier *v.* herbergier
herberc, *maison*
herberge, *demeure*
herbergier, -egier, herbiger, he-
  berger, *loger*
here, haire, *cilice*
heritage, heritaige, er- ; hire-
  tage, ir-, *héritage, propriété*
hertier, *réfl. faire des efforts, se*
  démener
het, hé, *haine*
het *v.* hait *et* haïr
hiaume *v.* helme
hier, ier, *hier*
hillot, *valet, serviteur*
hoc *v.* o ; ne por hoc, *pourtant*
hoir, heir, oir, *héritier*
home, homme, ome, omne,
  oume, hume, ume, omne,
  omen, *n.* huem, hom, homs,
  hous, om, hum, *homme ;* hou,
  on, an, en, um, l'hom, l'on,
  l'an, l'en, l'um, *on*
honeste, honn-, *honnête*
honir, honnir, hunir, *honnir,*
  déshonorer
honn- *cf.* hon-
honnourable, *honorable*
honor, -our, -eur, -ur, henor,
  enor, ennor, -ur, honnour,
  -eur, oneur, -ur, onnour, -eur,
  ounour, *honneur, avantage, fief,*
  royaume, grandeur, dignité,
  éclat, magnificence
honorer, -ourer, -erer, -urer,
  hounerer, honnorer, -erer,
  -ourer, henorer, ounrer, onur-
  rer, ounorer, ennorer, *honorer*
hons *v.* home
hontos, -eus, -eux, -us, *honteux*
hore, ore, heure, eure, hure, ure,
  heure, temps ; d'ures en altres,
  continuellement
horïon, horrïon, *coup*
host *v.* ost
hoste, oste, *hôte*
hostel, ostel, *n.* -eus, hostieux,
  logis, maison
hu, *huée*
huevre *v.* oevre
hui, hoi, ui, oi, *aujourd'hui ;* hui
  et le jour, *aujourd'hui*

huis, huiz, huys, hus, uis, us,
  porte, entrée
huissier, uissier, useire, *huissier*
huissier, vuissier, *bateau*
huit, huict, uit, oit, wit, *huit*
hum *v.* home
humblement, huml-, *humblement*
hume *v.* home
humelïer, um-, humilïer, *abaisser,
  humilier*
humilité,-eit, -iet, umilité, -eit,
  humelité, *humilité, soumission,
  modestie*
hun *v.* un
hunir, huntus, hure *v.* honir,
  hontos, hore
hus *v.* huis

I, *il*
i, hi, iv, *y*
ialz *v.* oil
iaue, iave *v.* aigue
ice *v.* iceo
icel, ichel, *ce*
iceo, iço, iceu, ice, *ce*
icest, ichest, icist, ichist, *ce*
ici, ichi, ycy, *ici ;* d'ici qu'a,
  jusqu'à
icil, *ce*
idonc, idunc, iduns, *alors*
ie *v.* jeo
ielz, ieuls, ieus, iex, iez *v.* oil
ier *v.* hier
iere, iert *v.* estre
iés, iestre *v.* estre
iex *v.* oil
il, illi, el, *f.* ele, elle, *il*
iloc, -oec, -uoc, -euc, -ec, -uec,
  illec, -euc, illo, ileques, -euques,
  -ueques, illueques, -ecques,
  -uekes, -uecques, *là*
image, imagene, ymage ; imagele,
  imagiele, ymagele, *image*
imaginatïon, *imagination*
impacïence, *impatience*
incarnacïon, *incarnation*
infourmer, *informer*
inobedïence, *désobéissance*
intelligence, *accord, entente des
  intelligences*
intentïon, -cïon, *intention*
interpretacïon, *interprétation*

interrompre, *réfl. s'entre-détruire*
ious *v.* oil
ire, *colère, tristesse*
ireement,irieement,*furieusement,
  tristement, avec colère*
ireist (= ireits), *fâché, triste*
irer, irier, *réfl. se fâcher ; part.
  pass.* iré, irié, *fâché, triste,
  chagriné*
irieement *v.* ireement
isnel, *rapide, vif, prompt*
isnelement, *rapidement*
issi *v.* ensi
issir, is-, isc-, yssir ; eiss-, eis-,
  esc-, exir, *sortir, s'en aller,
  jaillir*
ist, *f.* este, ce, *cette*
ister *v.* ester
itant, *tant, autant ;* a itant, *là,
  pour le moment ;* par i., *par là ;*
  pour i., *c'est pourquoi*
itel, *tel*
iver, ivier, yver, *hiver*

Ja, jai, *déjà, jadis, jamais, désormais ;* ja soit ce que, *quoique*
jacobin, *moine dominicain*
jaiant, gëant, gigant, *nom.* -ns,
  -nz, *géant*
jamais, -eis, -és, *jamais*
jambe, gambe, ganbe, *jambe*
jardin, gardin, -ing, *jardin*
jargon, *jargon*
jel = je le
jeo, jo, ju, *etc.* je
jeter, ge-, gi-, gie-, getter, jetter,
  gecter, *jeter, pousser, chasser,
  délivrer*
jeu, geu, gieu, giu, ju, *pl.* jeux,
  jeulx, *jeu*
jëuner, gëu-, ju-, *jeûner*
joene, -nne, jone, jouene, juvene,
  joesne, juesne, jenne, *jeune*
joenece, juenece, jeunece, -esse,
  jeunesse
joer *v.* jouer
joes = jo les
joiant, *joyeux*
joie, joye, *joie*
joindre, juindre, jundre, *joindre,
  unir, venir*
jointe, joincte, *joint, nerf*

joious, -eus, -us, -eux, -elux,
joyeux, *gai, joyeux*
joli, -y, *joli, joyeux, content*
jolif, *joyeux*
joliveté, *joie*
jone *v.* joene
jor, jour, jor, jorn, jurn, *jour,
clarté, assignation*
jornee, jour-, *journée*
jos = jo les
jos *v.* jus
joster, jouster, juster, *s'approcher,
tomber à, rassembler, se réunir,
lutter*
jou *v.* jeo
jou- *cf.* jo-
jouer, juër, jueir, *jouer, s'amuser,
s'ébattre ; réfl. s'amuser*
joy- *v.* joi-
ju, *je*
ju *v.* jeu
judeu, juïf, *n.* juys, juis, *juif*
juër *v.* jouer
jugëur, *juge*
juïf *v.* judeu
jur *v.* jor
jurer, *jurer, jurer par*
jus, *sève, sang*
jus, jos, *en bas, à bas, à terre,
par terre*
jusque, -es, jusche, jesque, ius-
que, *jusque*
just, juste, *juste*
juster *v.* joster
justice, -ise, *justice*
jut *v.* gesir

K = que
kankes *v.* quanque
kar *v.* car
ke *v.* que
ki *v.* qui

La, lai, lay, *là*
labour, -eur, -ur, *labeur, travail*
lacet *v.* laissier
lache, lasches, *inférieur*
lacier, lacer, lascier, lasser, *laccr*
Ladre, *Lazare*
lai *v.* la, loi-
lai, *laïque*
laid *v.* lait

laidir, lei-, *maltraiter, injurier*
laienz, -ens, -anz, -ans, *là, là
dedans*
lais *v.* las
laissier, -sier, -ser, laxier, lazsier,
lacier, leissier, lessier, -sser ;
laier, leier, *laisser, délaisser,
quitter, remettre, permettre,
s'abstenir, cesser, céder ;* je nel
lairrai que, je ne lairai ne, *je
ne manquerai pas de*
lait, laid, leit, let, *fatal, funeste,
triste, laid, méchant*
lamenter, *plaindre*
lance, *lance*
lancier, -chier, -cer, *lancer*
langue, languet, laingue, lengue,
langue, langage, parole
larai, larei *v.* laissier
large, *large, généreux, libéral*
largesse, -esce, *largesse ;* a l.,
en abondance
larme, lerme, *larme*
larmoier, -oyer, lermoier, -oyer,
pleurer
larron, -un, ladron, -un, lasrun,
lairun, learun, leron, *n.* lerre,
lere, *larron*
larronneau, *petit larron*
las, lais, *las, malheureux, pauvre,
épuisé, triste*
las *v.* laz
lasser *v.* lacier
lasseté, lascheté, *fatigue, lâcheté*
laudes (*lat.*), *chant d'église, actions
de grâces*
lavedure, *larure*
lavement, *ablution*
lay *v.* lai
laz, las, *lien, filet*
laz *v.* lez
lazsier *v.* laissier
lé *v.* lou
lé, let, *n.* lez, les, *large*
lëal, *etc. v.* loial
lëans, -anz *v.* leens
lëaus *v.* lëal
lechëure, *gourmandise*
ledece, -ice *v.* leece
lee *v.* lé
leece, léesce, l'iece, -esse, lyësse,
ledece, -ice, *joie, plaisir*

leens, -ans, -anz, *là dedans*
legier, leger, ligier, *léger, facile*
legierement, lig-, *facilement*
lei *v.* loi
lei- *cf.* lai-
lendemain *v.* endemain
lëon, lïon, -un, lyon, *lion*
lerme *v.* larme
lerrés *v.* laissier
les *v.* lé, lez
letre, lettre, *lettre, littérature*
leu *v.* lou
leu, lieu, liu, lou, *n.* lex, liex,
  lieu
leupart, liepart, *léopard*
lever, *lever, se lever, commencer*
levrete, *lèvre*
lez *v.* lé *et* lié
lez, les, leis, *côté; prép. à côté de*
li, le, lo, *fém.* la, li, le, *article le*
lié, let, *n.* liés, liez, lez, *gai,*
  joyeux
liede *v.* lié
liéament, lïem-, liedem-, *gaîment*
lïen, lïan, *lien, collier, rapports*
  d'amitié
liepart *v.* leupart
lïesse *v.* leece
lieve *v.* lever
liez *v.* lié
ligier *v.* legier
lign, ling, ligue, lin, *origine,*
  race
lignage, -get, -aje, linage, *famille*
linçol, *chemise*
lis, liz, *lis*
lit, lyt, *lit*
liu *v.* leu
lïun *v.* lëon
liverrai *v.* livrer
livraison *v.* livroison
livre, libre, *livre*
livrer, *livrer, délivrer*
livroison, -aison, -un, *livraison,*
  don, pension
liz *v.* lis
lober, *tromper*
loder *v.* loër
loöiz, *loué*
loënge, *louange*
loër, louer, loeir, loder, lauder,
  louer, conseiller, approuver, l.

ne conseiller, *conseiller; réfl.*
  se vanter
loger, lojer, *camper*
logis, -iz, *logis*
loi, loy, lei, ley, lai, *loi, loi sainte,*
  usage
loial, loyal, lëal, lëaul, *n.* -aul,
  -ax, loiax, loyaulx, *loyal*
loialment, loy-, lë-; loiaument,
  loy-, lëaumant, loiaulment,
  loy-, *loyalement*
loier, luier, luwier, *loyer, salaire*
loier, loïier, louer, luier, luër,
  louer, donner ou prendre à
  gages, payer; subs. prix
loingtain, lointain, -tein, *lointain*
loire, loisir, -xir, leisir, *être per-*
  mis; subst. loisir etc. loisir
loist *v.* loire
long, lonc, lung, lunc, *long, large*
longement, -a- *n.* longuement
longes *v.* longues
longuement, long-, lunge-, *longue-*
  ment, longtemps
longues, longes, lunges, *longtemps*
lor, lors, lores, *alors*
lor, lors, *pron. poss.* leur
lors que, *lorsque*
lorseïnol *v.* rosignol
los, loz, lous, *louange, consente-*
  ment, éloge, réputation
losange, -enge, *flatterie, perfidie*
losengëor, -etour, *flatteur, perfide*
losengier, *perfide*
losengier, *tromper, flatter*
lot *v.* loër
lou- *cf.* lo-
lou *v.* leu
lou, leu, lé, *n.* lous, lox, lus,
  loup
lox *v.* lou
loy- *n.* loi-
loz *v.* los *et* loër
luër, *souiller, barbouiller*
luier *v.* loier
luinz, *loin*
lumiere, -ere, *lumière*
lune, *lune*
lur *v.* lor
lus *v.* lou
luyant, *luisant*
ly- *cf.* li-

Madre, *espèce de bois*
madre *v.* mere
magne, *grand*
mahaignier *v.* meh-
mai, moy, *mai*
mail, *n.* maus, *mail, maillet*
main, mein, *main*
main, *matin*
maindre *v.* manoir
maine, *manière*
mainne *v.* mener
mains *v.* moins ; almains, *au moins*
maint, meint, *maint ;* maint grant, *maint grand coup*
maintenant, mein-, *aussitôt*
maintenir, *rester en place, se tenir*
mais, *le mois de mai*
mais, meis, maix, mays, mes, *mais, jamais, désormais, plus, encore ;* ne mais, *sinon ;* mès que, *sauf que, excepté ;* ne mais que sul, *rien de plus que, seulement*
maisniee, -nee, -nie, -niede, mesniee, maignye, *famille, maison, escorte*
maison, -un, meisun, meson, *maison*
maiseler, *meurtrir*
maistre, mestre, magistre, magestre, magister, *maître, seigneur, savant ; gouvernante, maîtresse ; adj. premier, principal, bon*
maistrie, *suprématie, supériorité*
mal, mau, mel, miel, *n.* maus, max, *mal, mauvais, méchant ;* de male part, *d'un mauvais caractère ; adv. mal ; subst. mal, souffrance, douleur, péché ;* por mal de, *en dépit de, malgré*
maladie, malage, *maladie*
maldire, mau-, maul-, maléir, *maudire, répliquer insolemment*
male, malle, *malle*
malement, mall-, *mal*
malëur, malheur, *malheur*
malfé, *mauvais destin*
malice, *méchanceté, malignité*
malmetre, mau-, *maltraiter ; mal employer*

maltalent, -ant, mautalent, -ant, *colère, mauvaise humeur*
maltalentif, *courroucé*
malvais, -eis, -és, mauveis, -es, mavais, maulvais, *mauvais, méchant, lâche*
malvaistié, -estiet, *méchanceté*
mamele, -elle, *mamelle*
mamelete, *petite mamelle*
manacer *v.* menacer
manche, mance, *manche*
mander, *commander, recommander, faire savoir, annoncer, convoquer, mander par, faire venir*
manent, -ant, *rentier*
maneviz, *intrépide*
mangier, -er, maingier, mengier, -er, *manger*
mangonial, *engin de guerre*
manicle, *gantelet*
maniere, -ere, meniere, manniere, *manière, façon ;* de grant m., *beaucoup*
manjuë *v.* mangier
manoir, menoir, *demeurer*
mantel, -eau, mentel, *n.*, -iax, -iaus, -ieus, *manteau*
mar *v.* mer
mar, mare, *à la male heure, par malheur, pour votre malh.*
marc, *nom.* mars, *marc*
marche, *frontière*
marchëant, -cëant, -chant, marchand
marchié, markié, *marché*
marchis, -iz, *marquis*
marés, *marais*
marescal, mareschaus, *maréchal*
margerite, margh-, *marguerite*
mari, -y, *mari*
mariage, -aige, *mariage*
marïer, marier, *donner en mariage*
marir *v.* marrir
marmiteux, *naïf, simple*
marrement, -iment, *affliction*
marrir, marir, *part.* marri, mari, *affligé*
mars *v.* marc
mars, marz, *mars*
martir, -yr, *martyr*

martire, -yre, -yrie, *tourment,*
  supplice
massonner, *maçonner*
mat- *cf.* met-
mater, *abattre, vaincre*
matinee, *matinée*
mattons *v.* metre
mau- *cf.* mal-
mau gre bieu, *mal gré de dieu,*
  imprécation impie
maugroiement, *malédiction*
mauparlier, *à la langue méchante,*
  médisant
maus *v.* mail *et* mal
mauvais, -és *v.* malvais
mauvis, *grive*
max *v.* mal
medisme *v.* meïsme
medre *v.* mere
meff- *v.* mesf-
mehaignier, mahaignier, *tour-*
  menter
mehaing, -aig, *tourment, mal,*
  maladie
mei *v.* mi
mei, *moi*
mei- *cf.* mai-, moi-
meiain, *celui du milieu, le*
  second
meie, *médecin*
meillor, -our, -eur, mellor,
  millor, meilur, *n.* mialdres,
  mieudres, miaures, *meilleur*
meins *v.* moins
meir, meire *v.* mer, mere
meis *v.* mois
meïsme, meïme, medisme, mees-
  me, mis-, mesme, *même*
meïsmement, mesm-, *également,*
  même
meïsse *v.* metre
mel = me le
mel *v.* mal *et* miel
membre, menbre, manbre, *membre*
membrer, menbrer, -eir, *réfl. et*
  impers. se ressouvenir, se rap-
  peler ; part. membré, *prudent,*
  sage
men *v.* mon
menace, ma-; manatce, *menace*
menacer, manacer, -ecier, -echier,
  menacer

mençonge, -çoigne, -songe,
  mançonge, *mensonge*
mençongier, mensonger, *menteur,*
  imposteur
mendre *v.* menor
mener, -eir, mainner, moneir,
  moiner, *mener, conduire*
menestrel, -eel, -eul, *n.* -eus,
  serviteur, chanteur, joueur
  d'instrument
mengier, -gué *v.* mang-
menor, -our, mineur, *n.* mendre,
  menre, *moindre, plus petit,*
  inférieur, plus jeune
mentir, mantir, *mentir, tromper,*
  manquer
menton, mantun, *menton*
menu, -ut, *menu, petit, fin,*
  rapide, en détail ; adv. souvent
menuisse du pié, *cou-de-pied*
mer, mier, *pur, vrai, sans mélange*
mer, meir, mar, *mer*
merci, mercit, mercid, -cy, -cet,
  mierceit, *merci, grâce, pitié*
mercier, *remercier*
mere, mered, medre, madre,
  mère
merveille, -oille, -elle, *merveille,*
  prodige, étonnement ; a.m. mer-
  veilleusement
merveillier, -er, -oiller, -iller,
  intr. et réfl. s'étonner
merveillous, -eus, -us, -eux, mer-
  vellex, *merveilleux, énorme*
mes, *maison*
mes, metz, *mets*
mes, *direction*
mes, *privé*
mes *v.* mais
mesaise, *malaise*
mesaisé, malaisé, *malaisé, mal-*
  heureux
mesaler, se mesaler vers, *se mettre*
  dans son tort envers
mesavenir, *mésarriver, arriver*
  mal à propos, arriver malheur
meschief, -chef, mischief, *mal-*
  heur
meschin, -cin, mischin, *jeune ;*
  subst. jeune homme, fém: jeune
  fille, servante
mescinete, *jeune fille*

mescroire, *croire à tort, se défier, douter de ; part. prés.* mescrëant, *mécréant ;* mescrëu, *mécréant, méchant*

mesdire, *médire*

mesel, meseau, mesiau, *lépreux*

meselerie, mezelerie, *lèpre*

mesfaire, -ere, meffaire, *méfaire*

mesfait, -et, meffait, -et, *méfait, crime ; adj. coupable*

meshui, -uy, *désormais*

mesler, meller, mcrler, mescler, moiler, *mêler ; réfl. se brouiller, s'engager*

mesme *v.* meïsme

meson *v.* maison

message, -aget, -aje, mesaige, *messager*

messe, misse, *messe*

messire, mesire, misire, *monsieur*

mestier, mistier, menestier, mestire, *métier, profession, emploi, devoir, besoin ;* mestier est, *il faut*

mestre, -rie *v.* maistre, -rie, *et* metre

metre, mettre, matre, mattre, mestre, mectre, *mettre, poser, placer, déposer, pousser, amener, persuader, envoyer, donner, employer, préférer, faire prisonnier ;* metrefors, *faire sortir ;* m. en. parole, *aborder ; réfl. s'abandonner, se ruiner ;* se metre en estant, *se dresser ;* si metre, *mettre en cet état*

meubles, *propriété mobilière*

meur *v.* mors

mëur, *mûr*

mi, mei, my, *demi, milieu, au milieu ;* par m., *par là*

mials, mialz *v.* mieus

miaus *v.* miel, mieus

mie, *amie*

mie, myr, mies, *miette, croûte ; adv., un peu, rien ;* ne . . . mie, ne . . . *point*

miel, mel, *n.* miaus, *miel*

miel *v.* mal

miels, -x, -z *v.* mieus

mien, men, *mien ; subs.* le bien que j'ai

mier *v.* mer

mieudres *v.* meillor

mieus, mieuz, miex, mius, mix, miez, mielz, miels, mielx, mels, melz, muels, muelz, muez, mials, miaus, mialz, miols, mieulx, myeulx, *mieux*

mignot, *mignon, joli*

mignotise, *gaieté*

mil, mile, mille, milie, miliet, *mille, mil*

mil, *charlatan*

millier, miler, *mille*

miols *v.* mieus

mire, *médecin*

mireor, *miroir*

mirer, *contempler ;* se mirer en, *se comparer à*

mise, *dépense*

misericorde, *miséricorde ; sorte de poignard*

misme *v.* meïsme

mist *v.* metre

mius, mix *v.* mieus

mocqu- *v.* moqu-

mocquerie, *moquerie*

moens *v.* moins

moi *v.* mui

moiain, meiain, moyen, *moyen, au milieu ; subst.* milieu, *moyen*

moie *v.* mien

moilier, -llier, moylier, muilier, -ler, -ller, *femme, épouse*

moilier, *mouiller*

moin- *cf.* men-

moine, -nne, moyne, *moine*

moineau, *terme de fortification*

moins, mains, meins, moens, *moins*

mois, meis, meys, *mois*

moitié, meitié, *moitié*

mollir, *devenir mou*

molt *v.* mout

mon, mun, men, *n.* mes, mis, *mon*

mondain, *parfait, noble*

monde *v.* mont

monde, *pur, net*

monnoye, *monnaie*

monosceros, *monocère, unicorne*

monstier, monstrer *v.* mostier, mostrer

mont, **munt, mond, monde, munde,** *monde*

mont, *beaucoup*

mont, **munt, munz, mont, mon-tagne**

montaigne, munt-, *montagne*

monter, -eir, munter, *monter ; monter à cheval: avancer; avoir de l'importance, profiter, faire monter, élever*

moquer, -ier, mocquer, *railler ; réfl. se moquer*

moralité, *morale, enseignement*

morir, mou-, mu-, mui-, *mourir ; tuer*

mors, meur, *mœurs*

morsel, *n.* -eus, -ieus, -iaux, -iax, *morceau*

mortel, -al, *n.* -ex, *mortel, qui tue*

mostier, moust-, monst-, must- ; muster, *cloître, église, monastère*

mostrer, mou-, mon-, mu- ; moustreir, *montrer, indiquer, commander, enseigner;* mostrer parole, *s'exprimer*

mot *v.* mout

mot, *mot, parole*

moult *v.* mout

mout, molt, mot, mult, mul, mut, moult, *beaucoup, très, fort*

movoir, mouvoir, muver, *mou-voir, agiter, se mettre en mouve-ment, en marche; réfl. même sens, s'éloigner; causer*

moy *v.* mai

moyen *v.* moiain

muable, -aule, *muable, mobile*

muder *v.* muër

muër, muder, *changer, toucher, varier;* ne pooir m. ne, *ne pouvoir empêcher que*

mui, moi, *muid*

muilier, -ler, *v.* moilier

muire *v.* morir

mun- *v.* mon-

mur, meur, muraille, *muraille*

murir *v.* morir

murmurer, -eir, *murmurer*

musart, *fou, sot*

museraz, *flèche*

musgode, *étui, trésor, provision*

must- *cf.* most-

mye *v.* mie

N *v.* en

nacele, *navire*

nafrer, naff- ; navrer, -eir, *blesser*

naie, *non*

naige *v.* neige

naigier *v.* najer, neger

naistre, nastre, nestre, *naître*

najer, *naviguer, nager*

nape, *nappe*

nascïon, nacïon, *naissance; nation*

nasel, *partie du heaume*

nate, *natte*

nature, *nature; habitude*

naturel, *naturel; légitime*

naturelment, -ellement, *de nature; naturellement*

navie, *flotte*

ne, ned, *ne, ni;* ne—ne, *ni—ni;* ne—que, *ne que, seulement;* ne *avec subj.; de peur que*

ne=en

né *v.* neïs

nëant, neent, nïant, nïent, naient, noiant, noient, neient, nent, rien, *néant; quelque chose; nullement;* por noiant, en vain; n'en fut nïent a dire, *il n'y eut rien à en dire*

necun, *aucun*

ned *v.* ne

nef, neif, *n.* nez, nes, neis, *nef, navire*

neger *v.* noier

neger, naigier, *neiger*

neient *v.* nëant

neif *v.* nef, noif

neige, nege, naige, *neige*

neir *v.* noir

neis *v.* nef

neïs, nes, nis, *même*

nel=ne le

nelui *v.* nul

nem=ne me

nemperro, *néanmoins*

nen=ne ; =ne me

nenil, nanil, nennil, nenny, *non*

neporquant, nun purquant, ne por hoc, nequedent, *pourtant*

nercir, noircir, *noircir ; devenir noir*

nes=ne se *et* ne les

nes *v.* neïs, nef *et* net

nes, nez, *nez*

nesun, nisun, *aucun* (*cf.* necun)

net, nect, *n.* nés, *pur*

neu=ne le

neue *v.* noër

nëul *v.* nul

neveu, -vu, *n.* niés, *neveu*

nez *v.* nes *et* nef

ni, *ni, et pas*

nïant *v.* nëant

niés *v.* neveu

nis *v.* neïs

nisun *v.* nesun

no *v.* non

no=ne le

nobileté, -et, noblelé, *noblesse*

noble, nobli, nobilie, *noble, pièce d'or d'Angleterre*

noblece, -eche, -esse, *noblesse ; magnificence*

nobleté *v.* nobilité

nodrir *v.* norrir

noër, nouer, *prés.* neue, *nouer*

noiant *v.* nëant

noier, noiier, neier, neger, nïer, *nier, renier ; réfl.* se démentir

noier, noiier, noyer, nayer, *noyer, submerger*

noif, neif, nief *n.* nois, *neige*

noir, neif, neyr, *noir*

noircir *v.* nercir

nois *v.* noif *et* noiz

noise, *bruit, querelle*

noiz, nois, *noix*

nol=ne le, ne li

nom, -n, num, -n, *nom ;* avoir a n., *avoir nom ;* par n., *nommé ; foi, religion*

nombre, *nombre, quantité, compte*

nomer, numer, nommer, *nommer, appeler*

nomeyement, *nommément*

non *v.* nom

non, nun, nom, no, *non*

noncier, nun-, *annoncer, indiquer*

none, -a, nune, *la 9e heure du jour*

nonne, nonain, nonnete, *nonne, petite nonne*

nonpurquant *v.* neporquant

nopce, *noces*

norrir, nou-, nu-; nodrir, *nourrir, élever*

nos=non se

nos, nus, nous, noz, *nous*

nostre, noz, nos, *notre*

notonnier, *matelot*

nou- *cf.* no-

nou=ne le

nourriture, nourreture, *nourriture*

nouvellet, novellet, *frais, jeune*

novel, nou-, nu-; nouviel, nouveau, *nom.* noviaus, -ax, noviaus, *nouveau, frais, jeune*

novele, -elle, nouvelle, nuvele, *nouvelle*

noveller, *recommencer*

nu, nud, *nu, dépouillé, débarrassé*

nuef, *neuf*

nuef, *n.* nués, *nouveau*

nuire, *nuire, faire mal à*

nuit, nut, nuyt, nuict, *n.* nuiz, *nuit*

nul, nuil, nëul, nïul, *n.* nus ; *subst.* nului, nelui, *nul, un, une, aucun ;* nul que, *personne sauf*

num-, nun- *cf.* nom-, non-

nur- *v.* nor-

nus *v.* nul

nuv- *v.* nov-

O, hoc, *ce, cela ; oui;* ne por hoc, *pourtant*

o, *interj.,* oh, o

o *v.* ou

o, *le*

o, ob, od, ot, *avec, auprès de*

obedience, obédience, obéissance

obeïssance, *obéissance*

oblïer, ou-, u-, oblider, *oublier*

obscur *v.* oscur

occirre, -ire, -ir, oïcirre, ocirre, -ire, ochire, oscire, *tuer, faire mourir*

ochier, *encourager*

ocoison, och-; aqoison, ach-; ockeson, *occasion, cause, prétexte, faute, accusation*

od *v.* o

odir *v.* oïr
odor, -our, -ur, -eur, *odeur*
odorer *v.* adorer
odurement, *odeur, odorat*
oe, *oie*
oés, ués, eus, obs, ob, *besoin, usage, service, profit*
oevre, uevre, ovre, ou-, oy-, eu-, oeu-, *œuvre, ouvrage, affaire*
oi *v.* avoir
oï *v.* oïr
oïe, *ouie*
oïl, ouïl, ouail, oï, ovy, *oui*
oil, oel, uel, oeil, ueil, oeul, ols, olz, euz, ex, ieus, iex, ieuz, iez, ious, oés, ialz, ielz, ieuls, eulz, euls, *oeil*
oingnement, *onguent, lotion*
oïr, ouir, oïir, oÿr, oyir, odir, *ouïr, entendre, écouter*
oisel, -eau, -iaus, -iax, -iaux, -eaulx, oyseaulx, eusel, *oiseau*
oisclé, *petit oiseau*
olifan, *trompette, clairon*
olt- *v.* out-
om *v.* home
ombre, onbre, umbre, *ombre*
ome, omme, omne *v.* home
on *v.* home
on- *cf.* hon-
onbre *v.* ombre
onc *v.* onques
onches *v.* onques
oncle, uncle, *oncle*
ongle, ungle, uncla, *ongle*
onnour *v.* honor
onques, -cques, -kes, -ches, unques, -kes, -ches, oncque, onke, unque, onc, oncq, unc, honc, *jamais*
or, *maintenant, or;* or avant, *désormais;* d'or en avant, *dorénavant;* or... or, *tantôt ... tantôt*
or, *or*
ora *v.* avoir
oraison, -un, *v.* oroison
ord *v.* ort
ordene, ordre, *ordre, congrégation religieuse, habitude*
ordener, -eir, ordoner, -onner, *ordonner, placer, instruire;* ordené, *ordonné prêtre*

ordoner *v.* ordener
ordre *v.* ordene
ordure, *vilenie, bassesse, malpropreté, désagrément*
ore, *vent*
ore *v.* hore; *adv.* ore, ores, *maintenant;* des o., *désormais;* ore *endroit, maintenant*
oreille, orille, *oreille*
orent *v.* avoir
orfavrerie, *orfèvrerie*
orfenin, orphelin, orphanin, orphelin
orgoel, -oil, -oill, -ueil, -ueill, -uel, -uil, *n.* -ueus, -ueulz, *orgueil*
orgoillox, orgueilleus, -eux, orguillos, -ous, -eus, *orgueilleux*
orie, *doré*
orient, -ant, *Orient*
oriflambe, oriflamme, *étendard d'armée*
oroison, oraison, oraisun, orison, ureisun, *oraison, prière*
orra *v.* oïr
orrible, or-, *horrible*
ors, ours, urs, *ours*
ort, ord, *impur, sale*
orteil, *n.* -ex, *orteil*
os, *interj.*
os, *osé*
os *v.* oser
os, *os*
os *v.* ost
osberc *v.* hauberc
oscur, obs-, *obscur*
oser, osser, ozer, oser, *s'enhardir*
ost, host *n.* oz, os, *armée*
ostel *v.* hostel
oster, osteir, *ôter; détourner; délivrer; réfl.* se soustraire
Osterice, *Autriche*
osterin, *pourpre*
ot *v.* huit, o, oïr et avoir
otroier, -oïer, -eiier, -eier, -ier, outroier, ottroier, octroyer, -ïer, *accorder, donner, consentir, octroyer, s'enhardir; réfl.* se donner
ottri, *consentement;* fruit de dous ottri, *baiser*
ou, o, u, *ou*

ou, o, u, *où;* ou que, *quelque
part que*
ou=el (en *avec l'art.*)
ou *cf.* o
oubli, -y, ubli, *oubli*
oul=où le
oult- *v.* out-
oultrance, outrance, *excès*
ouoit *v.* oïr
ours *v.* ors
out, oüt *v.* avoir
outrage, -aige, oltrage, *outrage,
outrecuidance, excès*
outrageus, olt-, oultrageux, *qui
passe les bornes, présomptueux,
insolent*
outre, oltre, ultre, utre, oultre,
*prép. et adv. outre, au delà, à
travers*
outremer, -eir, oltremer, *outremer*
ouvra *v.* ovrer
ovre *v.* oevre
ovrer, ou-, u- ; uverer, *faire,
agir, travailler, procéder*
ovrir, ou-, u- ; auvrir, *ouvrir,
s'ouvrir*
oye, *oreille*
oys *v.* oïr
oz *v.* ost
oz- *v.* os-
oz *v.* oïr

Pacïenment, pacientment, *pa-
tiemment*
paien, paiien, pagien, *païen*
paienisme, *païen*
paier, paiier, *calmer, payer; réfl.
se réconcilier*
paile *v.* pale
paile, palie, paliet, pale, *étoffe de
soie, manteau*
pain, pein, *pain;* pain pour dieu,
pain bénit
paindre, poindre, *peindre, broder*
paine, -nne, -ngne *v.* peine
paine *v.* pener
pais *v.* pas
pais, pes, paix, *paix, tranquillité*
païs, -iz, -ys, païs, *pays*
paistre *v.* pastor
paistre, pestre, *manger, donner à
manger, nourrir*

palais, -és, -aix, *palais, salle*
pale, paile, *pâle*
pale *v.* paile
palés *v.* palais
palie, paliet *v.* paile
palir, pallir, *pâlir*
paller *v.* parler
pan- *cf.* pen-
pan, *pièce, poitrine*
panre *v.* prendre
paor, paour, poor, poür, pëor,
pëur, pavor, *peur*
papelardie, *papelardise, hypo-
crisie*
par, per, *par, désigne le moyen, le
motif; à travers, sur, dans,
avec, à; adv. int. très, beaucoup,
bien;* de p., *au nom de, de la
part de;* par quoi, *en comparaison avec q.;* par humilité,
humblement
par *v.* per
paradis, -ix, paraïs, pareïs, *paradis*
parage, paraget, *noblesse, rang,
naissance illustre, famille*
parchemin, parchamin, **par-**
gamen, -in, *parchemin*
pardoner, -uner, -onner, per-
doner, *pardonner, remettre,
donner tout à fait*
pareil, -ail, *pareil, semblable, com-
parable*
pareïs *v.* paradis
parenté, -et, *parenté*
parer, *préparer, orner*
parfaire, *parfaire; part. pass.*
parfait, -eit, -it, -aict, *parfait,
destiné*
parfeitement, parfitement, *par-
faitement, sincèrement, pieuse-
ment*
parfont, *profond;* en parfont, *au
fond*
parfournir, *procurer, achever*
parler, pairleir, paller, *prs.*
parole, -olle, *parler; subst.
mot*
parmaindre, *rester*
parmi (*cf.* par *et* mi), *dans*
paroir, -eir, *paraître, apparaître;
réfl. se montrer*

parole *v.* parler

parole, -olle, *parole, parole sen-*
sée, discours, plaidoyer ; mos-
trer parole, s'exprimer

part, *part, côté, direction ;* quel
p., *où que ;* de male, de franche
p., *de mauvais, de bon caractère*

parti, party, *parti, manière,*
entreprise

partie, *part, partie, portion, côté,*
parti, procès ; amer sans p.,
aimer sans retour ; fait de
partie, *accusation ;* avoir partie,
avoir un procès

partir, pertir, *partager, départir,*
répartir, donner, séparer,
partir, s'en aller, crever, se
briser ; se partir de, *sortir*

partuer, *achever de tuer, donner*
le coup de grâce

pas, *pas, passage ;* aller plus que
le p., *aller très-vite ;* pas ren-
force la négation, pas ; isnel le
pas, *immédiatement*

pascor, *de Pâques*

pasle＝pâle

pasmer, *réfl. et intr. pâmer*

pasmoison, -eson, -exon, -eisun,
pamoison, *pâmoison*

passage, *passage, traversée*

passer, paisser, paser, *passer,*
traverser, faire le voyage de la
terre sainte, surpasser, re-
joindre, supporter ; réfl. passer,
se passer

passïon, -un, pasïun, *passion*

pastor, -our, -eur, paistre, *pas-*
teur, berger

pastore, -oure, *bergère*

pate, patte, *pièce de fer*

paterne, *personne du père, père*
céleste

pauvret, *pauvre*

paveillon, -un, -ellon, -illon,
pavillon, tente

pavement, -iment, *pavement, pavé*

pechié, -é, -iet, -ied, -ed, -et,
peciet, pecié, pecchié, *n.* pechez,
piez, *péché*

pecïer, peçoier, *briser*

pécune, *argent, trésor*

pedre *v.* pere

peer *v.* per

peer, empoisser, *enduire*

peez *v.* pié

pein *v.* pain

peine, -nne, paine, -nne, -ngne,
poine, -nne, *peine, effort, diffi-*
culté, fatigue

peise *v.* peser

pel, *pieu*

pel, peel, *n.* piaus, *peau, cuir*

pelerin, *pèlerin*

peleure, *peau, morceau de peau,*
lambeau

penant, *pénitent*

pendre, pandre, *pendre, sus-*
pendre, dépendre

pener, *prs.* paine, poene, *tour-*
menter, peiner, efforcer ; réfl.
se donner de la peine, se fatiguer

penevous, *pénible*

penitance, *pénitence, peine, châti-*
ment

penne, *plume*

penre *v.* prendre

pense, pensé, pansé, pensed,
pensee, pansee, *pensée*

penser, -eir, panser, -sser, penser,
penser, réfléchir, songer, croire ;
subst. pensée

pensif, *n.* -is, *pensif*

pëor *v.* paor *et* pïor

per *v.* par

per, peir, peer, pier, par, pair,
semblable, pareil ; subst. com-
pagnon, camarade, compagne,
épouse

percier, -cher, *percer, déchirer*

percevoir, *apercevoir ; part.* per-
cëu, *en possession de ses sens*

percutre, *frapper, percer*

perdre, pardre, *perdre*

pere, peire, pare, pedre, *père*

perece, *paresse*

perriere, *engin lançant des pierres*

peril, *n.* -iz, *péril, danger*

perillous, *périlleux*

perir, *périr*

perron, -un, *escalier, balcon,*
marche, pierre

pers, *bleuâtre, livide*

persecucïon, *persécution, infliction,*
épreuves, fléau venant de Dieu

persecuter, *persécuter*
pert, *habile*
perte, *perte, ruine*
pertuis, *trou, ouverture*
pervers, *pervers, fou*
pesance, *peine*
pesant, *lourd*
peschier, -er, pesxier, *pêcher*
peser, *prs.* peyse, poise, *peser, fâcher, chagriner, déplaire,* il me pese de, je regrette; *subst. poids*
pesme, *très mauvais, cruel*
petiot, *très petit, faible*
petit, *petit,* un petit de, *quelques; adv. peu; a p., peu s'en faut*
petitet, petitelet, *très peu*
peu *v.* po
peule, peuple *v.* pueple
phisicien, *médecin*
pié, piet, pied, *n.* piez, piés, pez, peez, *pied;* se mettre en p., *se redresser*
pieça, -cha, *il y a longtemps*
piece, *pièce, intervalle, espace de temps, moment*
piege, *piége*
piere, pierre, pere, perre, *pierre*
piet *v.* pié
pieté, -et, ed, *piété, pitié*
piez *v.* pechié, pié
piler, pillier, *pilier*
pillart, *pillard*
pincel, *pinceau*
pincer, pinser, *pincer*
pïor, -eur, pëor, poior, *n.* pire, *pire, plus mauvais*
pis *v.* piz et pius
pis, *pic*
pis, *pis*
pité *v.* pitié
piteusement, *pitoyablement*
piteus, -eux, *miséricordieux, pitoyable*
pitié, pitet, -é, -ez, -és, *pitié, miséricorde, attendrissement*
pius, pix, pis, *pieux*
piz, pis, peyz, *poitrine*
place, -che, *place*
plaidier, -er, pleidier, *plaider, traiter*
plaie, -aye, *plaie*

plaier, *blesser*
plain *v.* plein
plain, plein, *plain, aplani;* a pl., *clair; enfin; subst. plaine*
plaint, *plainte*
plaire, plaisir, pleisir, plesir, *plaire; subs. plaisir*
plaisance, *volupté, joie*
plaissier, *courber*
plait, -eit, -aid, -et, -ayt, plaiz, *procès, dispute, convention, assemblée où l'on juge les procès;* metre en plait, tenir p., a p., *parler;* prendre plait, *faire un engagement*
planche, plansque, *planche*
planchon, -çon, *branche, sorte de pique*
plante, *plainte*
planté *v.* plenté
plege, pleige, *répondant, caution, garantie, promesse*
pleige *v.* plege
plein *v.* plain
plein, plain, plen, *plein*
plenté, -anté, *plénitude, abondance*
plesir *v.* plaire
plevir, *promettre, garantir; part. fidèle*
ploier, ployer, *se courber*
plom, plum, plon, *plomb*
plommé, *plombé, massue*
plor, plour, *pleur, larme*
plorer, -ourer, -eurer, -urer, *pleurer*
ploros, *pleurant*
pluie, pluye, plueue, *pluie*
pluisor, -our, plusour, -eur, -ur, plusior, -ieurs, *plusieurs;* li p., *la plupart*
plurer *v.* plorer
plus, plux, *plus, davantage;* de p., *davantage;* le p., *la plupart;* sans p., *seulement, seul*
pluye *v.* pluie
po, pou, poi, peu, poc, pauc, pouc, *peu;* m'est p., *peu m'importe;* a p., por p., per p., *à peu près;* poi et poi, *peu à peu;* par un poi ne, a poi ne= *presque*

podéste v. poësté
poës v. pooir
poësté, podéste, poëste, *pouvoir, puissance*
poëstëif, n. poëstëis, poesté, *puissant*
poi v. po
poil, peil, peyl, *poil, cheveux*
poin, poing, poig, poyn, puin, puing, puign, pung, *poing, poignée*
poindre, puindre, *piquer, poindre, donner des éperons, aller au galop, s'élancer*
poïne v. peine
point, poent, punt, *point, pointe, instant, borne, fin, état, manière, position;* à point, *au moment critique, au temps voulu*
pois v. pués
poise v. peser
poisse v. pooir
poisson, -sçon, peysson, *poisson*
poiz, *poix, résine, glu*
polir, *polir; part. pass.* poli, polly, *poli*
pome, pume, pomme, *pomme*
pont, *pont, poignée*
pooir, povoir, pouvoir, podir, *pouvoir, avoir la force; subst. pouvoir, puissance, tout ce que l'on peut*
pople v. pueple
por, pour, pur, per, pro, *pour, à cause de, par le moyen de, au nom de, par crainte de;* p. ce que, *parce que;* p. coi, *pourvu que;* ne por hoc, *pourtant*
porparler, pour-, pur-, *comploter*
porpenser, pour-, pur-, porpanser, *penser, imaginer, méditer, réfléchir; réfl. réfléchir*
porrai v. pooir
porrir, pourrir, *pourrir*
porro que, *parce que*
port, n. porz, *port*
port, *les défilés des Pyrénées*
porte, -a, *porte, bonde*
porter, -eir, *porter, emporter, témoigner, obtenir; réfl. se porter, marcher; imp.* il porte, *il faut*

poser, pauser, *poser, placer, mettre, convenir*
postiz, -iç, *porte*
pot, n. poz, pos, *pot*
potence, *béquille*
pou v. po
poür v. paor
pour v. por
pour- cf. por-
pourmener, *promener*
pourpoinct, *pourpoint*
pous, *pouls*
pout v. pooir
poverin, *pauvre*
poverté, -eit, povreté, pouv-, pauv-; povérte, *pauvreté*
povoir v. pooir
povre, pou-, poi-, pau- poure, *pauvre*
praël, pre-, praiel, *fém.* praële, praielle, pray-, *petit pré*
praërie, *prairie*
praiel v. praël
prametre v. prometre
prandre v. prendre
preïus, precïeux, -eulx, precios, pretïeus, *précieux*
preder, *dépouiller*
pree, *prairie*
preier, preiere v. prïer, proiere
prelait, n. -aiz, *prélat*
premier, -er, primier, -er, -eyr, *premier*
premerain, prim-; primerein, *premier, aîné*
prendre, prandre, prindre, penre, panre, *prendre; réfl. et impers. commencer; réfl. se tenir, s'accrocher*
pres, prez, priés, *prép. et. adv. près, auprès, presque*
preschement, *prédication, sermon*
present, -ant, *présent;* de p., en p., *actuellement, maintenant*
presenter, -anter, *présenter*
presse, *presse, foule, mêlée, désordre*
prest, *prêt, disposé*
prester, *prêter*
prestre, prebstre, *prêtre*
presumtie, *présomption*
preu, n. pros, proz, prox, preuz,

prex, prud, pruz, *f.* preude, *prudent, brave*

preudome, -omme, prodomme, preudom, -oms, prodom, -on, prozdom, -uem, pruzdum, pruduems, *prud'homme, homme de bien, bonhomme*

prevost, -ot, provost, *n.* -os, *prévôt*

prex *v.* preu

prez *v.* pres

pri, *prière*

prïer, -ere, *v.* proier, -ere

prieuse, *supérieure d'un couvent*

priez *v.* pres

prime, *prime, première heure*

primerain *v.* premerain

primereinement, *premièrement*

prince, -che, *prince, seigneur*

pris, preis, *prix, valeur, avantage*

prise, *saisie*

prisier, priser, prixier, preisier, proisier, praiser, pretier, *priser, apprécier, estimer, évaluer, louer*

prison, -xon, *prison*

prisonier, -onnier, *prisonnier*

prist *v.* prendre

pro *v.* por

pro, prod, prot, prou, proud, prud, prout, pru, preus, *profit, quantité; adv. assez*

proceder, *procéder, avancer*

profession, *profession, vœu, promesse, témoignage*

profit, prouffit, *profit, vêtements*

proie, preie, *butin, proie*

proier, proiier, preier, preiier, prïer, priier, *prier*

proiere, priiere, praiere, prï-, prii-, *prière*

prometre, pra-, *promettre*

prophete, -ette, *prophète*

propos, -oz, *projet, dessein*

proposer, *mettre en avant, alléguer, proposer*

prot *v.* pro

prou- *cf.* pro-

proud *v.* pro

provendier = almosnier

prox, proz *v.* preu

pru, prud *v.* pro

pruzdum *v.* preudome

pucele, -elle, puch-, pulcelle, -ele, -ella, pulcellet, pucellet, *pucelle, jeune fille, femme de chambre*

pueple, poeple, pople, puple, poblo, peuple, peule, pule, *peuple*

puer, en, *en dehors*

pués, puez, puis, puys, pois, pos, poyst, post, *prép. et adv. après, puis, dans la suite; puis que, depuis que; pois de lui, après lui*

puet *v.* pooir

pui, *colline*

puign, puin, puing *v.* poin

Puillanie, *Apulie, la Pouille*

puin- *v.* poin-

puïr, *puer*

puis *v.* pués

puissant, poiss-, *puissant*

puist *v.* pooir

puit *n.* puiz, *puits, fontaine*

pulcelle, -a, -ele *v.* pucele

pung *v.* poin

punt *v.* point

pur *v.* por

pur- *cf.* por-

pur, *pur, unique; pur et simple, sans condition; en vostre pure voulenté, entièrement à votre discrétion*

purofrir, *offrir*

purquant *v.* nonpurquant

pute, puite, *puant, vil, méchant, vilain*

puyent *v.* pooir

Q *v.* qu

queue, *queue*

quanque, -es, -canque, canques, kankes, quant que, *tout ce que, autant que*

quant, cant, kant, *combien, tout ce que; conj.* quant, quand, quand; *ne pour quant, néanmoins*

quar *v.* car

quarantisme, *quarantième*

quarat, *carat*

quarrel, -eaulx, quarius, *carreau*

quart, -cart, quairt, *n.* quarz, *quatrième*

quasser *v.* casser

quatir, *cacher*
quatre, quatro, quaer, *quatre*
que, ke, k', c', qued, quet, quid,
 que,pourquoi; conj. car,jusque;
 relat et. interr. qui, que, quoi,
 combien
quei *v.* quoi
quel = que le
quel, kel, keil, *n.* quex, quieus,
 quiex, queuls, quis, *quel;* li
 quel, *lequel*
quenoistre *v.* conoistre
quens, quenz *v.* conte
queneu *v.* conoistre
quenu *v.* chenu
quer *v.* car *et* cuer
querele, -elle, *sujet de plainte,*
 procès, dispute, requête
querir, querre, quere, *chercher,*
 demander
queu *v.* chief
queu, queux, *cuisinier*
qui, ki, *là*
qui, ki, chi, *qui, si quelqu'un, que*
quider *v.* cuidier
quient *v.* cuidier
quier *v.* querir
quil = qui le
quis *v.* quel *et* querir
quistrent *v.* querir
quite, cuite, *quitte, hors de danger;*
 clamer cuite, *tenir quitte, ab-*
 soudre
quiter, quitter, cuiter, *exempter,*
 délivrer, abandonner
quoi, coi, coy, koi, quai, quei,
 quoi, quelque chose
quoi *v.* coi

Rachater, -apter, racater, racheter, raicheter, rechepter, *rache-*
 ter, gagner
racine, rach-, ras-, *racine*
radise, *sorte d'épices*
radoter, re-, reduter, *radoter*
raëmbre, redembre, *racheter*
rafreschir, *munir de nouveau,*
 rafraîchir
rage, raige, *rage, excès*
rai *v.* ravoir
rai, raid *n.* raiz, *rayon*
rai *v.* roi

raier, *rayonner, couler*
raïue *v.* roïne
raison, rei-, re- ; raixon, -zon,
 raisun, *raison, sens, motif,*
 sentiment, raisonnement,parole,
 compte ; metre a r., *aborder,*
 questionner
raler, -eir, *aller (de nouveau),*
 s'en aller, retourner, revenir
ramainsist *v.* remaindre
ramembrance, rem-, *ressouvenir*
ramier, *rameux, branchu*
ramier, *pigeon ramier*
ranconner, *rançonner*
rancune, ransc-, *rancune*
randon, *force, violence;* de grant
 randon, *à toute vitesse*
raporter, rapp-, *rapporter*
rasoager, *consoler, soulager*
rassaisir, *égayer*
rassëoir, ras-, *rasseoir*
raviser, *remarquer, observer*
ravoir, *avoir de nouveau, rega-*
 gner; rai-ge =ai-ge
rebrasser, *rebrousser*
receler, -eir, *cacher;* en recelée,
 en cachette
recercelé, rechercelé, *bouclé*
recercer, recercier, *rechercher,*
 fouiller
recesser, *cesser*
recevoir, rech- ; reciuure, re-
 cepvoir, *recevoir, accepter,*
 admettre
rechief, rechef, recief, de r., *de*
 nouveau
reciter, *réciter, raconter*
reclamer, *prs.* reclaime, recleime,
 appeler, implorer, déclarer, con-
 fesser
reclost, reclore, *refermer*
recoillir *v.* recueillir
recomencier, recomancer, recu-
 mencer, recommencer, recom-
 mencer
recommander, -ender, recu-
 mander, *recommander*
reconfort, *encouragement, satis-*
 faction
reconoistre, -onnoistre, -ongnoi-
 stre, -ognostre, -unuistre, *re-*
 connaître

recorder, *rappeler, se souvenir, conter*

recorre, recourir, *recourir, aider*

recoult, *échappé*

recovrer, -ouvrer, -uvrer, *trouver, recouvrer, revenir à soi*

recroire, *cesser, désister;* recréant, *lâche;* recrèu, -ut, *découragé*

recueillir, rek- ; recoillir, requieldre, *recevoir, accueillir*

recum- recun- *v.* recom-, recon-

redemptiun, *rédemption*

redenst *v.* raëmbre

redire, *redire, dire encore, répéter*

redoner, *donner aussi*

redoter *v.* radoter

redouter, -oter, -uter, -otter, -oubter, *redouter, craindre*

redrecier, -escier, *réfl. et intr. se redresser*

redunrai *v.* redoner

reduter *v.* radoter *et* redouter

reff- *v.* ref-

reflamber, *flamber*

refraindre, *modérer; réfl. renoncer*

refrener, *retenir, modérer*

refuser, -eir, reffuser, *refuser*

regarder, reguarder, rewardeir, *regarder, examiner, considérer*

regenerer, *régénérer*

region, *région, pays*

regne, renne, ren, **raine**, *règne, royaume, patrie*

regreter, *regretter, plaindre*

reguarder *v.* regarder

reis, reiz *v.* roi, roit

rejehir, *confesser*

rejoindre, *parvenir*

relief, *reste*

religion, *religion,* **maison religieuse**

reluire, *reluire, réfléchir*

remaindre, remanoir, *demeurer, rester, cesser;* il ne remaint pas . . . que, *il ne tient pas à . . . que . . . ne*

remanant, remenant, *reste, surplus;* aler remanant, *diminuer*

remander, *commander*

remembrer, *se souvenir, rappeler*

remener, *ramener*

remés, remest *v.* remaindre, remetre

remetre, remectre, *abandonner; réfl. se rasseoir, se rendre*

remonstrer, *remontrer, expliquer*

renc, -ng, *rang, file*

rencharger, *confier, recommander*

rendre, randre, redre, *rendre, donner, payer, livrer;* fame rendue, *religieuse*

reng *v.* renc

renge, range, *ceinture*

renom, -n, *renom, renommée*

renomer, -ommer, *renommer*

renommee, renumee, *renommée, honneur, pureté*

rente, *revenu*

rëont, rëunt, rëond, rond, *rond*

repaire, -ere, *demeure*

repairier, -eirer, -erier, -adrer, *retourner*

repaistre, *rassasier*

reparlance, *renommée*

repasser, *guérir*

reposement, repaus-, *repos*

reposer, repauser, *reposer; réfl. s'apaiser*

reprendre, repenre, *reprendre, réprimander*

reproche, -oce, -uce, -ouche, *reproche*

requerre, -eir, *requérir, demander, prier, rechercher, s'adresser à*

requeste, *requête*

resaillir, resailir, *reculer, sauter de nouveau, se relever*

rescorre, *regagner, rattraper*

resembler, -ambler, -empler, *ressembler, sembler*

resgarder, *regarder*

resgart, *soin*

resont *v.* restre

resortir, *s'enfuir; rebondir; part. ravi*

respit, *délai*

respondre, -undre, -ondret, *répondre*

response, *réponse*

restablir, *rétablir*

rester -eir, *rester*

rester *v.* reter

restorer, *rappeler à la vie*

restraindre, *retenir*

restre, *être de nouveau, être à son tour, être toujours*

resurdre, ressourdre, *ressusciter; réfl. s'élever*

resurrexis, = 2ème pers. sing. passé défini de ressusciter

resvigorer, -ourer, revigorer, *remettre en vigueur*

retaillier, *retrancher*

retenir, *retenir, tenir de l'autre côté*

retenue, *l'action de retenir; obligation*

reter, rester, *blâmer, accuser*

retor, retour, *retour*

retorner, -ourner, returner, -ar, *retourner, rendre, répliquer, détourner, faire retourner, congédier*

retraire, -eire, -ere, *retirer, détailler, rapporter, répéter, raconter, ressembler; en retraire sor, se venger sur; part. passé: abandonné*

revanche, *compensation, châtiment*

revenir, *revenir, redevenir*

revertir, *tourner, se tourner, résulter en*

revestir, *revêtir*

revoloir, *vouloir à son tour, vouloir de nouveau*

rewarder, reward *v.* reg-

riche, rice, *noble, puissant, riche*

rien, riens, ren, *chose, quelque chose, rien, être, cercle d'amis; est r., importe; de rien, aucunement*

rigoler, *plaisanter, se jouer de*

rigour, rigueur, *rigueur*

rire, *rire, sourire*

robe, *vêtement, tunique*

robëor, -ur, *larron*

rober, *voler, piller*

roche, roce, *rocher*

roe, *roue*

roge, rouge, *rouge*

roi, rei, rai, rey, roy, rex, *roi*

roial, royal, regiel, *royal*

roialme, roiame, -aulme, roy- aume, -aulme, *royaume, règne*

roiffe, *lèpre*

roïne, raïne, reïne, roÿne, *reine*

roit, reit, roide, *roide, dur, fort*

Romaine, *Romagne*

rompre, ron-, rum-, *rompre, déchirer, châtier*

rond *v.* rëont

rondel, *rondeau*

rosee, rousee, *rosée*

rosignol, rouss-; roisignor, lorseilnol, *rossignol*

rossel *v.* ruissel

rote, *instrument musical*

rote, route, rute, *troupe, route*

rouge *v.* roge

rous- *v.* ros-

rover, *prier, ordonner*

roy *v.* roi

ruele, *ruelle, passage, entrée*

ruissel, -eau, rossel, rusel, *n.* ruisiaus, *ruisseau*

rumpre *v.* rompre

rute *v.* rote

rut *v.* rompre

ruver *v.* rover

Sa *v.* ça

sac, *n.* sas, *sac*

sachier, -er, sacier, saichier, *tirer, ôter, arracher, crever*

sage, saige, saive, sapi, *sage, savant, prudent*

sagement, saigement, *sagement*

sai *v.* ça

saichant *v.* savoir

saichier *v.* sachier

saige *v.* sage

saillir, salir, *sauter, s'élancer, sortir, jaillir*

sain, *sein*

sain, *en bonne santé, sain et sauf*

Saine, *le fleuve la Seine*

sainement, sainn-, *en bon état, d'une bonne manière, sans accident*

sainier, *saigner*

sainglement, *séparément*

sainglier, sainier *v.* seignier

sainne *v.* saner

saint, *cloche*

saint, seint, sain, sanct, sant, sanz, sans, senz, *saint*; saintisme, sein-, *très saint*

saisir, seisir, sesir, *mettre en pos-session, prendre possession, saisir*
saison, *saison, temps*
Saisunie, *la Saxe*
sale, *salle*
sale, *sale*
sals *v.* sauf
salu, -ut, -ud, -udt, *action de sauver, salut*
saluer, saluder, *saluer*
salv- *cf.* sauv-
samaine *v.* semaine
sambl- *v.* sembl-
sanc, sang, *n.* sangs, sans, *sang*
sanct *v.* saint
saner, *guérir*
sanglant, sain-, sen-, *sanglant*
sans *v.* saint, sanc *et* sens
santé, -ei, *santé*
saolee, saoulee, *rassasiement, soûl*
saoler, saouler, soëler, *rassasier*
saoul, saül, *n.* saous, *rassasié; subst. rassasiement*
sapience, sapientia, *sagesse*
sarrasin, -zin, *sarrasin*
satiffaire, *satisfaire*
satisfaccion, *satisfaction*
sauf, saulf, *sauf*
saulter, *sauter*
saut, *saut*
saut *v.* sauver *et* saillir
sautier, *psautier*
sauver, salv-, salvar, saulver, *sauver*
sauveour, -eur, salvedur, -eur, *n.* salverres, salveires, *sauveur*
sauveté, salveté, -et, -eit, *salut, sûreté, rédemption*
savoir, -eir, -er- -ier, -ir, sçavoir, *savoir, apprendre, demander, avoir le pouvoir; subst. savoir, science, raison; part. prés. sachant, saçant, saichant, instruit, intelligent; du sceu du roi, avec la connaissance du roi*
savor, -eur, *goût, saveur*
savra *v.* savoir
sc- *cf.* s-
sceu *v.* savoir
se *v.* si
sëans, *situé*

sëans *v.* ceenz
sec *f.* seche, sesche, *sec*
secle *v.* siecle
secont, segont, secunt, **segunt,** *second, deuxième*
secorre, -ourre, soscorre, sucurre, *secourir, secourir*
secors, -ours, socori, *secours*
secret, secré, segroi, *secret*
sedeir *v.* sëoir
seder *v.* sëoir
seel, seaus, sel, *sceau*
seeler, sceller, *fixer*
sei *v.* soif
seignier, **-er,** signier, saingnier, sainier, *bénir, faire le signe de la croix*
seignor, -our, **-eur,** -ur, segneur, -ur, signor, -our, seinor, sennur, sennior, senior, *n.* sendra, mari, seigneur (sire), maître
seignori, segnouri, sign-, *magnifique*
sein, sain, *sein*
seinor, -ur *v.* seignor
sejorner, -ourner, **sojurner,** sujorner, sujurner, **surjurner,** *séjourner, demeurer, vivre, résider, reposer, hésiter*
sele, selle, *selle*
selonc, -unc, -on, sulonc, **-unc,** *selon, le long de, à côté*
semaine, -ainne, -aynne, -eine, samaine, sepmaine, *semaine*
semblable, sambl-, *semblable*
semblance, sambl-, *ressemblance, image, mine, apparence*
semblant, sam-, sau-, *air du visage, mine, semblant, image, apparence, extérieur, faux air; estre par semblant, se donner l'air d'être*
sembler, sam-, sen-, san-, *sembler, paraître, ressembler, assembler; part.* **senblansz,** *semblable*
semoing *v.* semondre
semondre, -undre, *inviter*
semonse, **semonce, somonse,** *appel*
sempre, -es, **semper,** *toujours, aussitôt*

semundre *v.* semondre

sen *v.* sens

senescal, *n.* -aus, seneschal, *sénéchal*

sengler, *sanglier*

sens, -z, sans, -z, sainz, semz, sen, *sans, excepté, sinon, sauf*

sens, -z, sans, *sens, esprit, manière*

sente, *sentier, voie*

sentir, santir, scentir, *sentir, s'assurer ; se sentir de, ressentir*

senz *v.* saint *et* sens

sëoir, sedeir, seder, soueir, *asseoir, être assis, convenir, seoir, plaire ; sëant, situé*

sepouture, sepult-, *sépulture*

sereine, *sirène*

serf *v.* cerf

serf, serv, *n.* sers, *serf, esclave*

sergant, sergent, sarjant, *serviteur, domestique ;* sergante, *servante*

seri, -y, serit, *tranquille*

sermon, *langage, discours, sermon*

seroge, *belle-sœur*

seronder, *entourer*

seror, -our *v.* soror

servage, *service*

service, -iche, -ise, -iset, *service*

servitor, -eur, *serviteur, prêtre servant*

ses *v.* son

ses=si les

set *v.* si

set, sept, *sept*

set *v.* savoir

seul, soul, sol, sul, *n.* seus, sos, *seul, unique ; adv. seulement*

seule *v.* siecle

seulement, seull-, sol-, sul-, *seulement*

sëur, segur, *sûr, ferme*

seur *v.* sor ; *amer*

seurcot, sorquot, *vêtement de dessus*

scure *v.* sor

sëurté, seureté, *sûreté, assurance*

seus *v.* seul

severe, *sévère*

sez, *assez*

si, se, *si, ainsi, aussi, comme ; che fu si, il arriva ; si com, comme, jusqu'à ce que ; se tant, si seulement ; se . . . non, sinon, sauf ; subst. oui, aveu*

si, se, set, *si*

si *v.* son

si, se, *soi*

siecle, secle, seule, *siècle, monde, vie, vie mondaine*

sien, suen, sien, son, al s., *à ses frais ;* le sien, *le bien qu'on a*

siene *v.* sien

sigle, *voile*

signe, *signe, indice*

signefiement, *signification*

signiffiance, *signification, promesse*

signifier, signefier, segu-, sen-, *signifier, déclarer, annoncer*

sil=si le

sim=si me

sim, *demi*

simplement, sinplemant, *simplement*

simplesse, *simplicité*

sire, -es, -et *v.* seignor

sis, six, *six*

sis *v.* sëoir

sis=si se

sis=si les

sit=si te

sivre, suivre, suir, suivir, *suivre, continuer*

soavet, sou-, *doucement*

sobre *v.* sor

soëf, sou-, su-; soueif, soweif, *doux, agréable ; adv. doucement*

soëler *v.* saoler

soferre *v.* sofrir

soffire, souff-, suff-, soffeire, *suffire*

soffisance, *suffisance, richesse, contentement*

sofrir, soff-, souf-, souff-, suf-, sosf-, soferre, *souffrir, tolérer, supporter, consentir, attendre ; se sofrir de, s'abstenir, se soumettre; faire ne soffrir, accepter, se contenter*

soi *v.* savoir

soie, *sa*

soie, soye, *soie*

soif, soi, sei, *soif*

soif, *haie*

soin, soing, *soin, souci, inquiétude, peur*

soissante, seiss-, soix-, *soixante*

sol, *soleil*

sol, *sou*

sol v. seul

solacier, -cer, -chier, *récréer, réjouir, se divertir*

soldre, sorre, saure, *payer*

soleil, -el, eill, n. solaus, -ax, -aux, -auz, -euz, -ex, soleiz, solleiz, soloil, souleuz, *soleil*

solement v. seulement

soler, soller, souler, *soulier*

soloir, sou-, su-, *avoir coutume*

som, son, sum, *sommet ;* en sum, *sur*

somme, summe, *somme ; teneur*

somme, sume, *charge, peine*

somme, *sommeil*

son v. som

son, som, sun, n. ses, sis, *adj. poss. son*

son, *son, air, chant*

soner, sonner, suner, *sonner, dire, proclamer, prononcer*

songe, *rêve, pensée*

songier, songer, sonjer, *rêver, penser, réfléchir*

sonner v. soner

sor v. soror

sor, sour, seur, sur, sore, seure, soure, sure, soure, *prép. et adv., sur, après, au-dessus, dessus, plus que*

sor, *jaune d'or*

sordre, sour-, sur-, *sourdre, jaillir*

sore v. sor

soror, seror, -our, -eur, n. sor, suer, seur, soeur, *sœur ;* belle s., *belle-sœur*

sorprendre, sour-, seur-, sur-, *surprendre*

sorse, sourse, surce, *source*

sortir, *sortir ;* sortis, *destiné*

sos v. son, soz

sospir, *soupir*

sospirer, sous-, sus-, sou-, *soupirer*

sostance, sus-, subs-, *substance, soutien, richesse*

sostenir, sous-, sus-, *soutenir, secourir, souffrir, supporter, conserver*

sot n. soz, *fou*

sot v. savoir

sou- *cf.* so-

sou v. soz

souci, -y, soussi, -y, sousci, *souci*

souëf v. soëf

souf- *cf.* sof-

souff- *cf.* souf-

soul- *cf.* sol-

soul v. seul

soupirer v. sospirer

sour- *cf.* sor-

sourcil, n. -cieus, *sourcil*

sourvenir, sur-, *venir, survenir*

sous- *cf.* sos-

souslever, soul-, *soulever*

souspicïon, suspicïum, suspezïun, souspesson, suspesson, soupeçon, soupçon, *soupçon*

sousprendre, sozp-, soup-, sopr-, *surprendre, attaquer*

soussi, -y v. souci

sout v. savoir

soutil, subt-, soutiff, n. soutieus, -iex, sultiz, soubtis, *subtil*

souv- *cf.* sov-

sovenir, sou-, su-, *pers. et impers., se souvenir ; subst. souvenir*

sovent, -ant, souvent, su-, *souvent ; adj.* soventes feiz, *souvent*

soverain, su-, souvrain, souverain, *supérieur, élevé, souverain, céleste*

soweif v. soëf

soye v. soie

soz- v. sous-

soz, souz, sos, sous, suz, sus, sou, sub, sost, soubz, *sous*

spose v. espouse

stile, *style, manière*

su- *cf.* so-

suëf v. soëf

sueil, *seuil*

sueil v. soloir

suen v. sien

süeur, suur, sudor, *sueur*

suf- *cf.* sof-
sufraite, souffrecte, *manque*
suir *v.* sivre
suire, *beau-père*
sul *v.* seul
sul- *v.* seul-, sol-
sulonc, -unc *v.* selonc
sujurner *v.* sejorner
sum-, sun- *v.* som-, son-
sur, sur- *v.* sor, sor-
surjurner *v.* sejorner
survenir *v.* souvenir
sus, suz, *prép et adv., sur, en haut;*
   sur le jour, *au jour;* en s., *en*
   arrière
sus- *cf.* sos-
sus *v.* soz
suv- *v.* sov-
suz *v.* soz *et* sus

Tabis, *vêtement de soie*
taillier, *tailler, trancher*
taire *v.* taisir
taisir, teisir, taire, *intr. et réfl.*
   taire
talent, -ant *désir, volonté, disposi-*
   tion, humeur
tancer, tançon *v.* tencer, tenson
tanser *v.* tencer
tant, *tant, si nombreux, si grand,*
   tellement; tant—tant, *plus—*
   plus; de t. plus, *d'autant plus;*
   en tant, *pendant ce temps;* de
   tant que, *d'autant plus que;* t.
   cum, *tant que, aussi longtemps*
   que; tant que, *jusqu'à ce que;*
   combien que, quelque . . . que,
   pour que
tantost, *aussitôt*
tanz *v.* temps
tapis, tabis, *tapis*
tappir, *cacher*
tarder, se tarder *v.* targier
targier, -jer, *tarder;* se targier,
   s'arrêter, se retenir
tart, tard, tairt, *tard; adv. tar-*
   divement, peu, jamais; lui ert
   tart qued, *il lui tardait que*
taster, *tâter, chercher en tâtant,*
   goûter de
teindre, taindre, *teindre, changer*
   de couleur; part. pâle

tel, teil, tiel, *n.* teus, tés, telx,
   tex, tieulx, teis, *tel; devant un*
   nom de nombre, quelque; adv.
   de telle sorte
tempéste, *tempête*
temple, *tempe*
temple, *temple*
temprer, *accorder;* tempré, tem-
   péré, trempé
temps, tamps, tiemps, tens, tans,
   tanz, *temps;* tout a tens, *au*
   bon moment
temptatïon, *tentation*
tencement, *protection, défense,*
   pardon
tencer, -cher, -ser, tancer, -ser,
   quereller, blâmer, protéger,
   défendre
tendre, taudre, tendre, *étendre,*
   viser (à), se rendre
tendre, *tendre, délicat, aimé*
tendrement, tenr-, *tendrement*
tenir, *tenir, soutenir, servir, pos-*
   séder, occuper, se tenir, rester,
   arrêter, observer, garder, croire;
   t. a, pour, *prendre pour;* tenir
   sa voie, *s'en aller;* a eulx en
   tient, *il dépend d'eux*
tens *v.* temps
tensement *v.* tence-
tenson, -zon, tançon, *dispute,*
   querelle
tente, tante, *tente*
terme, *terme, borne, temps préfixé,*
   destinée, coutume
terre, tere, *terre, pays, contrée;*
   prendre t. *aborder*
terrestre, terrien, *terrestre*
tes *v.* ton
teste, tete, *tête*
teus *v.* tel
tevor, *tiédeur*
tex *v.* tel
tien, tuen, *tien, ton*
tierce, *la 3ème heure du jour*
tierz, tiers, tierc, terc, terz,
   troisième
tirer, *tirer, traîner, arracher;*
   réfl. se glisser
tison, *pieu, poutre, planche*
tistre, *tisser*
tochier, tou-, tu-, toucher, tocer,

toucher, *porter, atteindre, jouer
(instrument), confiner, tourner*
toe, *adj. fém. v.* ton
toldre, tolir, tollir, *ôter, enlever,
arracher*
ton, tun, tum, ten, *n.* tes, tis, *ton*
ton, *ton, air*
tonnel, *tonneau*
tor, tur, tour, *tour, moyen, fois,
façon, manière*
tor, tour, *tour, château*
torbler *v.* trobler
torment, tour-, *tourment*
torner, tour-, tur-, *tourner, retourner, se changer, détourner ;*
torner a, *changer en*
tornoier, tour-, tur-, *tourner,
jouter*
tort, *injustice*
tort, *tortu*
tortrele, tourterele, torterelet,
tourterelle
tost, *vite*
tot, toth, tout, tut, *n.* toz, tos,
tous, *pl.* toit, tuit, *tout ; adv.
tout à fait ;* del tot, tout à fait ;
de tot en tot, *entièrement*
totevoies, totes- ; tuteveies, *toujours, cependant, toutefois, de
toutes manières*
tou- *cf.* to-
touaille, *serviette*
toucher *v.* tochier
toudiz, tosdis, *toujours, à jamais*
tour- *cf.* tor-
tous, touz, *toux*
touse, *jeune fille*
tousel, *jeune homme*
tout *v.* tot
touz *v.* tot *et* tous
trabuchier *v.* tresbuchier
trace, *trace*
traime, *trame, fil*
traïn, *queue*
traïner, *traîner*
traïr, trahir, *trahir*
traire, treire, trere, *tirer, lancer,
attirer, faire sortir, mener,
tendre, traîner, arracher, souffrir ;* se traire, *se tourner*
traistre, *traître*
trait, *tir*

traitis, -iç, *doux, joli, bien fait*
traïtor, -our, tradetur, *n.* traître,
traistre, *traître*
trambler *v.* trembler
trametre, *envoyer*
tranchee, *tranchée*
tranchier, -er *v.* trenchier
travaillier, -eiller, -ellier, -illier,
*tourmenter, se donner de la
peine, s'efforcer, travailler*
traveillement, *peine*
travers, *de travers ;* prendre en
travers, *prendre en mauvaise
part*
trecerie *v.* tricherie
trecher *v.* trichier
tref, *tente*
treis *v.* troi
trembler, tram-, *trembler*
tremper, temprer, *modérer, mêler
d'eau*
trenchier, -er, tranchier, -er,
trencer, *couper, tailler, trancher ;* faire trenchier, *aiguiser*
trente, trentre, *trente*
trere *v.* traire
tres, *derrière, depuis ; adv. int.
beaucoup, tout à fait, bien ;* tres
ci, *depuis lors ;* tres or, *désormais*
tresbuchier, -cier, -trebuchier,
cier, trabuchier, tresbucher,
*renverser, trébucher, tomber,
faire tomber*
treschier, tresquer, *sauter, dan-
ser*
trescorre, *parcourir*
tresgeter, trasgeter, tresjeter,
mouler, étirer
tresor, tressor, *trésor*
trespas, *trépas, mort, passage*
trespasser, trespesseir, trepasser,
trespeisseir, *passer, passer
outre, traverser, mourir ; passif
au sens intr. rester sans effet*
tresprendre, *prendre, saisir*
tresque, trosque, truske, *jusque*
tressaillir, tres-, *tressaillir,
sauter, sauter par dessus, trembler*
tressuër, *transpirer ; part. couvert
de sueur*

trestourner, -urner, *tourner, détourner, renverser*
trestot, -out, -ut, tretot, -out, *tout*
tribouillerie, *bavardage*
tribulatïon, -cïun, *tribulation*
tricherie trec-, *tromperie*
trichier, trechier, *tromper*
tristor, -our, -ur, *tristesse*
trive, trieve, treve, *trève*
trobler, troubler, trubler, torbler, tourbler, *troubler, devenir trouble*
troi, trei, troy, trois, treis, treys, troys, *trois*
trop, *très, bien, trop, tout à fait*
trover, trouver, truver, trovert, torver, *trouver, rencontrer, inventer, composer*
trubler *v.* trobler
truisse *v.* trover
truv-, truev- *v.* trov-
tu- *cf.* to-
tuër, *tuer*
tuit *v.* tot
tumbeaulx (*pl.*), *tombeaux*
tun- *v.* ton-
tut *v.* tot
tyreteinne, *espèce d'étoffe*

U- *cf.* o-
u *prov.* = un
u *v.* ou
ubli *v.* oubli
ublïer *v.* oblïer
ue- *v.* oe-
ui, ui- *v.* hui, hui-
ultre *v.* outre
um- *v.* om-, hum-
um *v.* home
un, ung, unt, hun, u, *un, un seul; un a un, par un e un, l'un après l'autre;* pl. *quelques, des*
un- *cf.* on-
unc, unches *v.* onques
un-corn, *licorne*
unkes, unque, -s *v.* onques
unt *v.* avoir
ur- *v.* or-
ure *v.* hore
user, *user, faire usage, employer, avoir l'habitude, souffrir;* subs. *usage, service*

usque, *jusqu'à ce que*
utle, *utile*
uv- *v.* ov-

Va, *eh bien, hé; cf.* diva
vaillains, *vaillant*
vaillance, *valeur, vaillance*
vaine *v.* veine
vair *v.* voir
vaïr *v.* vëoir
vair, veir, ver, *de diverses couleurs, gris-bleu; subs. fourrure, vêtement*
vaissel, vessel, vassel, *vaisseau*
vait *v.* aler
val, *n.* vaus, *val, vallée;* contre v., a v., *en bas*
vallet *v.* vaslet
valoir, valloir, *valoir, avoir du prix, de la valeur; être utile, aider, servir;* vaillant, vallent, vaillant, *valant, vaillant, précieux, aisé, excellent*
valt *v.* valoir
vant *v.* vent
vanter *v.* venter
vanter, -eir, venter, *réfl. et intr. se vanter*
vaslet, varlet, vallet, valet, vadlez, *garçon, jeune homme, écuyer*
vassal, vasal, *homme brave, vassal*
vasselage, *action de valeur, prouesse*
vaucel, vaucele, *vallon*
vedeir *v.* vëoir
vëeïr, vëer, *v.* vëoir
veer, *refuser, défendre*
veie *v.* voie
veincre, vain-, ven-, veintre, *vaincre*
veine, vaine, *veine*
veir *v.* vair *et* voir
veir- *v.* voir-
veistes *v.* vëoir
velle, *veille*
vencre *v.* veincre
vendra *v.* venir
vengance, rengeance, venjance, *vengeance*
vengier, -er, vanger, *venger*
venir, *venir, parvenir*
vent, venz, vant, *vent*

venter *v.* vanter

venter, vanter, *venter, souffler*

vëoir, veioir, vëeir, vëer, veïr, vaïr, veder, vedeir, *voir ; part.* veu, *considérant*

verai, vrai, vray, *vrai, véritable*

verdor, verdure, *verdure*

vergier, vregier, vergié, vregié, -iet, *n.* vergiez, vergez, *verger*

vergonder, -under, *déshonorer*

verité -et, -ei, -iet, verté, -eit, -et, vreté, *vérité*

vermeil, -oil, -el, -eul, *rouge*

vermeillet, vremellet, *rouge, rose*

veroiement *v.* vroiment

verrat, *sanglier*

verre *v.* voirre

verroi, *vrai*

verroillier, *verrouiller*

vers, viers, ver, *envers, contre*

vers, *couplet, verset, air*

vertat, -é, -eit, *v.* verité

vertu, -ut, -ud, virtud, *vertu, qualité, force, miracle*

vesconte, *vicomte*

vespree, *soir, soirée*

vessel *v.* vaissel

vestement, vestiment, *vêtement*

vestëure, vesture, *vêtement*

vestir, viestir, *vêtir*

vesqu *v.* vivre

vëue, *vue ; v.* vëoir

veuil *v.* voloir

vez *v.* foiz

vez, ves, *voici, voilà*

vi *v.* vëoir

vïande, *viande, vivres*

vice, visse, *vice*

victorïeu, *vainqueur*

videle, *espèce de manche*

vie, vide, *vie*

vieillece, -esse, viellece, -che, *vieillesse*

viel, vieill, veill, *n.* velz, viels, vieus, viex, viaus, vius, *vieux, laid*

vïele, *vielle*

viellart, *vieillard*

viellece, -eche *v.* vieill-

vierge *v.* virge

viers *v.* vers

vieus *v.* viel

viex *v.* viel

vif, *n.* vis, vius, vivs, *vif, vivant*

vigne, vinne, vine, *vigne*

vignet *v.* venir

vil, *n.* vils, vis, vix, *vil, bas, méprisable, abaissé*

vilain, vilein, villain, *habitant de la campagne, paysan ; adj. vil, grossier, bas*

vile, ville, *village, ville*

vilenie, -onie, -onnie, velonnie, villenie, -ennie, -enye, *grossièreté, impolitesse, injure, affront, tromperie*

villein *v.* vilain

vilté, *ignominie*

vindrent *v.* venir

vint, vingt, *obl.* vinz, *vingt*

vïoler, *violer*

virge, virget, virgene, -ine, vierge, *vierge*

virginité, -et, -ed, *virginité, vœux de religion*

vis *v.* vif *et* vil

vis, viz, *avis*

vis, viz, visage, visaige, *visage*

visïon, *vision*

visse *v.* vice

vivet, *vif*

vivre, *vivre, se comporter ; vivant, vivant, vie ; a son vivant, avant sa mort ; a tut vostre vivant, tant que vous vivrez*

voel *v.* voloir

voie, veie, voye *voyage, route, chemin ;* tenir sa voie, *s'en aller ;* tute v., *cependant ;* depescher la voie, *se hâter*

voir, veir, vair, *f.* veire, *vrai, véritable ; subst.* vérité ; de v., *per ver,* voir, voire, *vraiment, en vérité*

voirement, veir-, *vraiment*

voirre, verre, *verre*

vois *v.* aler

voisin, veisin, vicin, *voisin*

voiz, vois, voix, voz, *voix*

vol *v.* vuel

vol, *vol*

voleir *v.* voloir

volenté, -et, eit, volunté, -et, vulenté, voulenté, -anté, *volonté* volentiers, -ers, voulentiers, voluntiers, -ontiers, -unteyr, *volontiers*

voloir, -eir, vouloir, *vouloir, désirer;* v. bien, *vouloir du bien; subst. vouloir, volonté;* voillant, bien v. *ami, amical*

volontiers *v.* volentiers

volsissent *v.* voloir

volt, vult, *visage*

volu, arc v., *arcade*

volunt- *v.* volent-

vos, vous, vus, *vous*

vostre, voustre, vustre, voz, vos, *votre*

voul- *v.* vol-

vout *v.* voloir

voye *v.* voie

voys *v.* aler

voz *v.* voiz *et* vostre

vregié, -ier, -iet *v.* vergier

vroiment, *vraiment*

vueil *v.* voloir

vuel, vol, voil, *vouloir, volonté;* mon v. *etc., de bon gré*

vuellent *v.* voloir

vuissier *v.* huissier

vuit, veut, *vide*

W *cf.* g, gu

war- *v.* gar-

weit *v.* gué

welt *v.* voloir

wigre, *espèce de javelot*

Y *v.* i

y- *v.* i-

yaue *v.* aigue

ypocrite, *hypocrite*

Ysengrin, *personnification du loup*

yv- *cf.* iv-

yverner, *être hiver*

yvrongne, *ivrogne*

Zai *v.* ça

GENERAL INDEX

The numbers refer to the pages.

Index 389

www.ingramcontent.com/pod-product-compliance
Lightning Source LLC
Chambersburg PA
CBHW031350290326
41932CB00044B/870